Draumkvæde

Til Kirsten

STUDIA NORVEGICA ETHNOLOGICA ET FOLKLORISTICA - 16

No. 1. Scottish and Norwegian Ballads. By Knut Liestöl. 16 pp.
No. 2. The Dead and the Living. By Reidar Th. Christiansen. 96 pp.
No. 3. A Norwegian Visionary Poem from the Middle Ages. By Knut Liestöl. 144 pp.
No. 4. Light-Mother and Earth-Mother. By Nils Lid. 20 pp.
No. 5. On the Sources of the Ásmundursaga Kappabana. By E. F. Halvorsen. 57 pp.
No. 6. Studies in the Gisla Saga. By Anne Holtsmark. 55 pp.
No. 7. Studies towards a Theory of Sociological Transformations. By Sverre Holm. 119 pp.
No. 8. Horse-fight and Horse-race in Norse Tradition. By Svale Solheim. 173 pp.
No. 9. A Study of Cultural Change. Rural-Urban Conflicts in Norway. By Peter A. Munch. 104 pp.
No. 10. Primitive Scandinavian Textiles. By Odd Nordland. 1961. 154 pp.
No. 11. Falcon Catching in Norway. By Olav Bö. 1962. 80 pp.
No. 12. European Folklore in America. By Reidar Th. Christiansen. 1962. 124 pp.
No. 13. Norwegian Folktale Studies. By Warren E. Roberts. 1964. 88 pp.
No. 14. The Warp-weighted Loom. By Marta Hoffmann. 1964.
No. 15. Sjømann og håndverker. Seilmakere ved Oslofjorden og Skagerak 1850–1914. By Brit Berggreen 1973.
No. 16. Draumkvæde. By Michael Barnes. 1974.

Michael Barnes

Draumkvæde

An edition and study

UNIVERSITETSFORLAGET
Oslo – Bergen – Tromsø

Section: A. 20. 43 – 2 T

ISBN 82-00-08960-6

Omslag: Terje Mathisen

Printed in Norway by
E. Sem A/S, Halden

Preface

The aim of this book is threefold. First to survey in detail the history of *Draumkvæde* scholarship, second to define *Draumkvæde* more clearly and objectively than has been done previously, and third to make available to a wide audience a selection of the original texts. For this last purpose a glossary and notes on the language and matter of the texts have been provided.

I have done my best to weigh up the advantages and disadvantages of all the arguments about the genesis, nature and content of *Draumkvæde* which have been put forward by other scholars. Circumstances have not always allowed much more than summary discussion or dismissal, but I should like to temper the curt criticisms of some of my predecessors by an ample acknowledgement here of the strong stimulus I have received from their learning and enthusiasm.

It is a great pleasure to acknowledge the help and encouragement I have received while writing this book. Bengt Jonsson of Svenskt Visarkiv and Reimund Kvideland of the University of Bergen supplied me with some elusive pieces of information, and Bengt Jonsson read the complete manuscript. My colleagues, Peter Foote and Richard Perkins of University College London, gave me unsparingly of their time. Richard Perkins assisted me with the laborious task of checking and Peter Foote read the whole book in manuscript and in proof and made many valuable suggestions. Sigrid Liestøl of Institutt for folkeminnevitskap in Oslo provided me with xerox copies as and when I needed them and answered numerous questions with great patience. To all these my warmest thanks. To Ådel Blom, Olav Bø and the late Svale Solheim, all of Institutt for folkeminnevitskap, I owe a special debt of gratitude. They made me feel more than welcome on the frequent occasions I visited the Institutt and took a lively interest in my work. Ådel Blom and Olav Bø read the complete manuscript and offered much sound advice. All three helped in other ways too numerous to recount here, and it is largely thanks to their efforts and to Bengt Jonsson that this book is being published.

Finally I would like to express my thanks to Norges almenvitenskapelige forskningsråd for financial support, and to the printers, E. Sem A/S of Halden, for making an excellent job of a difficult manuscript.

University College London, 1972. *Michael Barnes*

Contents

1. Introduction

Draumkvæde[1] is usually considered to be a ballad (*folkevise*), but it has also been described as a poem (*kvæde*).[2] It is found only in Norway. Like so many other Norwegian ballads it was discovered in Telemark in the central southern part of the country in the 1840s and first written down in that decade (cf. Section 3.1, pp. 72–7). Unlike most of the other ballads it has a religious subject: it describes life after death, tells of heaven and hell and of punishments and rewards for deeds done on earth. In this *Dr* has more in common with medieval vision literature than with the bulk of Scandinavian ballads, and no other Norwegian ballad has such a theme.[3] Formally, though, *Dr* must be classed as a ballad; its metre, rhyme and general diction are part of a common heritage. In two important respects however it stands out: it appears to have more than one refrain, and, since it lacks a narrative thread, individual stanzas or groups of stanzas can appear in almost any order. The lack of a story, of a series of events one following on the other and each in some measure dependent on what precedes it, may possibly be responsible for the poor state of preservation of *Dr*. While there are well over a hundred variants or texts of the ballad, only fourteen contain ten or more stanzas and only three more than twenty-five while many consist of one or two, or sometimes only half a stanza or a single line.[4] Moreover the longer variants and texts differ widely among themselves both in length and content. The two longest consist of sixty-one and seventy-four stanzas respectively and contain much material not found in any of the others. The task of the prospective editor is not, therefore, an easy one. He is faced with a large corpus of disordered material and there is little to help him sort it out. He cannot, as in the case of ballads which tell a story known from other sources, use external criteria to guide him. It is true that *Dr* has been compared to and even thought to be based on certain medieval pieces of vision literature, but, as will become apparent in the following, the connection between the ballad and any one of these is tenuous. The lack of narrative thread makes it difficult to reduce the chaos on the basis of the material alone, for not only is it impossible to say in what order the stanzas should be arranged, but it is doubtful whether any objective limits can be put on the amount of material admissible as *Dr*. As Olav Bø has shown,[5] *Dr* has become inextricably mixed up with certain *gamlestev*, single four-line stanzas, which are identical with the stanzas of the ballad in form and sometimes very similar in content. He argues that a number of stanzas which have been attributed to *Dr* probably began their life as *gamlestev*, but it is equally possible to argue the reverse. The question which naturally arises – and it is surprising that until recently it seems virtually to have been ignored – is whether *Dr* ever existed as a single, unified ballad or poem at all.[6] Those who have edited texts of the ballad or written about it have mostly assumed that it did, and that it was composed at some date before the Reformation, but few of them have thought it necessary to prove their assumptions. Much of the energy expended on *Dr* in the last hundred and twenty years has gone into producing reconstructed texts of the ballad – most as different from each other as the originals on which they are based – and the impression given by each of these texts is certainly of a complete and unified entity. Unfortunately, however, enjoyable though such texts are in themselves, in seeking to impose order where there is mostly chaos their editors give a false impression of the real position and have in many ways stifled proper discussion of the textual problems. Moreover, in the absence of a diplomatic edition, almost all literary and folkloristic discussion of the ballad has been based on the reconstructed texts.

It is thus apparent that much basic work remains to be done on *Dr*. It is to be hoped that it will be included in one of the early volumes of the definitive edition of the Norwegian ballads which is in preparation. The present edition makes no claim to be definitive; its principal aim is rather to give the reader a clear idea of the nature and extent of the material that goes under the heading *Dr*, and to enable a wide audience to read a representative selection of the original texts. It is also intended as a general introduction to the ballad or ballad fragments, and Section 2 therefore consists of a brief survey of previous contributions to the subject, together with full bibliographical details.

For the sake of convenience I shall continue to refer to *Dr* (or 'the ballad') throughout most of the following discussion. The name should not, however, be thought of as referring to a single, clearly defined ballad or any of the well-known reconstructed texts, but to the heterogeneous collection of material which is the object of this edition.

2. A survey of Draumkvæde research

2.1 The discovery of Draumkvæde

Dr first came to the notice of the scholarly world in the 1840s. A reconstructed text, based on three principal variants and a number of fragments, was published in 1850 by the Norwegian folk-tale collector, Jørgen Moe.[7] Although Moe was the first to edit a text of *Dr*, it was the ballad collectors, the Reverend Magnus Brostrup Landstad and Olea Crøger, who seem to have been the first to write variants of it down, or have them written. Landstad's extensive edition of the Norwegian ballads, *Norske Folkeviser*, which was based on his and Crøger's material, was published in 1853.

Moe and Landstad were the only scholars who did significant work on *Dr* in the 1840s, and although there are MSS of the ballad in other hands from this decade, it is fairly certain that most of them were written for one or other of the two. The earliest dated MS of *Dr* that exists, however, and probably the oldest of all, was written for Crøger by the sexton of Vinje, Niels Svenungsen, in 1842 (V1a).[8] The text runs to sixty-one stanzas and is the second longest of all manuscript versions of the ballad. He wrote another version for Moe in 1846 (V1b) of which, unfortunately, only twenty-one stanzas now remain, but from these one can see that it differed considerably from his earlier version. Neither of Svenungsen's texts is a genuine variant in the sense that it comes from a single informant. In a letter to Crøger (printed in Section 3.7, V1a, note 5), which he sent together with his text, Svenungsen explains that it took him several years to piece the ballad together; first he had to visit informants from a number of parishes and then arrange the material in a suitable form. Not surprisingly his texts are something of a hotchpotch in which it is possible to identify stanzas from a number of different ballads as well as the odd *stev*. They are nevertheless among the oldest versions of *Dr* we possess and influenced both Moe (V1b) and Landstad (V1a) in their reconstructions of the ballad.

The only genuine variants of any length from the 1840s are those by a) Maren Ramskeid, written down by Landstad (K1), b) Anne Lillegaard, two versions, one written down by Olav Grasberg (L4), the other by Jørgen Moe in 1847 (L1), and c) an unknown informant, written down by Moe in 1847 (L2). In addition there are three variants containing eight, six and six stanzas respectively, the first two by unknown informants, written down by Landstad (T5 and T3), the last by Tone (Marteinsdotter?), written down by Moe in 1847 (L3), and a number of odd fragments.[9]

The three variants which form the basis of Moe's text are L1, L3 and V1b. Moe calls them A, B and C respectively and indicates from which source or sources most of the stanzas are taken. In one or two cases he has deviated slightly from the wording of his MSS. He may also have introduced material from at least one other variant (L2), but it is difficult to be certain of this since forty-one of the stanzas of V1b are now lost.[10] Moe's reconstruction has thirty-seven stanzas and L1 undoubtedly formed the framework around which it was built. In his preamble to the text Moe states that *Dr* is the Eddaic poem *Sólarljóð* remodelled as a 'romance' and that the hero, Olav Åsteson, is St Ólafr. He notes that the refrain varies according to the 'nature of the contents' and stresses the difficulty of reconstructing the text, not least because of the lack of a narrative thread; *Dr* is too far removed from *Sólarljóð* to use this as a guide: 'The difficulty is increased by the fact that all the *gamlestev* and a number of other heroic ballads have the same melody as *Draumkvæe*, and that manuscript C, for the sake of completeness, has included a lot of this heterogeneous material.'[11] Moe also comments on the fact that certain of the stanzas have been parodied, but points out that the parodies are not normally felt to be such and are usually included among the genuine stanzas by the unsuspecting informant.

Landstad printed two texts, one (A) a reconstruction, the other (B) Maren Ramskeid's variant (K1). Landstad B was thus the first genuine *Dr* text to be published, although the spelling was normalised and numerous small alterations were made to the wording. Landstad A takes its material from V1a and a number of variants; how many or exactly which we cannot be sure. There are some thirteen extant variants which are either in Landstad's hand or part of his collection and together with V1a these account for all sixty stanzas of his reconstructed text, though in the case of several, notably 12 and 60, one has to assume fairly extensive re-working, or that they are based on a variant or variants now lost.[12] A cursory examination reveals that K1 is closest of all the extant variants to Landstad A, and Landstad himself tells us that he used K1 as a model for his reconstructed text. He considered it 'the most complete and well ordered',[13] and for this reason included it as a B text. Landstad A is twice as long, but the ordering of the episodes, if one can call them such, is the same. In Landstad B we find: the introduction, stanzas 1–2; the sleep, awakening and visit to church, 3–6; the journey to the other world, including the *Gjallarbru* stanzas, 7–9, 11; the *sæl* stanzas, 12–16; the blue ice, the glimpse of paradise and the meeting with the *gudmor*, 17–20; the punishments, 10, 21–2; the hosts from north and south and the judgement, 23–8; the awakening and conclusion, 29–30. This, with the exception of the two final stanzas, which are in Danish, is the skeleton which Landstad fleshed out with his additional material.[14] None of the other pre-1853 MSS shows anything like as close a correspondence with Landstad A. The only other text apart from K1 which may have served as a model is V1a. Stanzas 1–14 of Svenungsen's compilation contain very much the same material as Landstad A 1–12, but in slightly different order.[15] Landstad informs us that this, together with K1, was the most complete version he had, but does not tell us how he used it.

Landstad, like Moe and other scholars, found a close connection between *Dr* and *Sólarljóð*. He describes it as an adaptation, an offspring of *Sólarljóð*, which he dates to the ninth or tenth century, because of 'the mixture of heathen and Christian ideas'[16] it contains. *Dr* itself he considers to be from 'the first centuries of Christianity in Scandinavia'.[17] He does not agree with Moe in identifying Olav Åsteson with St Ólafr, but finds much to suggest that St Ansgar is the hero of the ballad. There is the emphasis on dreams in Rimbert's life of St Ansgar and Landstad points to similarities between these dreams and parts of *Dr* (and *Sólarljóð*). He had also on one occasion heard the hero of *Dr* called *Ásgarðson*.[18] He further suggests that the refrain which begins: *I Ródelándo . . .* may refer to *Rolanda sokn* in 'Elfsborgs Len' in Sweden.[19] Although St Ansgar apparently never visited Norway, his fame, Landstad feels, must have spread there from Sweden and the Norwegians, who were wont to make poems about their religious beliefs and ideas, composed *Sólarljóð* basing it on Ansgar's dreams in which they found much that corresponded with their own ideas about life after death.

In attempting a reconstruction of the text of *Dr* Landstad was faced with more or less the same difficulties as Moe. Landstad did, however, have a greater number of variants, among them K1, which, as we have seen, he used as the basis for his reconstruction. He nevertheless points out in his introduction that the ballad consists only of fragments and that it is virtually impossible to be sure that every 'piece' occupies its proper place or to know what belongs to the ballad and what is spurious. He prefers to retain certain things about whose genuineness he is doubtful rather than risk omitting anything which might belong to *Dr*. This was no doubt due in part to reports he had heard that the ballad at one time consisted of 'several hundred stanzas'. It led him to include a section of what is generally regarded as an entirely different ballad, *Mitt belte* or *Beltevisa*, which V1a contains in its entirety, although he felt able to ignore certain other parts of Svenungsen's text: 'Niels Svenungsen had introduced much spurious matter, but since a large part of this could be recognised as belonging to other ballads, it was not so difficult to remove it.' Landstad also draws attention to the fact that *Dr* was once very well known in upper (i.e. western) Telemark and that 'almost everyone who is still interested in the old ballads has heard tell of it or knows a few stanzas. But these isolated and scattered stanzas are confused with and used as *stev*, and as such are liable to undergo any changes the *stev*-singer considers suit the place or the occasion.'[20]

It is in many ways unfortunate that Landstad chose to use reconstructed texts in his ballad edition, a practice for which he was in fact condemned at the time.[21] Jørgen Moe, as we have seen, had followed the same course a few years earlier, but in his case it was of less significance, since he was not publishing a full edition. Moe also gave a more detailed description of the process of reconstruction, indicating in many cases from which version a particular stanza was taken.

In Denmark the year 1853 saw the publication of the first volume of *Danmarks gamle Folkeviser*, but in Norway it marked the beginning of a long series of ballad editions, mostly purely popular, containing hardly a genuine variant among them. The effect of such editions in the case of *Dr* was to give the false impression that it was a homogeneous, rounded work, and many of those who wrote about it let themselves be so far influenced by this impression as to base their research on reconstructed texts rather than genuine variants. One cannot help agreeing with contemporary criticism of Landstad, and feeling that the tenor of Norwegian ballad research over the last hundred and twenty years might have been different and much more enlightening if he had simply reproduced the texts he wrote down in the field.

2.2 Landstad's first draft

Landstad's ballad edition of 1853 was the result of long preparation. He wrote his first draft MS as early as 1845 or 1846. For many years this MS was thought to be irretrievably lost, but it reappeared in the early 1920s and was published in 1925.[22] It contains a text of *Dr* called *Droumekvæi* which is fundamentally different from Landstad A. According to the editor, Knut Liestøl, this text (like the others in the MS) is 'not reconstructed – at least not to any appreciable extent',[23] and is thus one of the earliest variants of *Dr* we have. Examination, however, reveals that every stanza of *Droumekvæi* except 9 and 25 is found with almost identical wording in V1a.[24] Such striking similarity, together with the lack of any reference in Landstad's 1853 edition to such an important variant as *Droumekvæi* would constitute, strongly suggests that it is an abbreviated version of V1a. If this is the case, it is perhaps justifiable to say it is not reconstructed, although stanza 9[25] is not found in V1a or anywhere else and stanza 25 appears to have been altered, but it is hardly a genuine *Dr* variant in the sense Liestøl's words suggest. In this edition it will be treated as an abbreviated version of V1a, and as such requires no further separate comment.

2.3 Sophus Bugge's article

Shortly after the appearance of Landstad's *Norske Folkeviser* Sophus Bugge published an article on *Dr*.[26] His principal aim was to show that much of the material in *Dr* had parallels in medieval vision literature, various mythologies and popular beliefs. Bugge had, not unnaturally, read more widely than Landstad and was thus able to view the ballad in a broader perspective. He shed light on a great many things that were not mentioned in the notes of Landstad's 1853 edition and offered alternative solutions to some of the problems Landstad did discuss. Bugge's remarks were based entirely on Landstad A to which he suggested a number of emendations. It is difficult to criticise him for using this text, since the only others available to those reading his article were Landstad B and Moe (1850) and neither of these contained all that he wished to discuss.

Bugge apparently thought that *Dr* was in some way connected with *Sólarljóð*,[27] but he nowhere states that they are one and the same poem or that *Sólarljóð* is the source of *Dr*. He dismisses Landstad's suggestion that the visionary was Ansgar, and sees Rimbert's *Vita Ansgarii* as an instructive parallel, but totally unrelated to the ballad. As regards the identity of the visionary he makes no pronouncement: 'The name . . . is only of importance here in that through it the people themselves express a view as to the age of the poem.'[28]

Bugge offers new suggestions as to the identity of the *gullmór* (Landstad A 40, 42–4, SS.118–20)[29] and *grutte gråskeggi* (Landstad A 52–3, SS. 157–8). The former may be the Virgin Mary, God's mother; apart from the fact that the word *gullmor* or *gumoir* lends itself to this interpretation,[30] Bugge points out that there is a Norwegian folk-tale in which gold rings appear as an attribute of the Virgin Mary.[31] *Grutte graaskeggi* has, according to Bugge, a number of features reminiscent of Óðinn; there is the cognomen *graaskeggi*, the black hat and the black horse. However, while it is true that three of Óðinn's many names are *Hárbarðr* (greybeard), *Síðskeggr* (longbeard) and *Síðhǫttr* (broad-hat)[32] and that he often appears in medieval Norse literature in a broad-brimmed hat, there is no indication that this hat was black, and it is specifically stated that *Sleipnir*, which is presumably the horse Bugge is referring to, was grey.[33]

Bugge's most important contribution to the study of *Dr* lay not in the interpretation of individual words, but in setting the ballad in a broader context by drawing attention to many parallels. In the case of the 'heathen' Scandinavian elements such as *Gjallarbru* Bugge was chiefly emending and expanding what Landstad had already said, but reference to the visions of Gottskalk, Owain, Thurcill and Tundale and parallels from other parts of the Germanic world, Greece, India and elsewhere was a new departure. Some of the parallels were of uncertain value and more than a little strained, as Bugge himself was doubtless aware. Thus, his interpretation of Landstad A 34 (S.149) on the basis of certain religious beliefs in ancient India was: 'Those who in this life have generously given a cow to the poor now find on their journey to the realm of the dead a cow which leads them across *Gjallarbrú*; the unmerciful, on the other hand, find no guide, become dizzy and tumble off the high, steep bridge down into the deep *Gjallarhyl*.'[34] Nothing is said in *Dr* about a cow leading the visionary across *Gjallarbru*. In the vision of Tundale,[35] which many scholars consider to have influenced *Dr*, Tundale crosses a narrow bridge with a cow, but it is *he* who has to lead *it* and it is a hindrance, not a help, a punishment for stealing a cow in this life.[36] If, however, a work of such similar character to *Dr* with a similar motif cannot provide a parallel to S.149,[37] we should be wary of explaining anything in *Dr* on the basis of Indian mythology. The ox (or oxen) which stands and gores those who would cross *Gjallarbru* (Landstad A 26–7, SS.93–9) is compared by Bugge to the many terrible animals with iron horns in hell referred to in the Anglo-Saxon poem *Solomon and Saturn*,[38] and with the dream of Ólafr Geirstaðaálfr in the Legendary Saga of St Ólafr in which an ox is a portent of plague.[39] Both these parallels are, however, far removed from the ox on *Gjallarbru*; that in the dream of Ólafr Geirstaðaálfr is more closely comparable with the three lots of biblical oxen foreshadowing hard winters in *Jómsvíkinga saga*, or the *fylgjur* in *Ljósvetninga saga* and *Vápnfirðinga saga*.[40]

It also worth mentioning two assumptions in the article which Bugge makes no attempt to justify. First that Landstad A 38–9 (SS.116–7,121) and, apparently, 45–51 (SS.122–37) depict purgatory, an assumption already made by Landstad about A 38 in his 1853 edition; second that Landstad A 52–9 (SS.157–66) describe the Day of Judgement. Landstad considered his A 38 to refer to purgatory because of the phrase: *votno dei der ísanne brunno blá* '"*the burning lake of sulphur*" or . . . purgatory'.[41] Bugge does not give his reasons for seeing Landstad A 39 as a further 'purgatory' stanza, but these were presumably 1) because it follows Landstad A 38, 2) gives a general picture of misery and suffering, and 3) does not obviously belong anywhere else – except perhaps immediately before Landstad A 45–51 which Bugge would in any case move forward to follow 39. From this and certain other remarks it seems clear that he considered 38–9 + 45–51 to form a unit describing purgatory first in general terms, then in detail. Landstad makes no general comment on his A 52–9, but Bugge compares them first with stories in medieval French and German works about angels and devils fighting for the souls of the dead, implies that these can only be distant parallels since 'in *Draumekvædi* . . . it is on the Day of Judgement that the two armies join battle', and sees in this description of the Day of Judgement traces of 'the heathen myth about *ragnarøkr*'.[42] The true interpretation of Landstad A 38–9, 45–51 and 52–9 will doubtless never be known. Parallels can be produced to support the view that purgatory is depicted or to oppose it, to show that the Day of Judgement is meant, or simply a provisional judgement after death. Any interpretation will depend largely on the order in which the stanzas are arranged. Bugge followed Landstad A for the most part which had the merit of being based, if loosely, on the genuine variant, K1. Subsequent editors shunted stanzas around almost at will, so that their interpretations not unnaturally differed from his; indeed

Bugge's 'purgatory' stanzas appear not together, but in three widely different places in later reconstructions of the ballad. But even if one accepts that the order in Landstad A is original in the sense of being that of a medieval version of *Dr*, Bugge's reading of stanzas 38–9 and 45–59 was by no means so obvious that he was absolved from the duty of arguing a case for his views.

2.4 Minor contributions 1894—1902

After the publication of Bugge's article many years elapsed before any further contribution of substance was made to *Dr* studies. In an article dealing with popular beliefs about the journey of the soul after death the Danish scholar, Henning Frederik Feilberg, compared, as Bugge had done, the story of Hermóðr's ride across *Gjallarbrú* with the part played by the bridge in *Dr*,[43] but he said nothing new about the ballad.

Some remarks on *Dr* are to be found in Amund Helland's *Bratsberg amt* which are normally attributed to Moltke Moe.[44] The views expressed certainly agree with the results of Moe's investigations: *Dr* was composed about 1220 by a Norwegian who had travelled in the north of England; its most obvious models were the visions of Gottskalk and Thurcill; it was older than *Sólarljóð* and influenced the Icelandic poem rather than the other way round.

In a collection of essays entitled *Vort litterære liv* the author and journalist, Hjalmar Christensen, included a piece called 'Et moderne draumkvæde'.[45] It is essentially a rather superficial criticism of Garborg's *I Helheim*, but it also contains criticism of *Dr* which is said to have served as a model for Garborg's work. The chief value of *Dr*, according to Christensen, is as a historical and cultural document. It forms a connecting link between medieval and modern Norway. As a work of literature, however, it is 'devoid of style', although many parts of it are beautiful. The combination of heathen form and medieval Christian belief is 'more naive [than in *Sólarljóð*], but just as lacking in taste'. The philosophy expounded in the ballad consists of 'odd fragments of Christian belief and morality' and it 'makes no clear distinction between the Catholic purgatory and the so-called eternal fire'.[46] *Sólarljóð* is criticised for much the same reasons. Christensen does not appear to have been very familiar with either poem. He assumes that *Gjallarbrú* occurs in *Sólarljóð* and says, apparently of *Dr*: '*Helheim* is not, after all, a place of punishment for those who have not mortified their flesh with starvation',[47] but this must be a reference to *Sólarljóð* 71. The lack of familiarity with the material is unfortunate; worse is Christensen's willingness to make sweeping statements about a ballad of which he can have known only one genuine variant of the near hundred which existed at the time. The absurdity of his criticisms is most clearly seen in the remark about purgatory. As indicated above, it has not yet been satisfactorily demonstrated that *Dr* contains any reference to purgatory at all; whether or not one believes it does depends largely on the order in which the stanzas of certain variants are arranged.

2.5 The work of Moltke Moe

Around the turn of the century there appears to have been an upsurge of interest in *Dr*. Many editions were published – all containing reconstructed texts[48] – and a number of relatively insignificant contributions were made to the subject (cf. Section 2.4). The really important work to emerge from this period, however, was the planned edition of *Dr* and *Sólarljóð* by Hjalmar Falk and Moltke Moe. This work had a somewhat chequered and unhappy history. In 1891 and 1892 Moe lectured on *Dr* at the University of Christiania using Landstad A. In 1893 he began preparing a completely new edition of the ballad with an introduction on medieval vision literature, a reconstructed text quite different from both Jørgen Moe's and Landstad's and a commentary on the individual stanzas or groups of stanzas in his text. In the same year Falk wrote a commentary on *Sólarljóð* which, together with a text of the poem, was to be included in the work on *Dr*. In 1897 the MS was almost complete and part of Moe's introduction and much of his text and commentary were already in proof, but a fire at the printing works which entirely destroyed the type caused the publication of the work to be postponed indefinitely. Fortunately copies of the proof escaped the fire so we have a fair idea of what the work (hereafter referred to as FM) was like. In 1899 Moe published a text of *Dr* with short explanatory notes on certain words and grammatical forms for use at the University's 'landsmålskursus'. The text is in all essentials the same as that in FM. It was twice reprinted (in 1906 and 1912) without the notes and with one or two changes in the wording and in the number of stanzas.[49] Moe rewrote the commentary on *Dr*, and Forening for norsk bogkunst agreed to publish the text and the commentary in two separate volumes. The text was published in 1904, and part of the commentary got into proof, but the second volume was never completed owing to Moe's ill health at this time. In 1908 a short section of the commentary expanded into a separate article, 'Limbus puerorum', was published in *Sproglige og historiske afhandlinger viede Sophus Bugges minde*, and in 1911 the introduction to FM appeared in a revised and abbreviated form in a volume of *Maal og minne* dedicated to H. F. Feilberg, under the title 'Middelalderens visionsdigtning'. Falk's work on *Sólarljóð* was also revised and published in *Videnskapsselskapets skrifter* in 1914, and finally, in 1927, Moe's *Samlede skrifter* appeared posthumously, edited in three volumes by Knut Liestøl. Moe's work on *Draumkvædet* appears in vol. III. It contains the text of 1912 with a number of inconsistencies 'ironed out',[50] an expanded version of 'Middelalderens visionsdigtning', the commentary and the explanatory notes, culled from various sources,[51] and 'Limbus puerorum'.

Moe's reconstruction of *Dr* has been described by the Norwegian folklorist, Knut Liestøl, as 'a work of art' which '. . . will remain the representative of modern *Draumkvæde* tradition'.[52] Olav Bø, commenting on the fact that *Dr* lacks a continuous narrative thread, says: 'It is true that *Draumkvædet* as we know the ballad from Moltke Moe's masterly reconstruction is not without a framework, but this framework was little known and little used by the informants at the time the ballad was written down.'[53] These two quotations give some idea of the enormous impression Moe's reconstruction made on later scholars. Liestøl, in addition to praising its artistic merits, seems to imply that the text (being both good and representative of the sources ?) will be the one used by generations to come, but the English translation somewhat obscures his exact meaning. Bø suggests that the framework which emerges from Moe's reconstruction had been largely forgotten or was ignored by nineteenth-century informants, implying that the ballad did conform to it at some earlier stage. For this, however, there is no evidence. Bø also states that the variants K1, L1 and L4 (which he considers the most complete) have the same framework as Moe's reconstruction,[54] but this is hardly the case, however one understands the word 'ramme'.

Because of the importance attached to Moe's reconstruction and the influence it has had both on scholars and, through being printed in a great many popular editions, on the common conception of *Dr*, it will be useful to examine it in some detail.

Moe's text (hereafter abbreviated MM) is a radical reconstruction, not based on any genuine variant, but rather on his wide knowledge of medieval vision literature and his conviction that *Dr* was modelled on two visions in particular, those of Thurcill and Gottskalk.[55] In FM Moe is frank about the arbitrary nature of his reconstruction: 'The version of the poem presented here has not been arrived at without an arbitrary choice having to be made. But this has proved necessary in order to unify the divergent texts, which are often difficult to recognise as belonging to the same poem, and to create some continuity of thought in the arrangement of their stanzas which is disordered in various ways.'[56] No such statement accompanies MM elsewhere (it is most notably absent in *Samlede skrifter*, although Moe himself cannot be blamed for this omission). It nevertheless contains a most important revelation. Certainly a little information about the degree of reconstruction in MM can be gleaned from Moe's many references to 'stanzas' or 'variant stanzas' not included. But at best these only tell us something about the large amount of material which was omitted. The above statement speaks of unifying divergent texts and creating continuity of thought in the arrangement of their stanzas. Even this does not go far enough, however. In fact only *one* of Moe's fifty-two stanzas (MM 26) is to be found with identical wording among the extant variants (in V9 from 1910). In some cases the differences are slight, but in most they are substantial. This may in part be due to the fact that some of the variants used by Moe have since disappeared, but such an explanation can hardly account for all the discrepancies. Other possibilities are 1) that he heard variants which he memorised or only jotted down roughly or incompletely,[57] and that these jottings were subsequently destroyed or lost; 2) that certain words, phrases and stanzas are taken direct from Landstad's edition although unsupported by occurrences in existing variants; 3) that a number of things were made up by Moe himself. Of these possibilities 1) and 3) are not normally capable of demonstration, while 2) can rarely be proved conclusively.[58] In view of the doubtful origin of some of Moe's material and his radical reconstruction of the ballad, it will be of value to compare MM with the three longest among the oldest genuine variants, K1, L4, and L1,[59] and to list the corresponding stanzas of Landstad A, MM and these three variants. We can then discuss what MM has for which no original source can be found.

MM is almost twice as long as K1, and although the order in which individual stanzas are arranged is not markedly different, the order in which the various recognisable sections or episodes appear is not the same.[60] Thus the *sæl* stanzas are placed at the end in MM (MM 46–51, K1,12–16), while the judgement stanzas (MM 29–37, K1,23–8) precede the punishments (MM 38–45, K1,10, 21–2). Furthermore the introductory stanzas (MM 1–6, K1,1–6) are very different, and MM 7–15 are not found in K1 at all. Other substantial differences in the length, order and content of the various sections are found in K1,7–9 and 11 which correspond to MM 16–23 and K1,17–20 which correspond to MM 24–8.

MM is over twice as long as L4 and L1 which, coming from the same informant, are very similar in length and content. MM 1–5 shows a quite close correspondence to L4,1–4 and L1,1–5, but MM 7–15 is represented by only one stanza in L4 and L1 (5 and 6 respectively). MM 16–23 correspond very roughly to L4,6–7, 12–13, 16 and L1,7–9, 12–13, 16, and MM 24–9 to L4,20–3 and L1,19–22, although in the case of MM 24–9 especially the order and content of the stanzas is very different. The 'judgement' stanzas appear in the middle of those about *Gjallarbru* in L4 and L1 (14–15 in both variants), and the punishments are listed before *Gjallarbru* is mentioned at all and are somewhat different in content from those in MM (L4,8–11, L1,10–11). The *sæl* stanzas appear split up in L4 (17–19, 24) but together in L1 (17–18); they occupy a position different from that in MM, but more like that in K1.

The corresponding stanzas of Landstad A, MM, K1, L4 and L1 are as follows (the stanza numbering of this edition is given in round brackets; square brackets indicate that a different, though similar stanza is found in the text or variant concerned):

L.A		MM		K1	L4		L1	
1	(1)	1		–	1		1	
2	(3)	–		2	–		–	
3	(2)	–		1	–		–	
4	(5)	2		3	2		4	
5	(8)	3		–	–		3	
6	(17)	[4]	(18)	5	[3]	(18)	[5]	(18)
7	(–)	–		–	–		–	
8	(–)	–		–	–		–	
9	(–)	–		–	–		–	
10	(–)	–		–	–		–	
11	(36)	[5]	(37)	6	[4]	(34)	[2]	(35)
12	(24) ? (169) ?	6		–	–		–	
13	(5)	7		3	2		4	
14	(76)	9		–	5		6	

L.A	MM	K1	L4	L1
15 (83)	10	–	–	–
16 (84)	45	–	–	–
17 (111)	26	–	–	–
18 (86)	11	–	–	–
19 (87)	12	–	–	–
20 (89)	[13] (?)	–	–	–
21 (90)	15	–	–	–
22 (39)	17	7	6	8
23 (40)	–	8	[7] (41)	[7] (41)
24 (101)	18	–	12	12
25 (102)	–	–	–	–
26 (94)	–	9	–	–
27 (98)	20	–	13	13
28 (107)	21	–	[16] (105)	[16] (106)
29 (109)	22	11	–	–
30 (103)	23	–	–	–
31 (39)	17	7	6	8
32 (43)	16	–	[7] (41)	9
33 (147)	46	12	19	18
34 (149)	47	13	–	–
35 (152)	48	[15] (145)	24	–
36 (150)	49	14	18	–
37 (142)	[51] (144)	16	[17] (143)	[17] (143)
38 (116)	24	17	22	21
39 (121)	14	–	–	–
40 (119)	25	19	20	19
41 (115)	27	18	23	22
42 (119)	29	19	20	19
43 (120)	28	20	–	–
44 (118)	–	–	21	20
45 (122)	38	[21] (126)	8	10
46 (122)	–	[21] (126)	8	10
47 (124)	39	22	–	–
48 (129)	40	–	9	11
49 (132)	41	–	11	–
50 (134)	[42] (133)	[10] (135)	10	–

L.A	MM	K1	L4	L1
51 (?)	43	–	–	–
52 (?)	30	–	[15] (157)	[15] (157)
53 (158)	31	23	–	–
54 (159)	32	–	–	–
55 (160)	33	24	14	14
56 (161)	34	25	–	–
57 (162)	[35] (163)	26	–	–
58 (164)	36	27	–	–
59 (165)	37	28	–	–
60 (169) ?	52	–	–	–

There are no stanzas in K1, L4 or L1 corresponding to MM 8 (S.79), 19 (S.95), 44 (S.137) ? (S.136) ? and 50 (S.141).

The more important discrepancies between MM and the extant variants can be listed under five headings:[61] 1) stanzas or lines unknown in the variants; 2) words unknown; 3) grammatical forms or constructions unknown; 4) genuine stanzas combined; 5) slight alterations made on the basis of material in other variants. In the following list L signifies that the item concerned is found in Landstad A. Such items, if words, lines or complete stanzas, may well be genuine since it appears that although Landstad made many alterations to the readings of his MSS (contrast, e.g., K1 with Landstad B), it was not his normal practice to introduce extraneous matter into the texts of *Norske Folkeviser*. Unless otherwise stated the stanza numbers refer to MM (the text in *Samlede skrifter* 199–208).

1(*a*) stanza 6 (L 12): *Gamle mennar å unge/ dei gjev'e etti gaum'e,/ mæ han Olav Åsteson/ tel'e sine draume.* The nearest equivalents in the variants are V1a,14, V1b,6 and V1a,61 (cf. SS.24,169). It seems likely that stanza 6 is taken from L 12 and that Landstad constructed it on the basis of V1a,14 and 61. If this is true, certain features such as the 'inversion' of *mennar* and *å unge*, which Moe considered to be of philological interest,[62] must have been introduced by Landstad himself since they do not occur in either of Svenungsen's texts.

1(*b*) stanza 25 (L 40): *Eg va meg i auromheimi,/ ingjen der eg kjende,/ berre ho sæle gumor mi/ mæ raue gull på hendi.* The first two lines occur in K4 and T6 (in the former only by reference to Landstad A 40), but

Moe has substituted *auromheimi* for *Anheimen* (cf. 3(*a*) below). Line 3 appears to be pieced together from many different sources; S.119, with which we are basically dealing, shows the following variations: V9,11 (post-dates MM) *berre 'o gudmo' mì*, L1,19 *Bære mi goe Sjukmoer*, L2,6 *Bære mi gamle Sjukmo'r*, L4,20 *bare mi goe Gudmoer*, K1,19 *der kjænde æg atte Gudmo mi*, K4,1 [*der ság eg atte*] *mi sæle Gudmoer*, K5,17 *Eg saag atte Gudmo mi*, N1,10 *bare mi gamle gudmor*, T6,2 *der ság eg atte mi sælle gudmor*. Line 4 seems to be based on K1,19 *mæ røde Gul paa Hænde* with the substitution of *raue* for *røde*; K4,1 has *raue G. bar hó* [*pá hende*] and T6,2 *raude Gulli bar hon pá hænde*.

1(*c*) stanza 40.2: *dei bar på gloande jor* (cf. SS.123,129). Moe indicates in a note that he made up this line himself;[63] it first appeared in the three texts of *Dr* published in 1896, 1901 and 1902 (but word 4 *gloandes*),[64] and subsequently in Moe's text of 1904. His 1899 version had *dei vrei sine hendar i blo* which agrees with L5,7.[65]

1(*d*) stanza 43.2,4 (L 51): *dei bit'e kvòrare i spori :/ som gifte kvòrare på jordi*. The rhyme word in l.2 and the whole of l.4 are unknown in any extant variant, although the sense is the same as that of S.135 (cf. also SS.133–4). Moe may have taken the whole stanza from Landstad A; he seems convinced of its genuineness since he writes a note on the form *spori*.[66]

1(*e*) stanza 44: *Kjem eg meg āt Syslehusi,/ der va trollkjeringan inne :/ dei sto kjinna i raue bloi,/ de va so tung ei vinne*. The nearest equivalents in the variants are found in K3 and Sæl (cf. SS.136–7) of which 44 seems to be a combination, with *troll-* and certain other words supplied by Moe himself. It is worth mentioning that *trollkjeringhúse* and *trollkjeringanne* are given as an interpretation (apparently) of *sýslehúse* and *sýslinne* by Bugge in his fair copy of K3 (*trollkjeringh.* is also found in the original), and that in one of the MSS of Sæl Moe has entered two variant readings so that the third line *Der svaitta dai de kalle Bloi* could read *Der kjinna dai de raue Bloi*. It is doubtful, however, whether these readings come from an informant; they are probably taken from K3,3.

1(*f*) stanza 52 (L 60): *Gamle mennar å unge/ dei gjev'e etti gaum'e ;/ de va han Olav Åsteson,/ no hev 'en tålt sine draume*. This is presumably taken from L 60 which seems to be based on V1a,61 (cf. 1(*a*) above). Moe doubtless changed *fortolt* in Landstad A to *tålt* on analogy with stanzas 5 and 6 (cf. 5(*b*) below). The stanza is found in the continuous text in *Samlede skrifter*, but is omitted in the commentary section.

2(*a*) stanza 12.1: *færemo* (cf. S.87). In his notes on the text in FM Moe indicates that this word is his own construction.[67] The note was, however, omitted in later editions of the text. Thus MM (1899) simply states: '*Færemo* from Old Norse *ferðamóðr*, wearied by the journey.'[68]

2(*b*) stanza 13.4: *under* (cf. S.89). Moe tells us that this word is an emendation suggested by Bugge. As in the case of stanza 12.1 the note to this effect appears only in FM;[69] later editions print the word without comment.

2(*c*) stanza 18.3 (L 24): *gulli* (cf. S.101). No extant variant has *gulli* in this stanza, most have either the word *jønn* in place of *gull* or the phrase *fast me Krokar* in place of *òdd mæ gulli*, cf., however, S.102. Moe may well have taken *gulli* from L 24, note 29. The fact that Landstad notes it as a variant reading is presumably an indication of its authenticity.

2(*d*) stanza 21.2: *lei* (cf. S.107). In FM Moe originally had *brei*, which is the reading of all the extant variants, but in the proof *lei*, preceded by a dash, has been entered in the margin. The source of this word is unknown. It may have been introduced by Moe because *brei* conflicted with the statement of the visions on which he considered *Dr* was based.[70]

2(*e*) stanza 27.1: *vetterstig* (cf. SS.115–6). The variants have *Vetters Ti*, *betlarstyen* (*Betlarstigen*) and *Ventersti*. L 41 has *vette-stíg* (path of supernatural beings, gods, cf. Old Norwegian/Icelandic *vættr f.*, Aasen *vett*, *vetter f.*, *vette n.*) which, Landstad admits, is a guess. FM has the form *vetterstíg* and the commentary states: 'The path he travels is called *vetterstíg* (in Landstad distorted to *vetters ti*) or *betlarstígjen*.'[71] Landstad A, as we have seen, has *vette-stíg*; Landstad B has *vetters tið*. It is difficult to see what Moe is getting at here, unless he is referring to Landstad's notes 40 and 41 where *vetters tið* is discussed; in both these cases, however, the phrase comes from the genuine variant, K1, and gives good sense as it stands. One thing is certain: there is no extant variant with the form *vetterstig* and none was known to either Jørgen Moe or Landstad. It seems likely that it is Moe's own construction, although reading his note in the edition of 1899: 'Instead of *vetterstig* the variant *betlarstig* sometimes occurs',[72] one could be excused for thinking that it was a common form in the variants.

2(*f*) stanza 30.4 (L 52): *brass* (cf. S.157). The word is unknown in any extant variant, and it is certain that Moe took it from L 52. In *Samlede skrifter* he says: 'To Maren Ramskeid's version of the [judgement] section he [Landstad] has added two stanzas from another source which vary two of hers: 52 and 54.'[73] In his discussion of the judgement stanzas Moe lists all the sources of this section known to him (K1, K3, K5, L4 ?,

L1, L5). None of these contains the word *brass*, therefore the 'other source' which provided Landstad with his stanza 52 can only have been known to Moe from Landstad A.[74]

3(*a*) stanza 14.1 (cf. also stanzas 25, 48, 50–1): *auromheimi*. This form is accompanied by the following explanatory note in *Samlede skrifter*: 'in the other world; archaic dative singular masculine, Old Norse *í ǫðrum heimi*'.[75] Landstad has the form *ann'heimen* and suggests that the word may mean 'the spirit world'.[76] *Anheimen* is certainly the only form found in the extant variants which contain this stanza (K4 and T6, cf. S.121).[77] However, Moe doubtless introduced *auromheimi* here on the basis of forms occurring in the *sæl* stanzas, cf.: *Føesheimen – andre Heimen*, *F*[*øesheimen*] – *annen Heimen* K1,15–16, *denne Heimen – Annom Heimen* L4,17 etc., *dessi Væri – aurom Væri* M6,17 etc., *denne Heimen – Auroheimen* L3,3 etc. There is nevertheless no example of *auromheimi* in any extant variant, and no example of *annheimen* in the *sæl* stanzas; the closest we get to it is *Aen Hejmen* (*Heimen*) in T9,1–2. It is interesting to observe that in FM Moe originally had *aurom heime* in stanza 14 and *annheimen* in stanza 25 which he, like Landstad, interpreted as 'spirit world'.[78] There is, however, also a note which states that this interpretation is uncertain. It continues: 'I take *Annheimen* to be not "the spirit world", but "the other world". This is supported by *annheimen* v. 49.3[79] which is synonymous with and a variant of *aurom heime* in 50.3. It is also supported by the expression *i den anen heimen* in the variant [L6].'[80] In the proof Moe altered *annheimen* in stanza 25 to *aurom heimi* with a reference to the discussion in the MS of his lectures (of 1891–2).

3(*b*) stanza 15.1 (L 21): *kvòrjom* (cf. S.90). There is only one extant text in which this stanza occurs (V1a), and in it *qvorjum* is followed by *Viso*. It is impossible to say whether Landstad knew a variant without *Viso*, or whether he simply removed the word in an attempt to tidy the line up. In any event it seems likely that Moe followed Landstad A in this matter. If *Viso* has been omitted by an editor, Moe's note in *Samlede skrifter*: '*kvorjom* is an irregular dative singular neuter form of *kvar* (in Telemark *kvor*)'[81] is, of course, meaningless.

3(*c*) stanza 37.4: *burt* (cf. SS.165–6). FM has *hen*, but in Moe's edition of 1899 (and subsequent editions) *burt* is introduced in its place without comment. K1 is the only variant which contains this stanza, although a similar one is found in K5. Both variants have *hen*, and it seems likely that *burt* was introduced by Moe himself who possibly considered the form more in keeping with the language of his reconstruction.

3(*d*) stanza 39.3: *i dessom heimi* (cf. S.124). Moe's edition of 1899 has *i dessi heimi* (as have those of 1904 and 1906) together with a note to the effect that '. . . the older form [of the demonstrative] *dessom* also occurs in the ballads'.[82] This is true, but it does not occur in any extant variant of *Dr* and the likelihood is that Moe or Liestøl[83] introduced it from other ballads. According to a note by Liestøl,[84] stanza 39 and the commentary on it in *Samlede skrifter* are taken from Moe's lectures of 1891–2, but this must refer to the commentary alone since Moe used Landstad's A text in these lectures.

4(*a*) stanza 5: this appears to be a combination of SS.34 (and perhaps 35,36) and 37. The rhyme words *lange/ mange* do not occur in any extant variant with l.1 *Presten stend'e fyr altari*, or l.3 *Olav set seg i kyrkjedynni*.

4(*b*) stanza 16: apparently a combination of SS.43 and 39 or 40. The rhyme words *-mog* and *fot* occur in S.43, but only in SS.39 and 40 do we find the raw material for l.1.

4(*c*) stanza 35: apparently a combination of SS.162 and 163. Both occur in one variant only, K1,26 and K5,20 respectively; 35 is almost identical with K1,26 except for the final rhyme word *gange* which is found in K5,20.

4(*d*) stanza 42: apparently a combination of SS.133, 134 and 135. The rhyme words *tanne/ banna* are found in S.133, *Kjæm eg mæg at Podda Aa ormmen* in S.134 and something approaching l.3. in S.135.[85]

4(*e*) stanza 47 (L 34): this is almost certainly a combination of two forms of S.149; 47 is almost identical with K1,13 except for the first rhyme word which in that variant is *Rug*; *Ku* is found in V1a,56 which is otherwise somewhat unlike 47. Moe was doubtless chiefly influenced by the vision of Tundale in his preference for *ku*.[86]

5(*a*) stanza 3.1 (L 5) (cf. S.8): *han* is not found in this stanza in any extant variant, only *eg* or a radically different first line. The third person pronoun was doubtless introduced from S.5 (which has both *han* and *eg*), or another of the introductory stanzas that has this form.

5(*b*) stanza 5.4: *tel'e* (cf. L 11–12, SS.34–7). Only forms of the verb *fortelja* (or some entirely different verb) are found in the extant variants containing this stanza. There is one case in which *telja* is used with the same sense as *fortelja* (V1a,14 – S.24), and from here it doubtless found its way into MM 5, 6 and 52 and Landstad A 11 and 12.

5(*c*) stanza 10.1: *Eg hev vori meg upp mæ sky* (cf. S.83). Only two texts contain this stanza. V1a,33.1 runs *Egh hæv vori uponde Skye*, T8,5.1 *Thii heve fare fort fe meg*. Moe's first line must be borrowed from SS.76,

79 or 82, perhaps with support from a note by Landstad on his stanza 15 which states that the first line could run *Eg hev vorið up með ský.*[87]

5(*d*) stanza 11.4: *mune.* This stanza only occurs once (V1a,45) and the auxiliary verb used is not *mune,* but *maa.* Some variants containing S.87 (MM 12) have *monne* or *mone* and these are presumably the source of the word in MM 11.

5(*e*) stanza 19.2: *stend.* Two variants only contain this stanza and in neither does the word *stend* occur in l.2 (cf. S.95). It is presumably borrowed from one of the many *Gjallarbru* stanzas with the line *stuten stend aa stangar.*

5(*f*) stanza 22.1 (L 29): *Våsemyran.* The forms of the name occurring in the two variants which contain this stanza (S.109) are *Voxmyren* (K1,11), and *Vågsmýrann* (K4,3). *Våsemyran* was clearly substituted since it was the form of the name chosen for 21 as well, and an etymological explanation had been found for it.[88] The name occurs with varying forms in five stanzas altogether (SS.105–9), though only once do we find *Vosemyran* (T9,4).[89] In spite of the likeness it does not seem imperative to assume that *Voxmyren, Vosemyran* and the other forms all go back to a common original, cf. *Gaglemyran* in MM 23 (S.103, cf. also 104) which presumably refers to the same place.[90]

5(*g*) stanzas 35–7 (L 58–9 and cf. L 57): *sål, såline.* SS.162–6 on which 35–7 are based have only the forms *Sjæl, Sjæle, Sjæline* etc., although the epithet used about St Michael mostly appears as *Saale. Sål* and *såline* were no doubt introduced into these stanzas because of this, and perhaps also because some variants have such forms in other parts of the ballad (cf., e.g., L2,4, L4,9, K9,4).

5(*h*) stanza 39.1 (L 47): *manni dei.* This stanza (S.124) only occurs in two extant variants. In K1,22 the first line runs *Saa møte æg ein Man,* and in K5,12 *Saa kom eg til Mannen den.* The archaic *manni dei* may have occurred in a variant known to Landstad and Moe, now no longer extant, but it is just as likely that it was introduced from certain forms of SS.122 and 129. It is also worth noting that many of the punishment stanzas have a dative singular or plural in their first line.

5(*i*) stanza 50.1,4: *Sæl æ den i føisheimen/ anten fy hæ-i hell hat.* This stanza (S.141) occurs only in two variants (K2 and T9) where the wording is almost identical. In K2,4 ll.1 and 4 run *sæl æ' dæn i denne Heimen/ anten før Spott hell Hat.* Moe doubtless introduced *føisheimen* from other *sæl* stanzas in order to maintain the same first line throughout this section. *Hæ-i* appears to have been substituted for *Spott* on the basis of S.142

where 1.4 runs (K1,16) *anten for Spot hel Hæi.* Moe dismissed this as a variant reading of *fy håge kjellar-bræ-i* (51) partly because it '. . . does not accord very well with our stanza 50',[91] and having done so presumably felt free to use the native word *hæi* in place of the loan-word *spott* in his stanza 50.

It seems clear that Moe's contribution to *Dr* studies did not lie in the field of textual criticism. We would, however, be wrong to suppose he was not aware of some of the problems which face the would-be editor. The MS of his lectures of 1891–2 shows clearly how, by a careful process of sifting and arranging, he built up his text from the variants and texts known to him. Furthermore, and perhaps most important, he freely admits here that his proposed textual solutions may not be 'correct' (i.e., succeed in restoring to *Dr* the form he felt it once had). Unfortunately, however, there is no attempt to demonstrate the process of reconstruction or to express doubt about the 'correctness' of the result in any of Moe's published works on *Dr*, and an entirely false impression of the ballad's state of preservation is thereby given. This has had unhappy consequences for the work of later scholars, many of whom seem to have accepted MM without question, and few of whom have escaped its influence.[92] MM, however, is the product of a hypothesis which it is itself meant to confirm. Believing *Dr* to be based on a number of medieval visions, most notably those of Gottskalk and Thurcill, Moe arranged his text in such a way as to emphasise points of likeness with these visions, and matter not found in them was dismissed unless there were other cogent reasons for including it. It is therefore hardly surprising that he was able to demonstrate that his *Dr* had much in common with the visions of Gottskalk, Thurcill and others, and to give the approximate place and date of its composition.[93] On the other hand such fundamental questions as: 'What is *Dr* ?', 'How do I recognise it ?', were avoided. Far from being obvious, any satisfactory answers to these questions will be extremely involved; indeed it is arguable that a precise definition of *Dr* cannot be given.[94]

It would be wrong not to draw attention to the many positive aspects of Moe's work. His detailed comparison of *Dr* with medieval vision literature, the many parallels he demonstrated between it and other visions and the interpretations he was consequently able to offer of many difficult words, lines and stanzas in the ballad have proved of fundamental importance. Nevertheless, his very learning seems often to have got the better of him and diverted his attention from more mundane matters such as the state of preservation and the content of the variants we have. This is undoubtedly the reason for his inflexible approach to the ballad. Having read the relevant chapters in *Samlede skrifter* one is left not with an understanding of the folkloristic and textual problems which surround *Dr*, but with the impression of an unknown author sitting somewhere in the north of England in the early thirteenth century, piecing together a poem or ballad similar to Moe's (linguistic forms apart) from what he remembered of Gottskalk's, Thurcill's and other visions. The idea that the author himself might have had some original thoughts, or that *Dr* describes a real vision, does not seem to be countenanced, let alone the possibility that *Dr* may not be a medieval vision poem composed in the thirteenth century. A few examples will suffice to make Moe's approach clear:

1. MM 26 (cf. SS.110–13) runs: *Sume fór ivi Grimaråsen/ å sume ivi Skålestrònd,/ men dei som fór ivi Gjaddarhylen,/ dei kòme våte fram.* Moe notes that many visions contain descriptions of different paths in the world of the dead, but says: '. . . only Gottskalk's vision tells of these three paths: a steep one going up to Heaven shining like blazing fire, a broad and easy middle path leading to some beautiful houses and a stinking, steep and narrow path leading downwards, consisting of bottomless mud.'[95] In *Dr* the last of these paths was, according to Moe, confused with *Vose-* and *Gaglemyran* (MM 21–3, SS.103,107,109, cf. also 104–6,108 and 53–4): '. . . that is why the path with the bottomless mud has been replaced here by the wading across the netherworld river [of Gottskalk's vision].'[96] This is possible, but it already removes one of the similarities between the three paths of Gottskalk's vision and MM 26. *Grimaråsen* can hardly be compared with the shining path going up to the sky; *ås*, after all, means 'hill', 'ridge' and, as Moe himself points out,[97] medieval visions are full of descriptions of hills and ridges in the world of the dead. There remains *Skålestrånd* and the reference to houses in Gottskalk's vision. As Landstad, Liestøl and Bø have all pointed out, the names in this stanza vary greatly,[98] but this only applies to ll.1 and 3. In l.2 we almost invariably find *Skålestrånd.* However, to connect this with the path leading to beautiful houses in Gottskalk's vision, especially when it has already been stated without reservation that the image is borrowed from the Dialogues of Gregory the great,[99] seems far-fetched. It is more likely that *Skålestrånd*, like the names in ll.1 and 3 of this stanza, was originally a local place-name. *Skål*(*e*) is well-known as a first element in place-names and the south-eastern shore of lake *Totak* in Rauland is actually called *Skålestrondi*.[100] The opinion of the three scholars mentioned above is that the stanza is 'doubtful' or a *gamlestev*.[101]

2. MM 28–9 (SS.119–20) run: *Der såg eg att'e gumor mi ;/ meg mune 'kji bet'e gange :/ 'Reis du deg ti brokksvalin,/ der skò domen stande.' Kjem eg meg ãt pilegrimskyrkjun,/ der va meg ingjen mann kjend'e,/ berre ho goe gumor mi/ mæ raue gull på hendi.* Moe finds that stanza 28 is based on Thurcill's vision; *Broksvalin* is the church borne on pillars, the *animarum congregatio* built by God through the intercession of Mary herself and also called *basilica sanctæ Mariæ*. Moe considers that the Virgin's connection with this church provided '. . . one of the impulses for the role *Draumkvædet* assigns to Mary in the church beyond the grave'.[102] He also points out that the judgement which is to be held at *Broksvalin* is derived from the provisional judgement which in Thurcill's vision takes place at the *animarum congregatio. Pilegrimskjørkje* of stanza 29, we are told, is the same place as *Broksvalin*, but the name is based on a church in Gottskalk's vision near which a crowd of pilgrims congregate. The description of the pilgrims combined with Thurcill's *animarum congregatio* in the memory of the *Dr* author and this gave rise to MM 28–9. Some of these assumptions have been challenged by Liestøl. He sees MM 24, 27 and 28–9 as being based largely on the vision of Gundelin (or Gunthelm):[103] Gundelin meets Mary in a chapel close to paradise, and after he has promised to serve her she bids his guide, St Benedict, take him back whence he came. Liestøl considers there are three parallels with *Dr* here: the church with the Virgin Mary, its position close to paradise and the fact that Mary bids the visionary go. He also denies that *Pilegrimskjørkje* is the same place as *Broksvalin*: 'It is probably Thurcill's vision that led Moe to this conclusion, for there the preliminary judgment takes place by a church; but in *Draumkvæde* the godmother bids him go *from* the place where he met her to the trial-porch.'[104] Liestøl is correct in maintaining that Gundelin's vision is more like MM 28–9 than Gottskalk's (although if it is contended that these stanzas were based exclusively on Gundelin, the source of *Pilegrimskjørkje* remains unexplained). Moe's assumptions can, however, be criticised for a much more fundamental reason: they are based on his own text. The variants which contain the equivalents of MM 28–9 are something of a muddle. According to K1 the protagonist turns off to the right and sees paradise (18); from where he is looking towards paradise he meets his *Gudmo* (19); she tells him to go to *Broksvalin* 'for that is where the judgement is to be held'

(20); then follow two of the punishment stanzas. According to K5 the protagonist turns to the right and sees paradise (16); he then arrives at *Pelegrems kjørkje* where no one knows him, but he sees his *Gudmo* again (17); then follow four of the judgement stanzas which end this variant. According to L4 the protagonist arrives at *Pilegrims Kjørkje* (from *Jedarbroi*, with several *sæl* stanzas interposed) where he knew no one but his *Gudmoer* (20); no one there was kind to him except his *Gudmoer* who gave him new shoes (21); after this he arrives at the lakes 'where the ice burnt blue' (22); finally he turns off to the right and sees paradise (23); the judgement stanzas occur in connection with *Jedarbroi*. In L1 the sequence of events is the same. According to L2 the protagonist arrives at *Pilegrims Kyrkje* (from the lakes) where he knew no one except his *Sjukmor* (6); no one there was kind to him except his *Sjukmor* who gave him new shoes (7); the variant ends with one *sæl* stanza and two describing the loss of the scarlet cloak; the judgement stanzas are not included. The only other variants which contain material corresponding to MM 28–9 are V9 and N1,[105] but these post-date Moe's work by some years. In V9 the protagonist suddenly sees paradise from an unspecified place (the thorny moor ?) and there is no one he knows there except his *gudmo*' (11); an incomplete punishment stanza follows (12), then a judgement stanza (13) which is the last.[106] In N1 the protagonist arrives at *Pilegrimskjørkje* (10) from lands which burn blue (9); no one knows him there except his *gudmor*; three stanzas about *Gjeddarbroi* follow and complete the variant. As can be seen from this brief summary, the only variant which contains a reference to *Broksvalin* (K1) makes no mention of a *Pilegrimskjørkje*. The only connection between them is the enigmatic figure of the *gud-* or *sjukmor*. This may be a reason for thinking that they are one and the same place, or it may not. All we learn from the *Dr* variants is that the protagonist met his *gud-* or *sjukmor* (probably the Virgin Mary) at an unspecified place (the *Vetters Ti*?) and/or at *Pilegrimskjørkje* and/or in paradise, and was told to go from the unspecified place to *Broksvalin* where the judgement would be held. The meaning of *Broksvalin* is disputed[107] and the significance of *Pilegrimskjørkje*, whether the image is taken from Gottskalk or not, is surely only that of a church in the other world, common enough in medieval visions. We are hardly entitled on the basis of this evidence to draw the same conclusions as Moe. Indeed it is difficult to draw any conclusions at all.

3. Moe considered that the judgement stanzas in *Dr* (MM 30–7, SS.157–66) must originally have referred to a preliminary judgement, just as in Thurcill's vision, which in the process of oral tradition became confused with the Day of Judgement, not least under the influence of the Book of Revelation – hence the presence of Christ, the trumpet and the commandment that *all* the souls must go to the judgement. Moe found his belief confirmed by the way in which the judgement section is preserved in the variants.[108] According to his account in *Samlede skrifter* five contain a reference to the two hosts riding from the north and south (K1, K3, K5, L1 and L5). In fact there are four more: L4, which Moe may have included under L1, although probably he did not know this variant, V9, which dates from 1910 and S6 and T5, which he apparently did not know.[109] Furthermore, since none of these contains the rhyme word *brass*, we must assume there was at one time a tenth variant. Moe considered the fact that this section had only been preserved in a few variants suspicious; given the undeniable popular interest in the Day of Judgement and all matters connected with the end of the world, this part of the ballad would surely have been among the best preserved if it had clearly portrayed these things from the start. The judgement stanzas must either have undergone radical changes – a forgotten religious belief has adopted features of a related one still current – or they must be an interpolation. The former, according to Moe, was the correct interpretation since '. . . our section has preserved so many features of the beliefs of a bygone age – from *Grutte Gråskjeg* with his half-heathen attributes, reminiscent of Óðinn, to St Michael's scales – and because of the secondary part played by Christ which cannot be reconciled with the description in the Book of Revelation'.[110] The variants which have preserved the judgement section are divided by Moe into two classes: the first places the relevant stanzas at the end and includes the judgement itself (K1 and K5); the second depicts only the approach of the two hosts and places this at the beginning (K3) or at *Gjallarbru* (L1); L5 does not belong to either class, but represents a transitional stage in which the approach of the two hosts is depicted, but placed at the end (for the variants not mentioned in *Samlede skrifter* see below). Moe's theory is that K3 and L1 have the more original text. As in Thurcill's vision, on which this section of the ballad was modelled according to Moe, the hosts come to weigh the souls immediately after death and to decide where they are to go until the Day of Judgement. Moe notes that K3 begins with the approach of the two armies and that in L1 they arrive as the visionary is crossing *Gjallarbru* which '. . . in reality means the same, since the bridge after all simply depicts the crossing from the world of the living to that of the dead'.[111] L5, by placing the arrival of the hosts at the end, is moving away from the idea of a provisional judgement, but as yet contains no features suggestive of the Day of Judgement. In K1 and K5 the process is complete. Here the Day of Judgement rounds off the ballad. Moe certainly argues an interesting case, but there are a number of objections to be raised. As usual a medieval vision is taken as the starting point and *Dr* explained largely in accordance with it. We do not know, however, that *Dr* was based on the vision of Thurcill or any other vision; this remains to be demonstrated. If we examine more thoroughly the *Dr* variants which contain the section under discussion, we shall see better the difficulties facing anyone who wishes to demonstrate a literary connection between them and Thurcill. Moe's division of the variants into two classes gives no clear idea of the extent to which the sequence of events differs in each variant. This becomes even more apparent if those not included in his survey are analysed as well. In K1 we have the approach of the hosts and the judgement at the end after paradise, the meeting with the godmother, the mention of *Broksvalin* and the punishments; K3 begins with the approach of the two hosts but is really too short (seven stanzas) to allow any firm conclusions to be drawn from it; in K5 the approach of the hosts and the judgement comes at the end after the punishments, the ice, paradise and *Pelegrems kjørkje*;[112] L4 and L1 place the approach of the two hosts in the middle of the *Gjallarbru* stanzas; in L5 the hosts approach near the end between the *sæl* stanzas and one of the 'journey up to the clouds' group;[113] V9 places a single stanza about the host from the south at the end after two *sæl* stanzas, the meeting with the godmother and a punishment; S6 has only the host from the north between two *sæl* and two punishment stanzas followed by one about *Gjallarbru* which is the last; T5 devotes three of its eight stanzas to the hosts and the judgement, but the order is not entirely clear; in all likelihood the three occur between two stanzas about the loss of the scarlet cloak and two punishments. In such a muddle any clear resemblance to the preliminary judgement in Thurcill is hard to find. Quite another question is the correctness of the criteria by which Moe divides the variants into classes. The position of the relevant stanzas is obviously important, but the presence or absence of a judgement scene seems less so, since we cannot be sure of what judgement is being described. According to Moe himself it is the presence of Christ, the trumpet and the reference to *all* the souls which suggests the Day of Judgement.[114] Here the variants have: K1 all three; K3 Christ;

K5 all three; L4 and L1 Christ; L5 Christ; V9 none; S6 none; T5 Christ (in what appears to be a variant reading) and *all* the souls. A further objection to Moe's theory is his equation, for the purpose of classifying K3 and L1 together, of *Gjallarbru* 'the crossing from the world of the living to that of the dead' with the beginning of the visionary's journey. The journey must surely begin as soon as the soul leaves the body, but between this and the arrival at *Gjallarbru*, in Moe's own version as well as a number of variants, lie the thorny moor and the thorny hedge, or other tortures associated with the loss of the scarlet cloak. Furthermore, whatever their origin in popular or religious belief, *Gjallarbru* and the bridges in a number of medieval visions seem chiefly to serve as instruments of torture or punishment for wicked souls.[115] They can hardly be seen, at least not first and foremost, as the gateway to the world of the dead or the place where St Michael and the devil fight for possession of the souls of the newly dead and decide where they are to go. Finally there are the enigmatic third and fourth lines of MM 37 (S.165, cf. also 166): *so vog han adde synde-såline/ burt ti Jesum Krist.* Moe, contradicting his other arguments, gives these lines prophetic significance by comparing them with a belief in total salvation which seems to have arisen during the middle ages.[116] However, *Dr* does not otherwise have the appearance of being a prophecy (perhaps the soundest reason for arguing that the judgement stanzas do not depict the Day of Judgement). This is a point made by Liestøl who adds: '*All* the souls must therefore mean all those who were at that time gathered in *Brokksvaline*, and the passage, does not, as was the opinion of Moltke Moe, convey any teaching of a common salvation for all.'[117] What Liestøl presumably means is that, in contrast to the many other souls the visionary saw, the particular batch at *Broksvalin* were spared the tortures of purgatory and permitted to await the Day of Judgement in comfort and delight (on the *mons gaudii* of Thurcill's vision ?). But it accords ill with medieval vision literature in general and Thurcill's in particular that sinful souls should escape punishment. We can perhaps arrive at a more satisfactory explanation of these lines if we assume that although the scene described is specific, the implication is entirely general (as seems to be the case in many *Dr* stanzas). The inference of MM 37 (i.e. K1,28) would then simply be that St Michael is merciful and will help the souls of the dead,[118] but the scene which brings this home to the reader or listener is that of a judgement at which those weighed in the balance are not found wanting. Such an interpretation has the advantage that we are able to base it solely on *Dr* as we have it today and can avoid the necessity of seeking support in medieval visions for lengthy and confused arguments about whether the Day of Judgement or a preliminary judgement is meant. The judgement stanzas of *Dr* were doubtless abbreviated, lengthened and moved around according to the interpretation or whim of the individual singer and the quality of his or her memory. That is certainly what we would expect of oral literature and is the impression gained from a study of the variants. It is difficult to show, however, that they, more than any other stanzas, underwent a deliberate re-working of the kind apparently envisaged by Moe.[119] This being so, and given that the variant which deals with the judgement in most detail (K1) is one of the oldest, longest and most coherent, it would seem better to follow this in a reconstructed text by placing the judgement stanzas at the end. It is of course conceivable that these stanzas were once modelled on Thurcill's vision (and included a description of '. . . St Michael leading the souls of the righteous to glory'),[120] but there is nothing to suggest this now whichever variant one follows. We are confronted with yet another example of Moe's disposition to ignore existing variants in his commentary and text. Medieval visions were the primary source; the extant *Dr* in its many guises simply provided the raw material from which Moe fashioned his ballad.

4. Perhaps the most striking aspect of Moe's commentary to a modern student of *Dr* is the almost dogmatic certainty with which he declared large parts of the ballad to be loans, from Gottskalk, Thurcill or other medieval sources. Thus the structure of the punishment section was modelled on Thurcill, though MM 38 was taken from Gottskalk;[121] MM 43 '. . . is apparently a free, remarkable adaptation of a feature in Thurcill's vision';[122] the similarity between the *sæl* stanzas of *Dr* and the Scottish *Lyke-wake Dirge* can only be explained by a historical connection which, together with the Middle English loan-words, the strong influence of Thurcill's vision and other factors provides weighty evidence that *Dr* was composed in northern England;[123] 'I can see no other possible way of explaining our stanza [MM 47] than on the basis of the account in Tundale';[124] the description of *Grutte gråskjegg* approaching on horseback is based on Thurcill's vision, but when the author of *Dr* heard about the devil on horseback in Thurcill he immediately remembered Óðinn and his horse *Sleipnir* and instinctively altered his original,[125] and so on.

This brief analysis of Moe's contribution to the study of *Dr* has dwelt largely on its negative aspects. It is therefore only fair to stress that Moe himself never lived to complete his work; what we have are fragments pieced together from various sources. A thorough revision might have led him to many new conclusions and even prompted a different approach to the textual problems. In spite of its many deficiencies there is no doubt that Moe's work lifted *Dr* studies out of their infancy and created a firm foundation of knowledge on which other workers in the field could build and to which they often turn for inspiration and guidance.

Hjalmar Falk's work on *Sólarljóð* contains only a few brief references to *Dr*. After a careful study of both poems he came to the conclusion that any connection between them was not such as to suggest direct loans by the one or the other: 'the many similarities can easily be explained as reflections of a common source.'[126]

2.6 The notes of Fredrik Paasche

In 1914 the Norwegian literary historian, Fredrik Paasche, published a work called *Kristendom og kvad*, based partly on an article which appeared in *Edda* the same year.[127] Both deal, among other things, with certain aspects of *Dr*. Paasche attempted to revive the idea, first suggested by Jørgen Moe, that Olav Åsteson was St Ólafr. He mentions the fact that St Ólafr was 'highly visionary'[128] and sees the phrase *Olafr sagdi drauma sina* in *Flateyjarbók* as corresponding to the *Olav Åsteson tel'e sine draume* of *Dr*.[129] Of greater weight, according to Paasche, is the parallel, also in *Flateyjarbók*, between Ólafr, Ásta's son, and *Cristus Mariu son*. Such a parallel was doubtless intended by the saga writer since it is stated that Ólafr suffered his martyrdom *j eftirliking sealfs grædarans*.[130] Against this it can be argued that St Ólafr is nowhere in medieval sources called Åstuson. Moltke Moe, who believed that the name went back to the epithet *guðs ástsonr*, considered it '. . . unthinkable that St Ólafr, the national saint, could have been described other than as *St* Ólafr at the time *Draumkvædet* was composed, still less that he should be known by his *mother's* name'.[131] Paasche himself admits that ' . . . the negative argument – the objections which can be raised against other interpretations – is the strongest'.[132] But few objections can surely be raised against the suggestion that Olav was a real or fictional character from Telemark or some other part of Norway, who had a vision or played the main part in a visionary poem or ballad?

Paasche's main contribution to the study of *Dr* is his total rejection of the idea that the St Michael of the judgement stanzas, on his white horse and with his long horn, is modelled on Heimdall.[133] He shows that St

Michael's connection with the Day of Judgement, the horse and the horn is old and well established in Christian literature and argues plausibly that one need seek no further for an explanation of these attributes of *sankte såle Mikkjel*.[134]

2.7 The work of Ivar Mortensson

The 1920s saw the publication of a number of articles and books about *Dr*. The poet and pastor, Ivar Mortensson-Egnund, was responsible for several of these. His first article appeared in 1915 in *Vidar* and was followed a year later in the same periodical by a reconstructed text of *Dr* containing 107 stanzas.[135] In 1920 came the article 'Draumkvæde-skalden' in *Norsk aarbok*, in 1926 the poetic cycle *Gjallarbrui*, together with a reconstructed text of *Dr* containing 119 stanzas, and finally in 1927 the books *Grunnsteinen i norsk bokheim* and *Draumkvedet i ny uppsetjing med utgreidingar*, the latter nothing more than the reconstructed text of 1926.[136] Mortensson's main thesis is that the author of *Dr* laid the foundations of modern Norwegian (oral) literature;[137] indeed, so powerful was the influence of his work that it not only served as a model for all the Norwegian ballads, but lent much material to *Sólarljóð* and was the principal source of the visions of both Gottskalk and Thurcill '. . . which are merely uninspired copies by semi-learned monks'.[138] The texts of 1916 and 1926–7 are over twice as long as Moltke Moe's and differ from each other quite widely in both content and stanza sequence. Mortensson implies that his texts are constructed on 'inner, organic principles'.[139] What this in fact means is that all previous work on the ballad as well as the testimony of the variants themselves is subordinated to the results of his highly subjective 'investigations'. Liestøl had stated that '. . . so much [of *Dr*] must be lost that it is extremely difficult to piece the fragments together again and make any sort of complete work'.[140] Mortensson decided that this task would be much easier if some of the things that were lost could be rediscovered, and set about combing the Norwegian ballads and *gamlestev* for anything his investigations suggested might once have been part of *Dr*. He even went to the length of composing a stanza and a refrain on the strength of certain remarks in Landstad's introduction to the ballad in *Norske Folkeviser*.[141]

Mortensson's reconstructions bear little relation to the *Dr* variants we know. They can be said to be loosely based on them, but that is all. Breaking down one of his texts (1926–7) we find that about eighty-nine stanzas are taken from what in this edition is considered to be *Dr* material – an exact figure is hard to give because some of them are markedly different from anything we find in the variants – twenty-eight are taken from other ballads or collections of *gamlestev*, one is taken from a variant stanza in Landstad's notes[142] and one is composed by the editor himself (cf. note 141 above).[143] In reconstructing the ballad Mortensson, like Moltke Moe, was guided by the evidence of certain medieval pieces of literature. But this was not all he had to assist him. To Mortensson *Dr* was no ordinary poem, no simple vision; it was an initiation into a mystical cult, a test of admission to an occult, theosophical movement whose members were a group of mystics, most probably monks of the Cistercian order. The author was certainly a Cistercian – one Rúnólfr, who founded the monastery of Lyse (1146). He was also the visionary,[144] and Christmas 1147 was the likely date of his vision or initiation.[145] 'Initiation formulas and the guidance of the poet'[146] were thus of some importance for Mortensson's reconstructions, although he also relied on the visions of Gottskalk and Thurcill (and Tundale?) and the poem *Sólarljóð* (cf. above). Earlier vision literature was of little significance since the creator of *Dr* was '. . . an original poet, a man so rich and great that he would scarcely need to borrow much from others'.[147] But there *was* the belt which Hrani, St Ólafr's foster-father, fetched from the mound of Ólafr Geirstaðaálfr and gave to Ólafr together with the dead king's name;[148] Ólafr had lost the belt, so the story went,[149] and as a consequence things were going badly in Norway; perhaps it was God's will that he, the dreamer, the creator of *Dr*, should take the path that Hermóðr had once ridden, follow in Þórr's footsteps and retrieve the belt – that Ólafr, the protector of Norway, should be born a third time.[150] And so the belt was retrieved, Rúnólfr gained the name of Ólafr[151] – and Mortensson's *Dr* grew by some ten stanzas.[152]

This was not the only occasion on which the editor submerged in a sea of fantasy. In his search for the plan to which *Dr* was constructed he seized on the word *dyrering* which, as Landstad had pointed out, means the zodiac.[153] The refrain *Månen skine/ og vegjine falle so vide* '. . . must indicate that same path through the zodiac which is traversed by the moon as well. If we use this as a guide, the arrangement of the sections falls automatically into place; they correspond to the signs of the zodiac which the moon passes through from *Taurus* to *Sagittarius*.'[154] The ways in which Mortensson brings in the various signs are sometimes tortuous, often ingenious and always totally unconvincing, not least since the ballad which emerges is so utterly unlike any or all of the *Dr* variants we know. However, Mortensson is finally vindicated in his own eyes. The moon takes a little more than two days and nights to pass through each sign of the zodiac. Taurus and Sagittarius merely mark the places where the path the visionary took is crossed by the Milky Way, so the whole journey, following the moon, corresponded to the twelve days he slept. Mortensson is thus able to conclude: 'When I had pieced together *Draumkvede* stanzas which are found in various MSS and arranged them in sections according to this plan and removed what seemed to be mere variants and accretions, and in addition had expanded the poem with stanzas from *gamlestev* or ballads which I had reason to believe could or must be loans from *Draumkvedet*, I received confirmation, as it were, that I was on the right track, since there was a section for each day the visionary was away.'[155] This quotation is a good example of what is essentially wrong with the whole of Mortensson's work on *Dr*. He continually propounds theories and seeks to prove them right with the help of other theories or texts of his own construction; sometimes he makes no attempt at all to demonstrate the correctness of his ideas, but simply proceeds as if they were established facts. It is hardly sufficient to dismiss his publications as 'more the work of a poet than a strictly scientific treatise'.[156] Mortensson himself scarcely saw them as part of his poetic output (except, presumably, *Gjallarbrui*), and Torkel Ofteli in his article 'Draumekvæde-skalden'[157] presents a summary of Mortensson's conclusions as if they were the results of a thorough and scholarly investigation. It also seems likely that Rudolf Steiner was influenced by his theory about the signs of the zodiac (cf. Section 2.8, pp. 35–6).

In many ways Mortensson's work is simply an extreme example of the refusal by Norwegian scholars to treat seriously the variants they had. It is far removed from Moltke Moe's relatively careful studies, but it is part of the same tradition. An interesting question, for example, is raised by Mortensson when he says: 'An editor dare not now dismiss anything which according to tradition belongs to *Draumkvedet*, unless he has very good reasons.'[158] But what the possible criteria might be for including or excluding such material he never discusses. Instead we are treated to an explanation of the 'plan' of the ballad and a description of the author – the author, that is, of Mortensson's reconstruction; about the author or authors of the *Dr* variants we come from his books none the wiser.

At the end of the article 'Draumkvæde-skalden' Mortensson expresses his sentiments with a quotation (*Hávamál* 143, of which the fourth line has been replaced by two of the author's own): *For æser Odin,/ for alvar Daain,/ Dvalin for dvergar./ Ranulv for hordar/ og telar skar runer./ Eg sjølv riste sume.* ('For the Æsir Óðinn, for the elves Dáinn, Dvalinn for the dwarves. Rúnólfr for the men of Hordaland and the men of Telemark cut runes. I myself cut some.') Perhaps, in Mortensson's own spirit of enquiry, we could take his inclusion of the last line of this verse as a hint that he wrote his books and articles on *Dr* with tongue in cheek.

2.8 Some contributions in German

Outside Scandinavia it is only in the German-speaking world that *Dr* has received much attention. Rudolf Steiner, the founder of the Anthroposophical movement, was greatly interested in the ballad and lectured on it in the early 1910s using his own translation.[159] Erich Trummler, likewise an Anthroposophist, published a translation of *Dr* together with an introduction to the history of the ballad in 1927.[160] The occultist, Ludwig Hoffmann, who according to his own words spent many years of his life studying *Dr*, published three works on the subject, each of which included a 'literal' translation by himself.[161] It was from Lammer's Norwegian text[162] that the German translations were made in every case.

Steiner's, Trummler's and Hoffmann's approach to *Dr* is entirely uncritical and marked by an almost nonchalant disregard for factual detail. Their works are riddled with inaccuracies, and doubtful or fantastic interpretations of the ballad and details in or connected with it are offered as though they were undisputed facts. Steiner's lack of familiarity with the Norwegian language does not seem to have inspired in him the caution one might have expected. His translation (made on the basis of a word-for-word rendering in German by the Norwegian authoress, Ingeborg Møller) is often a tendentious paraphrase,[163] and although he is able to tell us that, for example, the Norwegian dialects (Volkssprache) contain much '. . . was hart herangeht an die Grenze der okkulten Geheimnisse',[164] he seems remarkably ill-informed about even basic facts of Norwegian language, literature and topography. Thus it was in 1850 that Landstad began to collect popular ballads in 'Telemarken, einem einsamen Gebirgstal';[165] *Dr* itself is a 'Legende',[166] and there is a movement in Norway whose aim it is '. . . die alte Sprache – die der ur-germanischen Sprache sehr nahe steht –, die nordische Sprache wieder aufleben zu lassen gegenüber der später eingedrungenen dänischen Sprache'.[167] Steiner seems to see Olav Åsteson as a clairvoyant and, by a rather fanciful interpretation of his name, as having inherited this gift from his forefathers: 'Aber wenn man alles berücksichtigt, was in Frage kommt, so heisst etwa *Olaf Åsteson:* der, der da noch ein Sohn ist jener Seele, die von Generation zu Generation heruntergeht und mit dem Blute, das von Generation zu Generation rinnt, zusammenhängt. So haben wir diesen Namen aber zurückgeführt zu dem, was wir so oft auf anthroposophischem Felde besprochen haben: daß in alten Zeiten das alte Hellsehen zusammenhing mit der Verwandtschaft des *Blutes*, das durch die Generationen rinnt. Und man würde etwa Olaf Åsteson übersetzen können mit: Olaf, der aus vielen Generationen Geborene und die Charaktere aus vielen Generationen noch in der Seele Tragende.'[168] No attempt is made to indicate that similarities with *Dr* are found in medieval vision literature, we are simply told that what Olav experienced '. . . der nordische Mensch in seiner Art als Vision empfinden kann', and '. . . während ganz sicher solche Visionen immer wiederum namentlich in germanischen Ländern erlebt worden sind, scheint vergessen gewesen zu sein dieses Traumlied'.[169] Concerning the identity of Olav Åsteson Steiner says: 'Viele Leute glauben natürlich, daß es anspielt an St. Olaf, der 1030 nach Christi das Christentum eingeführt hat und dessen Mutter Åste geheissen hat, die Liebe. Damit verhält es sich so wie mit vielem: daß zugleich Geschichtliches und Spirituelles vorliegt',[170] a statement which hardly clarifies the issue. However, in her notes which are appended to the text of the lectures, Ingeborg Møller states that Steiner advised her not to adhere to the view that St Ólafr (who fell in 1035!)[171] was the original Olav Åsteson: 'Es habe mehrere "Olaf Åsteson" gegeben, sagte Dr. Steiner. Es war dies eine Art Mysterien-Titel.'[172] This, and the interpretation of the name Olav, referred to above, is no doubt the basis of the view, attributed to Steiner in Møller's note, that *Dr* originated about A.D. 400. This dating was apparently the result of further research on the ballad, but was only communicated orally by Steiner to some friends during a visit to Norway in 1921 or 1923. The remainder of what he had to say to them, although attributed by Møller to Steiner himself, reflects familiarity with the views of Ivar Mortensson, discussed in 2.7: 'Damals [about A.D. 400] lebte ein großer, christlicher Eingeweihter hier im Lande. Er begründete eine Mysterienschule in Südnorwegen; der Ort wurde nicht genannt. Sein Mysterienname war Olaf Åsteson, und das Lied schildert seine Einweihung. Ursprünglich, so erzählte Dr. Steiner, war das Lied viel länger und hatte zwölf Abschnitte, einen für jedes Bild im Tierkreis.

Das Lied schildert Olaf Åstesons Wanderung durch den ganzen Tierkreis, was er dort sah und erlebte. Es sind nur Reste des ursprünglichen Liedes, die wir heute haben. Die erwähnte Mysterienschule bestand bis in das frühe Mittelalter hinein. Der Leiter wurde immer Olaf Åsteson genannt.'[173] It is inconceivable that Steiner could have arrived at such conclusions independently without some study of the variants, which, since he knew no Norwegian, it is highly unlikely that he undertook.

Beyond asserting that Olav Åsteson had his clairvoyant experience in a less materialistic age, when man lived in closer contact with the macrocosmos, and at a time of year when the human soul is most receptive of clairvoyant experiences, Steiner had little new to say about *Dr*. To *Dr* research he made no contribution whatsoever.

Trummler's translation is a reasonably accurate rendering of Lammer's *Dr* text. Hoffmann's 'literal' translation is grossly inaccurate in a number of places,[174] and the free rendition included in his 1954 work obscures the meaning of the original with even greater thoroughness. Neither author adds anything to our knowledge of *Dr* and both appear to belong to that category of people who put errors into circulation rather than to those who seek to eradicate them. Let one or two brief examples suffice. Trummler tells us in the space of a few pages, and without adducing any evidence whatsoever, that *Dr* existed in the middle of the first millennium after the birth of Christ, that *Grutte Graubart* is the god Hǫðr, Seljord (spelt *Saeljord* by the author) means 'Selig-Erde' and that 'Brokksvalin ist gleichbedeutend mit dem Fegefeuer des Mittelalters und dem Kamaloka der Inder.'[175] Some of the more delightful of Hoffmann's many assertions are that his literal translation was of 'des altnorwegischen Textes', that *gul mor* ('Goldmutter oder goldig strahlende Mutter') is identical with the Frau Holle of German folk-tale and legend ('das urmütterliche göttliche Prinzip, das *Ewig-Weibliche*'), that St Ólafr had the vision which *Dr* describes during Advent or the Christmas period in 1014 in Rouen, that *Gjallarbru* and *Bifrǫst* are one and the same, and 'Das Wort Brokksvalin war den Wikingern ein vertrauter Begriff.'[176]

2.9 The work of Knut Liestøl

Mention has already been made of some of the contributions of the Norwegian folklorist, Knut Liestøl, to the study of *Dr*. His most important work on the ballad was *Draumkvæde, A Norwegian Visionary*

Poem from the Middle Ages (1946) of which a summary in Norwegian appeared in the periodical *Syn og Segn* in 1948.[177] Some of the discussion and the conclusions found in *Draumkvæde* (1946) are based on two earlier articles which first appeared in 1924 and 1925.[178] Liestøl was also responsible for the introduction to *Dr* in the popular edition of the Norwegian ballads published in 1920–4, but this adds nothing to the study.[179]

The aim of Liestøl's 1946 monograph was partly to present *Dr* and the problems surrounding its origins to the English-speaking world, and partly to scrutinise and develop further some of the views and ideas expressed by Moltke Moe. Liestøl had intended to publish a critical edition of the Norwegian ballads, and as part of the preparatory work for this had examined all the *Dr* variants known to him. This, as he says, '... together with a geographical grouping and detailed comparison stanza by stanza has led to certain new and, as I believe, more reliable results with regard to what is genuine and original and what is secondary matter. Consequently, a systematic comparison with other visions led me to a view of the sources which differs somewhat from the one which has hitherto been common.'[180] Liestøl points out that, until all the variants have been printed, it is an 'indispensable prerequisite' of any detailed investigation of the sources to give a survey of all the material of which *Dr* is made up. He nevertheless feels it necessary to add, apologetically, that such a survey '... may be rather dull reading'.[181] In fact it is the most interesting part of the whole book, for it marks the first attempt by anyone to give even a limited account of the material which had been the subject of so much erudite discussion and whose merits had repeatedly been extolled in the most eulogistic, even fulsome terms.[182]

In the chapter which deals with the variants Liestøl makes a most interesting observation. The fact that the various editors of *Dr* each arrived at a different total number of stanzas '... proves clearly that there is no definite and indisputable limit as to how much of the matter contained in the records really belongs to the poem'.[183] Having made this statement, however, Liestøl seems not to grasp its full implications since he continues to accept or dismiss stanzas on the basis of little more than the views of previous scholars or his own intuition. Thus Anne Skaalen's variant (M6 – D in Liestøl, cf. Section 3.4–5) is said to contain 'much spurious and foreign matter'[184] apparently because Bugge, the collector, held this view, and presumably also because Moltke Moe failed to make much use of this variant.[185] Of three other stanzas not included by Moe we are told that the first '... has the true old ring', while the second is 'banal and evidently new' and the third '. . . must – in its present form – be a more recent verse'.[186] No reasons are given for any of these judgements. Nor is any attempt made to define 'spurious' in the context of *Dr*, which would seem a sensible precaution since we know nothing for sure about its origins. Finally, having earlier said that there is no definite limit to the amount of matter which 'belongs to' *Dr*, Liestøl informs us that: 'Excepting for a certain number of variations in single expressions this [Moltke Moe's text, with the addition of one or two (or three ?) stanzas] is the whole of the material.'[187]

Among the variants K1 and L1/4 are singled out as 'the principal versions'.[188] Landstad had already drawn attention to the qualities of K1, and Jørgen Moe used L1 fairly extensively in his reconstruction (although he had fewer variants than Landstad to choose from). Furthermore, in Liestøl's view, the information supplied to Moe and Landstad by the two informants made it possible to trace the history of these variants back to the middle of the eighteenth century or earlier.[189] Liestøl seems to assume that K1 and L1 remained relatively unchanged for over a century,[190] but Anne Lillegaard's two versions, which were written down within a few years of each other, differ both as regards the number of stanzas they contain and, to some extent, their order. Liestøl, oddly enough, ignores this altogether and talks as though there were only one variant. In his appendix he prints a text in which L1 and L4 have been combined and the orthography and linguistic forms partially normalised. He does indicate here that there are two MSS, but makes it appear that they are identical with each other and his printed version. As regards K1 there is no mention of the heading *Vil du mæg høire etc.* or the note *40 Vers* at the top of the right-hand margin (cf. Section 3.7, K1, text and note 7). The significance of these additions to the text are difficult to determine, but they could indicate that what we have is a very imperfect record of the tradition which 'extends to the earlier half of the 18th century' and is 'so complete and genuine'.[191]

Liestøl notes that K1 and L1/4 are markedly different, but states: 'Originally, of course, the sequence [of events] must have been *one*.' He visualises *both* as having deviated from a common original, but considers that where they have the same sequence '. . . an old connection has been preserved'. He also feels that there may have been 'hidden channels of communication' between the two lines of tradition, but points out nevertheless that the fact that they are markedly different suggests they '. . . diverged at an early date'.[192] This last point is, of course, of some importance if we could be sure that the two go back to a common original. To state this as a fact, however, is begging the question (cf. Section 3.3).

An important feature of Liestøl's survey of the variants ought to have been his arrangement of them in geographical groups, but the approach is unsystematic and lacking in detail. It was of some help to the author in deciding that *Draumkvæde* and not *Draugkveen* was the correct title of the ballad, and that the name of the visionary was originally Olav Åkneson.[193] Light was also shed on Moltke Moe's statement: 'The swamps in the other world are sometimes called *Gaglemyran* as well as *Våsemyran*.'[194] One is probably a geographical variant of the other.[195] Apart from this, however, Liestøl does not seem to have gained much from looking at *Dr* from 'the geographical point of view'.[196]

A decidedly unsatisfactory aspect of Liestøl's work is his treatment of vision literature and its relevance to *Dr*. He is able to dispute or develop certain of Moe's assumptions, but offers little that is basically new. It is true that he dismisses Gottskalk's vision as a possible source and introduces that of Gundelin instead,[197] but it was Liestøl himself who argued: 'The very fact that one has to search for the source of the individual features of *Draumkvædet* now in Gottskalk, now in Thurcill, shows that neither of these visions alone can have provided the inspiration'[198] – words which apply with equal force to his own theories. Indeed, in his article 'Til Draumkvædet' Liestøl pointed out that such similarities as there are between the visions of Gottskalk and Thurcill on the one hand and *Dr* on the other do not necessarily indicate knowledge of these visions by the author of *Dr*, but may be due to familiarity with other, similar visions we no longer possess. Yet in *Draumkvæde* (1946) he states: 'There appears to be no doubt that the author of *Draumkvæde* in some form must have known Tundal's and Gundelin's visions and borrowed from them important material for the building up of his own poem', and: 'Our poem is . . . in the main based on three visions: Tundal's, Gundelin's, and, last but not least, Thurkill's.'[199]

Liestøl's most useful contributions to the study of *Dr* (apart from his attempt to describe the variants) are to be found in chapters V and VI of his 1946 monograph. Chapter V is called 'General Vision Motifs in *Draumkvæde*'. Moltke Moe's reconstructed text is examined, and a number of such motifs revealed. In addition to this, however, certain stanzas (MM 11–13, 15, 26) are declared spurious, and it is suggested that at least some of them are *gamlestev*.[200] The confusion of *Dr* stanzas with *gamlestev* is a question of fundamental importance, and it is here for the first time that any real attempt is made to discuss the subject.[201] Liestøl notes that most of the stanzas he is in doubt about lack 'connection' with 'the visions'[202] (the same approach as used by Moltke Moe) and likens some of them to the so-called *ferdastev* (*gamlestev* which describe a journey). But there is no attempt to systematise the problem and to suggest what general criteria, if any, might be used for deciding what are *gamlestev* and what is *Dr*. Without some sort of systematisation, however, any pronouncements about the genuineness or otherwise of *Dr* stanzas must seem haphazard and lack conviction. Chapter VI is entitled 'Norse Matter in *Draumkvæde*' and includes a section on *Gjallarbru* which gives many examples of the occurrence of this name in Scandinavian ballads.[203] The chapter also contains Liestøl's interpretation of the name *Gaglemyrane*, which first appeared in 1924.[204]

As distinct from Moltke Moe, Liestøl was of the opinion that *Dr* was composed in Norway.[205] The date he gives for its composition varies from about 1300 in 'Til Draumkvædet' to 'the central sixty years of the thirteenth century' in his 1946 monograph.[206] In both cases, however, it is clear that this is a *terminus a quo*. As the Swedish literary historian, Karl-Ivar Hildeman, has pointed out, no real attempt is ever made to argue the case for a *terminus ante quem*.[207]

Taken as a whole, Liestøl's work on *Dr* is disappointing. He had access to virtually all the material and studied all the then known variants of the ballad, yet what he produced was in the main no more than a complement to Moltke Moe's earlier studies. His work is also marred, as was Moe's, by a certain carelessness in the treatment of factual detail. It would be less than fair, however, to dismiss Liestøl's work out of hand. It provides us with a number of fresh problems to think about, even if it fails to give us any satisfactory answers or lay a firm basis on which to discuss them.

2.10 Notes by Magnus Olsen, Rikard Berge and Anders Bugge

Three minor contributions to the study of *Dr* were made by the Norwegian scholars, Magnus Olsen, Rikard Berge and Anders Bugge.[208]

Olsen drew parallels between the practice of tying *helskór* to the feet of dead men and MM 46 (S.147), and considered that *Vosemyran* and *Gjallarbru* should be seen in the same light as the *heklemog* of this stanza: 'in the first period after the introduction of Christianity the journey across swamps and rivers in the other world was made easy for the person in whose memory a road had been cleared or a bridge made in this world.'[209] This idea is not, of course, specifically stated anywhere in *Dr*, but it could perhaps have been in the mind of whoever composed the *sæl* stanzas.

Berge discussed briefly the preservation of the ballad in the Vinje and Rauland districts of Telemark and printed a variant he had himself collected from the informant Margit Tveiten (V9)[210] who, according to him, represented a line of tradition which could be followed back to the late eighteenth century. Berge stresses the fact that the ballad was so popular in the west of Telemark that almost every ballad singer knew one or two stanzas. The general impression, however, was that no one knew all of it.

Bugge attempted to trace the *Broksvalin* image back to a certain type of church portico, specifically the Pórtico de la Gloria in the Cathedral of St James in Santiago de Compostela, and also to the entrance porches found in many stave-churches. The persuasiveness of Bugge's theory depends, of course, not least on the way one interprets the name *Broksvalin*. He suggests 'vestibules of the clouds' (*skysvalene*) as a modification of Landstad's 'halls of the clouds' (*Skyernes Sale*), but there is no certainty about the meaning of this word (cf. Section 5.2).

2.11 Dag Strömbäck's article

The year 1946 saw the publication not only of Liestøl's monograph, but also of a perceptive article by the Swedish folklorist, Dag Strömbäck,[211] who cast a critical eye on the arguments for an early dating of *Dr* and on the assumption that the author borrowed motifs and images from specific medieval visions. Strömbäck commences his article by stating that MM is 'acceptable'[212] and the text on which his remarks are to be based. This somewhat unpromising beginning fortunately proves to be of little significance for what follows. MM is clearly chiefly preferred because it is longer than the one genuine variant known to Strömbäck at this time (K1) of which he says: 'The various stages of the visionary's journey are depicted more clearly and consistently here than in the version [MM] whose contents we have just related.'[213] It was the raw material of which *Dr* was made up, in particular the *Gjallarbru* motif, rather than the way it was put together, which interested Strömbäck, and in the event MM proved as sound a basis for his discussion as any other available text could have done.

Strömbäck makes the same general point as Liestøl (in 1925), but with greater force, that such evidence as has been produced to show that *Dr* is based on one or more medieval visions is unconvincing. If any of the motifs do go back to the visions of Gottskalk, Thurcill, Tundale or Gundelin, they doubtless passed through many intermediate stages which are now unknown to us.

The larger part of Strömbäck's article is devoted to a discussion of the *Gjallarbru* motif and to demonstrating the occurrence of the name in medieval and post-Reformation sources. The material is virtually the same as that produced by Liestøl (cf. p. 40 above) with one or two additional examples of some importance. Strömbäck is able to show that *Gielle-broe* (various spellings) occurs in two Danish ballads of entirely different periods, and that the name *Gielde-myre* is found in a third. He considers it unlikely that all three occurrences can be ascribed to Norwegian influence. In Sweden a form *gille broo* is found among the prophecies and visions of the beggar and preacher Jöns Anderson who was active in the 1580s. Here it is stated: 'He has also seen *gille broo.* It is fifteen *milar* long and big, full of razors and the teeth of flax-combs and nails which are made on Fridays and Sundays; and all the knives and nails which are made on that day go thither from this world and increase that bridge. And the dark flame stands burning on all sides of the bridge, and there lies purgatory. Whosoever gives shoes in God's name, will not be compelled to cross that bridge.' The name also occurs in a contemporary satirical poem about the excesses of the Roman Church: 'If you worship the saints with steadfast faith, they will help you over *Gillebro*', and further: 'Teach your flock to believe in the gates of hell and *gillebro,* across which they needs must go barefoot upon the many iron pincers, unless they give you a pair of shoes with as much money in them as they can hold; in that case nothing shall harm their feet, although their purse must suffer a knock.'[214] Strömbäck considers Jöns Anderson's vision indicative of the fact that the detailed, almost systematic descriptions of the other world which were current in the later middle ages contrived to influence popular traditions about life after death up to and even after the Reformation. He makes no specific comment on the satire, but the fact that several of the motifs found in *Dr* are ridiculed, alongside holy water and the intercession of saints,[215] certainly suggests that they formed a significant part of religious belief up to the time of the Reformation. The Swedish evidence is undoubtedly of importance for the dating of *Dr.* It shows that the type of motif which might be taken as evidence of an early date of composition could as easily be indicative of late, even post-Reformation origins. On the other hand it is not proof that *Dr* was composed in the early fifteenth century – a date favoured by Strömbäck[216] – or at any other time. Rather it serves to increase our uncertainty.

Strömbäck sees *Dr* as a parallel to the Scottish *Lyke-wake Dirge* (not, like Moltke Moe, as a closely related work) and views both as products of intellectual and spiritual milieux similar to that which gave rise to Jöns Anderson's visions. He considers it not unlikely that *Dr* was a genuine vision or trance, inspired by the terrible descriptions of death and judgement, purgatory and retribution which were current at the time (the fifteenth century ?), and sees one of many parallels in the vision of the Icelandic woman, Rannveig, in the year 1199.[217] It is not quite clear how Strömbäck visualises the composition of *Dr*. He simply says: 'The poem was then constructed around these shattering experiences [the vision] which were related in the village, and was sung over the centuries to a ballad melody in Telemark.'[218] In addition he thinks it very likely that a number of things were added and lost in the course of oral transmission and stresses the interplay there must have been between *Dr* and *gamlestev*. This view of the genesis of *Dr* is certainly reasonable, but again no evidence is produced anywhere in the article which compels us to believe in it. It is only fair to stress, however, that Strömbäck is never dogmatic and gives his views no more than the status of suggestions.

On one point Strömbäck seems to have gone astray. He argues that traces of Nordic heathen belief in *Dr* are no evidence of an early date of composition; such 'reminiscences'[219] of the heathen past survived far into modern times. Clearly he is thinking chiefly of *Gjallarbru*. It is surely, however, as a symbol of Nordic-Roman Christianity that *Gjallarbru* survives. So much so that after the Reformation *gillebro* is satirised in Sweden together with other trappings of the Roman Church, and *Gieldebroo* in a Danish ballad was changed to *Himmerjge*.[220]

Strömbäck's article, although short, was an important milestone in *Dr* studies. Having no interest in raising *Dr* to the status of Norway's foremost literary product of the middle ages, he was able to perceive and to challenge many of the assumptions about the age and character of the ballad on which Norwegian scholarship had up to then been based. While providing no convincing answer as to when and in what circumstances *Dr* was composed, he demonstrated that it could be much younger than generally supposed – even post-Reformation – and thus threw open the whole question of the ballad's age and origins.

2.12 Hans Midbøe's literary-psychological study

In 1949 the Norwegian literary historian, Hans Midbøe, published what he described as a literary-psychological analysis of *Dr* entitled *Draumkvedet. En studie i norsk middelalder*. He considered that the detailed discussion of motifs and sources by scholars such as Moltke Moe, Liestøl and Strömbäck was insufficient to give us a full understanding of the ballad, since it told us nothing about 'the position of the author, his experience and most important of all: his intention'.[221] The burden of Midbøe's argument is that *Dr* is a didactic poem, a literary vision with a clear purpose, of the type used by the mendicant friars to impress on people the need to show charity towards the poor (cf. the *sæl* stanzas) and the spiritual dangers inherent in not doing so. Midbøe stresses '. . . the practical, down-to-earth attitude to which the description [in the ballad] continually gives expression'[222] and finds this reminiscent of the mendicant friars' style of preaching. He also sees a parallel between MM 8–27 and the wandering life of many of these friars (cf. SS.39,43,76,79, 83,86–7,89–90,95,98,101,103,107,109,111,115–16,119,121). He considers MM 5 and 45 (cf. SS.34–7,84) indicative of a less than friendly attitude to the secular clergy which was common among Franciscans and Dominicans, and uses the supposed venom of these stanzas to localise the author of *Dr* to the Franciscan monastery in Oslo which was built in the 1290s in the face of energetic opposition from the Bishop and Chapter. Midbøe even mentions a number of names of men active in the second half of the thirteenth century,[223] though without suggesting directly that any one of these may be the author of *Dr*.[224] He could not have thought seriously of attributing the ballad to any of them because he finally dates its composition to the middle of the fourteenth century.[225]

Midbøe raises a number of interesting points, but his work fails to establish anything new about *Dr*. There are two main reasons for this. First, he lapses into subjective reasoning, a fault which he rightly criticises in Ivar Mortensson; one hypothesis is often built upon another. Second, his literary-psychological analysis is based entirely on MM. This fact is not even stated, let alone discussed, yet its implications for Midbøe's study are far-reaching indeed.

One of the author's main hypotheses, as we have seen, is that *Dr* was composed in the fourteenth century by a member of the Church. He argues against Strömbäck's theory of lay authorship, accepting Liestøl's view that *Dr* was based on specific medieval visions emanating from

Britain – and therefore, if for no other reason, the work of a cleric.[226] The extent of the ballad's dependence on such visions is not always made clear. Thus it is stated, for example, that in the judgement stanzas the author '. . . by and large goes his own way',[227] yet later it is suggested that the differences between these stanzas and the description in Thurcill's vision upon which Moltke Moe thought they were based may be due to the fact that the author was using a different vision which is now lost.[228] However this may be, Midbøe plainly considers a number of features in *Dr* to have their origin in events of the late thirteenth and early fourteenth centuries rather than literary sources: MM 5 (cf. SS.34–7), for example, in which the exciting dreams of the visionary are contrasted with the tedium of the church service, may well symbolise the conflict between the established Church and the mendicant friars as seen by the latter;[229] typical of this conflict was the battle over the establishment of a Franciscan monastery in Oslo; a Franciscan connected with this monastery who had taken part in the struggle might well have composed *Dr*; it cannot have been one of the lesser, unknown friars – only a man of great intellect who had studied in Britain and become a leading member of his order could have written such a poem;[230] and so we arrive, perhaps, at a certain friar 'Ivar'. This series of hypotheses, against most of which serious criticisms can be made, stems ultimately from the first about the authorship and date of *Dr*, and this seems to owe much to an uncritical acceptance of Liestøl's views and an incomplete understanding of the arguments put forward by Strömbäck.

Midbøe presumably believed that the textual problems of *Dr* had largely been solved by Moltke Moe, and therefore did not realise how risky a task he was undertaking. It clearly will not do to build a literary-psychological analysis on a reconstructed text, in particular one so different from the individual variants on which it is based. Much of Midbøe's actual analysis is wholly or partly dependent on the order of the stanzas as they appear in MM,[231] but, as we have seen, the stanza sequence in *Dr* is one of the most uncertain features of the ballad. Midbøe is dependent on Moe's text in other ways too. He suggests at one point that the fact that there are six *sæl* stanzas may have literary significance. To those who object that the *sæl* section is rather poorly preserved in the variants and that there could, therefore, originally have been more, he can only say: 'This argument cannot . . . be decisive.'[232] According to the numbering of this edition, however, there are sixteen *sæl* stanzas (SS.141–56), although it is of course impossible to say how many are 'original'. The assumptions that MM 38–43 (cf. SS.122–35) depict purgatory and that the *Syslehusi* of MM 44 (cf. S.136) is 'very near the border between purgatory and hell itself'[233] also seem to be taken over from Moltke Moe.[234] Certainly no attempt is made to substantiate them. Midbøe's view of purgatory, on the other hand, appears to be his own: 'Should we not take this description of purgatory as emphasising that which *did not* lead to salvation?'[235] Our answer must be no. If it is indeed purgatory that is being described in *Dr*, the sinners are presumably being cleansed in preparation for their ultimate salvation. Midbøe, however, is not at his best on the subject of salvation and damnation. Having described Moltke Moe's interpretation of the lines *sá vóg han alle syndesjælene/ hen til Jesum Krist* (S.165) as 'theoretical and abstract',[236] he seems to suggest that they are an expression of the possibility of salvation offered by the mendicant friars and defined in the *sæl* stanzas.[237]

Two residual points of interest which emerge from Midbøe's book may be briefly mentioned. The author states that the most remarkable feature of the ballad in his opinion is '. . . the synthesis, the amalgamation of almost ecstatic visions and a practical and realistic view of life which finds expression in the descriptions'.[238] He never tells us in detail what is ecstatic and what practical and realistic or how they are synthesised, but one cannot help wondering how this statement might apply to individual variants; whether any of these contain primarily ecstatic or primarily practical elements. If this were so, it might have a bearing on the question of whether or not we are dealing with more than one ballad, but for Midbøe the question does not arise: 'If *Draumkvedet* is a distinctive, personal work of literature, and who would deny that . . . ?'[239] In a chapter called 'The Wanderer' Midbøe points out that the impression he is left with after reading MM 8–27 is that of a lone wanderer. This naturally accords with his theory of the Franciscan authorship of *Dr*. It is interesting to note, however, that in none of the visions on which Moe and Liestøl (and Midbøe?) considered *Dr* to be based does the visionary make his journey alone. To Midbøe this meant that it was a feature the author had introduced himself, although for the visionary to travel alone is by no means unknown in medieval vision literature. Whatever the case may be, it is certainly right to emphasise this as a point of difference between Gottskalk, Thurcill, Tundale and Gundelin on the one hand and *Dr* on the other.

A comparison between Midbøe's and Mortensson's work on *Dr*, which Midbøe invites,[240] reveals a difference only in the degree of subjectivity they exhibit. In some ways Midbøe is the less critical. He was content to base his book unquestioningly on Moltke Moe's text, and apparently never examined any of the genuine variants. The result speaks for itself.

2.13 Olav Bø's article

In 1955 the Norwegian folklorist, Olav Bø, published an article in the periodical *Norveg* entitled 'Draumkvædet og Gamle-stevet'.[241] As we have already seen, scholars had for some time been aware that the two had become intermixed, but, apart from Liestøl's brief treatment of the subject (cf. Section 2.9), Bø's article was the first attempt to assess the extent to which this had taken place and in particular to identify *gamlestev* among the *Dr* stanzas.

Bø bases his discussion, as many others before him, on MM, but gives the wrong impression that this text does not differ greatly from K1 and L1/4.[242] He suggests that MM 15 and 26 (SS.90,111) are *gamlestev*, and that MM 11–13 and 45 (SS.84,86–7,89) may be mixed stanzas, part genuine *Dr* material and part *stev*, or alternatively, that MM 11–13 at least may be more recent stanzas.[243] Bø then discusses the fact that *gamlestev* were often called *Draumkve'en* or *Draugkve'en*, and that collections of individual stanzas, mostly *gamlestev*, appear with names such as *Draugakvoi* or *Draugkvædet*. These are all, with the exception of *Draugakvoi*, titles which were sometimes given to the groups of stanzas we know as *Dr*. Bø also stresses the similarity of theme between many of the stanzas in *Dr* and large numbers of *gamlestev* which either depict a journey (*ferdastev*) or are gnomic in character (*frødestev*). An important point which is taken up is the occurrence of mythological names such as *Gjallarbru* in *stev* and ballads. It would appear that many of them were well known as late as the nineteenth century and used fairly indiscriminately in new compositions. Finally Bø deals with what he regards as clear examples of mixed stanzas, and concludes by discussing a number of *Dr* variants which contain such stanzas and drawing attention to MSS in which *Dr* stanzas and *gamlestev* are found side by side.

Bø's article sets out to deal with what is perhaps the most important textual problem of *Dr*. It would, however, seem fair to say that he only scratches the surface of the problem. Underlying his work is a supposition that has bedevilled *Dr* studies for over a century, namely that we know what *Dr* is, at least to the extent of being able to judge with some accuracy what is genuine and what is spurious. This allows Bø to talk about 'a *Draumkvæde* stanza with a strongly watered-down form',[244] and to observe that ' . . . the great similarity between genuine *Draumkvæde* stanzas and *gamlestev* caused the ballad to become diluted'.[245] It also underlies his remarks about 'rather free' and more recently composed stanzas.[246] The implication of such statements is that *Dr* had a fixed form which we are able to reconstruct. In fact, however, we know nothing for sure about the history of *Dr* until collectors began to write down ballads in the 1840s. This is not to say that there may not be arguments for declaring some stanzas spurious from a historical and literary viewpoint, and indeed Bø produces a number which merit attention,[247] but before they can be given proper weight, we must know what he considers genuine and why. Closely related to the problem of what is genuine and what is spurious is the question of the length of the ballad. Bø states that '. . . a great deal . . . is lost'[248] and that '. . . perhaps the greater part . . . was forgotten',[249] but what was lost or forgotten? Do we assume that if the collectors had begun their work a century earlier the material we have would be augmented by numerous stanzas, now entirely lost, that were once part of a unified ballad called *Dr*? Or are we to think of a number of existing *gamlestev* as having once, in some form or other, been part of the ballad?[250] Or of numerous *gamlestev* infiltrated among 'genuine' *Dr* stanzas?[251] The information given to collectors about the inordinate length of *Dr*[252] can certainly be explained in different ways. If we accept the second of the above assumptions, or both the second and the third, and these seem the most likely, we must reconcile ourselves to the fact that the clear distinction there may once have been between *Dr* and *gamlestev* had become so blurred by the 1840s that it may no longer be possible to define it exactly. It would not be easy to demonstrate that even most of the stanzas we now call *Dr* were originally not some form of *gamlestev*. If we accept the first of the assumptions, which Bø apparently does, it must be largely as an act of faith, since evidence of any kind is almost entirely lacking.[253]

Several of the points that emerge from Bø's article are of importance for the study of *Dr*, but one is of overriding significance. It is apparent that, when discussing the material as a whole, it is the stanza or group of stanzas rather than the variant that should be taken as the basic unit,[254] and it is clearly necessary for the literary historian and others interested in the genesis and development of *Dr* to try to establish general criteria for accepting or rejecting individual stanzas. The use of such criteria, if they can be found, would provide one means of extending our knowledge of *Dr* backwards in time.

2.14 Karl-Ivar Hildeman's article

A most important *Dr* study was published in 1958 by the Swedish literary historian, Karl-Ivar Hildeman. It took the form of a lengthy article and was entitled 'I marginalen till Draumkvædet'.[255] Unlike most of his predecessors Hildeman deplores the unavailability of genuine variants which has meant that the study of *Dr* has been based almost entirely on reconstructed texts. As he himself points out, in the absence of proper material his own contribution can only amount to a review of previous discussion of the ballad and must be based on the reconstructed texts used by earlier scholars. Hildeman contends that the question around which most of the discussion has centred is that of the date of composition. In an attempt to give his own answer to this question he reviews earlier theories which he notes have been based almost exclusively on the content of the ballad – the visionary and 'mythological' material. He then surveys certain formal features exhibited by the reconstructed texts of Jørgen Moe, Landstad and Moltke Moe and the variants K1 and L1/4.[256] Such features, though ignored by most earlier scholars, are clearly of major importance in dating the ballad.

Hildeman's article is refreshingly free of preconceived ideas. He considers *Dr* to be an important work of literature, but emphasises that the quality of the ballad can only be judged on the basis of its component parts since it no longer exists as a recognisable whole. He is uncertain whether the punishment stanzas depict purgatory or hell.[257] He even queries the assumption that *Dr* is a single ballad in the process of disintegration, and suggests that it may be 'an amalgamation of several related poems',[258] but stresses that such questions can only fruitfully be discussed after the whole of the material has been made available. In the absence of this material Hildeman seems to accept *Dr* as a unitary entity in the form given to it by Jørgen and Moltke Moe, since he discusses whether it is Olav or the author who in the *sæl* stanzas '. . . draws conclusions from the experiences Olav imparts from the other side'.[259]

Hildeman's approach to the question of dating is in keeping with his open-minded spirit of enquiry. In surveying the content of the ballad he asks both how old and how young it can be. He finds that the absolute *terminus a quo* must be the beginning of the thirteenth century, after the writing down of Thurcill's vision. He also thinks that 1250 is an important year since it was about this time that Gundelin's vision was included in Vincent of Beauvais's *Speculum Historiale*. As far as a *terminus ante quem* is concerned, Hildeman, taking in particular Strömbäck's arguments to their logical conclusion, finds 1550 a likely date, a year '. . . when the generation who joined the Archbishop, Olav Engelbrektsson, in the last revolt in support of Norway's old faith were doubtless no longer of any account'.[260] The reason for making the ending of state Catholicism the *terminus ante quem* is the undoubted pre-Reformation origin of such figures as *sankte såle Mikkjel* and the Virgin Mary, and the belief that marriage between cousins is sinful (cf. S.135). Hildeman makes the point that this stanza is found in K1 and that since it cannot be shown to have been borrowed from another ballad, it must be taken as belonging to *Dr*: 'And if *one* variant existed in the Catholic period, the *ballad* existed too.'[261] Hildeman finds nothing in the content of the ballad to suggest early rather than late origins. He underlines the doubts of several previous scholars, particularly Strömbäck, as to whether *Dr* borrowed from specific known visions which came into circulation in the twelfth and thirteenth centuries, and produces evidence to show that there was no falling off of interest in visions after this period. Indeed, one of those on which *Dr* is supposed to be based, that of Tundale, seems to have enjoyed great popularity in Sweden and elsewhere right up to the Reformation.

A criticism which can be made of the first part of Hildeman's exposition is that the *terminus ante quem* is too rigid. Strömbäck's study and Bø's evidence that mythological names were well known and used in the nineteenth century suggest that *Dr* need not necessarily have been composed before 1550. Furthermore, it was not until after 1600 that Lutheran ideas gained any widespread acceptance in Norway.[262] Apart from this, of course, we do not know that a single, clearly defined *Dr* ever existed. If, as Hildeman himself thinks possible, we are dealing with an amalgamation of several related poems, dating becomes a far more complex problem. We have to consider both the original poems and the amalgamation, and there is very little in the existing *Dr* material to help us decide when any of these may have originated. It is true that certain stanzas which form part of this material (and do not appear to belong to any other ballad) bear unmistakable traces of pre-Reformation origin, but this need not indicate that anything like what we know as *Dr* existed at that time. Nor does it necessarily show that a variant, such as K1, in which stanzas with pre-Reformation features are found 'existed in the Catholic period'. Indeed, Hildeman himself suggests that the changing refrain in K1 may indicate that this variant is '. . . a compilation, an attempt to rationalise of essentially the same kind as that made by Moltke Moe',[263] and thus virtually undatable.

Hildeman's investigation of the formal features of *Dr* led him to the conclusion that it was more likely to have been composed late than early. He notes that the introductory stanza (*Ja vi du lye eg kvea kann* etc.), the 'I' form (*Eg hev vori meg upp mæ Sky* etc.) and the varying refrain are features which mark ballads in Denmark and Sweden as late – after 1500 to all intents and purposes. He admits that we know nothing for sure about balladry in Norway at this time, but stresses that there is no evidence to show that the influence Norway undoubtedly had on the *genre* in Denmark and Sweden concerned such features as these. Indeed, it is clear that the introductory stanza and the 'I' form spread northwards from Germany into Denmark and Sweden. Whether the introductory stanza in *Dr* is in any way connected with the fairly widespread use of such a stanza in the Faroes and Iceland is, according to Hildeman, a matter for speculation. He regards the age and provenance of this feature in Faroese and Icelandic ballads as uncertain, and suggests that it may easily have been introduced from Denmark, and not from Britain as, for example, Liestøl apparently believed.[264] Whatever the truth of this, *Dr* appears to be unique among Norwegian ballads in having an introductory stanza, and there is no evidence to suggest it is 'an old custom'[265] in Norway or in any other Scandinavian country. The varying refrain is a feature of the reconstructed texts and of V1a, V1b, K1 and K11. V1a and V1b, however, are themselves compilations (cf. Section 2.1).[266] This leaves K1 and K11 as the only genuine variants in which there is more than one refrain. Hildeman considers it quite possible that *Dr* had, to begin with, a single refrain only, but that during the course of time others were composed or borrowed by singers and used with the particular variant they recited, so that each or at least several variants came to have their own, individual refrains, as happened in the case of many other ballads. This is what leads him to make the suggestion, noted above, that K1 may be a 'compilation', 'an attempt to rationalise'. There certainly seems to be no compelling reason to assume that *Dr*, if it was a single ballad, originally had more than one refrain.[267] Liestøl, who believed firmly that it did, failed, significantly, to produce any satisfactory arguments in favour of his view.[268] If, nevertheless, the varying refrain found in V1a, V1b, K1 and K11 is a feature which was originally part of a single ballad, Hildeman's evidence suggests that the ballad is more likely to have been composed after 1500, and is a further warning against dating *Dr* to the fourteenth century.[269]

In the last part of his article Hildeman examines the age of the religious ballad in Scandinavia. He finds that there are no good reasons for thinking it particularly old. The very paucity of religious ballads suggests that they are a late development, that the *genre* had little time to expand. It is also far from certain that *Dr* was among the earliest of the religious ballads. If there is a direct connection between *Sante Jakup*[270] and *Dr*, for example, it is more likely that the latter borrowed from the former; it would have been easier for *Dr* with its four-line stanzas to expand certain images than the reverse. Furthermore, it is surprising that a work of the power and quality of *Dr* exercised no influence whatever on the development of the religious ballad if it was itself one of the precursors of this *genre*, although of course this fact provides no definite evidence of anything. It could be due to chance.

In his summing up Hildeman emphasises, with typical caution, that although the weight of evidence is against it, the possibility still exists that *Dr* is from the high middle ages in Scandinavia. He makes it clear, however, that the burden of proof is on those who believe the ballad to be a thirteenth- or fourteenth-century work. Nothing has been produced so far, neither British visionary sources nor the cultural climate in the early fourteenth century,[271] which compels us to believe that *Dr* was composed as early as this, while there is much to suggest that it belongs to a considerably later period.

There are two small matters in Hildeman's article which call for criticism and emendation. 1) It is implied on several occasions that the less frequently a stanza occurs the more likely it is to be secondary.[272] Hildeman ought, however, to have made it clearer than he does that this is not a blanket rule which can be applied indiscriminately. It is only true when all other things are equal, and in *Dr* they seldom are. There is a fundamental difference, to take a straightforward example, between the unique stanzas of L1, L4 and L6 on the one hand and those of M6 on the other. The former are part of a clear narrative structure, are in Norwegian and are similar to stanzas in other *Dr* variants. The latter are not part of a clear narrative structure (many could be moved around freely or omitted altogether), they are sometimes in Danish or a mixture of Danish and Norwegian and have few or no affinities with stanzas in other *Dr* variants (cf. Section 3.3, pp. 97–9). Factors such as these are clearly of great importance and must always be taken into consideration when discussing frequency of occurrence. 2) In his summing up Hildeman suggests that if MM, Landstad A and Jørgen Moe's text give a correct picture of *Dr* as it was at an earlier period, then K1 has preserved and reflects the ballad's basic form.[273] What he must mean, however, is that all four texts are similar to the extent that they exhibit the features he has been discussing. In number and order of stanzas and in general content K1 is most unlike MM and Jørgen Moe's text, although it naturally resembles Landstad A somewhat, since it was on K1 that Landstad based his reconstruction. These comparatively minor points and the rigidity of his *terminus ante quem* apart, Hildeman's seems to be one of the most sensible and perceptive articles on *Dr* ever to appear.

2.15 An Italian contribution

In 1963 there appeared in the Proceedings of the First Congress of Scandinavian 'Italianists' an article by Giovanni Gonnet, the director of the Italian Institute of Culture in Oslo, entitled 'Il Draumkvaede e la Divina Commedia' or 'La Divina Commedia e il Draumkvaede'.[274] The article appeared in Norwegian translation in *Edda* in 1966 where it was reviewed by Mattias Tveitane.[275] It consists largely of a rehearsal of the main arguments in Moltke Moe's and Liestøl's works on *Dr*, together with a comparison of motifs in *Dr* and *Divina Commedia* between which, the author admits, there can be no connection.[276] The article adds nothing to our knowledge of *Dr* and indeed helps to spread a few errors. Tveitane's criticisms, to which the reader is referred, seem fully justified and obviate the necessity of going into the matter further here. It is worth noting, however, that Tveitane, with reference to his article 'En norrøn versjon av Visio Pauli',[277] states that the *Visio Pauli* is one of the sources of *Dr*.[278] If by this he means 'direct source', the examples he gives in *Edda* and in his article[279] are less convincing than those produced to show the dependence of *Dr* on the visions of Gottskalk, Thurcill, Tundale and Gundelin. It is, on the other hand, always possible that motifs from the *Visio Pauli* entered *Dr* after first becoming part of popular tradition.[280]

2.16 Magne Myhren's note on 'i uteksti'

In 1968 a short article by the Norwegian folklorist, Magne Myhren, appeared in *Maal og minne* entitled '"I uteksti" – eit utolka ordlag i Draumkvædet'.[281] Myhren dismisses as unlikely Moltke Moe's interpretation of *uteksti* (found in K1 and K5 in the forms *Uttexti* and *Ut*(*t*)*ext*) which in effect amounts to *(*ut*)*exitus* + *extasis* > *utekst*.[282] After discussing several possible explanations he concludes that it is a compound, *ut*

+ *eksti*, the last element being (originally) the *dat.sing.* of an otherwise unknown *i*-stem or *u*-stem equivalent of Icel. *akstur*, nynorsk *akster*. No comment is made on the loss of *r*. The *-i* of the ending is explained as a fossilised *dat.m.sing.* ending, or possibly the strong *f.def.art.*, the change of gender being on analogy with words such as *ferd*, *reis*, *rekst* which, if Myhren is correct, have a meaning similar to *Uttext(i)*. A different explanation of the *e* in *-eksti* offered by the author is that it comes from an *inf. eka* which is found instead of *aka* in eastern Telemark and parts of Agder. Myhren arrives at his etymology by combining, within the limits set by the form *Uttext(i)*, what is linguistically possible with what is semantically likely. He finds that visions and tales describing journeys to the other world or another existence, including *Dr*, operate largely with words which denote movement and travel. This is confirmed by variant forms of *Uttext(i)* in *Dr* where the second element is *-reis*, *-reise*, *-reysning* etc. Myhren does not state whether he considers such forms to be secondary, parallel or primary in relation to *Uttext(i)*, but a change from an unfamiliar word to a familiar one is, of course, more likely. (Cf. Section 5.1, general note 48.)

2.17 A reappraisal

In 1971 the Norwegian folklorist, Brynjulf Alver, published a book called *Draumkvedet, folkevise eller lærd kopidikting* (*Draumkvedet, ballad or learned imitation*). As the title suggests, the book is a total reappraisal of the arguments about the nature and genesis of *Dr*. Alver begins by criticising earlier scholarship which he considers, not without reason, to have had such a strong literary and historical bias that folkloristic and textual problems received little or no attention. He sees it as his principal task to give a proper account of the genuine *Dr* material and to discuss the problems it poses, and it is with this that the main part of his book is concerned. First there is an analysis of the contents of the individual *Dr* stanzas, followed by a detailed regional survey of the thirty 'most important'[283] variants (cf. Section 3.4–5), and notes on some fifty or sixty smaller fragments. The book then deals with the question of how the variants we have in manuscript form arose and their relationship with oral tradition, and this is followed by a brief discussion of the various names given to the ballad which, according to Alver, are *Draumkvedet*, *Draugkvedet* and *Draukvedet*. Finally the author goes through the whole of the material in order to detail the occurrence of the individual stanzas or episodes: how commonly they occur, whether they are restricted to specific areas and whether they appear in important or fragmentary variants. Alver's conclusion is that *Dr* is in all likelihood a product of the eighteenth century and consists partly of original stanzas modelled on *gamlestev* and partly of traditional *gamlestev* or loans from other ballads. The inspiration to put such a hotchpotch together came from visits to church where almost anyone listening to the pastor or admiring pictures could have gathered the necessary material and connected it with the moral and religious sentiments already expressed in individual *gamlestev*.

Alver's work is highly commendable in its intentions. In its execution, however, it leaves much to be desired. The book appears to have been put together in great haste. The number of factual mistakes and/or misprints is so great that they often seem to be jostling for room; several of these mistakes appear to be derivative and can be traced back to the preparatory work on a definitive edition of the Norwegian ballads begun by Knut Liestøl. The presentation suffers from a lack of clarity: many references, apparently to other pages in the book, lead nowhere at all, and on several occasions the point the author is trying to make becomes obscured, either because of the extreme brevity of the argument or a certain imprecision in the wording.[284]

More serious is the weak theoretical basis on which much of the argument about the nature of *Dr* and its origins rests.

In order to say with any confidence that *Dr* was composed or put together in the eighteenth century we must first of all be sure that we know what we mean by *Dr*. To say that it consists or consisted partly of traditional *gamlestev* and partly of stanzas modelled on *gamlestev* we must be able to define *gamlestev* in a way that will enable us to distinguish these from other four-line stanzas. Alver fails to give a definition of either *Dr* or *gamlestev* and the reader is therefore left to interpret these phrases, which have the appearance, but not the limitations of technical terms, as best he can. What the author often seems to suggest is that his thirty 'most important' variants are the (nineteenth- and twentieth-century) ballad *Dr* and anything else purporting to be a ballad of this name is in reality *gamlestev*. But what makes these thirty *Dr*? How does Alver recognise the ballad? Is it by the length of the variant? But then many 'groups of (*gamle*)*stev*'[285] with the title *Draumkveen*, *Draugkveen* or the like have been omitted. Is it the integrity of the variant? According to Alver they have none – except, perhaps, Maren Ramskeid's.[286] Is it the fact that the reciter conceived of the variant as a ballad? How do we demonstrate this? Alver does not. The problem is well illustrated by the author's variant 19[287] which according to him contains twelve *gamlestev*, four stanzas from other ballads, presumably with 'the function of *gamlestev*',[288] and three stanzas from *Dr* (these last are included in his analysis of the contents of individual *Dr* stanzas, so we must presumably regard them as belonging to the ballad). Yet this variant is described as an 'original MS'[289] (this it in fact is, but Alver clearly means 'MS of *Draumkvedet*', one of his thirty) which has borrowed a stanza from the religious ballad, *Agnus Dei*.

In the light of the uncertainty as to what Alver means by the phrases *Draumkvedet* and *gamlestev*, it is difficult to accept or even understand an assertion such as the following: 'The intermixture is so great that one can say without doubt that a large part of the *Draumkvede* tradition *must* be *gamlestev* or groups of *gamlestev*, and that most of them [the stanzas that make up *Dr*?] *could* be.'[290] What is 'the *Draumkvede* tradition'? What has become intermixed with what? The presupposition underlying such a statement is that there is a distinction between ballad stanzas, in particular *Dr* ballad stanzas, and *gamlestev per se* (because both have a clearly definable form or content?). But is this so? Elsewhere, as we have seen, Alver speaks of stanzas with 'the function of *gamlestev*',[291] and this certainly seems to be a more hopeful line of approach if we are to be able to distinguish adequately and objectively between *Dr* stanzas and *gamlestev*. We could say: when used outside a connected narrative, four-line stanzas of the type under discussion may be classed as *gamlestev*, when forming part of a narrative they can be termed ballad stanzas. This is the synchronic viewpoint which takes no account of supposed origins, and Alver might have done well to pursue it. One of his main points, after all, is that we are dealing with oral literature which has no fixed form. What should have been avoided was the confusion of the synchronic with the diachronic viewpoint whereby Alver talks on one page as though *Dr* stanzas and *gamlestev* are historically distinct, even though largely 'intermixed' and on the next as though the status of a stanza is determined by its function.[292] As regards the diachronic viewpoint, all we can say in the present state of research is that it is often extremely difficult to distinguish historically what scholars refer to as *Dr* and *gamlestev* and that, if we accept that there is a distinction, we must therefore agree that the two have become confused. As yet we cannot possibly determine the process by which this happened.

In support of his theory that *Dr* consists largely of *gamlestev*, Alver points out that the second element of the name, *-kvede*, appears in connection with both *Dr* and *gamlestev*, but is not found in the title of any other Norwegian ballad.[293] He suggests that since *kvede* can be either *sing.* or *pl.*, there is every reason to believe it may signify one or more individual stanzas, particularly in view of the fact that collections of *stev* may be called *Draumkvéen*, *Draugkvéen* and the like and often contain individual stanzas from ballads. It is possible that Alver is partly right about the use of *kvede*, but it is difficult to see why he only discusses this form when collections of *stev* he himself refers to and many of the variants of *Dr* are clearly headed *Draum-* or *Draugkveen*. Are we to take it that the second element of such names is *kvede*? The final *-n* makes it an unlikely dialect form. Most collectors clearly felt they were dealing with a different word (presumably the *pp.* of *kveda*) since they almost always use 'e' in *-kveen* and 'æ' in *-kvæde*, a distinction unfortunately obliterated in the latest *nynorsk* spelling.

Alver's theory that what we now know as *Dr*, or, at least, his thirty 'most important' variants, were inspired by things which eighteenth-century Telemark farmers saw and heard in their local church lacks credibility. Alver considers that in church they '. . . were able to hear about people who had been in the other world and seen what it was like there, that evil deeds in this life would have consequences for the after life and that good deeds here on earth would be counted to one's advantage when one had to cross over into the world of the dead'.[294] They would also, according to Alver, have heard Christ's sermon on the mount and have gained knowledge of St Michael, the weigher of souls, from things they both heard and saw. What remains to be demonstrated, however, is that these themes were such a prominent part of the religious experience in eighteenth-century Telemark that they would have inspired anyone to compose a ballad. It seems, to say the least, unlikely that Hans Mathias Abel, the parson who, according to Landstad,[295] was firmly opposed to the singing of *Dr*, would have placed great emphasis on journeys in the other world, specific rewards in the after life for good deeds done on earth and the role of St Michael as the weigher of souls.

Belief in the eighteenth-century origins of *Dr* becomes even more difficult when one considers the dissimilarity of the existing variants. Do these stem from one or more originals? Alver stresses that the only firm *Dr* tradition is to be found among individual informants and that even here there is often much variation.[296] He clearly regards it as impossible to find particular lines of tradition based on geographical or other factors. Several rather than one eighteenth-century prototypes therefore seem likely, given the short space of time that must have elapsed between composition and writing down. Indeed, Alver's thirty 'most important' variants can scarcely go back to less than fifteen to twenty originals. But what can have caused such a large number of people to compose or piece together ballads on the same or similar themes using a substantial corpus of common material? Possibly an otherwise unknown religious revival, but seemingly one with roots in the middle ages, or with antiquarian interests.

One of the principal difficulties in dealing with *Dr* is, of course, to explain why the variants are at once so similar and so dissimilar. The theory that they stem from one or more eighteenth-century compilations of *gamlestev*, 'original' stanzas and loans from other ballads, scarcely brings us closer to a solution.

Alver's book contains a number of positive features which deserve to be stressed. The very fact that he bases his discussion on genuine material, and is able to question the whole concept of a medieval *Dr*, represents an enormous advance on most previous contributions to the subject. His detailed exposition and analysis of the material[297] are two most important chapters which will be of assistance to all who wish to know something about the nature and extent of the material that has hitherto gone under the name of *Dr*. It is therefore a great pity that the work is marred by an unusual degree of carelessness over facts and references and by an insistence on an eighteenth-century date of composition, which, because of the almost total lack of evidence and supporting argument, seems quite as dogmatic as the assertion by Moltke Moe and other scholars that *Dr* was a medieval work.

2.18 Literary analysis of genuine variants

Shortly after the appearance of Alver's book the Norwegian folklorist, Ådel Blom, published a work entitled *Ballader og legender* which contains a chapter on *Dr*. Blom's principal aim is to give a brief commentary on *Dr* as a religious ballad. Unlike many previous scholars she is fully aware of the confused textual situation and the impossibility of using reconstructed texts, and therefore chooses a single variant, K1, as the object of her analysis. This needs some justification, however, and the first part of the chapter takes the form of an introduction to the textual and literary problems of *Dr*, and includes a survey of the more important contributions to the subject. Blom stresses the difficulty in identifying what we understand as *Dr* among the mass of recorded ballad material which exists, but points out that a collection of thirty-four variants has recently been excerpted by Svale Solheim of the University of Oslo's Institutt for folkeminnevitskap.[298] The criterion for inclusion in this collection is that the informants themselves felt that what they sang or recited was part of a definite ballad. How it is possible to decide this in each case is not stated.[299] Of Solheim's thirty-four variants there are, according to Blom, only thirteen which contain anything approaching a narrative (V9, R2a, M2, M3, M6, M9a, M15a (and b ?), L1/4, L3/5, L6, K1, K5, K9). Common to all these variants are two stanzas: one which tells that the protagonist fell asleep on Christmas eve and did not awake until the thirteenth day, and another which describes him standing in the church doorway or at the churchyard gate, or sitting on the churchyard wall, relating his vision while the priest stands before the altar or in the pulpit and reads, counts up or comments on some piece or pieces of Scripture. Blom argues that this second stanza (SS.34–6) cannot be a *gamlestev* with an independent existence, since it presupposes that an account of the visionary's experiences follows, and it must certainly be admitted that SS.34–6 (and 37–8) are very unlike any of the stanzas which have appeared in published collections of *gamlestev*. What follows after the scene at the church is so different in the individual variants that Blom considers it impossible to decide whether the thirteen belong to one and the same ballad or to several related ballads. To this it must be said that if historically we are dealing with more than one ballad, the nineteenth-century variants offer little evidence as to how the prototypes varied. They must have been very closely related indeed since, excluding M6, the bulk of the stanzas (however one defines stanza, cf. Section 3.2) are common to more than one variant. This is doubtless why Blom goes on to suggest (as an alternative ?) that visionary literature in *stev* and ballad metre, introduced by 'commonplaces'[300] describing the visionary's deep sleep and contrasting his dreams with the church service, may at one time have been widespread. The author is here presumably referring to improvisations based on a body of well-known material. A number of the written *Dr* variants we have today might well be the result of this type of literary activity, and to that extent the suggestion merits attention. There are four principal objections, however. First, it is an unparalleled phenomenon. Second, it would need to be demonstrated that interest in medieval visionary motifs persisted some three hundred years after the

Reformation.[301] Third, there is too great a similarity between many of the variants from Kviteseid and Lårdal and between most of Blom's thirteen variants to be explained as the chance result of improvisation – even allowing for the extensive use of traditional material. Fourth, in the case of L1 and K1 we hear of a tradition which stretches over three generations, and of many other informants it is said that they learnt their variant from someone else (cf. Section 3.5, notes). And while a number of variants look like just the kind of improvisation Blom apparently envisages (cf., e.g., T3), it is difficult to see why anyone should have taken it into his head to lump together, for example, the three stanzas of M1, unless the collector was somehow involved (cf. the title, *Suplemete ti Dromkve*).

Blom's survey of the material leads her to the conclusion that there is at least one variant with a narrative thread,[302] and the detailed and careful analysis of Maren Ramskeid's *Draumekvæi* which follows certainly gives weight to her view that this variant is not the result of some chance improvisation or the vagaries of tradition, but rather the careful and deliberate work of a single person. Blom maintains that since *Draumekvæi* was clearly shaped by a poet, even if he took some of his material from among traditional *stev* or ballad stanzas with visionary themes, *Dr* exists as a ballad. The stylistic features which Hildeman saw as a sign of degeneration when they occurred in the east Scandinavian area (cf. Section 2.14) clearly have a literary function in *Draumekvæi* : as a visionary poem it gains in intensity by the use of the 'I' form,[303] and the varying refrain is understandable in a long description of a journey divided into stages, as well as being an aid to the memory.[304] Blom is rightly cautious about the dating of *Draumekvæi*. She notes that according to the information given to Landstad it was sung in the beginning of the eighteenth century and must therefore be older than this.[305] However, the whole tone of the ballad, as well as an affinity with some of the sentiments expressed in a number of late medieval Swedish sermons, leads her to the view that it was probably composed before the Reformation.[306]

Blom's analysis and interpretation of *Draumekvæi* is this. Stanzas 3–28 form a connected narrative about a journey in the other world. Until the visionary's arrival at the church his actions are almost all described by a narrator (it is implied that this may also have been the case in stanza 6 originally), but as soon as the vision itself begins, the 'I' form is used. Stanzas 7–11 (possibly not 10) describe Olav's laborious journey to the world of the dead; having arrived there he has time to reflect (stanzas 12–16) and regrets not having been merciful in this life which would have spared him the suffering he has just experienced (12–14). His thoughts then turn to the world of the dead which he is about to enter (*andre/annen heimen*) and the rewards for merciful deeds one can expect there (15–16). Next he sees hell (17) and paradise (18) where he meets God's mother who, to his delight, tells him to go to *Broksvalin* where the final judgement is to be held (cf. the *def.* form *domen*). On the way to *Broksvalin* he meets dead people who are being punished for their sins, but this is not the eternal punishment in hell; they are being cleansed of their sins in purgatory and are heading towards *Broksvalin* and Jesus Christ, just like the visionary. Face to face with their creator the souls bewail their sins and tremble in fear of the judgement, but all who have reached this far are weighed away to Christ, i.e., united with their creator. This is the climax to which the poem has been leading up from the very beginning; each stage of the journey is linked to the next and the refrains emphasise the steady progression and unity of the narrative, beginning with the trance, moving on to the other world and finally taking up the words of stanza 20 and underlining the ultimate goal of the journey. K1, according to Blom, makes great use of contrasts, both within individual stanzas and in the way the stanzas are put together; even the various stages of the journey contrast with one another. We have, for example, the visionary and the priest in stanza 6, the sight of the blue ice (hell) in 17 and paradise in 18, the laborious journey and the terrors of *Gjallarbru* in 7–11 and the calm reflection of the *sæl* stanzas in 12–16, to name but a few. Nor is this all: if we examine the composition carefully, we notice that up to the *sæl* stanzas the verbs used to describe the visionary's progress are *fór*, *gange*, *gjængje*. From stanza 17 we find *såg* and *mødte*. In other words the visionary is actively involved in the first phase of the journey, but after entering the world of the dead he is a passive observer and is helped towards *Broksvalin* by God and the Virgin Mary. It is thus possible to see the first part of the ballad as an exhortation to religious activity; the road to salvation begins with the active will to turn away from the world and seek God in another life. The second part shows the knowledge and understanding the visionary gained because he was willing to struggle and conquer the difficulties which faced him during the early stages of his journey. *Draumekvæi* is more than a straightforward description of a journey in the other world which ended in salvation. It is a gospel.

This is a most ingenious interpretation[307] of a text which at first glance seems almost inscrutable. It must be admitted, however, that if it is correct, *Draumekvæi* is of a very different mould from most medieval visions where episode is piled upon episode, horror upon horror, with little apparent regard for coherence, progression or unity in the composition, let alone the possibility of understanding on more than one level. In many ways L4 and L6 remind one more of medieval visions than K1, and they can certainly be shown to form narratives as coherent as many of these.[308] Is *Draumekvæi*, then, a work in advance of its age, or was it composed later than Blom supposes? Is her interpretation open to doubt on any points?

Much in the interpretation, it can fairly be said, is uncertain. It is difficult to show that 'In *Draumkvæi* we find the official Catholic teaching about Heaven, hell and purgatory.'[309] Paradise is mentioned, but there is no direct reference to hell or purgatory. We cannot, therefore, be sure that those being punished in stanzas 21–2 (and 10?) were on their way to *Broksvalin* and the judgement. Does the visionary really cross over to the world of the dead after 11? It is, to say the least, doubtful (cf. Section 2.5, p. 28). Much of what Blom sees as the conscious work of a poet may be no more than the association of words or ideas by one or several informants. Her explanation of the position and wording of the *sæl* stanzas, for example, is attractive, but in the light of the complete lack of a fixed order in the stanzas of the *Dr* variants, is it not just as likely that they were placed after 7–11 because 13–14 include the name *Gjeddar Bru/Gjeddarbroi* and 12 shows some connection with 8? We can see that this is almost certainly what has happened in the case of 10 (cf. *Ormane*) which would seem better placed before, between or after 21–2. The author's view that K1 carries a specific religious message, a call to forsake this world and seek God in another life, though by no means impossible, perhaps assumes a degree of subtlety more in keeping with modern than pre-Reformation literature in Norway.

K1 may be the end-product of a long line of tradition stretching back into the sixteenth century or earlier, but we know nothing about this tradition or the prototype which was its source. A ballad not unlike *Draumekvæi* could have existed before the Reformation, but it is far from certain that Blom's interpretation accurately reflects the intentions of an unknown pre-Reformation author or compiler. Hildeman may well have been right when he suggested that K1 was 'an attempt to rationalise' (cf. Sections 2.14, pp. 50–1 and 3.3, p. 100). And there is no reason why this attempt should not have been made at any time after the Reformation.

As long as people continued to sing *Dr*, however many ballads or whatever this once was, there must have been some interest in what it meant and speculation as to how the various fragments fitted together. The literary analysis of a single variant presupposes, in fact, that that variant is some kind of rationalisation, since how otherwise can one ignore the remaining material, knowing little or nothing about the traditions which lie behind it?

Blom's chapter, although short, is one of the most interesting and thought-provoking studies of *Dr* to appear. In directing attention to the construction and possible meaning of a genuine variant, the author opens the way for further analyses of this kind which, if undertaken, may ultimately lead to a better understanding of the whole of the material, or at least of the longer variants and their relationship with each other. It is unlikely that we shall always be able to agree with the conclusions of such analyses, but given the nature of the material this is hardly to be expected.

2.19 A bibliography of Draumkvæde

Articles, monographs etc. (in alphabetical order according to the author)

Alver, Brynjulf, *Draumkvedet, folkevise eller lærd kopidikting* (1971). Cf. the reviews by Magne Myhren, *Edda LXXII* (1972), pp. 52–4 and by me, *Maal og minne* (1972), pp. 82–92.

Barnes, Michael, 'Draumkvæde – How Old Is It?', *Scandinavica 11* (1972), pp. 85–105.

Berge, Rikard, *Vinje og Rauland* (1940–4), I, pp. 142–4, 254, 257, 268–70.

Bergström, Richard & Höijer, Leonard, *Svenska Folkvisor utgifna af E. G. Geijer och A. A. Afzelius* (1880), II, p. 338.

Blom, Ådel, *Ballader og legender fra norsk middelalderdiktning* (1971).

Bugge, Anders, 'Dommedagssvalen ved verdens ende', *Museum I* (1948), pp. 56–7.

Bugge, Sophus, 'Mythologiske Oplysninger til Draumekvædi', *Norsk Tidsskrift for Videnskab og Litteratur VII* (1854–5), pp. 102–21, 192.

Bull, Francis & Paasche, Fredrik, *Norsk litteraturhistorie* (1924–55), I, pp. 485–8.

Bø, Olav, 'Draumkvædet og Gamle-stevet', *Norveg 5* (1955), pp. 77–102; English summary, pp. 103–4.

Bø, Olav, 'Draumkvædet', *Kulturhistorisk Leksikon for nordisk middelalder* (1956–), III, cols. 303–4.

Bø, Olav, 'Draumkvedet', *Utsyn over norsk folkedikting* (1972), pp. 46–54.

Christensen, Hjalmar, *Vort litterære liv* (1902), pp. 189–202.

Dal, Erik, *Draumkvædet* (1957), pp. 31–42.

Daae, Ludvig, *Norges Helgener* (1879), pp. 92–3.

Falk, Hjalmar, *Sólarljóð*, Videnskapsselskapets Skrifter. II. Hist.-filos. Klasse. (1914) No. 7.

Falk, Hjalmar & Moe, Moltke, 'Middelalderens visionsdigtning', *Festskrift til H. F.*

Feilberg, Maal og minne (1911), pp. 421–48. Reprinted in an expanded form under Moe's name alone in *Moltke Moes samlede skrifter* (1925–7), III, pp. 209–47.

Feilberg, Henning Frederik, 'Et kapitel af folkets sjæletro', *Aarbog for dansk Kulturhistorie* (1894), pp. 116–18.

Gonnet, Giovanni, 'Il Draumkvaede e la Divina Commedia', *Atti, I° Congresso degli Italianisti Scandinavi* (1963), pp. 63–78; in Norwegian translation in *Edda LXVI* (1966), pp. 25–40, together with a review by Mattias Tveitane, 'Draumkvædet og Divina Commedia . . .', pp. 217–22 and a reply by Gonnet, 'Réponse de Giovanni Gonnet', pp. 222–4.

Grundtvig, Svend, *Danmarks gamle Folkeviser* (1853–), II, p. 540.

Heggstad, Leiv & Grüner Nielsen, Hakon, *Utsyn yver gamall norsk folkevisedikting* (1912), pp. 28–9.

Hildeman, Karl-Ivar, 'I marginalen till Draumkvædet', *Medeltid på vers* (1958), pp. 216–55. Cf. the review by Olav Bø, *Historisk tidsskrift 39* (1959–60), pp. 180–2.

Hoffmann, Ludwig, *Das Traumgedicht* (*Der Traumgesang*) (1917, cf. note 161).

Hoffmann, Ludwig, *Licht aus dem Norden* (1924, cf. note 161).

Hoffmann, Ludwig, *Im Traumlicht der Ewigkeit* (1954).

Jørgensen, Ellen, *Helgendyrkelse i Danmark* (1909), p. 6.

Landstad, Magnus Brostrup, *Norske Folkeviser* (1853, reprinted 1968), pp. 63–96, 858–9.

Liestøl, Knut, 'Gaglemyrane', *Festskrift tilegnet førstebibliotekar A. Kjær av venner 26 sept. 1924*, pp. 65–9. Reprinted in Knut Liestøl, *Saga og folkeminne* (1941), pp. 200–5.

Liestøl, Knut, 'Til Draumkvædet', *Heidersskrift til Marius Hægstad* (1925), pp. 113–23. Reprinted in Knut Liestøl, *Saga og folkeminne* (1941), pp. 188–99.

Liestøl, Knut, *Draumkvæde, A Norwegian Visionary Poem from the Middle Ages, Studia Norvegica 3* (1946).

Liestøl, Knut, 'Draumkvædet', *Syn og Segn 54* (1948), pp. 49–65.

Liestøl, Knut & Moe, Moltke, *Norske folkevisor* (1920–4), I, pp. 191–4. Reprinted in Olav Bø & Svale Solheim, *Folkeviser I, Norsk folkedikting VI* (1958, 2nd edition 1967), pp. 253–5.

Liestøl, Knut (ed.), 'Aktstykke til soga um nordisk folkeminnegransking', *Maal og minne* (1923), p. 109.

Mannhardt, Wilhelm, 'Nachträge und Berichtigungen zu den "germanischen Mythen" ', *Zeitschrift für deutsche Mythologie und Sittenkunde IV* (1859), pp. 420–2.

Merry, Eleanor C., *The Dream Song of Olaf Åsteson* (1961), pp. 9–13.

Midbøe, Hans, *Draumkvedet. En studie i norsk middelalder* (1949).

Moe, Jørgen, 'Indberetning. . .', *Norske Universitets- og Skole-Annaler 2. R., V* (1850), pp. 272–86. Reprinted in Jørgen Moe, *Samlede Skrifter* (1877), II, pp. 96–118, and in *Tradisjonsinnsamling på 1800-talet, Norsk Folkeminnelags skrifter 92* (1964), pp. 47–62.

Moe, Moltke, *Forelæsninger over norske ballader og folkeviser fra middelalderen I*, pp. 79–186, & *II*, the handwritten MSS of Moe's lectures on *Dr*, preserved in the archives of Institutt for folkeminnevitskap, University of Oslo.

Moe, Moltke, 'Folkeviser' ('Befolkning'), *Norges land og folk VIII, Bratsberg amt* (1900), I, pp. 429–31.

Moe, Moltke, (*Draumkvæde, et digt fra middelalderen*), a planned commentary, to accompany the text of 1904 (in a separate volume), partially preserved in proof (cf. Section 2.5, pp. 11–12).

Moe, Moltke, 'Limbus puerorum. Et par vers av Draumkvædet', *Sproglige og historiske afhandlinger viede Sophus Bugges minde* (1908), pp. 247–57. Reprinted in *Moltke Moes samlede skrifter* (1925–7), III, pp. 346–56; English summary, pp. 398–400.

Moe, Moltke, 'Middelalderens visionsdigtning', *Moltke Moes samlede skrifter*, Instituttet for sammenlignende kulturforskning, Serie B, I, VI, IX (1925–7), III, pp. 209–47; English summary, pp. 385–7.

Moe, Moltke, 'Kommentar', *Moltke Moes samlede skrifter* (1925–7), III, pp. 248–345; English summary, pp. 387–98.

Moe, Moltke & Falk, Hjalmar, (*Draumkvædet* and *Sólarljóð*), a planned edition and commentary, partially preserved in proof (without title, but referred to as FM in this edition) and in later works by Moe and Falk (cf. Section 2.5, pp. 11–12).

Mortensson, Ivar, 'I andre heimen', *Vidar I* (1917), pp. 431–8; in *riksmål* translation, pp. 439–46.

Mortensson, Ivar, 'Draumkvæde-skalden', *Norsk aarbok* (1920), pp. 30–55.

Mortensson, Ivar, *Gjallarbrui* (1926).

Mortensson, Ivar, *Grunnsteinen i norsk bokheim* (1927).

Myhren, Magne, '"I uteksti" – eit utolka ordlag i Draumkvædet', *Maal og minne* (1968), pp. 59–62.

Myhren, Magne, 'Nokre problem i Draumkvædet', *Tradisjon 1* (1971), pp. 73–6.

Ofteli, Torkel, 'Draumekvæde-skalden', *Telesoga 46* (1920), pp. 3–10.

Olsen, Magnus, 'Gjøre bro for ens sjel', *Maal og minne* (1936), pp. 210–12.

Paasche, Fredrik, *Kristendom og kvad* (1914), pp. 33–5, 42–4. Reprinted in Fredrik Paasche, *Hedenskap og kristendom* (1948), pp. 62–4, 72–5.

Paasche, Fredrik, 'St. Michael og hans engle', *Edda I* (1914), pp. 46–51.

Sandvik, Ole Mørk, 'Melodier til Draumkvædet', *Kulturhistorisk Leksikon for nordisk middelalder* (1956–), III, cols. 304–5.

Skulerud, Olai, 'Utsyn yver åndslivet i Telemark', *Norsk aarbok* (1923), pp. 95–8.

Steiner, Rudolf, *Olaf Åsteson. Das Wachen des Erdgeistes* (1916, cf. note 159). Reprinted in *Welten-Neujahr*... (1958), pp. 38–44.

Steiner, Rudolf, *Weltenneujahr. Das Erwachen der Menschenseele aus dem Geistesschlaf der finstern Zeit* (1932). Reprinted in *Welten-Neujahr*... (1958), pp. 7–32.

Steiner, Rudolf, *Welten-Neujahr. Das Traumlied vom Olaf Åsteson* (1958).

Strömbäck, Dag, 'Om Draumkvædet och dess källor', *Arv 2* (1946), pp. 35–70. Reprinted in Dag Strömbäck, *Folklore och Filologi* (1970), pp. 1–33.

Strömbäck, Dag, 'Moltke Moe', *Biographica. Nordic Folklorists of the Past. Studies in Honour of Jouko Hautala* (1970), pp. 347–50. Also printed in *Arv 25–6* (1969–70), pp. 347–50, and *Leading Folklorists of the North*, ed. Dag Strömbäck (1971), pp. 347–50.

Thøgersen, Mogens, 'Han bles i luren lange', *Den iconographiske Post 1* (1971), pp. 11–13.

Trummler, Erich, 'Das Traumlied im Schicksal des Nordens', *Traumlied des Olav Aasteson* (1927), pp. 7–25.

Editions of Draumkvæde (in chronological order)

Moe, Jørgen, 'Indberetning...', *Norske Universitets- og Skole-Annaler 2. R., V* (1850), pp. 280–6, *Samlede Skrifter* (1877), II, pp. 109–18, *Tradisjonsinnsamling på 1800-talet, Norsk Folkeminnelags skrifter 92* (1964), pp. 56–62: Jørgen Moe's reconstructed text.

Landstad, Magnus Brostrup, *Norske Folkeviser* (1853, reprinted 1968), pp. 67–83 (A), pp. 84–9 (B): A is Landstad's reconstructed text, B is K1 with his normalised etymological spelling and some alterations to the wording.

Lindeman, Ludvig Mathias, *30 norske Kjæmpevisemelodier*... (1863), pp. 26–34: Landstad A, but without his etymological spelling.

Lammers, Thorvald ? Moe, Moltke ? A pamphlet containing six ballads (1896) of which the first (pp. 1–2) is *Draumkvæe*: an early version of MM ? The text has forty stanzas, the first twenty of which correspond to MM 1–7, 9–11, 13, 16, 18–22, 24, 27–8 in that order; stanza 21 = MM 14, then come the punishment section, the judgement and the *sæl* stanzas; the final stanza = MM 52.

Moe, Moltke, FM (1897 approx.), pp. 39–60c (interspersed with commentary): MM 1–37 (pp. 65ff. are wanting).

Moe, Moltke, *Nogen norske folkeviser ved universitetets landsmålskursus sommeren 1899*, pp. 1–17: MM minus 52.

Lammers, Thorvald, *Norske folkeviser* (1901–2, 1901 reprinted 1910, 1917, 1923, 1930), I, pp. 9–15: the text of 1896 which was doubtless largely the work of Moltke Moe.

Hægstad, Marius & Skard, Matias, *Af litteraturen før 1814* (1902, reprinted 1911, 1920, 1925), pp. 103–7: the text of 1896 with an additional stanza (MM 29) and with the *sæl* stanzas as 18–21 instead of at the end; new edition: *Eldre norsk og dansk litteratur* (ed. Leiv Heggstad & Eiliv Skard, 1933), pp. 82–6: MM.

Moe, Moltke, *Draumkvæde, et digt fra middelalderen* (1904): MM minus 52.

Lammers, Thorvald ? *Draumkvæe* (undated): two pamphlets marked *2det tusen* and *5te tusen* ('second thousand', 'fifth thousand') containing the text of 1896.

Moe, Moltke, *Draumkvæe* (1906): MM with the addition of two stanzas, 17a & 17b, which are found in Moe (1908) (cf. Section 5.1, general note 37).

Moe, Moltke, *Draumkvæe* (?) (1912): MM. (The copy of this text in Universitetsbiblioteket, the only one known to me, is missing, so it has been impossible to check the title or the contents. *Draumkvæe* is the form of the title given in the Universitetsbiblioteket catalogue, and the text in Moe (1925–7), III, pp. 199–208, according to Liestøl's notes (pp. 358–9), is more or less an exact copy of the 1912 version of MM.)

Mortensson, Ivar, 'Draumkvædet', *Vidar I* (1917), pp. 406–14 (also published separately in 1916): Mortensson's first reconstruction consisting of 107 stanzas.

Liestøl, Knut & Moe, Moltke, *Norske folkevisor* (1920–4), I, pp. 31–9: MM.

Liestøl, Knut & Semb, Klara, *Norske folkedansar* (1922–58), I, pp. 11–16: a shortened version of Landstad A which owes a number of details to MM. This text has appeared with few alterations in seven subsequent editions (the most recent was published in 1961, *Dr* pp. 17–21).

Garborg, Hulda, *Norske Dansevisur* (1923 – 4th edition), pp. 115–20: Liestøl's text of 1922.

M. B. Landstad, Folkeviser fra Telemarken, ed. Knut Liestøl (1925), pp. 23–8: apparently an abbreviated version of V1a (cf. Section 2.2).

Mortensson, Ivar, *Gjallarbrui* (1926), pp. 151–77: Mortensson's second reconstructed text consisting of 119 stanzas.

Mortensson, Ivar, *Draumkvedet i ny uppsetjing med utgreidingar* (1927): identical with the text of 1926.

Moe, Moltke, 'Draumkvædet', *Moltke Moes samlede skrifter* (1925–7), III, pp. 199–208: MM; pp. 248–343 (interspersed with commentary): MM minus 52.

Trummler, Erich, *Traumlied des Olav Aasteson* (1927), pp. (even) 28–62: the text of 1896.
Liestøl, Knut & Moe, Moltke, *Utval av norske folkevisor til skulebruk* (1928), pp. 17–24: MM which has appeared virtually unaltered in nine subsequent editions (the most recent was published in 1971, *Dr* pp. 23–30).
Munthe, Gerhard, *Norske folkeviser* (1933), no pagination: MM minus 52.
Berge, Rikard, *Vinje og Rauland* (1940–4), I, pp. 142–3: V9 (cf. Section 3.5, V9, note).
Liestøl, Knut, *Draumkvæde* (1946), pp. 134–7: a combination of L1 and L4; pp. 137–41: Landstad B.
Bø, Olav, 'Draumkvædet og Gamle-stevet', *Norveg 5* (1955), pp. 77–102: odd stanzas from a number of variants and the following in their entirety: V3 (p. 100), M12 (p. 99), M14 (except the single line of stanza 2, p. 99), T2 (p. 100), T11 (p. 99), By1 (p. 101).
Dal, Erik, *Draumkvædet* (1957), pp. 5–29: MM.
Christiansen, Reidar Th., *Norske folkeviser* (1957), pp. 37–48; Landstad A with stanzas 7–10 omitted and certain alterations to the text. The spelling is fairly close to standard *nynorsk*.
Bø, Olav & Solheim, Svale, *Folkeviser I, Norsk folkedikting VI* (1958, 2nd edition 1967), pp. 25–33: MM.
Liestøl, Aslak, *Norske folkeviser* (1964), pp. 9–17: MM.
Draumkvedet, J. W. Eides forlags julebok (1966): Christiansen's text of 1957.
Jonsson, Bengt et al., *European Folk Ballads* (1967), pp. (even) 198–208: Landstad B.
Alver, Brynjulf, *Draumkvedet* (1971): odd stanzas from a number of variants and the following in their entirety (though sometimes minus the refrain): V7 (p. 124), V8 (p. 65), V11 (p. 66), R1 (p. 69), M5 (p. 61), M14 (pp. 63, 99, on the second occasion minus the single line of stanza 2), M15a–b (pp. 12–13), M18 (p. 62), F1 (p. 70), L7 (p. 57), L11 (pp. 58, 104), K1 (pp. 48–52), K12 (p. 55), S2 (p. 72), S4 (pp. 67, 114), S8c (p. 101), H1 (p. 69), H3 (p. 69), T7 (p. 94), T8 (pp. 128–9), Sæ1 (pp. 72, 114), By1 (p. 75), By2 (p. 73), By3 (p. 74), He1 (p. 79); in addition: MM (pp. 21–9).
Blom, Ådel, *Ballader og legender* (1971), pp. 256–60: K1.
Barnes, Michael, 'Draumkvæde – How Old Is It?', *Scandinavica 11* (1972), pp. 94–5: R2a, M14, L4, T3.

Neither extracts from texts, whether reconstructed or genuine, nor reconstructed texts in general anthologies are included in this bibliography.

Translations of Draumkvæde (in chronological order)

English

Moe, Moltke, 'Summary in English', 'The Draumkvæde', *Moltke Moes samlede skrifter* (1925–7), III, pp. 387–98: MM (prose, interspersed with commentary).
Liestøl, Knut, *Draumkvæde* (1946), pp. 7–16: MM (verse).
Jorgenson, Theodore, *The Trumpet of Nordland...* (1954), pp. 139–49: MM (verse); pp. 150–176: Mortensson's text of 1926/7 minus stanza 107 (verse).
Merry, Eleanor C., *The Dream Song of Olaf Åsteson* (1961), pp. (odd) 15–41: the text of 1896, but translated from Erich Trummler's German version (verse). Samples of another verse translation, made by Benedict Wood, again from Trummler's German, are found on pp. 44–7 (stanzas 1, 7, 18, 21).

Jonsson, Bengt et al., *European Folk Ballads* (1967), pp. (odd) 199–209: Landstad B (verse).

Barnes, Michael, 'Draumkvæde – How Old Is It?', *Scandinavica 11* (1972), pp. 104–5: R2a, M14, L4, T3 (prose).

German

Steiner, Rudolf, *Olaf Åsteson* (1916, cf. note 159).

Hoffmann, Ludwig, *Das Traumgedicht* (*Der Traumgesang*) (1917, cf. note 161).

Hoffmann, Ludwig, *Licht aus dem Norden* (1924, cf. note 161).

Trummler, Erich, *Traumlied des Olav Aasteson* (1927), pp. (odd) 29–63: the text of 1896 (verse).

Steiner, Rudolf, *Weltenneujahr* (1932), pp. 4–14: the text of 1896 (verse).

Hoffmann, Ludwig, *Im Traumlicht der Ewigkeit* (1954), pp. 8–11: the text of 1896 (free verse translation); pp. 99–101: the text of 1896 (literal verse translation).

Steiner, Rudolf, *Welten-Neujahr* (1958), pp. 10–18: the text of 1896 (verse).

Danish

Dal, Erik, *Draumkvædet* (1957), pp. 43–52: MM (verse).

Czech

Babler, Otto F., *Píseň o snu Olava Aastesona* (1937): the text of 1896 (verse).

Select general bibliography

Rikard Berge, *M. B. Landstad, Norske folkeminnesamlarar II,2* (1920).

Rikard Berge, *Vinje og Rauland* I–II (1940–4).

Rikard Berge & Hallvard Gunleikson Heggtveit, *Olea Crøger, Norske folkeminnesamlarar II,1* (1918).

Sophus Bugge, *Gamle norske Folkeviser* (1858, reprinted 1971).

Olav Bø, *Stev, Norsk folkedikting V* (1957, 2nd edition 1964).

Erik Dal, *Nordisk folkeviseforskning siden 1800* (1956).

Johan Fritzner, *Ordbog over Det gamle norske Sprog* (1883–96, reprinted 1954).

Svend Grundtvig et al., *Danmarks gamle Folkeviser* (1853–).

Einar Lundeby, *Overbestemt substantiv i norsk og de andre nordiske språk* (1965).

Hans Ross, *Norsk Ordbog* (1895, reprinted with the six supplements 1971).

Hans Ross, *Norske bygdemaal II, Vest-Telemaal,* Videnskabs-Selskabets Skrifter. II. Hist.-Filos. Klasse. (1906) No. 3.

Oluf Rygh et al., *Norske Gaardnavne* (1897–1936, reprinted 1959–70), VII, *Bratsberg Amt.*

Johannes Skar, *Gamalt or Sætesdal* I–III (1961–3, 2nd edition).

Ivar Aasen, *Norsk Ordbog* (1873, reprinted 1918).

3. The texts

3.1 Variants

As the preceding history of *Dr* research has shown, earlier commentators, with one or two exceptions, were much concerned with the origins of the ballad, and their textual criticism, such as it was, presupposed the existence of an *Ur-Draumkvæde*. They naturally enough found it difficult to agree about the age, author and content of this early text, but it provided each of them with something fixed, if intangible, with which to compare the written variants of the nineteenth and twentieth centuries. They were to say the least saddened to see how ill this unique product of medieval Norwegian culture had survived the test of time. But their firm conception of what kind of poem it must once have been enabled them to reject much matter as spurious, and several managed to construct from the remaining material a work which they felt resembled the original poem more closely than any existing variant.

By no means all the scholars who have written on *Dr* talk in terms of an *Urtext*, but every statement about the genuineness or otherwise of a word, line or stanza assumes that such a text once existed and furthermore that we know approximately what it was like. In fact, of course, our knowledge of *Dr* does not extend beyond the 1840s when it was first written down. Jørgen Moe and Landstad give us information which suggests that something not unlike L1/4 and K1 was sung as early as the eighteenth century,[310] but how much the wording and content changed over the years we do not know. The differences between L1 and L4 and certain features of K1 (cf. Section 3.7, K1, note 7) suggest that what Anne Lillegaard's grandmother and Maren Ramskeid's grandfather sang may have been somewhat different from the variants we now possess. Speculation about the exact nature of a medieval or pre-1840 *Dr* is bound, therefore, to be an extremely subjective exercise and as such unrewarding. More crucial still: from a textual point of view it is totally irrelevant. We are dealing with oral literature which has no authorised form and may be constantly changed. The form only becomes fixed when the ballad is written down, and even then it may go on being remoulded, often under the influence of printed texts. It is wrong, however, where one can observe such influence, to talk of 'spurious' or 'less genuine' matter, just as it is wrong to talk of 'good' or 'bad' variants in terms of a supposed *Urtext*. Value judgements can really only be meaningful if applied to the individual text as a piece of literature.

The historical approach to *Dr* is not without justification since the variants contain a certain amount of historical matter and parallels with medieval vision literature can be observed. This is an entirely different matter, however, from applying a historical or diachronic approach to textual criticism and altering a given stage in the development of a piece of oral literature in order to make it approximate more closely to an assumed earlier stage. The variants we have must form the starting point of any historical or literary research. Moltke Moe and others have amply demonstrated what happens when literary and historical research is made the starting point of textual criticism. The dangers of this approach, however, are not only that the scholar often ends by writing his own poem, but also that terminological confusion arises when nineteenth-century texts are judged by ill-defined and possibly ill-understood medieval, Reformation or even eighteenth-century criteria. This is well illustrated by the discussion about the relationship of *Dr* and *gamlestev*. In this discussion it is always assumed that one knows what is meant by these terms and they are nowhere defined. Yet without such definitions it is extremely hard to follow the argument, and it becomes even more difficult when synchronic and diachronic aspects of the matter are confused. Brynjulf Alver, for example, talks, as we have seen, about MSS of *Dr* containing *gamlestev*.[311] This must mean not only that he considers it possible to distinguish between *Dr* stanzas and *gamlestev* on the basis of content, but, more significant, that the two are immutable – *stev* remain *stev* although they are included in a *Dr* variant and *Dr* stanzas are still *Dr* stanzas even where they appear in collections of *stev*.This is a diachronic viewpoint; it assumes an earlier stage of development than the one we know, when the *stev* had not yet been included in the *Dr* variant, and before the *Dr* stanza had been added to the collection of *stev*. In another part of the book it is stated repeatedly that the stanzas under discussion are, or are not, known or met with 'as *gamlestev*'.[312] This, however, is a synchronic viewpoint. The assumption underlying such statements is not that a ballad stanza or *stev* is something instantly recognisable as such wherever it appears, but rather that one's description of any given stanza is determined by its function. In this case all the MSS of *Dr* mentioned by Alver on pp. 45–79, if, like him, one accepts that they are MSS of *Dr*,[313] must by their very nature consist exclusively of material 'functioning as'[314] *Dr* stanzas. And if we agree, as Alver does,[315] that oral literature has no authorised form, at least until it is written down, material, irrespective of its origin, which functions as a stanza in a *Dr* variant becomes part of that variant and thereby part of *Dr*.

Recognition of the fact that we are dealing with oral literature, with all that this implies, creates almost insoluble difficulties for anyone wishing to edit *Dr*, but such recognition must, in my view, form the starting point of any approach to the vast collection of material which might be included under this heading.

The problem is this: we have many MSS headed *Draum- Drau(g)- -kvæde -kveen* etc. in the hand of the collector. A number of these contain variants in which some continuity of action, to say the least, can be observed, and it seems reasonable to regard this as ballad material. Others consist entirely of collections of unconnected stanzas or *stev*.[316] This fact alone causes little difficulty. There are, however, a good many MSS headed *Draum- Drau(g)- -kvæde -kveen* etc. which contain stanzas found in the coherent *Dr* variants, but where the text does not in itself form a connected whole. Such stanzas may be accompanied by others not found in coherent *Dr* variants, or otherwise in *Draum- Drau(g)- -kvæde -kveen* MSS at all. We also find that material identical with or similar to that which is headed *Draum- Drau(g)- -kvæde -kveen* in one MS appears in others with no heading whatsoever. Furthermore, we do not know in most cases whether a title is the informant's or the collector's. In theory, therefore, there is almost no limit to the amount of material admissible as *Draumkvæde*, *Drau(g)kveen* or the like. There *is* a limit to the amount of material admissible as the *Draumkvæde* (*Drau(g)kveen* etc.) ballad or ballads, but it is virtually impossible to define this limit objectively. Consider, for example, T8. It is short and without a title, but might be said to have continuity of action or narrative structure (cf. Section 2.18, note 308). It contains three stanzas (3–5) found in *Dr* ballad variants,[317] and two which are not otherwise connected with the ballad or ballads. Alver declares, after pronouncing T8 to be a 'group of connected *gamlestev*':[318] 'Many scholars have even considered this to be a variant of *Draumkvedet*.'[319] But why not? There are several of what must be classed *Dr* ballad variants that contain material which is either unique or only found elsewhere as *gamlestev*. One of Alver's thirty most important variants (cf. Section 2.17) contains, according to the author himself, sixteen non-*Dr* stanzas as opposed to three which (we must assume) form part of a *Dr* ballad.[320] Much criticism has been directed at M6 because it contains matter not found in other *Dr* ballad variants and is somewhat disjointed, but no one has ever denied that it is a *Dr* variant. There is no obvious reason, then, why we should reject T8, but ought we to exclude the first two stanzas? From a historical point of view perhaps we ought. We could say that they are *gamlestev*[321] and have simply been attracted to the other *Dr* stanzas by the similarity of situation and wording. If we wish to adopt a less subjective approach, we could attempt to define what a *gamlestev* is and accept or reject the stanzas according to this definition. There seem to be very few features the many stanzas described as *gamlestev* have in common, however, and the criteria would have to be fairly broad. A possible definition might be: a *gamlestev* is a four-line stanza with y-a-z-a end rhyme which is usually complete in itself; it is lyrical rather than narrative, the first two lines often contain a scenic description, while the second two carry the import of the stanza.[322] Further than this it is hard to go. Applying our definition to stanzas 1 and 2 of T8 we can still either reject or retain them, so we are no further on. From a synchronic point of view there is of course no problem about including the two stanzas if we accept that T8 is a *Dr* ballad variant. But are there any positive criteria we can use to establish this? In order to answer that question we must first try and delimit the material among which what we for the moment can call the *Dr* ballad is to be found. All of this material will provisionally be called '*Dr* ballad variants'.

Drǫugqveen! (V1a) was sent by Niels Svenungsen to Olea Crøger in October 1842. He presumably compiled it in that year, but points out in his accompanying letter to Crøger that he had been several years collecting the material (cf. Section 3.7, V1a, note 5). The information he omits to give is how he knew what to look for. All subsequent collectors and editors had not only his version to go by, but also his remarks on what the ballad was about. But how did Svenungsen arrive at his text and the interpretation he placed on it? It is possible that Crøger, who apparently[323] asked him to collect the ballad, gave him some idea of what he might expect to find, but from where did her knowledge come? The conclusion seems inescapable that either Crøger or Svenungsen or both heard parts of the ballad *Dr* sung and were told by informants or others what it was called, how they understood it, and that it had once been much longer and more complete.[324] Without some such guidance it is difficult to see how Svenungsen could have put together

V1a and decided that it was 'An ancient ballad, probably about the state of the soul after death . . .' (cf. Section 3.7, V1a, note 5). Once V1a (and V1b) had appeared, collectors knew more or less what they should be looking for. Naturally they too had access to informants' knowledge and views about the ballad, but we should not underestimate the influence of Svenungsen's MSS. Unfortunately our knowledge of the technique used by collectors in eliciting information is very scant. We know that Bugge, for example, carried a copy of Landstad's *Norske Folkeviser* around with him on his travels, and it seems very likely that he sometimes used it to jog his informant's memory. This was certainly the technique used by Rikard Berge who, for example, writes at the end of K11: 'Everything else in Landstad is unfamiliar.'[325]

V1a and V1b should clearly form the starting point of any attempt to delimit the *Dr* ballad material. However, as we have seen, both versions suffer from a serious drawback: they do not come direct from a single informant, but have been pieced together by Svenungsen. Unfortunately we know nothing about the guide-lines he used in constructing these texts, whether he simply included everything to which informants gave the name *Drougqveen* (*Draumkvæde* etc. ?), or whether he sifted through all kinds of ballad material, picking out those stanzas which, irrespective of their origin, seemed to fit in with whatever picture he had gained of the ballad. We can see today that much of the material in V1a forms part of other ballads.[326] What we do not know is whether any informant sang these stanzas in a coherent variant of the *Dr* ballad. On balance it seems better not to include them as part of the *Dr* ballad material and they are therefore omitted from this edition. Other stanzas included by Svenungsen which are omitted are those with a humorous content,[327] since this would seem to be incompatible, if not with a description of life after death, at least with the complete ballad as Svenungsen presents it. Further, two *stev* are excluded, the one (V1a,27) since we can be fairly sure that it began life as a *stev*,[328] the other (V1a,36) since it forms a continuation of the humorous stanzas V1a,34–5. What we are left with is thirty-six stanzas, twenty-four of which occur in variants of the *Dr* ballad. The following are unique: V1a,23 (S.92), 28 (42), 31 (77), 37 (52), 45 (86), 52 (90), 58 (146), 59 (148), 61 (169); three also occur in V1b: 14 (24), 15 (37), 22 (91).[329] Of these, however, only one (V1a,52) is totally unconnected with any other stanza which occurs in a *Dr* ballad variant, and some (V1a,15, 28, 31, 58, 59) are simply variations on stanzas which are found in a large number of variants. It should also be pointed out that many of the stanzas excluded also appear in *Dr* ballad variants, notably V1a,34–5 and variations on these. This presents something of a problem, since although such stanzas clearly were part of the *Dr* ballad in the 1840s and later, virtually all of them seem incompatible with what little we know about the ballad as a whole from Svenungsen and those variants which have a clear narrative structure, notably L1, L4, L6 and K1. The precedent established by omitting the stanzas where they occur in V1a is followed, reluctantly, throughout, but information about what has been excluded is found in Section 3.5, notes.

Unfortunately we do not know the exact date of many of the MSS in Landstad's collection, but it seems likely that virtually all of them were written before 1848.[330] We can also be fairly sure that most of the MSS of *Dr* he wrote himself pre-date 1847, since they do not exhibit the etymological spelling familiar to us from *Norske Folkeviser* which he probably began to use early in that year.[331] Jørgen Moe's MSS can be dated more exactly, since we know about the trips he made to Telemark to collect material. It is thus possible to date the three most complete variants of the ballad *Dr* which pre-date *Norske Folkeviser*, L1, L4 and K1, to 1847, 1840s (almost certainly before 1848) and before 1847 respectively. We know that these texts must be variants of the ballad a) because of their titles *Draumkve*, *Dromkvæen* and *Draumekvæi*, and b) because they have twelve stanzas in common with V1a. This may not seem very many, especially when one considers that the corresponding number for the individual variants is eight (L1 and L4) and seven (K1), but if one looks at the ballad in terms of episodes or sections, the three variants and Svenungsen's compilation cover very much the same ground. All describe the following: the hero's sleep, awakening and ride to church; the telling of his dreams at the church; the loss of the scarlet cloak; *Gjallarbru*; the punishments; the reward for good deeds (*sæl* stanzas). In addition L1/4 and V1a include the introductory stanza and the journey up to the clouds and down again, and K1 and V1a the description of the hero. Together V1a, L1, L4 and K1 contain seventy-two different stanzas and include almost all the sections of the ballad except those found only in M6. They form a nucleus that makes it possible to examine other complete[332] variants which pre-date *Norske Folkeviser*, to see if and how they are connected with the *Dr* ballad that has emerged. Those which can be considered are the following: 1) V2, 1840s, *Draumekvædet*; one stanza, not found in V1a, L1, L4 or K1, but describing *Gjallarbru*. 2) M1, 1847, *Suplemete ti Dromkve*; three stanzas, none are found in the three variants or V1a, but all describe similar events. 3) L2, 1847, *af Drougkvæ*; ten stanzas, all except one occur in L1 or L4, and all are found in one of the three variants or V1a. 4) L3, 1847, *Draugkve (Brudstykke)*; six stanzas, five are found in one of the three variants or V1a, the other describes a punishment. 5) S2, 1847, *Ole Oknesen 1ste Vers*; one stanza, found in the three variants and V1a. 6) T1, 1846; one stanza, found in L1 and V1a. 7) T4, 1840s; two stanzas (preceded by some fragments), one occurs in K1 and V1a, the other describes a punishment. 8) T5, 1840s, *Tilhører Dramekvæi*; eight stanzas, all except one occur in one of the three variants or V1a (cf. Section 3.5, T5, note), the one which does not describes the host from the south. 9) T6, 1840s, *af Draunekvædet*; two stanzas, one occurs in the three variants, the other describes the misery to be seen in the spirit (or other) world. It is impossible to date T7–12, but since T7–10 form part of Landstad's collection, it seems very likely that they pre-date 1848, and almost certain that they were written before the publication of *Norske Folkeviser*. Of these T8 and T9 are complete and contain five and four stanzas respectively. T8 has three stanzas in common with one of the three variants or V1a, the other two describe the protagonist drinking and falling asleep on Christmas eve. T9 has three stanzas in common with K1 or V1a, the fourth describes a reward for good deeds. Clearly almost all of these early variants are fragmentary. It is difficult to interpret them in such a way that a continuous narrative emerges,[333] and they lack most of the material found in V1a, L1, L4 and K1. Nevertheless they seem to be part of the same tradition. Even if the title could in each case be shown to have been added by the collector (and its varying form makes this seem unlikely), the fact remains that we have a large number of complete variants which describe exactly the same events as V1a, L1, L4 and K1 and in most cases contain largely the same stanzas. It therefore seems reasonable to include them as *Dr* ballad material.

Together V1a and the variants discussed contain eighty-three stanzas (slightly more or less if one accepts or rejects more of V1a) which could be part or the whole of a ballad or ballads about life after death. It is possible to argue that this material constitutes in itself an extended definition of the *Dr* ballad or ballads and is all that should appear in any edition. Other variants from the 1840s exist which contain identical stanzas, but these also include material which does not accord with the picture of *Dr* that emerges from V1a and the variants already discussed; some correspond closely with V1a etc. in all except one or two stanzas, while others consist largely or almost exclusively of unrelated material. We have three choices in respect of these variants. We can note their existence, but otherwise ignore them; we can include as part of the ballad those stanzas which also occur in V1a etc. or describe the same events as these texts; or we can include the complete variant. The first choice is the easiest and certainly consistent with a synchronic viewpoint. It is, however, unsatisfactory in cases where only 10–20% of the material appears to be unrelated to the ballad. The second choice is inconsistent with the synchronic approach, since one is often taking stanzas from a non-*Dr* ballad context where they have a non-*Dr* ballad function. The third choice is totally impractical since, having included a variant with, say, twenty-five new stanzas in addition to the two or three already known from *Dr* ballad variants, one would have to look for all the variants in which the new stanzas occur and include these too. In this way all Norwegian ballads and *stev* would soon become part of *Dr*. If we revert to the first choice, but decide to include variants where only a small amount of material is incompatible with what we know of the ballad, we are faced with the difficulty of deciding what constitutes a small amount of material and exactly where to draw the line. There is also the question of what to do with the incompatible material: whether to include or exclude it. Clearly, whatever one decides, objections can be raised. It would, however, seem to be the prime object of an edition to consider all material that is in any way relevant, even though, in the case of *Dr*, this means including as part of that material stanzas which do not seem to function as part of the ballad. The reader then at least has an opportunity to form his own judgement of what is and what is not *Dr* using the criteria he finds most appropriate. In accordance with this principle what in the present edition are described as S1, S3, T2, T3, T7 and T10 are included as 'variants' of the ballad *Dr*, but variant should be understood here not as a text in a MS identifiable as a separate item with a clear beginning and end and coming, as far as is known, from a single informant, but rather as *Dr* ballad material emanating directly from an informant (or informants) and not subject to alteration or re-arrangement by an editor.[334] This means in the case of T3, for example, that the second stanza has been omitted, since although this is so abbreviated as to consist of only one word, *oddar*, it is recognisable as the same stanza as V1a,34, which is humorous. The remaining stanzas are numbered 1–6 and it is these which are considered to form the *Dr* ballad variant T3.[335] In the case of S1 one stanza has been extracted from a collection of twenty since, although it does not function as a *Dr* ballad stanza, it is also found in V1a and has not been excluded as incompatible with what we know of the ballad. It is numbered 1 and considered to form the *Dr* ballad variant S1.

The complete and incomplete *Dr* ballad variants which pre-date Landstad's edition and almost certainly Moe's as well are thus: V2, M1, L1–4, K1, S1–3, T1–6. To these we can in all probability add: T7–10. It is clear from this that the bulk of *Dr* ballad material was collected after the appearance of *Norske Folkeviser*. In this edition such material has been treated in the same way as the variants already discussed in order that nothing of possible relevance should be left out. In practical terms this means the inclusion in their entirety of most variants which share a preponderance of stanzas or episodes with the pre-1853 *Dr* ballad. Stanzas which are incompatible with what we know of this ballad (e.g., those with a humorous content) have been omitted from a small number of variants of this type. MSS which consist partly of material identical with or related in theme or form to the pre-1853 *Dr* outlined above and partly of unrelated or incompatible material are divided up, only those stanzas being included which have a clear connection with the ballad. A serious difficulty arising from this procedure is the impossibility of deciding exactly where to draw the line. Approximately two-thirds of the stanzas in M6, for example, are not found in any other coherent or complete *Dr* ballad variant. Some of these stanzas describe the same events as other variants, but the majority do not. Nevertheless we seem to be dealing with a variant of the ballad *Dr*. It is called *Draugkveen*, has some degree of coherence and shares many of its episodes with other variants of the ballad. At the same time certain stanzas which are unique to M6 among coherent or complete *Dr* ballad variants (or in one case which M6 shares with one other complete variant and V1a) appear widely in collections of *stev* (cf. M6,23, 27–8, 40, V1a,38, By1,1).[336] The problem is not only confined to M6, although it is most noticeable in this variant. V1a,2 and K1,1–2 are found in the ballad of *Vilgår Hertugson*,[337] M9a,7 occurs in collections of *stev*, M9a,9 is found in almost identical form in *Margjit og Targjei Risvollo*,[338] M15b,3 occurs in the Danish ballad *Vidrik Verlandsens Viise*,[339] M20,1 appears in NFS Bugge k 67 in a somewhat shorter form which seems to be unrelated to *Dr*,[340] etc. Are these *stev* and ballad stanzas to be taken as part of the *Dr* ballad irrespective of where they appear and in what form? Clearly for practical reasons some limitation has to be imposed if the list of *Dr* variants is not to grow to unmanageable proportions. It therefore seems sensible, though in some degree arbitrary, to introduce the concept of central and peripheral stanzas. Central are those which describe events or situations common to a large number of complete variants. Peripheral are those which describe unique or rare events or situations. Normally only central stanzas are included in this edition when they do not function as part of a complete variant of what has emerged as the ballad *Dr*. Exceptions are S8c,1, S9a,1, T11,1 (possibly also S7,1 which forms a complete variant but whose only link with the ballad is V1a) (S.87) and Sæl,1 (S.137), which are included because of the important part they have played in *Dr* studies.[341] It should also be noted that S.111 occurs marginally more frequently in incomplete than complete variants (8:7 + V1a).

It is perhaps reasonable to ask at this point whether post-1853 variants, complete or incomplete, fragmentary or coherent can have the same value as those which pre-date *Norske Folkeviser*. The answer to this question will naturally depend on what one understands by value. As literature each variant must stand on its own merits irrespective of when it was collected and by what it was influenced. As examples of *Dr* ballad tradition all complete variants are of equal value provided they come directly from informants without any interference from a collector or scholar, but this is very difficult to demonstrate in the case of the post-1853 variants. First, they may have been influenced by Landstad A which is the product of an editor rather than oral tradition.[342] Second, and perhaps more important, with the appearance of Landstad's texts, and to a lesser extent that of Jørgen Moe, all collectors must have had a very clear idea of what they were looking for when they enquired of informants if they knew the ballad *Dr*. It is unfortunately impossible to judge how great an influence such texts had on their enquiries. Although Sophus Bugge took his copy of *Norske Folkeviser* with him when out collecting, we have no proof that he used it to prompt informants, although this seems likely.[343] He may, however, have been influenced to the extent of asking certain questions and not asking others, of doubting and querying information which did not fit into a particular pattern while readily accepting that which did. We have only to recall his attitude to Anne Skaalen's variant, M6, which, he tells us at the beginning of his fair copy, was 'very distorted', while dotted about all over the text are the expressions 'new', 'entirely new' etc., referring to individual stanzas.[344] Moltke Moe was perhaps the scholar who more than any other came to have a fixed idea of what *Dr* was and what it was not, but this seems to have had little influence on his activities as a collector. All of the complete variants of the ballad in his hand are very fragmentary. Half of the variants in this edition collected by him are incomplete, and although he (presumably) wrote them down in their entirety, Moe clearly did not consider the material we have excluded from them to be part of the ballad. He never used it in any of his editions, or even seriously discussed it in his lectures in which he took a much broader view of *Dr*. Where Moe does seem to have let his concept of the ballad run away with him is in his treatment of other collectors' MSS. Thus in Bugge II,165, a copy of Bugge k 67, mentioned above, Moe has written: 'Var. of "*Draumkvæde*"',[345] but it is strange that Bugge himself does not include this information if it was provided by the informant. In S.137 as it appears in Skar 1,16 Moe has substituted *kjinna* and *raue* for *svaitta* and *kalle*, but without any indication of where these 'variant readings' come from. Rikard Berge clearly used printed texts to prompt his informants. In addition to the example given above (p. 73) we find in V9,6 the word *Gjaddarhylen* with a note which states: 'only the form I used when asking'.[346] It appears that Torleiv Hannaas used this technique too. As has recently been suggested, he seems, by using MM, to have persuaded an informant in Sætesdal that he faintly remembered a judgement stanza.[347] Finally mention must be made of a long and coherent variant, K5, which may have been strongly influenced by Landstad's texts. One cannot fail to be struck by the similarity between this variant and K1 for which there are three possible explanations: 1) the informant represents the same line of tradition as Maren Ramskeid;[348] 2) he or she read Landstad B (and Landstad A?) and partially memorised it (or them); 3) the collector, Hallvard Heggtveit, put the text together, rather as Svenungsen had done earlier, using Landstad B as a model. This last possibility is suggested by Alver who finds evidence for it in the title *Stumper af Draumkvædet* ('Bits of *Draumkvædet*'), and in the fact that K6, by the same collector, is headed *Begyndelsen af Draumkvædet* ('The beginning of *Draumkvædet*').[349] Alver considers that Heggtveit discovered K6 after he had put together K5. That is why they occur separately. While this theory has much to be said for it, it is by no means certain that it is the correct explanation of the similarity between K1 and K5. What does seem likely, however, is that either Heggtveit's informant(s) or Heggtveit himself knew Landstad's texts fairly well.

It has now been shown how the selection of variants included in this edition has been arrived at. The way they have been classified requires one or two further words of explanation. The *Dr* ballad variants as each editor, prospective editor or scholar understood them have been classified four times already; first by Liestøl, then by those who continued his work on a definitive edition of the Norwegian ballads, and recently by Svale Solheim and Brynjulf Alver. Neither of the latter two systems could be used in this present edition because they take in relatively few variants. The former two suffer from a number of drawbacks, notably inconsistency and a certain unwieldiness, and naturally not even they include all the variants since some have only recently been made available. A criticism of all the systems is that they do nothing more than identify the variant. Regretfully, therefore, a fifth system has been introduced in this edition. It is based on the age and provenance of the variant. Age is clearly important, as has been shown above. Provenance also seems to be of some significance. The early variants from Mo, Lårdal and Kviteseid appear to form three more or less distinct groups, and it is not impossible that certain patterns of tradition could be demonstrated elsewhere.[350] Each variant is allotted a letter and a number. The letter describes the area of Telemark from which the variant in all probability comes[351] (rather than the area in which the informant lived at the time it was written down if a difference between the two is known), the number indicates its relative age. Where there is a clear connection between variants (normally if they share collector, informant and MS book or collection), they are given the same number and subdivided a, b, c etc. Copies of MSS are not given any status as variants. Where MSS exist containing identical stanzas by the same informant and collector and it is impossible to decide whether or not some or all but one of them are copies, the most original, if this is known, is chosen as the *Dr* ballad variant, but a note is made of the existence of the others in Section 3.5, notes. Where it is not possible to decide which text is the most original, an arbitrary choice has to be made.

3.2 Stanzas

In the preceding discussion, both in this section and Section 2, the term stanza has frequently been employed. It is of course used to describe the four-line units with end rhyme in the second and fourth lines of which the variants of the ballad *Dr* consist.[352] But this is not all. Previous commentators used the term rather loosely, never making entirely clear the distinction between different stanzas and variants of the same stanza. Such a distinction, however, is crucial to the way in which this edition is organised. Given that the *Dr* ballad variants are often very different in content, that many are fragmentary in the sense that they cannot conceivably form a narrative, and that the stanzas can appear in almost any order, it is clearly essential to have some kind of basic unit other than the variant when discussing the material as a whole. This unit could be the episode in a wide or narrow sense, or the stanza.[353] The stanza has been chosen here since it presents the most economical means of including virtually all the relevant material, and because it is a more precise concept and easier to define than the episode.

Study has shown that there is one simple, objective criterion by which stanzas can be distinguished: the final rhyme word. This causes few difficulties, can be applied consistently and leaves very little material unaccounted for. In this edition, therefore, to take two extremes, stanzas which are identical in every respect except the final rhyme word are considered to be separate, while those which differ considerably in their wording, but have the same final rhyme word are classed as one, provided, of course, that they describe the same event. In fact such extreme examples rarely occur; a change of rhyme words, particularly of the final rhyme, is a good indication that something fresh is being described, while stanzas which share the same rhyme word or words seldom differ greatly in other respects. It is true that stanzas are characteristically varied in Scandinavian ballads by changing the rhyme words and little or nothing else, but this does not occur to any great extent in *Dr*, and the whole point of the practice is to *vary* the stanza, i.e., not to repeat the same one (cf. the *sæl* group).

The implications of using final rhyme to distinguish stanzas need to be examined more closely in certain cases.

1. Different grammatical forms of a single word or homonymous related words are not considered to give more than one stanza, e.g., S.135 *dei mone kvorare ægte* (K1,10), *i denne Heimen dei tok kvorandre te Egte* (K5,14), *som ha kvorare ægtað* (T4,2). A word which appears both on its own and as the second element of a compound is considered to give two or more stanzas since the ideas expressed in such cases may be entirely different, e.g., S.145 *fe lie noko Nau*, S.146 *fø qvasse Heklenou.* This does not apply in the case of S.149 where *Gjæddar bru* (V1a,56), *Gjeddar Bru* (K1,13) etc. and *haddanbrú* (L6,6) are considered to express the same idea if not to refer to the same place (cf. L6,3 – S.93 and Section 5.2). *Hæklebro* (V1a,59 – S.148), on the other hand, introduces a new idea, that of spikes on the bridge, and has overtones of the thorny moor, cf. S.147 *Heklemoe* (K1,12), *Tynermo* (L4,19), which are considered to be one and the same place. Occasionally two or more stanzas may have one and the same rhyme word, but can be classed as different because thcy describe different events or are otherwise totally dissimilar. Examples are: SS.16,24,36 *fortællje vil æg Draumo mi* (K1,4), *æg theele af Droumane meene* (V1a,14), *fortællje vil æg Dramæn min* (K1,6); SS.125,129 *aa myre Mannen i Skog* (K5,11), *hae Flutte deild i Skog* (L4,9); SS.6,42 *daa Fokje i Kyrkja drog* (V1a,5), *ho va ny æg Heyma drog* (V1a,28).

2. In V4,1 and V5,1 ll.1–2 appear as 3–4 and 3–4 as 1–2. These stanzas are nevertheless considered to belong to S.34 (cf. also M6,15).

3. One disadvantage of using final rhyme to distinguish between stanzas is that the method allows considerable variation in the wording of the rest of the stanza. It must be stated, however, that any other method, if applied consistently, seems to produce even greater variation or an unreasonably high number of stanzas. Naturally there is a point where the variation in all but the final rhyme word becomes so great that the material must be classed as two stanzas rather than one, but this point can be difficult to determine. It seems clear that SS.16,24,36 must be classed as separate,[354] but consider S.119 which has three possible first lines, exemplified by L4,20 (thus L1,19, L2,6, K5,17, N1,10), K1,19 (thus V9,11) and T6,2 (thus K4,1), and two possible second lines, exemplified by L4 (thus all except K1) and K1. The third and fourth lines show some variation, but all express the same idea. There seems good reason to talk of one stanza rather than two where three lines (including the fourth) are identical or very similar and/or express the same idea (cf. SS.115–16), but if we class V9,11 as S.119, we can hardly exclude K1,19 since V9,11 and K1,19 also have three lines in common. Other stanzas in which a certain amount of variation is found, particularly in the first rhyme word, are those describing the destruction of the scarlet cloak (SS.39–41,43; 42,44–5 are unique) and some of the *sæl* group (SS.143–4,147,149–50,152). It has been suggested, principally by Liestøl, that the variation in the pronoun (*eg* or *han*) in the stanzas describing Olav's sleep and ride to church is significant.[355] It is not considered so in this edition since the variants show no consistent pattern in this matter. Occasionally a stanza may occur twice in one and the same variant where something other than the final rhyme word is modified. Examples are: V1a,3 and 6, 24 and 25, M6,8 and 72, 12 and 68 and L6,9 and 11.

4. Sometimes stanzas are found which consist of lines from two different stanzas according to the numbering of this edition. Where the first two lines (or sometimes four in the case of a six-line stanza) are from one and the second two (or four) from another, the stanza is divided into two parts, a and b, and each part is given its appropriate S. number, e.g., M6,26a and b – SS.5,122. This is also the practice adopted where a separate half- or part-stanza has a form compatible with one or two lines, e.g., M6,16a *Tunge va dæn Granastigjen(/) å gange*, or for one reason or another is not included in the numbering of this edition, e.g., K5,6b (the final two lines of a six-line stanza), S4,2b, T5,5a. If, for whatever reason, the fourth line of a stanza is wanting, and there is a choice of final rhyme words, it is of course impossible to say exactly to which of the stanzas of this edition it belongs. This is the case with V9,10 (fourth line missing), R2a,5a, M8,1 (one line only), M18,1a, M18,2 (fourth line abbreviated *&c.*) etc. (cf. Section 3.6).

Many collectors, notably Bugge, abbreviate stanzas, sometimes to the extent of writing only one or two words. Often this is accompanied by a reference to Landstad A. Alternatively, the lines or words omitted can be inferred from a preceding stanza. In this edition abbreviated stanzas are given the same status as those written in full, but when quoted, the missing material, whether taken from Landstad A or another stanza in the relevant variant, is always placed in square brackets. In one or two extreme cases a stanza can consist of no more than a reference to Landstad A. This occurs in M3 which theoretically has twelve stanzas, but from which two (10 and 12 in the original sequence) have been omitted in this edition since all we have is Bugge's laconic remark: 'In addition he recited Landstad A 24, variant reading 2, 17 (*Eikjaråsen, jólehylen*), 14.'[356] Landstad A 17 is included (as stanza 10) since two words are given and this is elsewhere considered sufficient. A problem arises in respect of S6. This variant is found in Bugge's copy of *Norske Folkeviser* and S6,3, 9 and 10 consist of no more than the remarks: 'Leiuf. V.3, Leiuf V.9., Leiuf V.10' written next to the appropriate stanza in Landstad A. In many ways this is an exact parallel to the abbreviations in M3, but since the text, although printed, does actually appear here, it has been decided to include these stanzas.

Sometimes it is impossible to distinguish between a variant reading and an abbreviation. It seems fairly clear that the words in the margin opposite K1,6 should be taken as variant readings rather than an invitation to repeat the whole stanza substituting these words. The position is not quite so clear in T5,4 where repetition of the first three lines and the substitution of *næste Jesum Christ* for *han rei paa kvitan Hest* seems possible. T3,3, on the other hand, is almost certainly an abbreviated stanza (cf. Section 3.7, T3, text and variant readings, also Section 3.5, K2, note).

The stanzas in this edition are numbered 1–169. This, with the exception of some unnumbered half- or part-stanzas discussed in Section 3.5, notes, comprises all the material known to me which accords with the description of the ballad *Dr* given above. The order in which the stanzas have been arranged does not purport to represent a likely or even possible sequence of events, but is based on the principle of grouping together stanzas which have something in common, e.g., those which mention *Gjallarbru* or begin with the word *sæl.* It will be found that the majority of stanzas belong to a recognisable group or section, although there are a number which are difficult to place. These have been fitted in anywhere that seemed appropriate. The resulting sequence is as follows:

1. Introduction S.1.
2. Description of Olav SS.2–4.
3. Olav falls asleep on Christmas eve, awakes on the thirteenth day and rides to church SS.5–23.
4. He arrives at the church during service, tells of his sleep and dreams and describes in general terms how he feels SS.24–38 (1–4 together are sometimes referred to as 'the introduction' or 'the introductory stanzas' in agreement with the practice of earlier commentators).
5. The loss of the scarlet cloak coupled with various injuries SS.39–45.
6. The *smådrengjir* SS.44–7.
7. The journey *norafjølls* (*Gaglemyr* in By1) SS.48–55.
8. Various adventures involving a hind, a serpent, lions, birds etc. SS. 56–75.
9. The journey up to the clouds and down again SS.76–83.
10. Hell S.84.
11. Heaven S.85.
12. The waters under the earth SS.86–7.
13. The journey up a river S.88.
14. The silence S.89.
15. The horror of death S.90.
16. *Gjallarbru* SS.91–109.
17. The three (or one or two) paths SS.110–14.
18. Paradise S.115.
19. The blue ice SS.116–17.
20. The godmother in a (or the) pilgrims' church, the spirit world or elsewhere SS.118–20.
21. The many miseries in the spirit world S.121.
22. The punishments SS.122–37.

23. A reward S.138.
24. The spiteful human tongue S.139.
25. A warning for those who are not merciful? S.140.
26. The *sæl* stanzas SS.141–56.
27. The hosts from the north and south SS.157–61.
28. The judgement SS.162–66 (27 and 28 together are sometimes referred to as 'the judgement' or 'the judgement stanzas' in agreement with the practice of earlier commentators).
29. Reflections on awakening SS.167–8.
30. Conclusion S.169.

In tying the various recognisable groups together, and in determining the order within and outside these groups, it is chiefly the wording of individual stanzas that has been used as a guide, and, where this fails, common sense. Thus S.1 is clearly best placed at the beginning, with SS.2–4 not far behind; S.5 or some other stanza with the first line (normalised): *Han* (*Eg*) *la seg* (*meg*) *ned um joleftan* must also come fairly near the start, and once one of these is included, all the others with the same first line follow as a group (SS.5–11); SS.12–15, with the first line: *Dæ* (*De*) *va no um Joleftanen* (*Jolef.*) seem a natural appendage to SS.5–11, as do SS.16–19 which begin (normalised): *Han* (*Eg*) *vakna ikkje fyrr um trettanddagjen*; SS.17–19 and 21–3 talk of the protagonist's horse, so it seems reasonable to place the stanza beginning: *Hesten min stende på Nórnesi* somewhere amongst these, and by making it S.20 it is possible to split up SS.17–19, which share the same first line, and SS.21–3, which have different first lines, but in part describe the same events as SS.17–19. SS.24–169 have been numbered following a similar line of reasoning. Occasionally it is difficult to place a stanza because it shares a concept with one section or group, but is more like another in its general description and wording. S.115, for example, clearly belongs near to SS.116–19 if we consider the wording, but could well form a group with S.85 (Heaven) in terms of ideas. S.85, however, is best placed next to S.84 since Heaven provides a contrast to hell; and since hell is also mentioned in S.83, which is the last of 'the journey up to the clouds' group, SS.84–5 can hardly be moved anywhere else.

A table indicating the stanzas which occur in each variant will be found in Section 3.6. Each of the hundred and sixty-nine stanzas is printed at least once in Section 3.7, and Section 5.4 comprises an index of stanzas showing in which of the variants printed in this edition they can be found.

3.3 The Draumkvæde ballad past and present

In Section 3.1 it was shown how the selection of variants included in this edition was arrived at and an attempt was made to justify the selection. Inclusion in Section 3.5–6 does not, however, automatically confer *Dr* ballad status on a variant. It would be difficult by any criteria to demonstrate that the amorphous collection of material listed in 3.5 is *a* or *the* ballad *Dr*, and that absolutely nothing else qualifies for this title. Nevertheless, if one or more such ballads exist, they are clearly to be found among this material.

'Ballad' has been defined in a Scandinavian context as a song (*visa*) which narrates a story in stanzas with end rhyme and includes a single or double refrain.[357] In addition to this definition it is stated that the ballad tells its story from an objective point of view, is dramatic in its presentation, concentrating on important events with rapid changes of scene, and is composed of dialogue and descriptive stanzas in varying proportions. This seems an appropriate definition and description of the Scandinavian ballad, and if the material included in Section 3.5–6 satisfies these criteria, *Dr* must clearly be regarded as one or more ballads.

Roughly the position is this: all the material consists of stanzas with end rhyme, and many variants have a refrain; a small number of variants can be interpreted in such a way that a narrative structure emerges; the presentation is by no means always objective, but it seems mostly to be dramatic; there is very little dialogue. Certain variants may thus satisfy most of the criteria of a ballad, but the material as a whole cannot. This raises a problem. Four-line stanzas of the type we are dealing with which do not form part of a ballad can hardly be anything but *gamlestev*. While it is often not difficult to distinguish between a ballad and a group of *gamlestev*, there will always be uncertainty over such distinction where the ballad variant is fragmentary or the ballad itself lacks a clear story. Since this is the case with the material in this edition, we shall have to accept the fact that there can be no clear-cut dividing-line between *gamlestev* and ballad, and therefore no clear-cut definition of the ballad or ballads *Dr*. It does seem possible, however, to show which variants are most or more likely to be ballads and which *stev*. There are a number of features which are normally found in ballads, but which are rare or non-existent in *stev*.

1. Ballads usually tell a story. This may not be the case with *Dr*, but if we are to class part of our material as a ballad or ballads the variants concerned must have some sort of narrative structure. This is of prime importance.

2. As Ådel Blom has pointed out (cf. Section 2.18), the stanza which describes the protagonist standing in the church doorway relating his dreams while the priest stands before the altar or in the pulpit conducting the service can hardly be a *gamlestev* with an independent existence since it presupposes that some account of the dreams follows. Certain variants which include this 'narrative stanza' (SS.34–8) do not appear to have narrative structure, and should therefore probably not be classed as ballads, but it would be unreasonable to describe those which have both narrative structure and one of SS.34–8 as collections of *stev*.

3. The distinction between complete and incomplete variants (cf. Section 3.1, pp. 74 and 76 and notes 332 and 334) cannot normally be applied to *stev*. The essential point about this type of poetry is that it consists of independent units each complete in itself. It is true that many, perhaps most, *stev* are found in collections with a clear beginning and end, but the stanzas in such collections are normally unconnected, as is one collection with another. Even the connected groups of *gamlestev*, the so-called *stevrekkjer*, appear frequently as part of large collections and seldom as separate items in a MS. Ballads, on the other hand, even in fragmentary variants, have a beginning, a middle and an end. What in Section 3.5 are described as incomplete variants type a and d must therefore be classed as *stev* which (for whatever reason) have the same form as certain *Dr* ballad stanzas. This ought probably to apply to most incomplete variants of type c as well, though it is difficult to be dogmatic about this. Complete variants which have narrative structure and one of the narrative stanzas should almost certainly be considered part of the *Dr* ballad or ballads, but completeness is insufficient by itself to confer *Dr* ballad status on a variant.

4. As pointed out by Jonsson, ballads are normally accompanied by a single or double refrain. *Stev* normally lack this feature. Although exceptions to both these rules can be found,[358] the presence of a refrain indicates that we are more likely to be dealing with a ballad variant than a collection of *stev*.

5. Where *stev* are given a title in a MS it is usually no more than *Stev*, *Gamlestev* or the like. They were, however, also known as *Draumkvéen* or *Draugkvéen*.[359] At the same time there is only sparse evidence that *stev* were called *Draumkvæde* or *Drau(g)kvæde* except to the extent that certain variants with these titles included in this edition have more features in common with *gamlestev* than with ballads. The presence of the title *Draumkvæde* or *Drau(g)kvæde* may therefore be indicative of a ballad rather than a collection of *stev*, but we must remember that after Jørgen Moe's and Landstad's editions *Draumkvæde* at least was a heading often supplied by the collector (cf. Section 3.5, notes). It does not seem that the titles *Draumkveen* or *Drau(g)kveen* necessarily indicate that we are dealing with *gamlestev*, although much of the material in this edition which bears these headings has more features reminiscent of *gamlestev* than of ballads.

6. According to Jonsson the ballad tells its story from an objective point of view. On the other hand it is probably true to say that most *gamlestev* are subjective (they express the view or feeling of the composer and are often in the first person). Most variants of three stanzas or more among the material in this edition appear to contain both objective and subjective matter, although in the case of many individual stanzas it is difficult to state positively that they are either objective or subjective. In view of this, objectivity as a criterion for distinguishing ballad variants from *stev* is abandoned.

7. Another feature of the ballad, according to Jonsson, is that it consists of both descriptive stanzas and dialogue. Few *stev* contain dialogue in the strict sense of the word, although many are addressed to a (now) anonymous *du*. Dialogue is also absent from most of the variants included in this edition. Those which do contain the odd snatch are: R2a, K1, K3, K5, K11, S6 and possibly H3. Dramatic presentation, also mentioned by Jonsson as a feature of the ballad, is of no use as a criterion for distinguishing ballads from *stev*. All the material included in this edition can be said to concentrate on important events with rapid changes of scene.

There are thus five basic features, the presence or absence of which can help us to decide whether or not a given variant should be classed as part of the *Dr* ballad or ballads. Narrative structure would seem to be the most important, but the least concrete and therefore most difficult to demonstrate. The 'narrative stanza' is also of great significance. The presence of these two features in addition to two of the others, especially if these are the complete variant and the refrain,[360] may be counted sufficient to confer ballad status on a variant. The presence of narrative structure alone, where this is clearly demonstrable, makes a variant more like a ballad than a collection of *stev*, but in general the fewer the ballad features, the further we can be said to move from the ballad and the closer to *stev*.

The distinctive feature matrix on pp. 90–3 will show, with due regard to the reservations expressed above, which of the variants in this edition may be considered part of the *Dr* ballad or ballads. $\pm$ against the narrative structure feature indicates that narrative structure may exist, but is difficult to demonstrate. A letter against the complete variant feature indicates that the variant is incomplete and in which way (cf. Section 3.4, pp. 104–5). A number against the title feature indicates the presence of a title and gives information about its approximate form (individual spellings may vary considerably): 1 = *Draumkvæde*, 2 = *Draugkvæde*, 3 = *Draukvæde*, 4 = *Draumkveen*, 5 = *Draugkveen*, 6 = *Draukveen*, 7 = *Draumkvaen*, 8 = *Ole Oknesen*, 9 = *Jedlarbrunæ*, 10 = *Jolkvæe*. (For further information about individual variants cf. Section 3.5.)

The matrix shows that the following variants may be classed as part of the *Dr* ballad or ballads: M3, L1, L4, L5, L6, K1, K5, K9 and N1. A very strong case can also be made out for V9, M2, M6, M9a, L9, L12, L13 and S6. Less obviously ballads, but hardly collections of *stev* are: M15a, L2, K3, K4, K11, T5 and T8. The remaining material seems to have more in common with the *stev* than the ballad *genre*, although, of course, the actual stanzas are often the same as those found in the ballad variants.

We have so far referred to the *Dr* ballad *or ballads*. We now have to decide whether V9, M2, M3, M6, M9a, M15a, L1, L2, L4, L5, L6, L9, L12, L13, K1, K3, K4, K5, K9, K11, S6, N1, T5 and T8 should be classed as one or more ballads. Just as there seemed to be no established criteria for distinguishing between variants of the same stanza and different stanzas, so also there appear to be few guide-lines to help one distinguish between variants of the same ballad and different ballads. Fairly extensive differences are often allowed between what are given as variants of a single ballad in *Danmarks gamle Folkeviser* and by Sophus Bugge in his *Gamle norske Folkeviser*. At the same time the sharing of a number of stanzas or episodes is clearly not always sufficient to allow us to talk of one rather than several ballads. We need only mention the *leikvoll* (sports field) scene, known in many Scandinavian ballads, in which a young man is spurred on by the taunts of his competitors to discover his father's true identity or to avenge his death.[361] *Dr* itself shares certain stanzas with other ballads (cf. Section 3.1, p. 77), and it is arguable that NFS Landstad 1b,92 (cf. Section 3.5, T7 and note) is a variant of *Beltevisa* which shares three stanzas with *Dr*.

It would perhaps seem reasonable to say that, all other things being

	V2	V3	V4	V5	V6	V7	V8	V9	V10	V11	V ?12
narrative structure	—	—	—	—	—	—	—	±	—	—	—
narrative stanza	—	—	+	+	+	—	—	+	—	—	—
complete variant	+	d	+	d	c	+	+	+	b	a	a
refrain	+	—	—	—	—	—	—	+	+	+	—
title	1	—	—	3	6	—	—	6	6	5	—

	R1	R2a	R2b	R3	R ?4	R ?5
narrative structure	—	—	—	—	—	—
narrative stanza	—	+	—	—	—	—
complete variant	+	c	+	+	c	d
refrain	—	—	—	—	—	—
title	—	7	—	6	5	6

	M1	M2	M3	M4	M5	M6	M7	M8	M9a	M9b	M10	M11	M12	M13
narrative structure	—	+	+	—	—	±	—	—	±	—	—	—	—	—
narrative stanza	—	+	+	—	—	+	—	—	+	—	—*	—	—	—
complete variant	+	+	+	+	+	+	+	+	+	d	+	+	d	+
refrain	—	—	+	+	+	+	+	—	+	—	—	+	—	+
title	1	—	1	—	—	5	1	—	6	6 ?	4/5	—	5	1

* Consists of one line from one of SS.34–6.

	M14	M15a	M15b	M16	M17a	M17b	M18	M19	M20	M21	M22	M ?23	M ?24
narrative structure	—	—	—	—	—	—	—	—	—	—	—	—	—
narrative stanza	—	+	—	—	—	—	—	—	+	—	—	—	—
complete variant	+	+	+	+	+	+	d	a	a	a	c	d	+
refrain	—	+	—	+	—	—	—	+	—	+	—	—	—
title	1	5	6	5	5	5	5	—	5	5	5/1	5	5/1

	F1	F2
narrative structure	—	—
narrative stanza	—	—
complete variant	+	+
refrain	—	—
title	1	1

	L1	L2	L3	L4	L5	L6	L7	L8	L9	L10a	L10b	L11	L12	L13
narrative structure	+	±	—	+	+	+	—	—	±	—	—	—	±	±
narrative stanza	+	—	—	+	+	+	—	—	+	—	—	—	+	+
complete variant	+	+	+	+	+	+	+	+	+	+	+	+	+	+
refrain	+	—	+	+	+	+	—	+	+	—	—	+	+	+
title	1	2	2	4	1	1	—	—	—	—	—	—	4	6

	K1	K2	K3	K4	K5	K6	K7	K8	K9	K10	K11	K12
narrative structure	+	–	±	±	+	–	–	–	+	–	–	–
narrative stanza	+	–	–	–	+	–	–	–	+	+	+	–
complete variant	+	+	+	+	+	+	+	a	+	d	+	+
refrain	+	+	+	–	–	+	–	–	–	+	+	–
title	1	–	–	1	1	1	–	10	1	1	1	1

	S1	S2	S3	S4	S5	S6	S7	S8a	S8b	S8c	S9a	S9b	S10
narrative structure	–	–	–	–	–	±	–	–	–	–	–	–	–
narrative stanza	–	–	–	–	–	+	–	–	–	–	–	–	–
complete variant	a	+	a	+	+	+	+	a	a	a	a	a	a
refrain	–	+	–	+	–	+	–	+	–	–	+	–	–
title	–	8	–	–	1	–	–	–	–	–	–	–	–

	S11	S12	S13	S14
narrative structure	–	–	–	–
narrative stanza	–	–	–	–
complete variant	+	d	+	a
refrain	+	–	–	–
title	–	1	1	–

	N1	H1	H2	H3	B1
narrative structure	+	–	–	–	–
narrative stanza	+	–	–	–	–
complete variant	+	a	a	+	a
refrain	–	–	–	–*	–
title	1	–	–	–	–

* Two lines which have been taken to be a half-stanza could conceivably be a refrain.

	T1	T2	T3	T4	T5	T6	T7	T8	T9	T10	T11	T12
narrative structure	–	–	–	–	±	–	–	+	–	–	–	–
narrative stanza	–	–	–	–	–	–	–	–	–	–	–	–
complete variant	+	a	b	+	+	+	c	+	+	a	d	+
refrain	+	–	–	–	–	–	+	–	–	–	–	+
title	–	–	–	–	1	1	–	–	–	–	–	1

	Sæl	By1	By2	By3	By4	By5	He1
narrative structure	–	–	–	–	–	–	–
narrative stanza	–	–	–	–	–	–	–
complete variant	a	+	+*	b*	+	+	+
refrain	–	–	–	–	–	–	–
title	–	1	–	–	1	–	9

* Also found in a big collection of *stev*.

equal, where well over half the stanzas in a variant X are not known in any other variants of what appears superficially to be the same ballad, it is right to class variant X as a separate ballad. If this criterion is adopted it means that all but two variants of the *Dr* ballad or ballads as defined in this Section belong to one and the same ballad since they share the majority (in many cases all or nearly all) of their stanzas with at least one and very often more than one other *Dr* ballad variant. The exceptions are M6 and T8. Fifty-four and a half of the stanzas in M6 (total seventy-four) and three in T8 (total five) do not occur in V9 etc. However, before these two variants are declared to be different ballads, account must be taken of any similarity of episode or situation which may exist between them and the others. Four stanzas in T8 and approximately[362] forty-five in M6 seem to have something in common with matter in V9 etc., but often the connection is somewhat tenuous, as witness, for example, M6,3–5, 33, 43–5. There hardly seems to be sufficient common ground between M6 and the other variants to class them all as one ballad and accordingly M6 will be regarded as separate from V9 etc. T8 is too short to allow any firm pronouncements to be made, but since it has as much in common with M6 as with V9 etc., it would be wrong to class it with either.

We emerge then with three separate but related ballads. A suitable name for V9 etc. would seem to be *Draumkvæde*, since this is the title which predominates in the MSS.[363] M6 is called *Draugkveen* in the original and *Draukveen* in the fair copy; the original is of course to be preferred. T8, which has no heading, will be termed *The Short Visionary Ballad.*

The description so far has been concerned solely with *Draumkvæde*, *Draugkveen* and *The Short Visionary Ballad* as we know them today. What of earlier times?

It has repeatedly been stressed that we know virtually nothing about the history of what up to now has been called *Dr* or 'the *Dr* material' before about 1840, and it would certainly be wrong to indulge in the wild speculation of some earlier commentators. Nevertheless, a few tentative suggestions about the development of the three ballads before the 1840s are perhaps permissible, provided they are based firmly on existing material and are not confused with facts.

There seem to me to be three basic questions to which one would like an answer:

1. How old are the ballads we have identified as existing in the nineteenth century?

2. Have there always been three ballads, or was there originally only one?

3. What is the age and what was the form of the earliest ballad or ballads similar enough to the variants we have today to be counted their forerunner?

The answer to any one of these questions is in some measure dependent on the answers to the others, so it will be easiest to discuss all three together. Starting with the whole of the material described in Section 3.5, but concentrating on the ballad variants, I shall attempt to work backwards in time as far as possible.

Study of the variants indicates that only in three areas was there demonstrable oral transmission of a visionary ballad over any length of time. These are Mo, Lårdal and Kviteseid.

From Vinje there are but three texts of any length: V1a, V1b and V9. The first two are not genuine variants and the stanzas in them may have been collected anywhere. V9, in my view, is suspect. It is true that the collector, Rikard Berge, guarantees its pedigree (cf. Section 3.5, V9, note), but there are three factors which should make us cautious: 1. No earlier collector, as far as we know, found anything like a visionary ballad in Vinje. What we have are odd stanzas and fragments some of which may once have formed part of *Draumkvæde*, *Draugkveen* or *The Short Visionary Ballad*, but which now can no longer be distinguished from *gamlestev*. 2. Berge seems to have used either a specific printed text or his knowledge of such texts to prompt the informant (cf. Section 3.1, p. 79). 3. V9 contains a number of rare stanzas and episodes (SS.80,84,103,119,159) some of which seem otherwise only to be known in early variants from Lårdal and Kviteseid (cf., however, the remarks on Nissedal below).

None of the three visionary ballads seems to have been known in Rauland at the time the collectors were active. It has only provided one text of any length which contains stanzas also found in the three (cf. Section 3.5, R2a and note), but this text has more in common with the *stev* than the ballad *genre*. Some of its stanzas may of course at one time have formed part of one or more visionary ballads.

The three stanzas from Fyresdal must clearly be regarded as *stev*, although these too, like all the other incomplete or wholly fragmentary 'variants' listed in Section 3.5, may once have belonged to a visionary ballad.

Seljord has only one variant of any length: S6. This is found in Bugge's copy of Landstad's *Norske Folkeviser* and is heavily abbreviated with reference to the printed text. Since Bugge had Landstad's text with him when he interviewed the informant, it is also possible that he used it to prompt him. This may explain the occurrence in S6 of a number of stanzas not otherwise recorded in Seljord in connection with a visionary ballad. The informant may have been familiar with them, but possibly in a different context. SS.3–4 in S6, for example, could equally well have been known to him from the ballad of *Vilgår Hertugson* (cf. Section 3.1, p. 77); Bugge's note does not extend to the actual name of the person described in these stanzas. S.158 might have been known to him as the *stev*: *Norðan koma Norðmennann/ deð tottest meg vera verst,/ fyri reið grutte gråskeggi/ på sin svarte hest.*[364] Not only this stanza, but the whole episode of the two hosts in *Draumkvæde* is otherwise unknown in Seljord. Just as in the case of V9, it seems doubtful whether S6 can help us much in a study of the pre-literary history of *Draumkvæde*, *Draugkveen* and *The Short Visionary Ballad.* All the other texts from Seljord appear to belong to the *stev genre.* Many are extracted from large collections of *stev*, and those which form complete sections in MSS can in no way be classed as ballads.

Nissedal is unique in having one fairly long variant of *Draumkvæde*, but no *stev* with identical or similar content. As with V9, it is puzzling, if N1 has a long history in Nissedal, that no collector before Berge found *Draumkvæde* in this area. N1 has a lot in common with the slightly earlier variant K9. SS.19, 97 and 128 are unique to these two variants and all the seven stanzas of K9 appear in N1. On the other hand K9 has little in common with other variants from Kviteseid. In the absence of evidence to the contrary we must assume that N1 represents a genuine line of tradition. However, the fact that it has seven stanzas in common with K9 and two more which otherwise are probably only found in Kviteseid and Lårdal (SS.116,119) suggests that this line ultimately goes back to Kviteseid, possibly the Morgedal district where K9 was recorded.

The odd stanzas from Hjartdal and Bø can clearly only be regarded as *stev*. This also applies to most of the texts whose provenance cannot be established with any certainty. T3 might be the remains of a visionary ballad of which almost all the motifs but one (*Gjallarbru*) had been forgotten. But it could, at least in part, be an example of improvisation on a familiar theme. T5 seems to be a fragmentary variant of *Draumkvæde*. With its emphasis on the hosts from the north and south and the judgement, it is probably from Kviteseid. The former motif does not seem to have been known at all outside Lårdal and Kviteseid and the latter is only found in K1 and K5. T8, as has been shown, is a short visionary ballad related to *Draumkvæde* and *Draugkveen.* It is impossible to say from what part of Telemark it comes. The *stev* in T6 are found in almost identical, but abbreviated form in the *Draumkvæde* variant K4. If the abbreviations really are to be expanded word for word on the basis of Landstad A 39–40, K4,1–2 and T6,1–2 become so similar that they could be from the same informant. The *stev* in T11 is otherwise found only in Seljord and V1a. T11 may therefore also be from Seljord.

The texts from Sætesdal, Bygland and Helleland are clearly *stev.* It is difficult to say whether any visionary ballad ever existed in these areas. By1 shares S.54 with *Draugkveen* (and V1a) and By2–5 have S.5 in common with all three visionary ballads, but these may have been commonplaces or *stev* which were used in the ballads. Alternatively, of course, they may originally have been part of one or more of the ballads and only later have been sung independently as *stev.* S.7, because of its similarity to S.5 and a number of other stanzas, could well have been part of the ballads at one time, but it could also be a new stanza modelled on S.5. He1 clearly cannot have arisen independently of the *Gjallarbru* stanzas which appear to be a central motif in *Draumkvæde.* However, something like this stanza (S.94) is widely used as what appears to be a nursery rhyme in Vest-Agder (cf. Section 3.5, p. 118) and may have spread to Helleland from there.

Of the many texts from Mo, Lårdal and Kviteseid listed in Section 3.5 it is clearly the ballad variants which can be of most help in an investigation into the pre-literary history of *Draumkvæde*, *Draugkveen* and *The Short Visionary Ballad.*

Draugkveen consists of a single variant: M6. This, coupled with the fact that the majority of the stanzas in M6 are not known from any other source, suggests that the ballad itself may not be very much older than the variant. As a rough and ready rule one can say that, all other things being equal, a rare or unique ballad or stanza is more likely to be recent than a common one. There are other reasons for thinking that *Draugkveen* is not particularly old. Intermixed with stanzas in Norwegian we find the occasional one in Danish or a combination of both languages (e.g., M6,57–9). Apart from this, a number of Danish or what appear to be Danish words and forms occur, more than is usual in a Norwegian ballad of Norwegian origin (e.g., *Klippi* (29), *foraktar* (35), *enlig* (37), *Øine* (38), *grumme Løver* (39), *Løvernes* (39); cf. also Section 5.1, general note 25). These bits of Danish scattered throughout the last two-thirds of M6 in stanzas unknown from any other source make it unlikely that *Draugkveen* is older than the seventeenth century and probable that it is much younger. The most important clue we have to the relationship of M6 to the *Draumkvæde* variants lies in the many stanzas in M6 which contain a motif, line or word also found in a stanza *Draugkveen* shares with *Draumkvæde*, but which are otherwise partly or wholly different. These stanzas (2–5, 17, 22, 32–3, 35, 37–8, 43–9, 51, 55–6, 59–61, 63–4, 69–71, 73–4), which as far as I know are only found in M6 (cf., however, below), bear all the marks of improvisations on a familiar theme. So also do most of those beginning: *Eg va' meg hær nórafjølls.* Of these only M6,40 seems to occur elsewhere, although a number of well-known *stev* are found which have approximately the same first line.

Taken together these facts make it seem improbable that *Draugkveen* can have existed for very long before it was written down. Indeed, I would be surprised if anything like M6 was being sung much before 1800. The ballad may be even younger than this. Brynjulf Alver lays great stress on certain evidence which suggests that the *Draugkveen* Anne Skaalen sang was part of a living tradition.[365] He does not argue a convincing case, however, and this is hardly surprising, for the evidence is not very strong. Bugge first wrote in his fair copy that Anne had learnt M6 from 'Hallvor Bjaaen', but later crossed it out. A reasonable inference is that Bugge found strong reason to doubt the correctness of the statement which presumably came from Anne herself. Alver considers it quite probable that Anne did learn *Draugkveen* from Hallvor, since, according to him, 'large parts'[366] of M6 resemble connected groups of *gamlestev* from Vinje (Hallvor's birthplace) headed *Drougkvéen* or *Draumkvéen.* It would be more exact to say that a few of the stanzas in M6 are well-known as *gamlestev* and that they sometimes appear in connected groups with the above titles. As regards Hallvor, he was one of the most famous of Norwegian ballad-singers, and given the keen interest of collectors in *Draugkveen*/*Draumkvæde* it is strange, if he taught *Draugkveen* to Anne Skaalen, that no one ever recorded it from him. Hallvor is known to have composed ballads himself. One is called *Draugafæri* and contains one or two (two-line) stanzas faintly reminiscent of *Draugkveen* and *Draumkvæde*, but taken as a whole it is most unlike M6.[367] Three singers, Alver seems to suggest, learnt *Draugkveen* directly or indirectly from Anne.[368] Apart from two stanzas (SS.44–5) printed by Moltke Moe in his article of 1908, however, we have nothing in the least reminiscent of her *Draugkveen* (cf. Section 3.5, M20–1 and notes, and Section 5.1, general note 37). Moltke Moe's statement, quoted by Alver, that Hæge Leirebrekk, following Anne Skaalen, introduced stanzas from *Orm Aaseland* and *Agnus Dei* into *Drougkvéen* is baffling, since, as far as I know, M6 contains no stanzas from either ballad. There is thus very little to show that *Draugkveen* as sung by Anne Skaalen was part of a living tradition which existed both before and after her time. Was she lying when she told Bugge she had learnt the ballad from Hallvor Bjaaen? We cannot tell for sure, but Bugge clearly thought so. Why should she lie? The most likely explanation is that it was she who put together the mixture of *Draumkvæde* stanzas, *stev* and improvisations that *Draugkveen* seems to consist of.

The Short Visionary Ballad is, as the name suggests, very short. This makes it difficult to say anything about its possible history. It could be the remains of a line of *Draumkvæde* tradition from which most of the stanzas known in existing *Draumkvæde* variants have been lost. At the other end of the scale it could be an improvisation on the spur of the moment – a putting together of well-known *stev* to form a sequence of events. Whatever the case may be, it is impossible to show that it is the remains of a separate visionary ballad.

Draumkvæde is known in a number of widely differing variants from Mo, Lårdal and Kviteseid. If it is accepted that we are dealing with a single ballad, these variants must clearly be related. The way in which they are related is not, however, at all clear. It seems fair to say that the firmest tradition is found in Lårdal. Lårdal has the greatest number of *Draumkvæde* variants and no large collections of *stev* containing stanzas also found in *Draumkvæde*. Allowing for the fact that L1 and L4 are by the same informant, there is a greater degree of similarity in the wording of individual stanzas in Lårdal than in Mo and Kviteseid, and the ratio of *different* stanzas to the *total number* of stanzas in *Draumkvæde* variants from Lårdal is somewhat less than in variants from the other two areas. Lårdal occupies a central position between Mo and Kviteseid with regard to the stanzas and episodes the variants contain. This is perhaps natural considering its geographical position. While Lårdal has a large number of stanzas and most episodes in common with both Mo and Kviteseid, the latter two differ quite considerably with regard to both stanzas and episodes.

Tradition in Mo seems to have been relatively stable. None of the variants is noticeably different from the others in content except possibly M3 which has slightly more in common with *Draugkveen* than the others. There is no fixed sequence of stanzas, but this is not found in any other area either.

Lårdal appears to have three separate lines of tradition represented by a) L1, L2 and L4 (L1 and L4 by the same informant), b) L3 and L5 (L3 does not satisfy the criteria of a ballad variant but is almost certainly by the same informant as L5) and c) L6. It is difficult to determine the relationship of L9, L12 and L13 to these lines of tradition. They could be the remains of a fourth line, or simply improvisations on a familiar theme.

Tradition in Kviteseid presents a more complicated picture. In the centre we have K1 and K5. K1 has long been held to be the best of all the *Draumkvæde* variants, and as a piece of literature it does seem to stand out above the others. Ådel Blom's analysis (cf. Section 2.18) has shown it to be a tightly-knit, coherent work of a kind very different even from L1, L4, L5 and L6. Does K1, then, give us a text not very different from the 'original' *Draumkvæde*? In my view this is unlikely. If K1 represented a line of tradition which had been preserved intact from the very beginning we would expect it to contain many more stanzas than it actually does (cf., however, Section 3.7, K1, note 7). Furthermore it would be odd if it were preserved in Kviteseid which has by no means as firm a tradition as Lårdal. The close relationship there seems to be between K1 and K5 may not be of much significance since it is uncertain whether K5 represents a single genuine line of tradition (cf. Section 3.1, p. 79). It is certainly not a work of literature in the same way as K1, although it contains very much the same stanzas. With its varying refrain, its explanation *Æg drøimde* before stanza 7, its conclusion in Danish and its uniquely clear narrative structure K1 appears to me most likely to be a re-working or reconstruction. This might have been undertaken by anyone who knew one or more fragmentary variants of *Draumkvæde* and was interested enough to speculate about their meaning. He or she may also have added stanzas from other sources, e.g., K1,1–2 (cf. Section 3.1, p. 77) which form a neat introduction. Since K1 still has a very clear narrative structure, the reconstruction is unlikely to have taken place very long before the 1840s. On the other hand this version of the ballad seems to have been in the informant's family for three generations. Perhaps Maren Ramskeid's grandfather was the one responsible (cf. Sections 3.7, K1, note 6, and 2.18, p. 60 and note 305). K3, K4 and K11 are probably the remains of the tradition from which K1 was forged, although K11 may well have been influenced by the collector and should be regarded with some circumspection (cf. Section 3.1, p. 73). All three are short. K3 and K4 have not a single stanza in common, but both share stanzas with K1. K11 has all six stanzas in common with K1, one with K4 and none with K3. K9 shares only one stanza (S.5, the commonest of all) with the other Kviteseid variants. If it represents Kviteseid tradition at all, this line must have parted company with the mainstream at a very early stage. As pointed out above, K9 shares all its stanzas with the one *Draumkvæde* variant from Nissedal.

In order to make clear the relationships between the *Draumkvæde* variants from Mo, Lårdal and Kviteseid, I have drawn the following stemma. It is intended to show in the crudest way the lines along which the variants we have today may have developed. It should be noted that M2, M9a and M15a can change places and that the position of L6 close to K3 and K4 is fortuitous. These variants have very little in common, but L6 has slightly more in common with variants from Kviteseid than Mo, and K3 and K4 have more in common with variants from Lårdal than K1, K5, K9 and K11. The rather odd line of tradition given to K9 is meant to indicate that this variant has more in common with those from Lårdal than K1, K5 and K11, but somewhat less than K3 and K4.

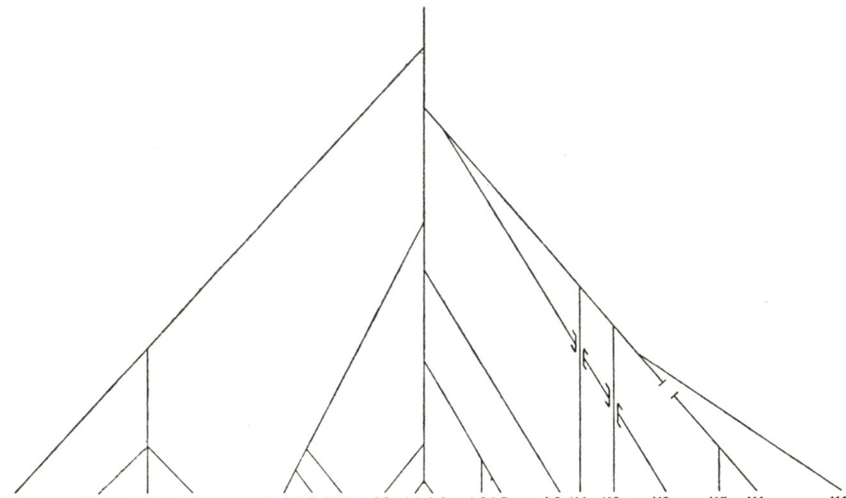

How far back in time do the various lines of tradition go before they meet? Can we be sure that they meet at all? Was the ballad we presume to have existed at this point anything like the variants we know today?

There is little doubt, in my view, that *Draumkvæde* goes back at least to the sixteenth century. The variants we have may not all stem from a single feat of composition – several variants may have existed almost from the very start as singers added to a nucleus and gradually built up their own forms of the ballad – but they cannot belong to more than one ballad in the widest sense. There are three factors which suggest considerable age.

1. The content. It is hard to believe that a singer in post-Reformation Norway (1600 +) would have had the knowledge, interest and inspiration to compose a ballad about St Michael, the Virgin Mary (?), *Gjallarbru* (cf. Section 2.11), the sinfulness of marriage between cousins (although such marriage was forbidden by law for several centuries after the Reformation), otherworld punishments which in medieval fashion reflect and illustrate the sin for which they are imposed and the many rewards one could expect in the after life for giving gifts to the poor on earth.

2. The great differences between the variants, and their fragmentary nature.

3. The language. First, one cannot fail to be struck by the difference between the language of *Draumkvæde* and the many stanzas of Anne Skaalen's *Draugkveen* which seem to be nineteenth-century improvisations on the *Draumkvæde* theme. *Draumkvæde* is in an archaic Norwegian (the odd Danish form or spelling may be due to the collector); Anne's stanzas are a mixture of Norwegian and Danish (Danish was also the language used by the singer who provided a conclusion for K1). Second, there are many expressions in the variants which are extremely difficult to understand and were doubtless incomprehensible to the informants themselves (cf., e.g., Section 3.7, L6, note 3). It is hard to believe that *betlarstyen*, *Vetters Ti*, *Broksvalin*, *Føesheimen*, *sýslehúse*, *Uttexti* etc., nearly all of which appear to be an integral part of the ballad, are words which were well-known and understood in eighteenth- or even seventeenth-century Telemark. It is also unlikely that the stanzas containing the expressions *annen Heimen* (K1,16), *den anen heimen* (L6,9), *Annom Heimen* (L4,17), *auro heimen* (L5,9) etc. were composed as late as the seventeenth century, yet these stanzas are among the commonest and quite central to the ballad. *auro heimen* corresponds to Old Norwegian *ǫðrum heimi* with the substitution of the *m.* common case *def.* ending *-en* for the old *m.indef.dat.* in *-i.* Aasen notes that both the *dat.* form *aurom* and *heim* in the sense of 'world' were used in Telemark, but he gives no sentences where they occur. In the case of *heim* he refers to Landstad's *Norske Folkeviser*. The likelihood is that both were exclusively ballad usages. In *Draumkvæde* (M3) and *Draugkveen* as well as some of the non-ballad variants (e.g., S5; also V1a) we can see that *vær* (i.e., *verd*) occurs in place of *heim*. A newer usage has clearly been substituted for an older, less familiar one. In Old Norwegian/Icelandic, however, *annarr heimr* was an extremely common expression.[369] The use of *an(n)en* with the *def.* form of the noun also seems to be old, and has in some cases been replaced by the more modern forms *andre* (e.g., K1,15) or *are* (e.g., L1,17). *Den annen* + *m.* or *f.subst.* or *annen* + *m.* or *f.subst.* + *def.art.* appears originally to have been a Danish construction, although it occurs in written Norwegian from the sixteenth century.[370] What we are dealing with here, however, is surely the Old Norwegian *í ǫðrum heimi* which has changed, to a greater or lesser degree, in step with the development of spoken Norwegian in Telemark.

Such little evidence as there is suggests to me that in *Draumkvæde* we have the remains of an old ballad. How old it is impossible to say with any accuracy, but I would imagine that something not unlike L1, L2 and L4, though longer and with a clearer narrative structure, was sung in at least parts of Telemark before the Reformation.

3.4 General notes on Section 3.5–7

The table in Section 3.5 contains twelve columns which give the following information:

1. The letter (= area) and number (= relative age) of the variant as defined in Section 3.1, according to the classification of this edition (cf. Section 3.1, p. 80). The geographical division is based on the old *herred* boundaries and is the same as that found in *Norske Gaardnavne*. V = Vinje, R = Rauland, M = Mo, F = Fyresdal, L = Lårdal, K = Kviteseid, S = Seljord, N = Nissedal, H = Hjartdal, B = Bø, T = Telemark, Sæ = Sætesdal, By = Bygland, He = Helleland. The position of the various areas vis-à-vis each other is illustrated by the schematic map opposite the next page.

2. The letter or number of the variant according to Liestøl's system of classification. The numbers are prefixed by D* in Liestøl's work (his 1946 monograph, the original Norwegian MS from which it was translated and various notes in the archives of Institutt for folkeminnevitskap, University of Oslo). It is possible that the classification is incomplete, or that we have incomplete knowledge of it. Thus we find A* and D*–F*, but no B* or C*, and V11, which Liestøl himself collected, has no letter or number that I have been able to discover.

3. The letter and, in some cases, number of the variant according to the system of classification adopted at one time for the planned definitive edition of the Norwegian ballads and found in MSS made in preparation for this edition in the archives of Institutt for folkeminnevitskap, Oslo.

4. The number of the variant according to the system of classification adopted by Svale Solheim for the forthcoming critical edition of the Norwegian ballads.

5. The number of the variant in Alver (1971).

6. The name of the informant. These are often spelt in different ways, even by one and the same collector, e.g., K1: *Marn Ramskeid* (p. 1), *Maren Ramskei* (p. 2). The form found in an original MS of a *Dr* variant (as defined in Section 3.1) is always preferred both in the table and throughout the edition, but where this is lacking, fair copies or other sources are used.

7. The surname of the collector(s). These are, with the addition of the Christian name(s) by which they are commonly known: Rikard Berge, Sophus Bugge, Tallef and Wetle Dyrland, Olav Grasberg, Hølje Gaange, Torleiv Hannaas, Hallvard Heggtveit, Hallvard G. (initial only known) Kaldbast, Magnus Brostrup Landstad, Knut Liestøl, Ludvig Mathias Lindeman, Jørgen Moe, Moltke Moe, Ivar Mortensson, Hans Ross, August Schneider, Johannes Skar, Aasmund Smedal, Niels Svenungsen, Hans Jacob Aall.

8. The year or approximate date at which the variant was written down.

9. The refrain. There are seven basic refrains and a number of minor variations as follows (each is represented by a typical example of the type; other examples may vary somewhat in spelling and wording):

1. Aa dæ va Olaf Aaknesonen som sove hæve saa længje (K1,3).
1a. Stat up du Olav Aasteson som hævæ sovi solænje (V1a,61).
1b. Vakre deg Olav Aasteson, no hev du sove lengje (S9a,2).

2. For Maanen skjine aa Vægjene fadde saa vie (K1,7).
2a. fe maanen s (L11,1).
2b. Lykylen synge å Løva springe Månen skine å Vegjinne fadde vie (M5,1).
2c. Sole skenne, aa Vejine fadde so vie (V1b,19).
2d. Min frende og din vin Maanen skine og vegine fadde vie (V2,1).

3. I Broksvalin der sko Domen stande (K1,21).
3a. På Gjæddarbrúinne der ska' dómanne stande (K3).
3b. På Åmlivollen der sko' dómen stande (L6,1).

4. I villand hei hogt upp i lande der kjenne dei meg (M13,1).
4a. I villande Heyo, i Rodelaande der kjænne dey mæg (V1a,3).

5. Snoren gaar under ø (M21,1).

6. Tonga talar, aa Sannong svarar paa Domedag (V1a,56).

7. Månen skín úti lunden så fagert (S6).

For four refrains which stand on their own cf. Section 3.5, p. 118.

10. The title of the variant (or of the whole text in the case of incomplete variants, cf. 11 below). Brackets indicate that it is only mentioned incidentally and does not appear as a heading. Where part of the title is in brackets, however, the words concerned are also bracketed in the MS. It is usually difficult to tell whether a title is the informant's or the collector's. Where it is bracketed in the MS (indicated in Section 3.5, notes) or preceded by such words as *Vers*, *Stev*, *Stumper*, *Lidt af* (*av*), or just *Af* (*Av*), it is perhaps more likely to be the collector's, although variation of the name of the ballad by a collector (e.g., M15b *Af Droukvéen*, M17a *Af Drougkvéen*, S13 *Af Droumkvæi*) suggests involvement by at least some of the informants.

11. The number of stanzas contained in the variant. $\frac{1}{4}$, $\frac{1}{2}$, and $\frac{3}{4}$ = one, two or three lines respectively. Stanzas which have a form compatible with three or four lines

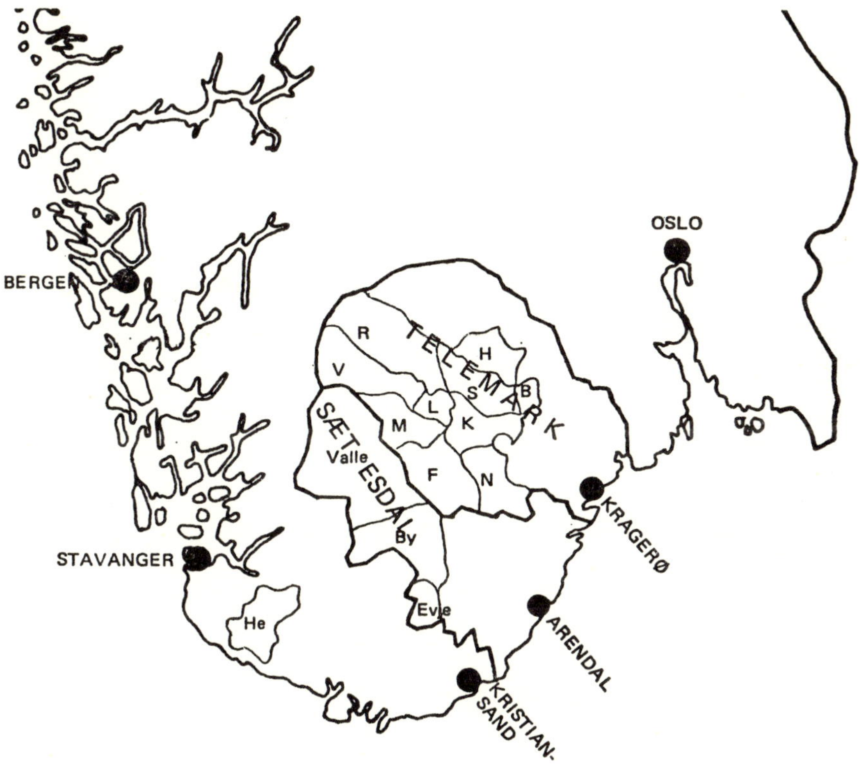

8. **Draumkvæde**

(e.g., M6,18) are counted as one. Where not all the matter belonging to a clearly defined ballad, unit or section in a MS is considered for the purposes of this edition to be *Dr* material (i.e., a variant is 'incomplete', cf. Section 3.1, pp. 76–7), the stanza total is marked a, b, c, or d.

a = variant extracted from a collection of *stev* and/or ballad stanzas.
b = one or more stanzas omitted – less than the *Dr* stanzas remaining.
c = one or more stanzas omitted – the same number as the *Dr* stanzas remaining.
d = variant extracted from odd notes and/or fragments in prose or verse (maximum non-*Dr* material three stanzas).

12. The collection in which the MS is preserved, its catalogue number and the pages on which the *Dr* variant occurs.

BFS = Bergen folkeminnesamling (University of Bergen).
NFS = Norsk folkeminnesamling (University of Oslo).
TFM = Telemark fylkesmuseum.
UB = Universitetsbiblioteket (Oslo).

Some variants appear in more than one MS or more than once in the same MS. Usually an original and a copy is involved. Only one text of each variant is entered in the table, but those texts not entered are mentioned in Section 3.5, notes, a) where it is not certain which, if any, MS is the original (apart from the fact that the original may now be lost, we must remember that collectors sometimes recorded variants on more than one occasion), b) where one of Bugge's fair copies is involved, c) if a copy contains any information not found in the original or otherwise of interest.

A blank space in the table means:

cols. 2–5: the variant concerned is not included or (cols. 2–3) not known to have been included in the particular system of classification.

cols. 6–8: the person or date is not known.

cols. 9–10: a refrain or title is wanting. No account is taken of headings such as *Stev* or *Gamlestev* where these occur over a collection of stanzas from which a *Dr* variant has been extracted (cf. 11 above).

In Section 3.6–7 the stanza numbering followed in the individual variant is that of the MS(S), or, failing this, the order in which the stanzas occur in the MS(S).

The spelling and punctuation of the texts in Section 3.7 is that of the MSS on which they are based. The sign / in the middle of a word indicates that in the MSS it is carried over to the following line without a hyphen. Occasionally it is difficult to distinguish between two letters (especially 'i'/'e' and 'a'/'æ') and more often between capitals and non-capitals (especially 'A'/'a', 'D'/'d', 'G'/'g', 'L'/'l', 'Q'/'q', 'S'/'s' and 'Æ'/'æ'). Alterations are very common in the MSS. These are mentioned in the notes that follow each text a) if they have any textual or linguistic interest, or b) if there is any doubt as to the reading. Straightforward corrections of mistakes (e.g., *faadde* > *fadde* K1,20*refr.*) and alterations which totally obscure the original spelling or wording are normally ignored.

3.5 A survey of the Draumkvæde variants

1	2	3	4	5	6	7	8	9	10	11	12
V1a	O	G2a	XXVIIa	21	various	Svenungsen	1842	1a, 2, 4a, 6	Drougqveen	61[b]	UB fol. 1803e
V1b	O	G2b	XXVIIb	21	various	Svenungsen	1846	2c, 4a	Drougqveen	21[b]	NFS Svenungsen 1–4
V2					Aslak Aartveit	Landstad	1840s	2d	Draumekvædet	1	UB fol. 1803e
V3	28	H2			Aslak Aartveit	Bugge	1867			1[d]	NFS Bugge c 164
V4	4	J2a			Margit Tveiten	Skar	1898			1	NFS Skar 3,9
V5	4	J2b			Saavi Bjaane	Skar	1898		Drau'kvæe	1[d]	NFS Skar 20,18
V6	4	J2c			Knut Tveiten	Skar	1898		Drau'kve'en	1[c]	NFS Skar 20,25
V7	27	K2			Gunnhill Negar	Skar	1898			1	NFS Skar 59,2
V8	A*	I2			Svein Hovda/ Tveiten	Skar				3½	NFS Skar 3,5
V9	E*	L2	XXVIII	22	Margit Tveiten	Berge	1910	2	(Dròukvéen)	13	TFM Berge LXI,81–5
V10					Kjetil Jonsson	Berge	1910	1	Dròukvéen	2[b]	TFM Berge XCVIII,18–19
V11		M2			Gunhild Haagehov	Liestøl	1916	2	Drougkvéen	1[a]	NFS Liestøl 8,15
V ?12						Berge ?	1904			2[a]	TFM Berge XXXIX,50, 52
R1	24	W2	XXIX		Aslak Kosi	Bugge	1857			1½	NFS Bugge g 27–8
R2a	P	X2	XXX	26	Steinar Gibøn	Bugge	1867		(Draumkvaen)	5[c]	NFS Bugge c 127–9
R2b	14	Y2			Steinar Gibøn	Bugge	1867			1	NFS Bugge c 138
R3					O. Trovatten	Berge	1906		Draukveen	2	TFM Berge CXLVII,30b
R ?4					Øli Berge	Berge	1908		Draugkvéen	1[c]	TFM Berge CXLVII,108
R ?5					Øli Lid	Berge	1910		Dròukvéen	1[d]	TFM Berge XLVI,18
M1	I	R	XIV	13		J. Moe	1847		Suplemete ti Dromkve	3	NFS J. Moe 10,7
M2	A	S	XV	14	Hæge Aarmote	Bugge	1856			8(9)	NFS Bugge l 66–7
M3	B	U	XVI	16	Bjørguf Rofshus	Bugge	1856(7 ?)	2	Draumkvæe IV	10	NFS Bugge I,207–8
M4	1	Va			Ingebjør Sandvik	Bugge	1857	2		1	NFS Bugge k 70
M5	9	W			Ingebjør Troddedal	Bugge	1857	2b		1	NFS Bugge k 86

M6	D	T	XVIIa–b	15	Anne Skaalen	Bugge	1857	2	Draugkveen	74	NFS Bugge k 118–26, 128–9 and III,1–10
M7					Olav Syning	Lindeman	1861	2	Draumkvæe	1	UB Musikksaml. eske 203, Hs. 2456
M8		Æ			Olav Syning	Bugge	1863			$\frac{1}{4}$	NFS Bugge d 105
M9a	C	Ya	XVIII	17	Hermod Larsen Dalen	Bugge	1863	2	Draukveen	9	NFS Bugge d 108–10
M9b	C	Yb			Hermod Larsen Dalen	Bugge	1863		Draukv.	1[d]	NFS Bugge d 197
M10		Z			Anne Bruhær	Bugge	1863		Draumkveen (ret) og Draugkveen	$\frac{1}{4}$	NFS Bugge d 193
M11					Ingebjør Kastedalen	Lindeman	1863 ?	2b		1	UB Musikksaml. eske 203
M12	17	Q3			Thone Mule	Schneider	1860s		Af Draugkveen	1[d]	NFS Schneider 1,34
M13		X				Landstad ?		4	Draumekvæde	1	UB fol. 2128
M14	16	Ø				Mortensson	1870s ?		Av Draumkvæe	$1\frac{1}{4}$	NFS Mortensson 11,8–9
M15a	E	Åa	XIXa	18a	Torbjør Ripilen	M. Moe	1890	2	Vers af Drougkvé'en	$3\frac{3}{4}$	NFS M. Moe 25,97–8
M15b	E	Åb	XIXb	18b	Torbjør Ripilen	M. Moe	1890		Af Droukvéen	3	NFS M. Moe 25,113
M16	F	A2	XX		Gró Sjåheim	M. Moe	1890	2	Vers af Drougkvéen	2	NFS M. Moe 25,168
M17a	Ga	B2a			Ånund Sigursli	M. Moe	1891		Af Drougkvéen	2	NFS M. Moe 27,72–3
M17b	Ga	B2b			Ånund Sigursli	M. Moe	1891		Af Drougkvéen	1	NFS M. Moe 27,84
M18	Gb	D2		20	Targjei Djuvi	M. Moe	1891		Af Drougkvéen	$1\frac{3}{4}$[d]	NFS M. Moe 28,3
M19	6	E2			Gónill Søistòg (Feddand)	M. Moe	1891	2		1[a]	NFS M. Moe 28,21
M20	H	C2		19	Nils Hougjen	M. Moe	1891		Drougkvéen	4[a]	NFS M. Moe 29,2–3
M21	8	F2			Hæge Kleivi	Liestøl	1910	5	Drougkvæen	2[a]	NFS Liestøl 7,84–6
M22					A. H. Slettetveit	Kaldbast	1924		Draugkven / – Draumkvædi	1[c]	TFM Berge DCIV,93
M ?23					M. Tjønnestøyl	Kaldbast	1926		Nokle Stev av Draugkveen	1[d]	TFM Berge DCIV,52

3.5 A survey of the Draumkvæde variants (cont.)

1	2	3	4	5	6	7	8	9	10	11	12
M ?24					J. O. Seljehammen	Kaldbast			Draugkveen / = Draumkvædi	2	TFM Berge DCIV,94
F1		Æ2	XIII		Gjermund Veum	Hannaas	1914		Draumekvæe	2	BFS Hannaas 396,5
F2		Ø2 ?			Margitt Haugan	Hannaas	1914		Draumekvee	1	BFS Hannaas 397,3
L1	J	Kb	XXIb	8b	Anne Lillegaard	J. Moe	1847	2	Draumkve	22	NFS J. Moe 8,25–8
L2	L	L	XXII	9		J. Moe	1847		af Drougkvæ	10	NFS J. Moe 5,27–28b
L3	Kb	Mb	XXIIIa	10b	Tone (Marteinsdotter ?)	J. Moe	1847	2	Draugkve (Brudstykke)	6	NFS J. Moe 8,38–9
L4	J	Ka	XXIa	8a	Anne Lillegaard	Grasberg	1840s	2	Dromkvæen	24	NFS Landstad 1b,21–5
L5	K	Ma	XXIIIb	10a	Tone Marteinsdotter	Bugge	1856	2	Draumkvæe I	14	NFS Bugge I,46–7
L6	N	N	XXIV	11		Bugge	1859	3b	Draumkvæi	14	NFS Bugge h 13–16
L7					Tone Marteinsdotter	Bugge	1863			1	NFS Bugge i 343
L8					Tone Marteinsdotter	Lindeman	1863 ?	2		1	UB Musikksaml. eske 203
L9	M	O	XXV	12	Olav Lofthus	Bugge	1867	2		3	NFS Bugge c 5–6
L10a	15	Pa				Ross	1874			1	NFS Ross 3,76
L10b	15	Pb				Ross	1874			1	NFS Ross 3,76
L11		Q				Mortensson	1879	2a		3	NFS Mortensson 7,7
L12	F*	I	XXVI	7	Hæge Kjelan	Hannaas	1914	1	Draumekvèen	3	BFS Hannaas 396,41
L13					Nils Turrgronflaten	Berge		2	Dròukvéen	3½	TFM Berge LXIV,46–7
K1	R	A	VI	1	Maren Ramskeid	Landstad	1840s	1, 2, 3	Draumekvæi	30	UB fol. 1803e
K2	T	Ca	VIII	2a	Birgit Lintveit	Bugge	1857	1		4½ ?	NFS Bugge m 18–19
K3	W	E	VII	4	Aslaug Askedalen	Bugge	1857	3a		6½	NFS Bugge g 300–2
K4	U	D	IX	3	Hæge Kastedalen	Bugge			Draumkvææ VIII	5	NFS Bugge III,79
K5	S	F	XI	5		Heggtveit	*c.* 1870		Stumper af Draumkvædet	20½	NFS Heggtveit 1,1–3
K6	2	G	X			Heggtveit	*c.* 1870	1	Begyndelsen af Draumkvædet	2	NFS Heggtveit 1,13

K7	V?	Hc			Aase Fürst	Aall	1892 or 3			1	NFS Aall 1,7
K8	V	Hb			Torvil Tollefsen Midbø'n	Aall	1892 or 3		Jolkvæe	1ª	NFS Aall 1,39
K9	V	Ha	XII	6	Tone Nuten	Aall	1892 or 3		Lidt af Draumkvæde	7	NFS Aall 1,70–2
K10					Signe Hanslid	Berge	1906	2	Draumkvæe	2ᵈ	TFM Berge CXLVII,58d
K11					Aslak Østnaa	Berge	1909	1, 2	Draumkvæde	6	TFM Berge LXVI,18–19
K12		J			Olav Reinskos	Hannaas	1914		(draumkvæi)	1	BFS Hannaas 396,127
S1		N2				Smedal	1845			1ª	NFS Landstad 1b,86–7
S2		E3	I			Gaange	1847	1	Ole Oknesen. — 1ˢᵗᵉ Vers	1	UB fol. 1803b
S3	25	O2				Dyrland	1840s			1ª	NFS Landstad 3,58–9
S4	10	T2	V		Aase Hallvorsdotter	Bugge	1874	1		2	NFS Bugge b 36
S5	Q	R2	IV	24	Else Li	Bugge			Draumkvæe IX	3	NFS Bugge III,79
S6	Y	Q2	III	23	Leiuf Gotenborg	Bugge		7		10	Bugge's copy of *Norske Folkeviser* (1853)
S7	11	S2b			Gunnild Mógann	Bugge				1	Bugge's copy of *Norske Folkeviser* (1853)
S8a	Xa	U2a		25a	Liv Huse		*c.* 1876?	1b		2ª	NFS M. Moe 51,1–2
S8b	Xa	U2b		25b	Liv Huse		*c.* 1876?			1ª	NFS M. Moe 51,5
S8c	Xa	U2c		25c	Liv Huse		*c.* 1876?			1ª	NFS M. Moe 51,9
S9a	Xb				Halvor Sondbø	M. Moe	1878	1b		3ª	NFS M. Moe 4,1a
S9b	Xb				Halvor Sondbø	M. Moe	1878			1ª	NFS M. Moe 4,1h
S10	12				Lavrans Øveland	Mortensson	1878			1ª	NFS Mortensson 4,5
S11	3	V2			Halvor Brennemo	Mortensson	1878	1		1	NFS Mortensson 5,82
S12	Xc				Hilleborg Brække	M. Moe	1891		Til Droumkvæe	1ᵈ	NFS M. Moe 30,42
S13	Xd				Lavrans Øveland	M. Moe	1891		Af Droumkvæ̅i	1	NFS M. Moe 30,70
S14					Knut Skarde	Berge	1910			1ª	TFM Berge XCI,23
N1					Hæge Postmyr	Berge	1906		Draumkvæde	13	TFM Berge CXLVI,1–3
H1	23	B3			Margjit Killingdokk	Bugge	1863			1ª	NFS Bugge i 178
H2	13	C3			Søvei Hågåviken	Bugge	1863			1ª	NFS Bugge i 225

3.5 A survey of the Draumkvæde variants (cont.)

1	2	3	4	5	6	7	8	9	10	11	12
H3		A3			Lars Lofthus	Bugge	1863			1½	NFS Bugge i 285
B1	5	Å2			Ola Storemyr	M. Moe	1880			1^{a}	NFS M. Moe 19,36
T1	7	L3				J. Moe	1846	2d		1	NFS J. Moe 6,30b
T2	26	M3				J. Moe	1846			1^{a}	NFS J. Moe 7,107
T3		H3	XXXI	28		Landstad	1840s			6^{b}	NFS Landstad 2,18
T4		G3	XXXIII			Landstad	1840s			2	NFS Landstad 7,19
T5		F3	XXXIV	27		Landstad	1840s		Tilhører Dramekvæi	8	NFS Landstad 8,1–2
T6			XXXV			Landstad	1840s		af Draunekvædet	2	UB 4to 740
T7	Æ	J3		30				4a		3^{c}	NFS Landstad 1b,92
T8	Ø	K3								5	NFS Landstad 2,17
T9	Z	I3	XXXII	29						4	NFS Landstad 3,45
T10										3^{a}	UB fol. 1803f(B)
T11	11	S2a								1^{d}	NFS M. Moe 66,16a
T12						Lindeman		2	Draumkvæde	1	UB Musikksaml. eske 582, Hs. 6975
Sæ1		R3				Skar	1874			1^{a}	NFS Skar 2,3
By1		O3			Thorbjønn Ljosstog (Skaamdal)	Schneider	1860s		Av Draumkvèe	2	NFS Schneider 1,114
By2		S3			Taddeiv Liè (Skaamedal)	Skar				2	NFS Skar 3,21
By3		U3a			Olav Odda (Austad)	Skar				2^{b}	NFS Skar 3,16
By4		U3b			Olav Odda (Austad)	Hannaas	1911		Draumkvæe	2	BFS Hannaas 421,3
By5		U3c			Olav Odda (Austad)	Liestøl	1917			2	NFS Liestøl 9,30
He1	22	Æ3			Lars Gjya	Hannaas	1910		Jedlarbrunæ	1	BFS Hannaas 434,13

Notes

V1a & b The sixty-one and twenty-one stanzas do not all belong to *Dr*, but since these are reconstructed texts and not true variants, the normal practice of marking only the number of *Dr* stanzas which occur is not followed (for full details of V1a cf. Section 3.7, V1a). V1b is incomplete. According to Svenungsen, the collector, it originally consisted of sixty-two stanzas (possibly only sixty-one stanzas, in fact, since stanza 18 is wanting), but, except for those printed by Jørgen Moe (1850), stanzas 23ff. are now lost. Of what remains 1–6, 12–15 and 22 are *Dr* stanzas, while 7–11, 16–17 and 19–21 belong to *Beltevisa* and correspond closely to the same stanzas in V1a.

V5 The informant lived in Bykle, Sætesdal, but probably came originally from Vinje where the variant was recorded.

V6 The stanza omitted is from *Beltevisa* and is followed by a refrain somewhat similar to 4a.

V7 This variant is also found in NFS Skar 20,58 with the information that Gunnhill had learnt the stanza from Knut Eddann.

V8 Parts of what appear to be this variant are also found in NFS Skar 18,70, 18,93–4 and 42,53. In Skar 18,70 stanza 1 stands by itself; in the other two cases stanzas 2–4 and 1 and 4 respectively occur in collections of *stev*. The informant lived in Bykle, Sætesdal, but his family came from Vinje where he himself lived for a time. V8 contains the following half-stanza, not included in the stanza numbering of this edition: *Anten vi eg ive Gjallarbrui/ ellau dau ette Søylen hange.* Two very similar lines form part of a whole stanza found in a variant collected by Torleiv Hannaas from the same informant (BFS Hannaas 425,31, 33) and headed: 'Lause vers til *Drauga-kvǫ́i* eller til denne visa' ('Odd stanzas belonging to *Drauga-kvǫ́i* or to this ballad [*Sigurd svein*]'). It is unfortunately not clear to which of these the stanza belongs, but in printed texts (apparently based partly on this variant, cf. *Norsk aarbok* (1921), pp. 141 and 146–50, stanzas 11, 30–3, 6) it appears as the final stanza of *Sigurd svein*, preceded by S.96. In the original it runs: *Men de va unge Sigur-svein/ han snører (gjurer) den salen trange/ 'Anten so ri eg den Gjeddarbrui/ hell dau innmæ salen hange.*

V9 The text of this variant referred to in the table is a fair copy which has recently been made available. It is however the printed text in Berge (1940–4), I, pp. 142–3 to which E*, L2, XXVIII and 22 refer. According to Berge this text is based on the MS we now have, but in fact the two versions are somewhat different, especially as regards the number and order of the stanzas (cf., however, Berge (1940–4), I, p. 599, where it is stated that the informant had no fixed stanza sequence). The printed version has eleven complete stanzas; in the fair copy 10 and 12 each appear to have a line missing, and between 10 and 11 there is a reference to a fourteenth stanza: 'V. 39 = L. [Landstad]'. A note states that the informant learnt this variant from Knut Eddan, and in another it is said that he was one of Niels Svenungsen's informants. In the first note the ballad is called *Dròukvéen*, apparently the form used by the informant, in the second *Draugkveen.*

V10 A fair copy. A note states that the informant learnt this variant from Tjodvor Steffasdotter from Vinje, who knew the whole of *Draugk.*[*veen* ?]. The stanza omitted is one of the humorous *Eg hev vori meg upp med sky* group (hereafter called humorous *Dr*).

V11 *Drougkvéen* is the heading of a large collection of *stev* (NFS Liestøl 8,12–31). A note states that the informant had learnt *Drougkvèen* from her mother who was from Vinje and was called Taaraand.

V?12 A fair copy by Berge. Across the second stanza is written *Draugkv.* Towards the bottom of Berge XXXIX,49 there is the following heading: '*Stev* (Uppskr. av Steffa T. Tjønn)' ('*Stev* (collected by Steffa T. Tjønn)'). Whether this applies to the final stanza on p. 49 only or to the whole of the following collection is difficult to say.

R1 This variant is also found in a fair copy by Bugge (NFS Bugge IV,153), where it is headed *Vers af Draumkvæde.* This is likely to be the collector's own title, as in most other cases where a title is lacking in the original but appears in the fair copy.

R2a Of the stanzas omitted three are humorous *Dr* and two are from *Beltevisa.* The title, found at the end of the ballad, is almost certainly the one given by the informant since Bugge draws attention to the form *-kvaen.*

R3 This variant is also found in a fair copy by Berge (TFM Berge LI,18). In both MSS there is a note, presumably emanating from the informant, in which the form *Dròukveen* is used.

R?5 A fair copy. Of two stanzas omitted one is humorous *Dr.*

M2 This variant is also found in a fair copy by Bugge (NFS Bugge I,115–16) which has an extra stanza (S.111) written in the margin and is headed *Draumkvæe II.*

M3 A fair copy. Most of the stanzas are abbreviated with reference to Landstad A. As well as the ten marked in the table two more stanzas are mentioned solely by reference to this text: 'Endnu meddelte han Landst. A V.24 Var.2 . . . 14' ('In addition he recited Landstad A 24*var.*2 . . . 14').

M4 In a fair copy (unconnected with M4, NFS Bugge I,151) Bugge notes that Ingebjør Sandvik's refrain in *Draumkvæe (III)* was 2b. Quite what this refers to is uncertain; it is possible that Bugge confused Ingebjør Sandvik and Ingebjør Troddedal.

M5 This variant is also found as a variant reading (partially abbreviated) in Bugge's fair copy of M6 (NFS Bugge III,2).

M6 This variant is also found in a fair copy by Bugge (NFS Bugge III,1–10) headed *Draukveen VII.* In the original the title is in brackets (for full details of M6 cf. Section 3.7, M6).

M7 The title is written in pencil, apparently by Lindeman, although the text itself is in ink.

M8 In a note by Moltke Moe (NFS M. Moe 25,110) it is stated that according to Olav Syning refrain 2 belonged to the whole of *Droukvéen.*

M9a The title appears in brackets at the top of p. 110 between stanzas 6 and 7.

M9b The title is in brackets.

M10 *(ret)* in the heading is written above the line; *Draum-* has been altered from *Dram-* and the *-en* of this word is almost certainly a later addition.

M12 This variant is one of three *gamlestev*-type stanzas headed *Af Draugkveen* in a collection of *nystev.* Earlier in the collection (NFS Schneider 1,32) there is a humorous *Dr* stanza by the same informant which, it is implied in a note, belongs to *Draugkvæe* (altered from *Draumkvæe*). The wording of the title, *Af Draugkveen,* suggests that it may have been supplied by the collector. This applies to many of the variants below as well. The variant was recorded in Sætesdal, but the informant came from Mo. A marginal note opposite the humorous *Dr* stanza on p. 32 states that she learnt it from 'Aanund Norgaren i Froland [Mo]'.

M13 Although UB fol. 2128 consists largely of MSS by Lindeman, the collection of which this variant forms a part is in Landstad's hand.

M15a In a note the ballad is called *Droumkvéen.*

M15b In the title *Drou-* appears to have been altered from *Drau-*. A note states '("*Drou'kvéen*") sill' dæ véra, trur eg"]' ('I think it was *Drou'kvéen* it was called').

M16 A note states that the informant had heard a few more stanzas, but could not remember them with any certainty. According to her the old people in Mo always called the poem *Drougkvéen*.

M17a In NFS M. Moe 32,26 stanza 2 is found by itself in a slightly different form; the informant is the same.

M18 In the second stanza of this variant ll.2 and 4 are missing, but l.4 is indicated by *&c*.

M20 The first of the stanzas in this variant has six lines. In a fair copy of his MS (NFS M. Moe 29,3b) Moe states that the informant is Anne Skaalen's nephew (with a query), and that he, like his sister, Hæge Leirebrekk, includes much extraneous matter in the ballad. Moe also notes that he once heard Hæge sing the ballad, but was unable to write it down at the time; her version was not unlike Anne Skaalen's (two stanzas of this version appear in 'Limbus puerorum' (1908), p. 248, (1927), p. 347, here with the statement that Moe was unable to write it down in its entirety). In NFS M. Moe 25,194 Moe states that Hæge [Leirebrekk], following Anne Skaalen, introduced stanzas from *Orm Aaseland* and *Agnus dei* into *Drougkvéen* as well as a large number of *gamlestev*.

M21 In a note in the MS of the ballad edition he was preparing (TSB 38. XCVI) Liestøl states that the informant learnt this variant from Hæge Leirebrekk. This information is not found in NFS Liestøl 7,84–5 and, since Liestøl was the collector in this case, was presumably a piece of information he had written down elsewhere or simply remembered.

M22 A fair copy. The stanza omitted is humorous *Dr*. It is difficult to interpret the double heading. Conceivably the collector considered both names equally correct; it is also possible that one title was given by the informant and the other supplied by the collector.

M?23 A fair copy. The heading given in the table is incomplete; in full it runs: 'Nokle Stev av Draugkveen, eller den bakvende Visa' ('A few *stev* of *Draugkveen*, or *den bakvende Visa*').

M?24 A fair copy.

F2 The informant lived in Fyresdal, but came from Mo, and it is possible that she learnt this variant there. The stanza concerned (S.5) occurs independently in Fyresdal and Mo (cf. F1 and, e.g., M6,7), as well as many other parts of Telemark and elsewhere, so there is little to guide us.

L1 The name of the informant given in the MS is Anne Aanensdatter. It is certain that she and Anne Lillegaard, the informant of L4, are one and the same. They are both mentioned as living at Eidsborg (L4: Esborgberget), the two variants are remarkably similar and in his ballad edition of 1858 Bugge writes the name in full: Anne Aanundsdatter Lillegaard. According to the order in which the stanzas are written in this variant 2 should be 5, but in the margin opposite the fifth stanza the collector has placed a 2, making 2–4 in the written sequence 3–5.

L3 The name of the informant is given in the MS as Tone and (what is presumably) the place as Lardal. Five of the six stanzas of this variant (1–4, 6) show a remarkable similarity to stanzas 3, 4, 8, 9, 11 of L5, and it has generally been considered that Lardal Tone and Tone Marteinsdotter are one and the same.

L5 A fair copy. The order of the stanzas was altered by the collector after the MS was written and a new stanza added in the margin opposite 10. These alterations suggest that Bugge heard the informant sing the ballad more than once. It is clear from L7 that he visited her on more than one occasion (the fact that the one stanza of this variant (S.111) is not included as part of L5 suggests that the informant did not consider it to belong there). L5 refers to the fair copy in its original form, though with the additional stanza included after 10 (resulting in 11–13 being re-numbered 12–14).

L6 This variant is also found in a fair copy by Bugge (NFS Bugge V,150–2) headed *Draumkvæe.* In the original the title is in brackets.

L7 Cf. the note to L5.

L8 The full name of the informant given in the MS is Tone Marteinsdotter Kolberg. There seems little doubt that she is identical with the Tone Marteinsdotter of L5. It is, however, worth noting that Lindeman's record of S.1 has the form *Aasneson* whereas Bugge's has *Åknison.*

L10a & b These are almost certainly two separate variants. They are divided by a vertical line in the MS and each marked 'Laardal'.

L12 The informant lived in Fyresdal and was born and brought up in Kviteseid, but she stated that she had learnt this variant from her grandmother who came from Lårdal. The MS has a sub-heading: *Olav Aakneson.*

L13 A fair copy. L13 contains the following half-stanza not included in the numbering of this edition: *Den som skò gange Gjallarbroi/ ho æ baate bratt aa lang.* These two lines show affinities with SS.97,107,108, but are clearly not part of any of them. Above the first line is written: *Gjallarbroi ho va,* but it has been crossed out. A note in TFM Berge LXIV,45 states: '*Dròukvéen* daa Lammers va' her a aa bruka di mykje tì ei fyllevise' ('*Dròukvéen* was used a lot as a drinking song when Lammers was here'). However, the words 'daa Lammers va' her a aa' have been crossed out.

K2 Part of this variant is also found in a fair copy by Bugge (NFS Bugge II,98) headed *Stumper af Draumkveen V.* The fact that original and fair copy vary in length suggests that Bugge may have heard the informant sing these stanzas more than once. However, Bugge II,98 is almost identical with half-stanza 3 and stanza 4 of the original and it seems improbable that an informant who could memorise individual stanzas so well would forget over half of the material. Half-stanza 3, which is not included in the numbering of this edition, runs: *Dær slepp ingjen dær førbi,/ dæn som Dómmen felle trångt.* It shows affinities with S.98, and to a lesser extent with SS.91,92,96,100. The stanzas are not separated in Bugge m 18–19 and it is possible that the last two lines of 2 (S.94) are meant to be repeated to give a complete stanza. S.94 does not occur in Bugge II,98, however, where the two lines quoted above appear as the beginning of a six-line stanza.

K3 This variant is also found in a fair copy by Bugge (NFS Bugge IV,221–2) headed *Draumkvæde* and with the note: 'Kvædersken kjendte ikke Visen ved Navn' ('The informant did not know the ballad by name'). Stanzas 6–7 of K3 also occur in another original MS (NFS Bugge h 147).

K4 A fair copy; all the stanzas are abbreviated with reference to Landstad A. Above the text is a sub-title: *Ôlav Åkningjen.* A note under the heading, *Draumkvæe VIII,* states that Hæge was used by Landstad.

K5 Two of the stanzas in this variant (3, 6) have six lines. The last two lines of 6, which are not included in the numbering of this edition, run: *Ingjen sleppe naa derin/ for Domene felle for Mange,* and show affinities with S.98 (cf. the note to K2).

K8 Above the text is a sub-heading: *Enkelte Vers.*

K10 This variant is also found in a fair copy by Berge (TFM Berge LIV,61–2) headed *Draumkvæde.* In both original and fair copy there is a note which states that the informant was not sure whether *Draukveen* (fair copy *Dròukveen*) or *Draumkveen* (*Dròumkveen*) was the correct title; she had heard both. After the final stanza in the original Berge has written in brackets: 'Ho segjer Draugkveen' ('She says *Draugkveen*'), presumably a reference to the informant. According to both original and fair copy Signe learnt this variant from Hermod Finesand. She herself came from Kviteseid, but lived in Vinje; Hermod's place of origin and abode is unfortunately not known for certain. In the fair copy this variant forms a sub-section consisting of three stanzas in a collection of *gamlestev.* One of the stanzas omitted in the original (the one stanza in the fair copy) is humorous *Dr.*

K11 A fair copy. A long note in TFM Berge LXVI,20 implies that the informant learnt this variant from his father, who in turn learnt it from his uncle who was a *lensmann* (district official and police officer) in Seljord. The provenance of the variant is therefore difficult to establish with certainty, but it seems to have existed in Kviteseid for some time.

K12 According to a note in the MS the informant learnt this variant from Tov Reinskos, his father. Olav thought he remembered his father's saying that *draumkvæi* contained thirty-eight or forty stanzas, but although Tov claimed to know the whole ballad Olav never heard him sing it, only fragments.

S1 Three of the stanzas omitted are humorous *Dr.*

S2 Hølje Gaange lived in Seljord and was a cripple who was unable to get about, so although his source for this variant is unknown, it seems likely that he or she also came from Seljord. Hølje himself described the MS in which the variant is found as 'Afskrevet' ('copied'), but he may simply have meant that it was a fair copy or, less probably, that the contents were 'copied' from an oral source or written down from memory. Before the heading, *Ole Oknesen.– 1ste Vers,* he writes that this is one of a number of references to ballads which he does not know by heart and is therefore unable to write down. Under the text he notes that the ballad consists of many stanzas.

S4 The second stanza of this variant appears to be something of a mixture in relation to the readings of other variants. The first two lines clearly represent the first half of S.76. The second half of the stanza, which is not included in the numbering of this edition, runs: *dær såg eg mi gode gullmor/ hó stó kinna bló* (*stó* altered from *ysta å*) and shows affinities with SS.118–20 and 136–7.

S5 This variant was possibly written down as early as 1857; the informant, although born in Seljord, lived in Øyfjell, Rauland which was visited by Bugge in that year. He was also in Rauland in 1867.

S6 This variant exists in the form of additions to Landstad A made by Bugge in his copy of *Norske Folkeviser.* Most of the stanzas consist of only a few words (three are no more than a note to the effect that Leiuf sang the stanza concerned) and Landstad A must be used to expand them (cf. S.4 = S6,2); stanza 8 is written out in full. The refrain occurs only by Landstad A 13, but was presumably the one used by Leiuf throughout the ballad.

S7 This variant exists in the form of additions to Landstad A 19 made by Bugge in his copy of *Norske Folkeviser.* It presumably has no refrain since none is specifically mentioned. Landstad A 19 has refrain 2.

S8a–c These variants were possibly recorded independently by Moltke Moe. There are two loose sheets of paper in Moe's hand marked '13)' and 'M Moe 51,1–2' which contain (13) the note: 'Først de samme strofer som efter Liv Huse i 1876; derpå:' ('First the same stanzas as by Liv Huse in 1876; then:'), followed by S.87 in full (with a slight difference in wording from S8c), and (51) S8a–b (including two humorous *Dr* stanzas in M. Moe 51,1 omitted in this edition). The informants and dates are given as (13) Halvor Sundbø and Liv Huse, 1878, and (51) Liv Huse, *c.* 1876. The second sheet is probably a copy of the relevant stanzas in NFS M. Moe 51,1–2, 5, although usually Moe's copies are marked *b* in addition to the numbering of the original (i.e. we would expect 51,1–2b, 5b). The normal practice in this edition would be to include the 1878 record of S.87 as a separate variant, but it is not entirely clear what this represents. It gives every appearance of being a copy too, and the collector may not therefore be Moe at all.

S9a–b These two variants are found in a large collection of *stev* and ballad fragments headed *Stev*. There has been an attempt to group some of the stanzas together; stanza 1 of S9a is divided by a line from 2–3 which are 1 and 4 in a group of four stanzas with refrain 1b (2 and 3 in this group are humorous *Dr*). S9b appears as a stanza on its own, preceded and followed by a line.

S11 This variant consists of one five-line stanza. The usual first line of S.5 is l.3; l.1 runs: *De va han Olav Oknesi* which is very similar to the first line of S.5 in K12.

S12 This variant contains two humorous *Dr* stanzas which have been omitted.

S13 In NFS M. Moe 30,68–9 there appear two stanzas in a slightly different metre from *Dr* headed *Af Drougkvǣi*. According to a note which follows them the informant told Moe that his father had said that *Drougkvǣi* and *Droumkvǣi* were two different ballads. The two stanzas he had just quoted belonged to *Drougkvædet*; it was *Droumkvædet*, on the other hand, which spoke of *Ólav Åknésón, som heve sovi så længje*. In view of this it is interesting that S.111 in M. Moe 30,70 is headed *Af Droumkvǣi* (cf. Section 3.1, p. 78), though we can by no means be sure that this is the informant's title.

S14 A fair copy. This variant is found in a large collection of *stev* by various informants. Knut Skarde is apparently the informant for this and the preceding stanza, a *gamlestev* in which *Gjallarbru* is mentioned.

N1 A note states that the informant learnt this variant from Tormod Heimdal who lived in Nissedal.

B1 The collector has written *Draumkvæ?* in the margin of a fair copy of this variant (NFS M. Moe 14–15,38).

T1 *Draumkvææ* has been added as a heading by Moltke Moe.

T2 The collection of *stev* in which this variant is found is headed *Gamle Stev*. In NFS J. Moe 7,108 there is a humorous *Dr* stanza.

T3 One humorous *Dr* stanza has been omitted from this variant.

T4 The two stanzas marked in the table are preceded by what appear to be fragments of three others: *fyryheimen/ annan heimen/ vai hev eg vogsmyrann/ gamle graa Grutteskeg* (or *-skg*). It is, however, by no means clear to which stanzas these fragments belong. The first could be part of any of SS.124,130,135 or 141–56 and the second part of S.130 or SS.141–56 or possibly S.119 or 121; the third belongs to one of SS.105–9 and the fourth to either S.157 or 158.

T5 The order of the stanzas in this variant is uncertain. Stanzas 6–7 follow 1–2, but there is a sign which seems to indicate that 3–5 should be moved from their position after 6–7 to one immediately after 1–2. Stanza 8 is found alone in NFS Landstad 8,2 with a heading which seems to read *Draumikvaet*. The first two lines of stanza 5, which are not included in the numbering of this edition, run: *dæ va Ste. Saale Mechael/ tok han te aa rie.*

T6 The title of this variant is doubtless meant to read *af Draumekvædet*; 'u' and 'm' are run together and comprise four vertical strokes instead of five. The title is almost certainly the collector's; it is preceded by a large N.B.

T7 The three stanzas omitted are from *Beltevisa*. The final stanza of the complete text, which is headed *Øl Stev*, is in a different hand from the first five.

T7–11 The fact that T7–10 are found in Landstad's collections, together with the evidence of the linguistic forms in all five variants, suggests that Telemark is their place of origin. It is difficult to be absolutely sure, however, since so little is otherwise known about them.

Sæl This variant is also found in NFS Skar 1,16, 46,2, 51,16 and 62,58, in each case as part of a collection of *stev*. In Skar 2,3 Moltke Moe has written *av Draumkvae* in the margin.

By2 This variant is also found in NFS Skar 21,115 and 46,27–8. In Skar 21,115 the order of the stanzas is reversed; in Skar 46,27–8 the two stanzas are found in a large collection of *stev*. In Skar 3,21 the collector notes that Olav Eivindsson (Austad) probably learnt this variant from Taddeiv (cf. By3–5).

By3 This variant also occurs in NFS Skar 20,178 and 46,27. In Skar 20,178 the two stanzas are found in a collection of odd fragments and are followed by prose; in Skar 46,27 they form part of a large collection of *stev* (cf. By2). In Skar 62,58–60 stanza 2 of By3 (l.2: *eg ville no barre kvile*) is followed by stanza 1 (stanza 2 of By2) which is in turn followed by stanza 1 of By2 (l.2: *de va i so go 'n Timi*). The names of the informants do not always accompany these stanzas; however, where Taddeiv Liè is mentioned the second line of S.7 is always *de va i so go 'n Timi* and where Olav Austad is given as the informant it is *eg ville no berre kvile*, or something very similar. It is thus usually possible to distinguish By2 from By3 even when they appear in collections of *stev* (cf., however, Skar 62,58–60).

By4 A note in BFS Hannaas 421,2 implies that the informant learnt this variant from his mother. It is stated that she sang 'this' ('detti') when the family were alone at Christmas, but knew only a few stanzas. The title, which is in square brackets, is doubtless the collector's. A note which follows the text states: 'Minnest at det var vers um *gjeddarbrune*. Og um ein som reid paa ein *svårte hest*. Og um *Sæle såle-Mikkjål*' ('He remembers [or: I remember] that there were stanzas about *gjeddarbrune*. And about someone riding on a black horse. And about *Sæle såle-Mikkjål*'). And below this we find: *35. . . . han bles i langelu/ . . . no ska domen stande.* 35 doubtless refers to stanza 35 in MM.

By5 A note states that the informant learnt this variant from his mother (cf. By4).

Other variants than those listed in the table have been connected with *Dr*. It will be sufficient here to mention the following: 1) three variants containing humorous *Dr* stanzas (NFS J. Moe 10,31, NFS Bugge i 115, NFS Schneider 1,32 (cf. M12 above), Liestøl's classification: –, *Folkeminne* classification: B, D3, P3); 2) a single stanza similar to ll.1, 4–6 of M20,1 (NFS Bugge k 67, II,165, Liestøl: D*1, *Folkeminne*: Vb); 3) two stanzas which have refrain 2, mention *Gjallarbru* and are headed *Af Draumkvadet*, but which otherwise appear unconnected with the ballad (NFS M. Moe 65,8, Liestøl: –, *Folkeminne*:

N3); 4) a number of what appear to be nursery rhymes about *Brillands-* or *Bjellandsbru*, collected in Vest-Agder, of which the following (NFS Ross 32,21) may serve as an example: *Den Bjellandsbruna, den Bjellandsbruna/ Den æ vond aa ganga/ Kattann klora, hunnann bide/ Dei store studann stanga.* Liestøl included these rhymes in his classification of *Dr* variants (D*18–21) and they also occur in the *Folkeminne* classification (V3–Z3). It is clear that they are in some way connected with certain of the *Gjallarbru* stanzas in *Dr* (cf. He1), but in the form in which we know them now, there seems little reason to include them as part of the material.

A number of MSS in Berge's collection contain humorous *Dr* stanzas and other material which some scholars may well consider part of *Dr*, but in this edition all such variants which do not comply with the criteria set up in Section 3.1 have been ignored.

Among Liestøl's preparatory work for his projected definitive edition of the Norwegian ballads we find a slip of paper containing S.111 and a note to the effect that the stanza is taken from 'Knut Laupedalen's collections' ('Knut Laupedalens samlingar'). Since we know nothing about Laupedalen's original, and it now no longer appears to be extant, his variant has been omitted from this edition.

Finally mention must be made of four refrains which do not occur as part of any ballad.

1. refrain 1; *Folkeminne* classification: P2, Ballad Edition: variant II; informant: Krestens Trae (Traa ?), Seljord; collector: Olea Crøger; date: probably 1853; MS: UB fol. 1803a. The collector asked the informant about the refrain of *Dr* and Krestens produced refrain 1.

2. *tunga talar å såli svarar på dómma*; unclassified; informant: Aaste Espeli, Lårdal; collector: Bugge; date: 1857; MS: NFS Bugge a 372. In the MS this refrain is not connected with *Dr* or any other ballad. It is the one used in the religious ballad, *Maria*, but it also shows a remarkable similarity to refrain 6, found only in V1a.

3. *Uppetter mæ Å, dær rinder dei Urtinne bróne å blå*; *Folkeminne*: Z2 ?; informant: Dagne Li, Fyresdal, born in Kviteseid; collector: Bugge; date: 1857; MSS: NFS Bugge m 52, II,101. The original is headed *(Draumkv.)* and the fair copy *Draumkvæde. VI.*

4. *lykjylen heng å slírinne sleng å vegjinne dei fedde víe*; unclassified; informant: Aslak Aartveit, Vinje; collector: Bugge; date: 1867; MS: NFS Bugge c 176. This refrain is not connected with *Dr* in the MS, but shows some similarity to 2b.

3.6 A survey of the stanzas found in each variant

Those stanzas marked in the table with an asterisk have either more or less than the normal four lines, and the way in which they vary from the normal is described in the notes preceding the table. 'Mixed' stanzas, which are divided into two parts (a = ll.1–2, b = ll.3–4), are also considered to come into this category. The first two lines of such stanzas are often difficult to place since there may be a choice of several rhyme words.

Stanzas, or complete variants, are sometimes abbreviated. The abbreviation may affect anything from part of a word to most of a stanza, and, broadly speaking, takes one of four forms: 1) straightforward omission of common words and/or lines (it is occasionally difficult to tell in such cases whether an abbreviation is intended or whether part of the stanza was lacking when it was sung); 2) omission of words and/or lines with reference to the corresponding stanza in Landstad A; 3) omission of words and/or lines which are identical with those in the or a preceding stanza written in full; 4) writing only the first letter of each word (normally words which have already appeared in full in the same MS). Stanzas abbreviated to any extent by the first or second method are marked [ ] and ( ) respectively in the table (where a variant or stanza is written in full in one MS, original or copy, and abbreviated in another, only the full version is taken into account). Abbreviation by methods 3 and 4 is not indicated, since the material the stanza contains is to be found in the MS.

The bold vertical lines which divide the table correspond to the episodes or sections of the ballad outlined in Section 3.2. A + sign instead of a figure indicates that the variant concerned has only one stanza or less.

Notes

V9,10 lacks l.4, the rhyme word in l.2 is *bròu*; 12 lacks l.2.

R1,2 lacks ll.1–2.

R2a,5a = ll.1–2 of SS.105–6; 5b = ll.3–4 of S.98.

M6,16a consists of one or two lines: *Tunge va dæn Granastigjen å gange*; 16b = ll.3–4 of S.104; 18 consists of three or four lines, ll.1–2 = 16a (with slight changes in wording); 26a = ll.1–2 of S.5; 26b = ll.3–4 of S.122.

M8 consists of one line: *Bikkja meg bít å ormen (meg) stinge.*

M9a,5 consists of three or four lines, ll.1–2 run: *Vónde so æ' dei gaglemýranne å gange.*

M10 consists of one line: *lese han tekstinne véne.*

M12 consists of three or four lines, ll.1–2 run: *Dei e saa blaute dei Gaglemyrann aa gange.*

M14,2 consists of one line: *eg hev vore paa Gallarbrue.*

M15a,4 lacks l.3.

M18,1a = ll.1–2 of SS.105–6; 1b = ll.3–4 of S.98; 2 lacks l.2, l.4 is indicated by *&c.*

M20,1 has six lines, cf. Section 3.5, p. 117 and 3.1, p. 77.

M ?24,2 consists of three or four lines, ll.1–2 run: *Ja, Gaglemyrane va bloute å gange.*

L5,5a = ll.1–2 of SS.101–2; 5b = ll.3–4 of S.39.

L11,1a = ll.1–2 of SS.96–9 or ll.3–4 of SS.93–4; 1b = ll.3–4 of S.139.

K2,2 consists of three or four lines, ll.1–2 run: *Ho æ tunge dæn Gjæddarbrui å gange.*

K3,4 lacks ll.1–2.

K5,3 has six lines, ll.1–2 (3a) = ll.3–4 of S.16; 6 has six lines, cf. Section 3.5, K5, note; 13 lacks ll.3–4.

S4,2a = ll.1–2 of S.76; for 2b cf. Section 3.5, S4, note.

S11 has five lines, cf. Section 3.5, S11, note.

H3,1 lacks ll.3–4.

T5,5b = ll.1–2 of S.164; for 5a cf. Section 3.5, T5, note.

	1	2	3	4	5	6	7	8	9	10	11	12	13	14	15	16	17	18	19	20
V1a	1		2		$^{3}/_{6}$	5		4												
V1b	1		14		$^{2}/_{3}$	4														
V2																				
V3																				
V4																				
V5																				
V6																				
V7																				
V8																				
V9					1															
V10					1															
V11					+															
V ?12																				
R1																				
R2a					1			2												
R2b																				
R3					1															
R ?4					+															
R ?5					+															
M1																				
M2					1			2												
M3	1				(2)			(3)												
M4	+																			
M5																				
M6	1				$^{7}/_{26a}$*			$^{6}/_{25}$	69	70	71	2	3	4	5					
M7					+															
M8																				
M9a	1				4			3												7
M9b																				
M10																				
M11								+												
M12																				
M13	+																			
M14																				
M15a					1															
M15b																				
M16	1																			
M17a																				
	1	2	3	4	5	6	7	8	9	10	11	12	13	14	15	16	17	18	19	20

Continued p. 122

Continued p. 126

23	24	25	26	27	28	29	30	31	32	33	34	35	36	37	38	39	40	41	42	
	14												12	15		29			28	V1a
	6										13		12	15						V1b
																				V2
																				V3
											+									V4
											+									V5
											+									V6
																				V7
																				V8
											2									V9
																				V10
																				V11
																				V ?12
																				R1
											3									R2a
																				R2b
																				R3
																				R ?4
																				R ?5
																				M1
											3									M2
											(4)					6				M3
																				M4
																				M5
				33	36	37	57	59	27	28	$^{8}/_{72}$				73	10				M6
																				M7
																				M8
											2									M9a
																				M9b
											+*	+*	+*							M10 (bracketed together)
																				M11
																				M12
																				M13
																				M14
											2									M15a
																				M15b
																				M16
																				M17a

23 | 24 25 26 27 28 29 30 31 32 33 34 35 36 37 38 | 39 40 41 42

Continued p. 123

	1	2	3	4	5	6	7	8	9	10	11	12	13	14	15	16	17	18	19	20
M17b																				
M18																				
M19					+															
M20																				
M21					1															
M22					+															
M ?23																				
M ?24					1															
F1					1															
F2					+															
L1	1				4			3										5		
L2																				
L3					1															
L4	1				2													3		
L5	1				(3)															
L6					1															
L7																				
L8	+																			
L9					1															
L10a																				
L10b																				
L11																				
L12					1															
L13					1															
K1		1	2		3											4	5			
K2					1															
K3																				
K4																				
K5					1											3a*	2			
K6		1	2																	
K7					+															
K8					+															
K9					1														2	
K10					1															
K11		4	5		1											2				
K12					+															
	1	2	3	4	5	6	7	8	9	10	11	12	13	14	15	16	17	18	19	20

Continued p. 124

Continued p. 126

23	24	25	26	27	28	29	30	31	32	33	34	35	36	37	38	39	40	41	42	
																				M17b
																				M18
																				M19
													2							M20
																				M21
																				M22
																				M ?23
																				M ?24
																				F1
																				F2
												2				8		7		L1
																		9		L2
																				L3
											4					6		7		L4
											2					(5b*)				L5
											2									L6
																				L7
																				L8
											2									L9
																				L10a
																				L10b
																3	2			L11
											2									L12
											2									L13
													6			7	8			K1
																				K2
																				K3
																				K4
													3b*			5	4			K5
																				K6
																				K7
																				K8
											3									K9
													2							K10
													3							K11
																				K12
23	24	25	26	27	28	29	30	31	32	33	34	35	36	37	38	39	40	41	42	

Continued p. 125

	1	2	3	4	5	6	7	8	9	10	11	12	13	14	15	16	17	18	19	20
S1																				
S2					+															
S3																				
S4					[1]	[1]						[1]								
S5					⏟	⏟						⏟								
S6			(1)	(2)	(3)															
S7																				
S8a					1															
S8b																				
S8c																				
S9a					2															
S9b																				
S10																				
S11					+*															
S12																				
S13																				
S14					+															
N1	1				[2]														3	
H1																				
H2																				
H3					[2]			1*												
B1					+															
T1								+												
T2																				
T3																				
T4																				
T5	8																			
T6																				
T7					1	2		3												
T8					3			4												
T9																				
T10																				
T11																				
T12					+															
	1	2	3	4	5	6	7	8	9	10	11	12	13	14	15	16	17	18	19	20

Continued p. 126

23	24	25	26	27	28	29	30	31	32	33	34	35	36	37	38	39	40	41	42	
																				S1
																				S2
																				S3
																				S4
																				S5
													(4)							S6
																				S7
																				S8a
																				S8b
																				S8c
																				S9a
																				S9b
																				S10
																				S11
																				S12
																				S13
																				S14
4											5					7		6		N1
																				H1
																				H2
																				H3
																				B1
																				T1
																				T2
																				T3
																				T4
																1	2			T5
																				T6
																				T7
		1	2																	T8
																				T9
																				T10
																				T11
																				T12
23	24	25	26	27	28	29	30	31	32	33	34	35	36	37	38	39	40	41	42	

	43	44	45	46	47	48	49	50	51	52	53	54	55	56	57	58	59	60	61	62
V1a										37		38								
V1b																				
V2																				
V3																				
V4																				
V5																				
V6																				
V7																				
V8																				
V9	8																			
V10																				
V11																				
V ?12																				
R1																				
R2a																				
R2b																				
R3																				
R ?4																				
R ?5																				
M1																				
M2																				
M3	(5)																			
M4																				
M5																				
M6	9	47	46	44	45	64	65	66	67			40	41	42	31	16a*/18*	29	49	50	
M7																				
M8																				
M9a																				
M9b																				
M10																				
M11																				
M12																				
M13																				
M14																				
M15a																				
M15b																				3
M16																				
M17a																				

43 44 45 46 47 48 49 50 51 52 53 54 55 56 57 58 59 60 61 62

Continued p. 128

Continued p. 132

65	66	67	68	69	70	71	72	73	74	75	76	77	78	79	80	81	82	83	84	
											30	31		32				33	60	V1a
																				V1b
																				V2
																				V3
																				V4
																				V5
																				V6
																			+	V7
															1					V8
											3				4				5	V9
															2					V10
																				V11
											2									V ?12
																				R1
											4									R2a
																				R2b
											2									R3
																				R ?4
																				R ?5
													1							M1
											5			4						M2
																				M3
																				M4
																	+			M5
39	38	30	48	51	55	54	32	52	53	58	12/68			11			13			M6
																				M7
																				M8
											8									M9a
																				M9b
																				M10
																				M11
																				M12
																				M13
																				M14
																				M15a
											1			2						M15b
																				M16
											1									M17a
65	66	67	68	69	70	71	72	73	74	75	76	77	78	79	80	81	82	83	84	

Continued p. 129

	43	44	45	46	47	48	49	50	51	52	53	54	55	56	57	58	59	60	61	62
M17b																				
M18																				
M19																				
M20																				
M21																				
M22																				
M ?23																				
M ?24																				
F1																				
F2																				
L1	9																			
L2	10																			
L3																				
L4																				
L5																				
L6																				
L7																				
L8																				
L9																				
L10a																				
L10b																				
L11																				
L12																				
L13																				
K1																				
K2																				
K3																				
K4																				
K5																				
K6																				
K7																				
K8																				
K9																				
K10																				
K11																				
K12																				
	43	44	45	46	47	48	49	50	51	52	53	54	55	56	57	58	59	60	61	62

Continued p. 130

Continued p. 132

65	66	67	68	69	70	71	72	73	74	75	76	77	78	79	80	81	82	83	84	
																				M17b
											[2*	2*	2*	2*	2*]					M18
																				M19
											3			4						M20
											2									M21
																				M22
											+									M ?23
																				M ?24
																				F1
																				F2
											6									L1
											1									L2
																				L3
											5									L4
											(14)									L5
											12									L6
																				L7
																				L8
											3									L9
																				L10a
																				L10b
																				L11
																3				L12
											3									L13
																				K1
																				K2
																				K3
																				K4
																				K5
																				K6
																				K7
																				K8
																				K9
																				K10
																				K11
																				K12
65	66	67	68	69	70	71	72	73	74	75	76	77	78	79	80	81	82	83	84	

Continued p. 131

	43	44	45	46	47	48	49	50	51	52	53	54	55	56	57	58	59	60	61	62
S1																				
S2																				
S3																				
S4																				
S5																				
S6																				
S7																				
S8a																				
S8b																				
S8c																				
S9a																				
S9b																				
S10																				
S11																				
S12																				
S13																				
S14																				
N1																				
H1																				
H2																				
H3																				
B1																				
T1																				
T2																				
T3																				
T4																				
T5																				
T6																				
T7																				
T8																				
T9																				
T10																				
T11																				
T12																				
	43	44	45	46	47	48	49	50	51	52	53	54	55	56	57	58	59	60	61	62

Continued p. 132

65	66	67	68	69	70	71	72	73	74	75	76	77	78	79	80	81	82	83	84	
																				S1
																				S2
																				S3
											2a*									S4
																				S5
																				S6
																				S7
											2									S8a
																				S8b
																				S8c
											3									S9a
																				S9b
																				S10
																				S11
											+									S12
																				S13
																				S14
																				N1
																				H1
																				H2
																				H3
																				B1
																				T1
																				T2
											[1]									T3
																				T4
																				T5
																				T6
																				T7
																		5		T8
																				T9
											3									T10
																				T11
																				T12

65 66 67 68 69 70 71 72 73 74 75 | 76 77 78 79 80 81 82 83 | 84

	85	86	87	88	89	90	91	92	93	94	95	96	97	98	99	100	101	102	103	104
V1a		45	44		51	52	22	23						39			24/25			
V1b							22													
V2																			+	
V3																				
V4																				
V5																				
V6																				
V7																				
V8					4							2								
V9																			7	
V10																				
V11																				
V ?12															1					
R1														2*			1			
R2a														5b*						
R2b																				
R3																				
R ?4																				
R ?5																				
M1											3									2
M2											7			8						6
M3														(9)						
M4																				
M5																				
M6														14						15/16b*
M7																				
M8									+*	+*	+*	+*	+*	+*	+*					
M9a				9										6						5*
M9b																				
M10																				
M11																				
M12																				+*
M13																				
M14	1									2*						2*	2*	2*	2*	
M15a														4*						3
M15b																				
M16														2						
M17a																				2
	85	86	87	88	89	90	91	92	93	94	95	96	97	98	99	100	101	102	103	104

Continued p. 134

Continued p. 138

107	108	109	110	111	112	113	114	115	116	117	118	119	120	121	122	123	124	125	126	
26				43																V1a
																				V1b
																				V2
																				V3
																				V4
																				V5
																				V6
																				V7
																				V8
				6								11								V9
																				V10
																				V11
																				V ?12
																				R1
																				R2a
				+																R2b
																				R3
																				R ?4
																				R ?5
																				M1
				(9)																M2
				(10)																M3
																				M4
																				M5
				24	74		43								26b*					M6
																				M7
																				M8
																				M9a
				+																M9b
																				M10
																				M11
																				M12
																				M13
2*	2*																			M14
																				M15a
																				M15b
																				M16
																				M17a
07	108	109	110	111	112	113	114	115	116	117	118	119	120	121	122	123	124	125	126	

Continued p. 135

	85	86	87	88	89	90	91	92	93	94	95	96	97	98	99	100	101	102	103	104
M17b																				
M18														1b*						
M19																				
M20																				
M21																				
M22																				
M ?23																				
M ?24																				2*
F1																				
F2																				
L1														13			12			
L2																	2			
L3																				
L4														13			12			
L5														6			(5a*	5a*)		
L6									3											
L7																				
L8																				
L9																				
L10a																				
L10b					+															
L11									1a*	1a*		1a*	1a*	1a*	1a*					
L12																				
L13																				
K1										9										
K2										2*										
K3																				
K4																				
K5										6a*										
K6																				
K7																				
K8																				
K9													7				6			
K10																				
K11																				
K12																				
	85	86	87	88	89	90	91	92	93	94	95	96	97	98	99	100	101	102	103	104

Continued p. 136

Continued p. 138

107	108	109	110	111	112	113	114	115	116	117	118	119	120	121	122	123	124	125	126	
				+																M17b
																				M18
																				M19
			1*																	M20
																				M21
																				M22
																				M ?23
																				M ?24
																				F1
																				F2
								22	21		20	19			10					L1
									5		7	6								L2
2																				L3
								23	22		21	20			8					L4
4																				L5
7										13					10	8				L6
				[+]																L7
																				L8
																				L9
						+														L10a
																				L10b
																				L11
																				L12
																				L13
		11						18	17			19	20				22		21	K1
																				K2
								7	6						4*					K3
		(3)										(1)		(2)						K4
								16	15			17					12	11		K5
																				K6
																				K7
																				K8
5																				K9
																				K10
																				K11
																				K12
107	108	109	110	111	112	113	114	115	116	117	118	119	120	121	122	123	124	125	126	

Continued p. 137

	85	86	87	88	89	90	91	92	93	94	95	96	97	98	99	100	101	102	103	104
S1																				
S2																				
S3														+						
S4																				
S5																				
S6																				
S7			(+)																	
S8a																				
S8b																				
S8c			+																	
S9a			1																	
S9b																				
S10																				
S11																				
S12																				
S13																				
S14																				
N1													13				12			
H1										+										
H2																				
H3																				
B1																				
T1																				
T2														+						
T3														[5]		4	2	3		
T4																				
T5																				
T6																				
T7																				
T8																				
T9																				
T10														1						
T11			+																	
T12																				
	85	86	87	88	89	90	91	92	93	94	95	96	97	98	99	100	101	102	103	104

Continued p. 138

107	108	109	110	111	116	117	118	119	121	122	123	124	125	126	
				+											S1
															S2
															S3
															S4
															S5
(10)															S6
															S7
															S8a
				+											S8b
															S8c
															S9a
				+											S9b
				+											S10
															S11
															S12
				+											S13
															S14
11					9			10							N1
															H1
				+											H2
															H3
															B1
															T1
															T2
	6														T3
															T4
										6/7					T5
								2	1						T6
															T7
															T8
4															T9
				2											T10
															T11
															T12

107 108 109 | 110 111 112 113 114 | 115 | 116 117 | 118 119 120 | 121 | 122 123 124 125 126

	127	128	129	130	131	132	133	134	135	136	137	138	139	140	141	142	143	144	145	146
V1a									53											58
V1b																				
V2																				
V3																				
V4																				
V5																				
V6																				
V7																				
V8																				
V9									12*										10*	10*
V10																				
V11																				
V ?12																				
R1																				
R2a																				
R2b																				
R3																				
R ?4																				
R ?5																				
M1																				
M2																				
M3																		7		
M4																				
M5																				
M6													23	56				19/34		
M7																				
M8																				
M9a																				
M9b																				
M10																				
M11																				
M12																				
M13																				
M14																				
M15a																				
M15b																				
M16																				
M17a																				
	127	128	129	130	131	132	133	134	135	136	137	138	139	140	141	142	143	144	145	146

Continued p. 140

149	150	151	152	153	154	155	156	157	158	159	160	161	162	163	164	165	166	167	168	169	
56	57																			61	V1a
																					V1b
																					V2
	+																				V3
																					V4
																					V5
																					V6
																					V7
																					V8
			10*							(13)											V9
																					V10
																					V11
																					V ?12
																					R1
																					R2a
																					R2b
																					R3
																					R ?4
																					R ?5
																					M1
																					M2
	8																				M3
																					M4
																					M5
	20	17	21	61	35	22	60														M6
																					M7
																					M8
																					M9a
																					M9b
																					M10
																					M11
																					M12
																					M13
																					M14
																					M15a
																					M15b
																					M16
																					M17a
149	150	151	152	153	154	155	156	157	158	159	160	161	162	163	164	165	166	167	168	169	

Continued p. 141

	127	128	129	130	131	132	133	134	135	136	137	138	139	140	141	142	143	144	145	146	1
M17b																					
M18																					
M19																					
M20																					
M21																					
M22																					
M ?23																					
M ?24																					
F1																					
F2																					
L1			11														17				
L2			4						3								8				
L3					5	6															
L4			9			11		10									17				
L5			7			8															
L6				9/11								14									
L7																					
L8																					
L9																					
L10a																					
L10b																					
L11													1b*								
L12																					
L13																					
K1									10							16			15		
K2															4						
K3	5									3											
K4																	(5)				
K5							13*		14							7					
K6																					
K7																					
K8																					
K9		4																			
K10																					
K11																					
K12																					

127 128 129 130 131 132 133 134 135 136 137 138 139 140 141 142 143 144 145 146

Continued p. 142

8	149	150	151	152	153	154	155	156	157	158	159	160	161	162	163	164	165	166	167	168	169
																					M17b
																					M18
																					M19
																					M20
																					M21
																					M22
																					M ?23
																					M ?24
																					F1
																					F2
									15			14									L1
																					L2
		4		3																	L3
		18		24					15			14									L4
		11		9					12			13									L5
	6	4		5																	L6
																					L7
																					L8
																					L9
																					L10a
																					L10b
																					L11
																					L12
																					L13
	13	14								23		24	25	26		27	28		29	30	K1
		5																			K2
										2		1									K3
		(4)																			K4
	10	9								18		19			20			21			K5
																					K6
																					K7
																					K8
																					K9
																					K10
		6																			K11
																					K12
8	149	150	151	152	153	154	155	156	157	158	159	160	161	162	163	164	165	166	167	168	169

Continued p. 143

	127	128	129	130	131	132	133	134	135	136	137	138	139	140	141	142	143	144	145	146
S1																				
S2																				
S3																				
S4																				
S5																1				
S6							8		(9)											
S7																				
S8a																				
S8b																				
S8c																				
S9a																				
S9b																				
S10																				
S11																				
S12																				
S13																				
S14																				
N1		8																		
H1																				
H2																				
H3																				
B1																				
T1																				
T2																				
T3																				
T4							1		2											
T5																				
T6																				
T7																				
T8																				
T9															2					
T10																				
T11																				
T12																				
	127	128	129	130	131	132	133	134	135	136	137	138	139	140	141	142	143	144	145	146

149	150	151	152	153	154	155	156	157	158	159	160	161	162	163	164	165	166	167	168	169	
																					S1
																					S2
																					S3
																					S4
			3																		S5
	(5)								(7)												S6
																					S7
																					S8a
																					S8b
																					S8c
																					S9a
																					S9b
																					S10
																					S11
																					S12
																					S13
																					S14
																					N1
																					H1
																					H2
																					H3
																					B1
																					T1
																					T2
																					T3
																					T4
									3	4					5b*						T5
																					T6
																					T7
																					T8
1																					T9
																					T10
																					T11
																					T12

149 150 151 152 153 154 155 156 | 157 158 159 160 161 | 162 163 164 165 166 | 167 168 | 169

	1	2	3	4	5	6	7	8	9	10	11	12	13	14	15	16	17	18	19	20
Sæl1																				
By1																				
By2					2		1													
By3					1		2													
By4					1		2													
By5					1		2													
He1																				

	43	44	45	46	47	48	49	50	51	52	53	54	55	56	57	58	59	60	61	62
Sæl1																				
By1											2	1								
By2																				
By3																				
By4																				
By5																				
He1																				

	85	86	87	88	89	90	91	92	93	94	95	96	97	98	99	100	101	102	103	104
Sæl1																				
By1																				
By2																				
By3																				
By4																				
By5																				
He1										+										

	127	128	129	130	131	132	133	134	135	136	137	138	139	140	141	142	143	144	145	146
Sæl1											+									
By1																				
By2																				
By3																				
By4																				
By5																				
He1																				

23	24	25	26	27	28	29	30	31	32	33	34	35	36	37	38	39	40	41	42	
																				Sæl
																				By1
																				By2
																				By3
																				By4
																				By5
																				He1

65	66	67	68	69	70	71	72	73	74	75	76	77	78	79	80	81	82	83	84	
																				Sæl
																				By1
																				By2
																				By3
																				By4
																				By5
																				He1

107	108	109	110	111	112	113	114	115	116	117	118	119	120	121	122	123	124	125	126	
																				Sæl
																				By1
																				By2
																				By3
																				By4
																				By5
																				He1

8	149	150	151	152	153	154	155	156	157	158	159	160	161	162	163	164	165	166	167	168	169	
																						Sæl
																						By1
																						By2
																						By3
																						By4
																						By5
																						He1

3.7 Drougqveen, Suplemete ti Dromkve, Draugkveen, Dromkvæen, Draumkvæi, Draumekvæi, Lidt af Draumkvæde, two unnamed texts and twenty-nine individual stanzas

V1a

Drougqveen!

(1) 1. Vhii du mæg høyre ægh qvea ful kan,
alt om dey nyttan Drenjir,
alt om æn Olav Aasteson,
som hævæ sovi so lænje.
Maanen skjeene aa Vejine faddæ so viiæ.

(3) 2. Olav han æ i voxtro veenæ,
som ein Seljeteine;
Far aa Moer dey onto væl,
fraa dhee han kom i Heimee
Maanen skeene, aa Vejine etc

(5) 3. Egh drak en Dryk om Joleftan
stærkan Svævnen fæk,
vakne kje fø om Trettandajen;
daa Fokje i Kyrkja gjæk.
I villande Heyo, i Rodelaande der kjænne dey mæg.

(8) 4. Egh la mæg nee om Joleftan,
no hæv æg sovi solænje,
vakna kje fø om Trettandajen,
Fuglanæ skokæ Vænjo. etc.

(6) 5. Egh la mæg nee om Joleftan,
egh stærkan Svevnæn tok,
vakna kje fø om Trettandajen
daa Fokje i Kyrkja drog. etc.

(5) 6. Egh la mæg nee om Joleftan
stærkan Svevnæn fek,
vakna kje fo om Trettandajen
Fokje i Kyrkja gjæk. etc.

7. Egh sto up ein Sondagsmorgo
aa ville ti Kyrkja riæ;
Egh sprætte paa mæg Belti mit,
dhe glema i Værn so viæ. etc.

8. Som egh kaam at Kyrkje Lee,
Egh studdæ mæg enat Stette.
so mangæ som paa mith Belti fæk sjaa,
dey lyfte paa Hat aa Hette. etc.

9. Som ægh mægh i Kyrkja kaam,
Ægh monne paa Knæ fallæ
somangæ som paa mit Belti fæk sjaa,
dey gløymde paa Gud aa kalla etc.

10. Egh gjæk mægh i Kyrkja eend
som Fokje paa Knæ villæ fallæ
som Klokkaren paa mit Belti saag
han gløymde paa Gut aa kallæ. etc:

11. Præsten som fram fø Altari sto—
alt mæ see lærde Tongæ
aa ret som han mit Belti saag,
han gløymde baa læsa aa sjungæ. etc:

---

(36) 12. Præsten gjæk paa Prækestolen
aa las up leksunæ seenæ,
so sættæ ægh mæg i Kyrkje Dynne
aa fortaaldæ om Droumanæ meene etc.

(21) 13. Dee va aarli om Morgonæn
Sole tog ti skeene.
Olav salar Gangareen seen,
aa lægge paa gylden Greeme etc

(24) 14. So riæ han sæg at Kyrkja
fortæl af Droumane seenæ
Gamle aa Ongæ gjæv Attegoume
æg theele af Droumane meene. etc.

(37) 15. Præsten stænde paa Prækestolen
gjære han lexune lange.
Olav han sitæ i Kyrkje Svo/lo
aa fortælæ Drouman mange. etc

---

16. Dey bou mæg tvo Stutar,
aa baaæ so vha dey qviitæ,
Ægh ville kje sælje mit Bælti burt,
ægh totte dhæ va for lite. etc.

17. Dey bou mæg tvo Rollar,
aa baaæ so vha dey likæ,
æg ville kje sælje mit Belti burt
æg totte dhæ va for lite. etc.

18. Dey bou mæg Fjosi sit,
mæ qvorjum Ku i Baase,
daa ægh inkje sælde Belti mit
daa jore æg som ein Taapi. etc.

19. Dey bou mæg Gulli,
aa mælte dhe up i Skaalir,
daa æg inkje sælde Belti mit
daa joræ ægh som ein Daari. etc.—

20. Egh gjæk mæg i Vejen fram,
ægh kom i so galnæ Tankar,
egh sælde mit Belti burt fo reengt,
aa dhe fø eit fille Par Handskar etc.

21. Dhe va kje so mæt Belti mit,
som dhe vha sjaaande paa,
dhe vha gjort af Kalverompur
og fora mæ Halmestraae etc.

---

(91) 22. Egh sala ut meen kaate Rou
ægh ville Præsten sjuse,
egh slap kje ivi Gjeddar Broe
fødey Hougetussar.
Maanen skene og Vejine faddæ so vie.

(92) 23. Egh sala ut meen kaate Rou,
ægh ville thi Kyrkja riæ,
æg slap kje ivi Gjeddarbroe,
fø dey Drouganæ niæ. etc.

(101) 24. Gjæddarbro den liggæ so høgt
mot Nora Veende,
ho, æ, i Enda mæ Jønni slejæn,
og Soum i qvorjum Teende. etc

(101) 25. Egh hæv gjænji Gjeddarbro
den liggæ so høgt i Veende,
ho vha addæ mæ Jøn besleje
aa Soum ette qvorjum Teende. etc.

(107) 26. No hæv æg gjænji Gjæddarbro,
dæn æ baadi vii, aa brey—
naa hæv æg vat VaaæMyran
no æ, egh qvittæ dey. etc.

---

27. Doguren aat egh i Haaraang,
aa Ondaalen giæk paa Gletti,
Netværen aat egh i Tindalen
utænkt so ha egh detti etc.

---

(42) 28. Dhe va me fyste Utreysning
igjænom dæn Tyner Skog
sondæ sleyt æg me Skarlakkens Kaapæ,
ho va ny æg Heyma drog. etc.

(39) 29. Dhe va me fyste Utreysning,
igjenom den Tyners Reendi
sondesleyt, æg me Skarlakens Kaapæ,
aa Neglan af qvorjum Fingre. etc:

(76) 30. No hæv æg vori upmæ Skye,
aa neat paa Havsens Gronne
den som fulnar meene Fotspore
han læer kje af blie Mon/ne. etc:

(77) 31. Egh hæv vori uponde Skye
aa jupt i Havsens Gronne
den som fyjer meene Fotspore
han læer kje af Hjartas Gron/nee. etc.

(79) 32. Egh hæv vori uponde Skye
aa neat paa Dikje svarte
den som vhi meene Fodspor fyje,
den læer kje af bliæ Hjarta. etc.

(83) 33. Egh hæv vori uponde Skye
aa neat paa svarte Dikje,
egh hæv seet ad heyte Helviti,
aa Ejendeyl i Hemmerikje. etc

---

34. Egh hæv vori uponde Sky,
aa neat paa Havsens Oddar,
den som vhi meene Fotspor fyje
den maa kje danse paa Loddar. etc.

35. Egh hæv vori uponde Sky,
aa neat paa Havsnns Øyar
fire Gaangur hæv egh vori gift
aa altid fænji Møyar. etc.

36. Den æjne fæk Egh i Øyefjød,
dæn aræ fæk æg paa Soheye,
dæn treeæ fæk egh paa Hadeland,
dæn fjoræ i villande Heyo. etc.

---

(52) 37. Egh va mæg eingaang Norafjøls,
egh ville hogge Kasir.
dher møttæ Egh tvo villan Dyr;
eit Jkon aa ein Jasii, etc.

(54) 38. Egh va mæg Eingaang Norafjølds,
dher kaam so stor ein Snjoræ,
Kjærinje laantæ mæg Øyro sheeh
ti lappæ meene Skoe. etc.

(98) 39. Ormen stik, aa Bikja bitæ,
aa Stuten stændæ stangar,
dheer feer injen Jeddarbro
som fæller Domanæ vrange.
Tonga talar aa Sannong svarar paa Domedag.

---

40. Soom egh kaam i fyste Hodde
dher va so ondelæg vori,
Dukjen va otto Bloi dræjen,
aa Ormen spillar ette Bore.

Maanen skeene og Vejine faddæ so viæ.
Maanen skeene etc.

---

41. Som egh kom i den are Hodde
egh vha i so stor ein Vaai
Gaangekjæri paa Golvi sto
aa Trodde ivi dey raai. etc

42. Egh kaam ti den treæ Hodde,
Egh mone dher betæ likæ
der va veene Sænjir opreyde
aa breyde mæ Silkje qvitæ.

---

(111) 43. Soomæ foer ivi TveitarAasen
aa soomæ Skaalæstraand,
mæn dey som foer ivi Jolehylen
dey kom so vaatæ fram. etc.

(87) 44. Egh æ so trøyttæ av Heere mo,
aa ennaa maa me brænnæ;
æg høyrer Vatne aa fær dhee inkje,
ondæ Jore so maa dhee rænnæ. etc.

(86) 45. Egh hæv fari ivi vigde Votne,
aa ivi jupæ Dalar,
høyrer Vatne, aa seer dhee inkje
ondæ Jore so maa dhee fara etc

---

46. Islands Galten aa FraanarOrmen,
baaæ so æ dey douæ,
attæ livær den lisle Guten
han raaer ivi Gulli rouæ. etc

47. Islands Galten aa Fraanar Ormen,
dey baaæ hæve laati liv,
atte liver den lisle Guten,
han raaer ivi veene Viv. etc.

48. Stæinfin liggæ onde Sotæhalsæn
sotan Sænje saknar,
so knæja Sotæn i Skremslo,
so mone Stæinfin vaknæ. etc:

49. Stæinfin tekæ sæg inkje anna fø,
paa virke Vikun tri,
hel han skjærper up Pilinæ seene,
han jære baadi slipar aa gnier etc.

50. Stæinfin villæ løynæ sæg,
hjelmar Kampen leytæ
so løyntæ han sæg i Skjer-Egje
længst i villandeHeyo. etc.

---

(89) 51. Enkje knejar Sotæn meen,
enkje jøyr meen Hond,
enkje gala dey Ottefuglan
dhee tikjes mæg væra vont. etc:

(90) 52. Egh kan noko af qvorjum Viso
dherfø tikjes æg fro
Eg va laangæ i Molle moka;
ha egh tot den Douen goe. etc:

(135) 53. Egh mødte tvey Ormar,
dey hojis uti Kjæfte;
dæ dey tvo søndugu Syskjenboonne
som heera qvoraræ vhi ægte. etc

---

54. Egh hæv vori paa vori paa svarte Havsgroond,
aa stomdom paa Skye svengar,
men den som tooræ kloras mæ mæg,
den maa hava Kløer og Vengar.

Stat up du Olav Aastesonen som hæve sovi so lænje.—

---

55. Egh hæv vori paa svarte Havsgrond
aa stomdom i Skye svarte
deen som torræ kloras mæ mæg
han maa kje ha Kalvehjarta. etc.

---

(149) 56. Shæl æ den i denne Være
som Fattikæ hæv gjevi Ku,
den tar kje ræddas i aannaa Være
fø, gange ivi Gjæddar bru.
Tonga talar, aa Sannong svarar paa Domedag.

(150) 57. Sæhl æ den i denne Være,
som Fattikæ hæv gjevi Koon,
den tar inkje ræddas i aanno Være
fø qvasse Stutehon. etc.

(146) 58. Shæl æ den i denne Være,
som Fattikæ hæv gjevi Brou,
den tar inkje fælæ i aanno Være
fø qvasse Heklenou. etc.

(148) 59. Shæl æ den i denne Være
som Fattikæ hæv gjevi Skoe
den tar inkje ræddas i aanno Være
fø qvasse Hæklebro. etc.

(84) 60. Dher æ heyt i Helviti,
heytar hel nokæn hyggæ,
dey hængde pivi en Kjøru Kjættil,
aa brykja ni, ein Styjeengs Rygge.
Tonga talar, aa Sannong svarar paa Domedag.

(169) 61. Gamle Mænnar aa onge Mænnar,
maa gjæva Attegoumme,
mæ Olav Aasteson
fortaalt hæv seene Droumme.
Stat up du Olav Aasteson som hævæ sovi solænje.

Alterations: heading: meqvee *written above* gqvee *by different hand*; 7.1 u *of* up *altered from* o*(?)*; 9.2 fallæ *altered from* falle; 9.3 somangæ *altered from* somange; 10.2 ll *of* fallæ *altered from* dd*(?)*; 11.2 *Roman* ee *altered from Gothic* ii*(?)*; 12.2 u *of* up *altered from* o; 12.3 i *and another letter(?) written before* i, *but second letter obscured by ink mark*; 16.2 baaæ *altered from* baae; 17.3 kje *altered from* kji; 22.refr. etc. *written after* vie., *but crossed out*; 24.2 mot *altered from* mod*(?)*; 24.4 q *of* qvorjum *altered (twice?) from* g; 25.1 G *of* Gjeddarbro *altered from* Jed; 25.4 ette *written over* i; 28.3 *first* k *of* Skarlakkens *altered from* g; 29.2 Reendi *altered from* Reende; 30.4 e *of* læer *altered from* r; 33.2 neat *first written* nedat *or* nedt, *but* ed(a)t *rubbed and crossed out and* eat *written after this*; 37.3 møttæ *altered from* møtte*(?)*; 37.4 *mark after* eit *appears to be first stroke of an abandoned* J *rather than a comma*; 38.2 *Gothic* S *altered from Roman* S; 38.3 *first* h *of* sheeh *almost certainly added after word was written*; 39.4 D *altered from* s*(?)*; 41.2 Vaai *altered from* Fari; 42.3 veene *altered from* vene; 42.4 oto*(?) written immediately before* mæ, *but crossed out and partly obscured by first stroke of* m; 43.1 e *of* foer *altered from* o; TveitarAasen *first written* Tveitastraande *(*-Straande*?)*, Aasen *written over* straande *and* r *added before* A; 46.1 *first* a *of* aa *altered from* og; 49.3 u *of* up *altered from* o; 50.4 Heyo *altered from* Heye*(?)*; 51.2 *a letter (*d *altered from* e*?) between* y *and* r *of* jøyr *crossed out*; 51.4 æ *of* væra *altered from* e; 53.3 b *of* boonne *altered from* o*(?) and first* o *begun as* n*(?)*; 54.2 r *of* svengar *added after word was written*; 54.3 *second* o *of* tooræ *altered from* r, *or possibly begun as* r; 54.refr. S *of* Stat *written over* et *or* et *and a partially written* c; Olav *altered from* Olaf; 55.1 d *of* Havsgrond *added after word was written*; 55.2 mdom *of* stomdom *altered from* ndom; 55.3 æ *of* torræ *altered from* e; 55.4 v *added to* ha *after word was written, but crossed out*; 56.refr. etc *or* etc. *written before* Tonga, *but crossed out*; 57.2 k *of* Fattikæ *altered from* g*(?)*; 57.3 n *of* inkje *begun as* k; 57.4 fø *altered from* før*(?)*; 58.4 fø *added above line with a sign indicating its position in text*; 59.4 *second* s *of* qvasse *added after word was written*; 60.4 Styjeengs *altered from* Styjeens; 61.3 e *of* Aasteson *altered from* a; *in one or two cases refrains seem to have been added after the text was written: this applies to stanzas* 40 *(second refrain)*, 56 *and* 60*: the* etc *after stanza* 13 *may also have been added later.*

Other notes on the MS:

1. 8.3 *sjaa* may read *sjoa*; 15.2 *gjære* may read *gjære*; 30.2 *e* of *Havsens* more or less illegible, may be altered from *n* (cf. 35.2); 30.3 *t* of *Fotspore* uncertain, apparently altered from *d*, but difficult to see either *d* or *t*; 31.2 cf. note to 30.2; 31.3 cf. note to 30.3; 32.4 *k* of *kje* altered and rendered more or less illegible; 33.3 *ad* may read *at*; 34.2 cf. note to 30.2; 39.*refr. svarar* may read *svaear*, it appears to have been written *svaeer* or *svarer* first, then the final *er* was altered to *a* and a new *r* added: the fourth letter is difficult to read, it looks more like *e* than *r*, but in that case it is surprising it has not been altered with other parts of the word; 41.3 *Gaangekjæri* may read *Gaange kjæri*; 60.3 *hængde* may read *hængdæ*, both *d* and the final letter appear to have been altered.

2. It is occasionally difficult to distinguish a comma from a full stop. In such cases a comma is printed after ll.1, 2 and 3 and a stop after l.4.

3. The stanza numbering 1–61 is found in the MS, but has undergone some alteration: stanzas 9–27 were first numbered 8–26, and stanzas 28–60 37–69, though from stanza 28 the original numbering is not clear in every case and it is at least possible that stanza 28 was first numbered 27. The figures 61 above the last stanza do not appear to have been altered. No separation of the stanzas into lines has been made in the MS and this feature has been added by the editor.

4. Svenungsen's comments on the content of the text have been omitted.

5. Between the heading and the first stanza there is a long sub-heading which says: 'An ancient ballad probably about the state of the soul after death, which shows: that the old Norwegian heathens and Papists had accepted the transmigration of souls in the most mystical, fanatical, superstitious and horrifying portrayals and terrifying images; collected by Niels Svenungsen, 19 October 1842.' ('et Ældgammelt Omqvad, formodentlig, om Sjælens Tilstand eftter Døden, som viser: at de gamle norske Hedninger og Papister have antaget Sjelevandringen i de mest mystiske, sværmeriske, overtroiske og gyseligste Fremstillinger og Skrækkebilleder; samlede ved Niels Svenungsen den 19 Octbr 1842.') The MS was sent by Svenungsen to Olea Crøger together with the following letter (slightly abbreviated): 'In accordance with your request which has reached me on several occasions, the last time via my old friend and acquaintance, S.T. Lieutenant Landstad, I enclose with this letter an Old Norse ballad called *Drougqveen* which seems to portray the ideas of the old heathen Telemark farmers concerning the state of the soul after death, and which, as far as I am aware, is not yet generally known. I have taken great pains to collect this ballad and have visited the oldest inhabitants who could give me any information about it in several different parishes. It has taken several years to arrive at the collection I now send to you, and it has not been sufficient just to collect, there has also been work to do putting what I had collected into order, since at one time the material was in something of a muddle and there was no cohesion in the contents of the ballad. It is possible that it would have been much more readily accessible two or three hundred years ago when the old people were still alive for whom this was a much loved song and therefore more commonly heard at their festive gatherings. I have been bold enough to add a few notes at the edge of each of the pages on which I have written this collection, as I understand it [in accordance with my interpretation of the text ?], and I hope this well-intentioned effort of mine will please you. I have still more Old Norse songs . . . If you desire more you must let me know – I shall be most happy to serve you in this matter . . .' ('Eftter Deres Forlangende ved flere Budsendelser, den sidste ved S.T. [salvo titulo ?] Leutenant

Landstad /: min gamle Ven og Bekjendt :/ fremsender jeg herunderlagt et oldnordisk Omqvad: Drougqveen kaldet; der sandsynligviis fremstiller de gamle hedenske Tellebønders Forestillinger om Sjelens Tilstand eftter Døden, og som jeg troer ei endnu er kommen for Lyset saavidt jeg derom kan viide. [new §] Jeg har havt megen Umag med at samle dette Omqvad, og det i forskjellige flere Præstegjelde har jeg opsøgt de ældste Oldinge som har kunnet underrette mig herom, og det har varet i flere Aar, inden jeg kunde komme til den Samling deraf som jeg her leverer Dem, og har det ikke været nok med at samle, men ogsaa har det været Arbeyde i at ordne det Samlede som forhen laae spredt omhinanden, saa at man havde ingen Forbindelse i de fremsatte Materier i dette Omqvad. Maaskee at man for 2 a 3 Hundrede Aar tilbage i Tiden havde kommet meget lettere dertil, da de Gamle endnu levede for hvem dette var en Yndlingsang, og derfor mere almindelig og brugbar ved deres høytidelige Sammenkomster. Jeg har vovet at tilføye nogle enkelte Notitzer – ved Bredden af hvert Blad, hvorpaa jeg har nedskrevet denne Samling, saaledes som dette forekommer mig. Og ønsker det maatte behage, dette mit velmeente Arbeyde. Jeg har endnu flere oldnordiske Sange . . . Ønsker De Flere, maa De lade mig det viide – jeg er glad beredvillig til heri at tjene Dem . . . ')

M1

Suplemete ti Dromkve.

(78) 1. Eg hev vore ponde Skye
Aa ne me Mjødde kvite
Den som mine Fotspor ska fygie
Han ler kji a Monne blie

(104) 2. Dei æ saa blaute dei Gaglemyrann
De kan dei Ingjen gange
Men enddaa vær' ive Jæddarbroe
Den tyst onde Skye hange—

(95) 3. Ormen haag aa Bikja bit
Aa Stuten midt i Lei
Tri æ Tingji paa Gjæddarbroi
Aa adde æ gramme aa vrei

Alterations: 2.1 Dei *written above line over* he*(?)*, han*(?) which is crossed out*, e *is difficult to read and* i *appears to have been added after word was written*; 2.2 Ingjen *altered from* ingjen*(?)*; 2.3 Jæ *of* Jæddarbroe *altered from* Ga.

Other notes on the MS:

1. 2.1 *Gaglemyrann* may read *Gaglemyrane*; 3.2 *midt* may read *mitt*; the rhyme words in 3.2 and 3.4 and *-broi* in 3.3 cannot be deciphered with certainty. They could read *Lé* or *Lée*, *-broé* and *vrée*. It is perhaps more likely that they were first written *Lee*, *-broe*, *vree* and subsequently altered to *Lei*, *-broi*, *vrei* by the addition of a dot/accent over the *e* which in each case is otherwise indistinguishable from *i*. Against this, however, there are the *-e* endings in, e.g., 1.1 *Skye*, 1.2 *Mjødde*, 2.3 *Jæddarbroe*, the position of the accent in 3.2 and 3.4 and the fact that *vrei* is ungrammatical.

2. Two crosses precede stanzas 1 and 2, and a line (in pencil – a later addition?) runs down the left-hand side of stanza 3 beneath which there is a single cross.

3. The stanza numbering 1–3 does not occur in the MS and has been added by the editor; the separation of stanzas and lines is clear throughout.

4. *Mjødde* 1.2 and *Gaglemyrann* 2.1 are explained in two separate notes as *Nysne* (fresh snow) and *Gaaremyrene* or possibly *Gaaramyrane* (the awful mires) respectively.

5. M1 appears to have been written in haste. The reading of a number of words is doubtful and there are several alterations (apart from those noted above) which obscure the original text, although it is difficult to tell whether any or all of the alterations were made as the MS was being written or later. It seems likely that M1 is an original.

M6

(Draugkveen)

(1) 1. Ja vi du lye eg kvea kann,
eg kve um dei nyte Drengjir
eg kve um en Olav Åknesi
som sovi heve så lengje.
Månen skine å Veginne fedde så vie.

(12) 2. De va no um Joleftanen
sterkan Svevnen fekk,
ingjen av mine Vinir
som kunna meg uppvekkje.

(13) 3. Dæ va no um Jolef.
dei Laugevatni bar,
då måtte eg på Havsensbotnen
mæ salte Tårir har.

(14) 4. Dæ va no um Joleftanen
dei bar inn Kling å Kakur,
så m. eg p. H.
å sjå mæ Fiskjen vakjer

(15) 5. Dæ va no um Joleftanen
dei bar inn Øl i Skål,
men ingjen av mine Vinir
kunna høyre på mitt Mål.

(8) 6. Eg la meg ne um Joleftanen
då sov eg så lengji,
eg vakna kje fyrr um Trettandagjen
då Fuglan*n*e skóke Vengjir.

(5) 7. Eg l. m. n. u. J.
sterke Svevnen fekk,
eg v. k. f. um T.
då Fókkje i Kyrkja gjekk.

(34) 8. Presten stende på Predikstolen
legg ut Tekstinne sine,
Olav han stende fyr Kyrkjedynni
fortel utav Drauman*n*e sine.

(43) 9. Dæ va fyste utreisa mi,
igjenom ein Tynnyrmóge,
eg sleit sunde mi Skarlakskåpa,
å Hui av kvor min Fóte.

(39) 10. Dæ va are Utreisa mi,
igjenom ein Tynnyr(e)ring'e,
eg sleit s. mi Skarlakskåpi
å Hui av kvor min Finge.

(79) 11. Eg hev vori meg upp mæ Sky
å ne mæ Havi Svarte
dæn som mi' Fotspori fydder
lær 'kje av bliom Hjarta.

(76) 12. Eg h. v. m. u. m. Sky,
å ne mæ Havsens Bunne,
d. s. m. F. f. — Munni.

(82) 13. Eg hev v. m. u. m. Sky
å ne på Havi júpe,
de ville eg ynskje utav Gud
at eg kunna fjúke.

(98) 14. Ormen stinge å Bikkja bite
å Stuten stend å stangar,
dær kjeme ingjen ivi Gjæddarbrói
fyr Dóman*n*e fedde vrånge.

(104) 15. Håge æ den Gjæddarbrói
hó tist punde Skýi hange,
men endå verre dei Gaglemyranne
som eg måtte gange.

(58) 16a. Tunge va dæn Granastigjen å gange
(104) b. men endå verre den Gjæddarbroi
ho tist punde Skýi hange.

(151) 17. Sæl æ dæn i dessi Væri
fatike låner Hús,
han tar 'kje ræast i aurom Væri
å høyre på Ulvetút.

(58) 18. Tunge så æ dæn Granastigjen å gange
men endå verre den Lindarormen,
som tist meg i Hælan*n*e hange.

(144) 19. Sæl æ dæn i dessi Væri
fatike hev gjevi Klæi,
han tar ikkje ræast i aurom Væri
fyr håge Kjellar Bræi.

(150) 20. Sæl æ dæn i d. V.
—Konn, – Væri
bli stanga av Stútehonn.

(152) 21. Sæl æ. d. i d. V.
Konnmåli den kan auke
d. t. kje r. i a. V.
på store Hundegaule.

(155) 22. Sæl æ. d. i d. V.
Vikti kan hadde ne
h. t. k. r. i a. V.
fyr Løveten*n*an*n*e å se.

(139) 23. Ingjen Fugle fýke så høgt
som Gråduva mæ sine Ungar
ingjen Orme stinge så kvast
som falske Man*n*etungur.

(111) 24. Sume fere Eikjaråsen
sóme den Skålestrånd,
men dei som fara Jólehylen
dei koma væl våte fram.

(8) 25. Dæ va' så tungt um Joleftanen
at eg sille Sova så lengji
eg vakna 'kje fyrr um Trettand.
då Fuglan*n*e skóke Vengjir.

(5) 26a. Dæ va meg um Joleftanen
sterkan svevnen fekk
(122) b. då møtte en Manne mæ Båne på Armen bar
som gjekk i Jori te Knes.

(32) 27. Sutinne å så Sorgjin*n*e
dei blandar eg alt isama,
Mun*n*en lær å Hjarta'i græte
de æ' no 'kje alt så Gama.

(33) 28. Sutin*n*e å så Sorgjinne
dei trøer eg unde min Fot,
ti glaere sko eg halle meg
ti mei dæ gjeng meg imót.

(59) 29. Eg gjekk upp den Granastigjen
den va' så tung å fara,
eg måtte upp dei store Klippi
å neri Bergedalar.

(67) 30. Eg såg meg den Fugleflokk
som Ørnekløar krøkte,
men endå verre den Løverkúla,
som adde på meg søkte.

(57) 31. Så såg eg ei liti Hind
ho ville mæ meg svala,
så kom dær fram tvo Lindarormar,
som hæna ville kvele.

(72) 32. Så gjekk eg upp på en Bergeknapp,
å tenkte at eg skulle vin*ne*,
me bære dæn i Svevnen sko fara,
dæ gjenge meg addi av Min*ne*.

(27) 33. Eg æ dæn eismadd i Verden
som sterkan Svevnen fanga,
men alli noken av mine Vinir
som kunna løyse meg oto Båndo.

(144) 34. Sæl æ dæn i dessi Væri
sine Foreldri ærer,
han tar kje ræast i aurom Væri
fyr håge Kjellar Bræi.

(154) 35. S. æ d. i d. V.
dæn Fatike ei foraktar,
h. t. k. r. i a. V.
fyr Løvenes Tann upptraktar.

(28) 36. Eg va som en Fugl i Bur
som gjønni vil vera fri,
her veit ingjen livandes
hot i annensmans Hjarta'i búr.

(29) 37. Eg æ nok den einaste,
som sterke Svevnen fanga,
som den enlig Fugl på Kvist
i Fugleburi fanga.

(66) 38. Så gjekk eg meg på Havets Strand
å mine Føtan*n*e kvesste,
Salte Tårir av Øine rann
å ingjen kun*n*a meg vekkje.

(65) 39. Så gjekk eg meg på Havets Strand
grumme Løver på meg sette,
så kjeme Lindarormen fram
å Løvernes Tennar knekte.

(54) 40. Eg va' meg hær norafjølls
dæ dreiv så mykje Snjore,
fekk eg fat i Hindehamen
ti lappe mine Sko.

---

(55) 41. Eg va' meg hær nórafjølls,
dreiv 'en Snjóren kvíte,
fekk eg fat í dæn Bjønnehamen,
som aldri hae noken Líkje.

(56) 42. Så fekk eg fat í dæn Hindehamen
å sveipte dæn kringum min Fót;
så kom hó fram dæn lisle Hind,
som Huggormen jaga ífrå.

(114) 43. Så gjekk eg fram dæn Skålestrånd
å Hundanne tók ti gjøy;
men dæn som í Svevnen sko' fara,
d'æ som 'en kunna døy.

(46) 44. Så fór eg fram dæn Gaglemýr,
hó va' no så vónd å gange;
så kom fram ein líten Smådreng,
unde míne Føtanne helle.

(47) 45. Så kjæm dei fram Smådrengjinne
å fesla míne Føtar;
men dæn som mí Fótspori fydder,
dæ blí 'kje gløymt, fyrr 'en dør.

(45) 46. Så kjæm dei fram Smådrengjinne
å míne Finganne feslar;
eg sleit sunde mí Skarlakskåpa,
í Tynnyrringjen meg refsa.

(44) 47. Eg sleit sunde mí Skarlakskåpa
ígjenom dæn Tynnyrmóg'e;
fram kjæm adde Smådrengjinne,
dei helt unde kvor min Fót'e.

(68) 48. Så såg eg dæn Fugleflokk,
som Ørnefjøirir bar;
men dæn, som mí' Fótspori fydder,
dæn blíve så sjellan gla.

---

(60) 49. Så gjekk eg meg på viddan Hei
i store Berg å Dalar,
men dæn som mi Fotspori fydder,
dæn må mæ Tunga tala.

(61) 50. Så gjekk eg meg på viddan Hei
eitt Skógesnar så tykt,
dæ møtte meg bå Løvir å Bjønnir
men Livi behelt eg trygt.

(69) 51. Så gjekk eg meg i Rosenslund
mæ fagre Gaukan*n*e leika,
men dæn som mi Fótspori fydder,
han gjer 'kje an*n*ten kve hell kjeimar.

(73) 52. Så sat eg upp i ei Lindegrein
Som Fuglan*n*e ha'e sitt Reii,
eg tenkte eg sille 'kje gjera Mein,
men Gaukjen fyrutta Meining.

(74) 53. Så sat eg unde ei Lindegrein
Som Fuglan*n*e hae si Føa,
men den må inkje gjera Mein,
som Fuglan*n*e gjer ti Nøgjes.

(71) 54. Så va' eg uppå den Bergetopp
som Skorpejonen mon*n*e fara,
dæ va dæn største Glei,
mæ fagre Gaukan*n*e gala.

(70) 55. D'æ dæ meste eg beer um
at ingjen mi Fotspori fydder,
men d'æ den støste Glei eg veit,
at fagre Gaukan*n*e gala.

---

(140) 56. Eg hørde på dæn Hundegaul
i míne langsomme Dagar;
men eg æ' dæn einaste í Verden,
som så hev blivi plaga.

(30) 57. Mine Foreldres Opdragelse
så gó dæn monne vera,
men enten i Plage hell stóre Ve,
som mig i Verden erfaret.

(75) 58. Så såg eg dæn Fugleflokk
í Lindegreininne fara;
Gud give jeg måtte i min Faders Går
fullende mine Dage!

(31) 59. Den største Sorg i Søvnen bær,
som smerter end mit Hjerte,
at min Fader og Moder kjær
av Søvnen mig ei kan vekke.

(156) 60. Sæl æ' dæn í dessi Væri
Vigt å Mål de ei vrakar,
han tar 'kje ræast í aurom Væri
i Ørnekløanne taka.

(153) 61. Sæl &c,
Fatike dæn kann gjeva,
han tar &c
dæn hægste í Himmerig vera.

(63) 62. Eg såg no dæn Løveflokk,
som ville dæn Slangjen uppeta;
i min Søvne jeg tenker om,
at jeg í min Heim monne vera.

(64) 63. Eg gjekk meg í Rósenslund,
som adde dei Løver mon vera;
men tungt æ' dæ í dessi Væri
míne Skjæbnen bera.

(48) 64. Eg va' meg hær nórafjølls
í så stór ein Kull;
dæn som mí' Fótspori fydder,
han æ meg vist tró å hull.

(49) 65. Eg va' meg hær nórafjølls
í så stór ein Kvíe;
Ormevrimlen í Føtanne stakk,
eg måtte på Hesten ríe.

(50) 66. Eg va' meg hær nórafjølls
mæ stór Sorg å Harm;
dæ va' meg te Møia lagt
í stór Sút å Savn.

(51) 67. Eg va' meg hær nórafjølls
alt på dei Bjørgeklippi;
dær høyrde eg mæ Lerken sang,
dæ va' meg te Letti.

(76) 68. Eg va' meg hær upp mæ Ský
å ne mæ klare Grunnar;
men dæn som mí Fótspori fydder,
han lær 'kje av blíom Munne.

(9) 69. Eg la' meg ne um Jóleftanen,
mæ dei andre túra;
men dæn som mí Fótspori fydder,
dæn må 'kje av Hjarta stúre.

(10) 70. Eg la' meg ne um Jóleftanen,
sat í myrke Hús,
vakna 'kje fyrr um Trettandagjen
mæ stór Sorg å Sút.

(11) 71. Eg la' meg ne um Jóleftanen,
dær va' væl mange, meg saknar;
eg vakna 'kje fyrr um Trettandagjen,
då Fókkji dæ va' samla.

(34) 72. Presten stende på Predikstólen,
legg út Tekstinne síne;
Ólav han stende fyr Kyrkjedynni,
han græt útav Draumanne síne.

(38) 73. Presten stende på Predikstólen,
på alt Fókkji han staggar;
Ólav han stende fyr Kyrkjedynni,
mæ síne Draumar uppvaknar.

(112) 74. Dei som fere Eikjaråsen,
dei fara mæ Tút å Skrål;
men dei som fara Jólehylen,
dei fara mæ tunge Mål.
Månen skíne å Vegjinne fedde så víe.

The above text is based on Sophus Bugge's original MS as far as this goes, but pp. 127 and 130ff. (stanzas 41–8 and 56–74) are missing. The complete text is preserved in his fair copy, and this is used here to supplement the original where it is defective. The breaks in the original are marked in this edition by horizontal lines.

Variant readings: Bugge included a number of variant readings in his fair copy, but several of these came from other informants and do not thus properly belong in M6. There remain a few for which no source is given and which therefore presumably came from Anne herself, although they are not found in the original. These are: 16.1 for den, som den sko' gange *(possibly not a variant, written above* å gange *in pencil in square brackets, but not marked* var.*)*; 19.4 av *written above* fyrr *and the two words bracketed together*; 27.2 dæ blandast alt í dæ sama. *(marked* var.*)*; 27.4 eg tiss dæ så líti Gama. *(marked* var.*)*; 28.3 så æ' eg oddu glaeste *(marked* var.*)*.

Alterations: 16.1 Tu *written over* Sa; 17.3 æ *of* ræast *altered from* e; 21.3 k. *expanded to* kje; 23.2 mæ *altered from* me; 26.1 D *altered from* d; 26.3 ø *of* møtte *altered from* å; 29.3 pa *written before* dei, *but crossed out*; 32.1 knapp *first written* knatt, *but* tt *crossed out and* pp *written above*; 33.4 kunna *altered from* kunne*(?)*; løyse *altered from* løse; 34.3 ræast *first written* ræddast, *but* dd *crossed through*; 36.1 Eg *altered from* Je; 39.2 dei *written before* grumme, *but crossed out*; 39.3 *first word originally* fram, *but crossed out and* så *written above*; kjeme *altered from* kom; 40.3 eg *written before* fekk, *but crossed out*; 46.3 Skarlakskåpa *first written* Skarlaksskåpa, *but second* s *crossed out*; 50.2 *first word originally* de *(*dæ*?)*, *but crossed out and* eitt *written above*; *before* Skógesnar *is a single* S *which has not been crossed out*; 58.2 g *written before* fara, *but crossed out*; 66.2 *final word originally* Sút, *but crossed out and* Harm *written above*; 66.4 Ha *written before* Savn, *but crossed out*; 68.2 klare Grunnar *underlined apparently with different ink from that in the text, but seemingly the same as Bugge used to write some of the notes and variant readings*; 70.2 myrke Hús *underlined: the underlining is in pencil as are a number of Bugge's notes and comments*; *both underlinings seem to refer to notes in the margin.*

Other notes on the MS:

1. 6.4 *Vengjir* could read *Vengjer* (cf. also 25.4); 14.3 *dær* could read *Dær*; 55.3 *støste* could read *støsti.*

2. It is occasionally difficult to distinguish a comma from a full stop. In such cases a comma is printed after ll.1, 2 and 3 and a stop after l.4.

3. The stanza numbering 1–40 and 49–55 does not occur in the original MS and has been added by the editor (all stanzas are numbered in the fair copy); the separation of stanzas and lines is clear throughout.

4. The fair copy contains a number of notes. Opposite the heading (' "Draukveen". VII.') and stanza 1 Bugge has written: 'A very distorted but extremely interesting variant.' 'The order of the last six lines uncertain according to her [Anne Skaalen's] own statement.' 'Anne is unreliable and untruthful. She may well have made up a few things herself here and there.' ('Meget forkvaklet, men særdeles mærkelig Optegnelse.' 'Versordenen i sidste 6 Linier efter hendes eget Sigende ikke sikker.' 'Anne er upaalidelig og ikke sanddru: hun kan vel have lavet noget hist og her paa egen Haand.') Under the heading there appears the name of the informant, Anne Skaalen, and then the following which has been crossed out: 'who had learnt it [*Draukveen*] from Hallvor Bjaaen of Bykle, born in Vinje' ('som havde lært den af Hallvor Bjaaen i Bykle, født i Vinje'). There are explanatory notes to 1.3 *Åknesi*: 'A man in Vinje: (Olav) *Aasnesi*, that was the name, he said, of a farm on Raulandstranden' ('En Mand i Vinje: (Olav) *Aasnesi*, saa hed, sagde han, en Gaard paa Raulandstranden'); 15.3 *Gaglemýranne*: 'The informant took this to be swamps, the home of birds who like the other beasts torment Olav' ('Kvædersken opfattede det som: Myrer, hvor Fugle holde til, der ligesom de andre Udyr plage Olav'); 24.2 *Skålestrånd*: 'Said to be the name of a place on Raulandstranden' ('Saa skal et Sted hede paa Raulandstranden'). Bugge's many comments on the text in his fair copy have been omitted.

5. Near the top of p. 128 in Bugge's original, amongst one or two notes and ballad titles, we find: 'Anne Skaalen Mo, Draumkvæen'. The title of Anne's variant is thus given three different forms by Bugge: *Draugkveen* (original), *Draukveen* (fair copy) and *Draumkvæen*.

6. An attempt has been made to follow Bugge in his use of accents. This has not, however, been done in the case of *i* in the original, since it is not always possible to distinguish an accent from a dot in this MS.

L4

Dromkvæen

(1) 1. Vi du mæg Lye eg Qvæa Kan
alt om dei Kaate Drænjr
Alt om en Olav Aakneson
som Sove heve sa Lænje
Maanen Skjn aa vejne dei falle vie

(5) 2. Eg la meg ne om Joleftan
Sterkan Svevnen eg Fek
eg vakna kie fe om Trettandajen
Folkje te Kjørkjune gek

(18) 3. Eg vakna kje fe om Trettan dajen
soli ho Rye i lie
daa salar Olav ut Fjottan Folen
aa vil at Kjørkjune Rie

(34) 4. Presten han sto fe Altaren
aa las up Textine sine
Olav Aakneson stend i Kjørkje dynni
fortele Droumane sine

(76) 5. Eg Hæve vore baate up mæ Sky
aa neat mæ Havsens bonnar
den som mine Fotspor vi Fye
han lær Kje af blie monar

(39) 6. De va mæ den Fyste utreisi
eg drog i giænom tøner Ring
sonde lout mi Skarlags Kaapa
Aa nagelen af kvor min Fing

(41) 7. De va mæ den Andre utreisi
eg drog igienem tønner mog
sonde lout mi Skarlags Kaapa
Aa ny e Heimate for

(122) 8. Kiæm eg mæg at manne dei
de blei mæg daa Fyste ve
Lite baan i Fanie bar
Giek i Jori alt unde Kne

(129) 9. Kjæm eg meg at mann dei
ha Hændan utav blo
Herregud søndige saaline
hae Flutte deild i Skog

(134) 10. Kjæm eg mæg at Podda Aa ormmen
dei Hoie verandre i Skjæfte
de va sandeleg Syskjni
dei vil hinaen nægte

(132) 11. Kjæm eg mæg at bonno dei
di Stoge so Høgt paa Gloe
Herre gud søndige Saaline
dei ha bana bort Faer Aa Moer

(101) 12. Kjæm eg mæg at Jeddar broi
ho Hænge so Høgt i vinde
ho va Fast mæ krokar sleji
Aa nagle mæ Kvorjom tinde

(98) 13. Bikia beit aa ormen Stak
Aa stuten Sto aa stanga
eg slap ikje af Jedarbroi
fe domane dei kom vraange

(160) 14. Her Kjæm i fær her sonnate
Aa den Rei naa so tvist
fyri Rei St. saale Mikjel
Ete kom Jesom Christ

(157) 15. He Kjæm ei Fær her Norate
den Rei naa so Qvast
Fyri Rei Grutte graasiæje
alt mæ sin svarte Hat

(105) 16. Gjænje Hev eg Jedarbroi
ho Tose uponde Skyi hange
vassa hev eg vossemyran
Aa vejne falle lange

(143) 17. Sæl æ den i denne Heimen
den Fatike gjæve Klæi
han tar inkje i Annom Heimen
Qvorkjen bibre hel siæve

(150) 18. Sæl æ den i denne Heimen
den Fatike giæve kon
han tar inkje i Anom heimmen
Rædas fe Stuttehon

(147) 19. Sæl æ den i denne Heimen
den Fatike giæve Sko
han tar inkje bærføte gange
i Qvase Tynermo

(119) 20. Kjæm eg mæg at Pilegrims Kjørkje
der va meg injen man kjænd
bare mi goe Gudmoer
mæ Rødegulband ikring hænde

(118) 21. Kiæm eg mæg te Pilegrims Kjørkje
der va meg injn man go
bare mi snille Gudmoer
ho gav meg nye Sko

(116) 22. Kjæm eg meg at votno dei
der isanne brone blaa
gud Skout mæg so got i Hujen
eg vænte meg derifraa

(115) 23. Rest eg mæg paa betlarstyen
eg vente meg paa mi Høgre haand
daa saag Eg ini Paradis
utivi dei vene Laand

(152) 24. Sæl æ den i denne Heimen
den Fattike gieve brou
han tar inke Rædas i Anom heimen
for store Hondegoul
Maanen Skjn Aa vejne falle vie

Alterations: 1.refr. *a* u *appears between* j *and* n *of* vejne, *but seems to have been crossed out*; 6.1 De *altered from* Eg; 7.4 e *altered from* æ; 8.1 manne *altered to* manno *by Landstad who also added a fresh* e *above* o; 10.2 oggje *written above* oie *by Landstad*; 10.4 n *of* nægte *underlined by Landstad*; 12.1 æ *of* mæg *altered from* e*(?)*; 14.2 tvist *underlined by Landstad*; 16.3 e *of* hev *altered from imperfectly formed* æ*(?)*; 22.1 *comma added by Landstad after* dei; 22.2 brone *altered to* bronne *by Landstad*; *comma added by Landstad after* blaa; 23.1 betlarstyen *altered to* betlarstigjen *by Landstad.*

Other notes on the MS:

1. It is very difficult to distinguish between *L* and *l* and *G* and *g*. In the case of *g* a capital is printed if the letter is somewhat larger than the other *g*s in a given stanza.

2. The stanza numbering 1–24 does not occur in the MS and has been added by the editor; the separation of stanzas, though not lines, is clear throughout.

3. *Njupe Tøn* (wild rose) written above *tøner* in 6.2 by Landstad, presumably as an explanation.

4. A note by Landstad on the first page of the MS attributes the variant to Anne Lillegaard.

5. L4 does not appear to have been written in haste. It may therefore be a fair copy, or it may be the result of slow and careful work with Anne Lillegaard.

L6

(Draumkvæi)

(5) 1. Olav la' seg ne um joleftá'en
sterken svevnen han fekk
han vakna 'kje førr um 13 dagjen
folkje i kyrkja gjekk.
På Åmlivollen der sko' dómen stande.

(34) 2. Presten stend på predikstolen
utlegg han tekstin*n*e sine,
Ó. stend i kyrkjedynni
fortel drauman*n*e sine

(93) 3. Som eg kom ette haddanbrúi
der va' den gnýren mange,
ormanne hoggje å bikkjunne beit
å stóre stúten den stanga.

(150) 4. Sæl æ' dei i den*n*e heimen
dei fatike gjeva konn,
dei tar 'kje i den anen heim
å ræddas for stútehonn.

(152) 5. Sæl— brau; —hundegau—

(149) 6. Sæl— skó, —før den haddanbrú.

(107) 7. Som eg kom meg te haddanbrúi
den va' bratt å brei,
gjengji hev eg Vågslimýrann
sluppi hev eg dei

(123) 8. Som eg kom meg te manni der
då blei eg fyste grý,
han bar på glóands jórtorvun*ne*e
å gjekk mæ ei kåpe av blý.

(130) 9. Så æ' de i denne heimen
de snakar jór av andre,
so må dei i den anen heimen
lie so stór en vande.

(122) 10. Då eg kom meg te manni der,
då blei eg fyste ve,
han– — torvunne
å gjekk i jóri te knés.

(130) 11. So æ' de — snakar skóg—

(76) 12. Eg hev vori uppunde skýi
å neatt på havsens bunni
den som mine fótspor sko' trøa
den lær 'kje av glae munni

(117) 13. Som eg kom meg te isen der,
den va' brunnen blå,
Gud skaut de i hugjen min
eg kom der inkje utpå.

(138) 14. Som eg kom meg te silkjesen/gji
den va' væl uppreidd,
der låg i dei festarfolkji
i festingji ha' dei døytt.

Alterations: 1.3 vakna *altered from* vakne; ø *of* førr *altered from* y; 1.4 då *written before* folkje, *but crossed out*; 6 dd *of* haddanbrú *altered from* ll*(?)*; 7.1 meg te *altered from* ette *(cf.* 3.1*)*; 12.2 neatt *altered from* nel*(?)*; 13.1 kom *added above line with a sign indicating its position.*

Other notes on the MS:
1. 7.3 *Vågslimýrann* may read *Vågslimýrane*; 12.2 *neatt* may read *neætt*, the third letter resembles *æ* more than *a*, but this may be due to an attempt to smother the *l*(?) over which it is written.

2. The stanza numbering 1–14 does not occur in the MS and has been added by the editor; the separation of stanzas and lines is clear throughout.

3. Over the word *grý* in 8.2 appear the words *ikke ellers* (not otherwise); in Bugge's fair copy of L6 this remark is expanded: 'the informant did not otherwise know this word' ('Kvædersken kjendte ikke ellers dette Ord').

4. An attempt has been made to follow Bugge in his use of accents. This has not, however, been done in the case of *i* since it is not always possible to distinguish an accent from a dot.

5. The text of L6 printed above is from Bugge's original MS.

K1

Draumekvæi (40 Vers)

Vil du mæg høire etc.
Af Marn Ramskeid

(2) 1. Olaf han va i Voxtern
han va som ein Selljuronne
Far aa Mor dei ont en væl
ifra en tala konne.

(3) 2. Olaf han va i Voxtern
han va som ein Seljuteine
Fair aa Moir dei ont ho væl
fraa en kom i denni Heimen.

(5) 3. Han la sæg ne om Jolæftansqvællen
den stærkan Svevnen fæk
han vakna inkje før om Trettandagjen
daa Folkje i Kjyrkjun gjæk
Aa dæ va Olaf Aaknesonen som sove hæve saa længje.

(16) 4. Han vakna kje før om Tr. dagjen
daa Solli ran i Li
Idag vil æg te Kjyrkjune
fortællje vil æg Draumo mi.
Dæ va o. s. v.

(17) 5. Han vakna kje før om Tr Dagjen
daa Soli ran i Lie
daa salar han ut fljotan Folen
aa la paa dei forgjylte Milir.
Dæ va o. s. v.

(36) 6. No stænde du før Altraren
aa læg ut Texten din
saa stænde æg i Kjyrkjedynni
fortællje vil æg Dramæn min.

Æg drøimde

(39) 7. Fyst va æg i Uttexti
æg for ivi Dyrering
sonde va mi Skarlakens kaape
aa Neglan a kvor min Fing
For Maanen skjine aa Vægjene fadde saa vie

(40) 8. Saa va æg i Uttexti
æg for ivi Dyretraa
sonde va mi Sk. kaape
aa Neglan a kvor mi Ta.

(94) 9. Aa Gjeddarbroi den æ vond
aa inkje go aa gange
Bikkjune bite aa Ormane sting
aa Stutæne stænd aa stangar.
For Maanen skjine etc.

(135) 10. Der saag æg dei Ormane tvei
dei hoggje kvorare i Kjæfte
aa dæ va Syskjenboni i denni Heimen
dei mone kvorare ægte.

(109) 11. Æg hæv gjængje Voxmyren
dæ hæv kje stai mæg nokon Grund,
No hæv æg gjængje Gjeddarbroi
mæ rapa Mod i Mun.

(147) 12. Sæl æ dei i Foesheimen
den Fattike gjæve Skor
han tar no inkje bærføtte gange
paa kvasse Heklemoe.

(149) 13. Aa sæl æ dæn i F
dæn Fattige gjæve Rug
han tar inkje somloug gange
paa hoge Gjeddar Bru.

(150) 14. Aa sæl saa æ en i F
den Fattike gjæve Kaan
han tar inkje ræddas paa Gjeddarbroi
fe kvasse Stute Hon

(145) 15. Sæl æ dei i Føesheimen
den Fattike gjæve Brau
han tar inkje ræddas i andre Heimen
fe lie noko Nau.

(142) 16. Sæl æ den i F
den Fattike gjæve Klæi
han tar inkje ræddas i annen Heimen
anten for Spot hel Hæi.

(116) 17. Saa tok æg paa ein Vetters Ti
der Isæne vore blaa
men Gud skaut dæ i Hugjen min
æg vendte der ifraa.

(115) 18. Saa tok æg paa ei Vetters Ti
alt paa mi Høgre Haand
saa saag æg ne te Paradiis
der lyser ivi vie Laand.

(119) 19. Saa saag æg mæg te Paradiis
dæ mone mæg inkje bære hænde
der kjænde æg atte Gudmo mi
mæ røde Gul paa Hænde

(120) 20. Saa saag æg atte Gudmo mi
dæ mone mæg kje bete gange:
reis du dæg te Broksvalin
fe der sko Domen stande.
Maanen skjine aa Vegjine fadde saa vie

(126) 21. Saa mødte æg Mannen,
aa Kaapa den va Blo
han bar eit Barn onde sin Arm
i Jori han gjæk te Knio
I Broksvalin der sko Domen stande.

(124) 22. Saa møte æg ein Man,
Kaapa den va af Bly
dæ va honoms arme Sjæl i denne Heimen
va trang i dyre Ti
I Broksvalin—

(158) 23. Der kom Færi norate
dæ tottes æg væra værst
fyry rei Grutte Graaskjæggje
han rei paa svartan Hest.
I Broksvalin etc.

(160) 24. Saa kom den Færi sonnate
dæ tottes mæg væra bedst
fyry rei sancte Saale-Mechael
aa næste Jesum Christ.—
I Broksvalin der sko Domen stande.

(161) 25. Saa kom den Færi sonnate
ho tosse me væra traa
aa fyry rei St. Saale Mechael
aa Luren onde Armen laag.
I Broksvalin

(162) 26. Dæ va St Saale Mechael
han blæs i Luren den lange
aa no sko alle Synde-Sjæline
fram fe Domen stande.

(164) 27. Men daa skolv alle Synde Sjæline
som Aaspelauv for Vinde
aa kvor den, kvor den Sjæl der va
dei gret for Syndine sine.
I Broksvalin—

(165) 28. Og det var St. sále Mikkjel
han vóg med skálevigt
sá vóg han alle syndesjælene
hen til Jesum Krist.

(167) 29. Saa vaagnede jeg den Trettende
omtrent ved Midnatstid
aa Gud bevare En og Her
for at vandre i saadan Tid
Dæ va Olaf Aakneson som sove hæve saa længje

(168) 30. Saa vaagner jeg om Trettandagjen
af den lange Søvne
det er en Sjælefristelse
at falde i saadan Drømme.
Aa dæ va etc.

Variant readings: 1.1 Voxtern: Voxtrun; vene *added above line after* Voxtern, *but cf. Landstad (1853), p. 84*; 6.1 Gak no dæg te; 6.2 din: dine; 6.4 aa fortæle Dr mine.; 13.3 gange: væra; 19.3 Gudmo: Gulmo.

Alterations: 1.3 æ *of* væl *altered from* e*(?)*; 5.4 r *of* Milir *underlined and* e *added in margin*; 16.1 den *altered from* dei; 17.3 Hugjen *written* Hgjen *and attempt made to insert* u, *mainly recognisable by diacritic mark*; 17.4 at *written before* æg, *but crossed out*; 21.2 Blo *altered from* blaa*(?)*; 22.2 Bly *altered from* Blo; 25.1 *first* a *of* Saa *written over* de; 25.2 h *of* ho *altered from* d; 27.4 sine *written between* for *and* Syndine, *but crossed out*; 29.1 vakna æg *written first, but crossed out and replaced by* vaagnede jeg *above the line*; 30.2 S *altered from* s.

Other notes on the MS:
1. 7.heading *drøimde* may read *droimde*, there is no stroke above or through the *o*, but one precedes it; 7.*refr.* final *a* of *saa* is difficult to read; 9.3 *Ormane* may read *Ormæne*; 21.4 *æ* of *gjæk*, altered from *j*, may read *e*; 22.4 *trang* may read *trong*, it is sometimes difficult to distinguish between *a* and *o* in the MS; 24.3, 25.3, 26.1 *Mechael* may read

Michael, *i* and *e* can often only be distinguished by the presence or absence of a dot, and this is not used consistently.

2. Between 5 and 6 the sign > appears in the left-hand margin, and between 16 and 17 in the right-hand margin; a line separates 20 and 21, 22 and 23 and 27 (28) and 29 and also occurs after the final stanza.

3. 28 is added below the final stanza and a note, and its position after 27 indicated by a cross; this stanza and the words 'Af Marn Ramskeid' at the beginning are written in a different colour ink from the rest of the MS and were presumably added later, considerably later (after 1846) judging by the etymological spelling of 28.

4. The stanza numbering 1–30 does not occur in the MS and has been added by the editor; the separation of stanzas and lines is clear throughout.

5. Landstad's attempts to explain difficult words in the text have been omitted.

6. After the final stanza there is a note which says: 'By Maren Ramskei, learnt from her father, Ole Gulliksen Ramskei who died 15 years ago, 77 years old. He learnt it from his father' ('af Maren Ramskei lært af sin Fader Ole Gulliksen Ramskei død for 15 Aar siden 77 Aar gl – han lært den af sin Far').

7. It is difficult to say for certain whether K1 is an original MS written down in the field, or a fair copy. It is much more carefully written than Sophus Bugge's originals, but nevertheless contains a fair number of alterations and improvements. The addition of stanza 28 indicates that Landstad heard Maren sing *Draumekvæi* more than once, but it is hard to tell whether the reference to 'forty stanzas' in the top right-hand corner of the first page, the sub-title(?): *Vil du mæg høire etc.*, and the marginal signs > are later additions, made as Landstad began to construct a text of *Dr* for *Norske Folkeviser*, or whether Maren did at some time sing forty different stanzas of the ballad for him, the first of which began *Vil du mæg høire*. On the whole the former seems more likely, since Landstad would surely not have neglected to write any additional stanzas down, particularly from an informant he prized so highly, and they would then have been added to K1 as was stanza 28. With the exception of this stanza the MS could be contemporary with Landstad's first visit to Maren, but should in this case probably be seen as the final result of a number of sessions with her.

K9

Lidt af Draumkvæde.

(5) 1. Olav la seg om Joleftan,
han sterkan Svevnen fek;
han vakna 'kje før hell om Trettandajen
Folkje i Kjyrkjunne jek.

(19) 2. Han vakna 'kje før hell om Trettandajen
Soli skjein i Stette
saa sala Olav sin Gangare graa
aa resste te Kjyrkja ette

(34) 3. Prèsten sto paa Predikstolen
aa lae ut Tekstinne sine.
Aa Olav sto i Kjyrkedynni
aa fortalde av Draumane sine

(128) 4. Eg saag naa dei, som jek omkring
aa vaddi Jori under Knè
Gud bère dei syndige Saalinne
sin Gud dei kjende ikje te

(107) 5. Eg hev jengji Jeddarbrui
ho e baate brat aa brei
vat saa heve eg Vaasmyrane
aa sluppe heve eg dei

(101) 6. Eg heve jengji Jeddarbrui
ho henge saa haagt me Vinde
ho er all me Jønno slejen
aa ein Krok paa kvòr den Tinde.

(97) 7. Ormen stak aa Paadda beit
aa Stuten stend aa stangar
Den som vi gange Jeddarbrui,
den maa'kje vera banga.

Variant readings: 4.2 under: onder, o *added above* u; 4.3 syndige: søndige, ø *added above* y.

Alterations: 1.4 y *of* Kjyrkjunne *altered from* o *or possibly* ø; 2.4 y *of* Kjyrkja *altered from* ø; 3.3 y *of* Kjyrkedynni *altered from* o; 4.3 inne *of* Saalinne *expanded from* in; 4.4 sin *first written* sig, *but* g *crossed out and* n *written after it*; G *written after* ikje, *but crossed out*; 6.2 *second* a *and* g *of* haagt *altered from* g *and incomplete* t; 7.2 den *written after* Stuten, *but crossed out*.

Other notes on the MS:

1. The stanza numbering 1–7 does not occur in the MS and has been added by the editor; the separation of stanzas and lines is clear throughout.

2. 7.2 *Stuten* is interpreted in a note: 'That signifies a lot of wicked people' ('De betyr mange vrange Folk, de'). A postscript states: 'Tone does not consider that stanzas 8,

9 and 10 in Landstad A belong to the ballad. She remembers that her father had *Draumkvæde* on large sheets of paper (almost three quarters in length) which were rolled up. However, with continual use they went to pieces. Olaf Okneson was the name of the lad.' ('Vers 8, 9, 10 i Landstads No. A. mener Tone ikke hører til. [new§] Hun mindes, at Faren havde Draumkvæde paa store Papirer (næsten 3 Kvarter lange), som blev rullede sammen; men paa Grund af megen Brug gik de istykker. [new§] Olaf Okneson hedte Gutten.')

3. It is difficult to tell whether or not K9 is an original. It is neatly written, but contains a number of alterations. These may, however, have been made necessary by careless copying.

T3

(76) 1. Æg hev vore uponde Skjye—grunnar

—————————

—oddar

—————————

(101) 2. Æg hev fari ivi Gjeddarbroi
ho ligge sá høgt i vinde—
den var med jonni slæjæn
aa Spiker i kvor ein Tinde.

(102) 3. aa gulli er etter Straumo lagt
og tann etter kvorjum Tillje.

(100) 4. Æg hev fare ivi G. B.
der er sá farleg ein Gang
den som einki dømer domane ret
han kjæm der aldrig fram.

(98) 5. Bikkja bit etc
som dømer domane vrange.

(108) 6. Æg hev fari G. B.
den er báte hág og breid
vassa hev eg dei Vásmyran
og endá sá kom eg heim.

Variant readings: oddar *is written immediately below* grunnar *in MS, but the dash preceding it indicates repetition of the whole stanza (with rhyme word* loddar, *cf. V1a,34)*; 3.1–2 *are begun between* 2.2, 3 *and* 4, *but extend beyond these into the margin: the dash after* vinde *suggests repetition of* 2.1–2 *rather than the status of variant reading for* 3.1–2.

Alterations: 1 j *of* Skjye *added after word was written*; 2.2 in *of* vinde *altered from* ei*(?)*; 2.4 v *of* kvor *altered from* o.

Other notes on the MS:

1. 1 *u* and first *n* of *grunnar* appear to be run together; 3.2 *tann* may read *Saum*, the first letter resembles *S* more than *t*, but the final two letters can only read *nn* or *un*, unless the last stroke of *u* and first of *m* have been run together (cf. 1 *grunnar*); 4.3 first letter of *den* consists of two strokes slanting upward from left to right, the inner stroke is shorter and the two seem to be an imperfectly formed *d*; it is sometimes difficult to distinguish between capital and small letters and it is possible that 1 *grunnar*, non-*Dr* stanza *oddar* and 4.3 *domane* should read *Grunnar*, *Oddar*, *Domane*.

2. The stanzas are not numbered in the MS and this feature has been added by the editor (*—oddar* is omitted from the numbering since it is not considered to represent a *Dr* stanza, cf. Section 3.1); apart from what has already been noted about *—oddar* and 3.1–2 the separation of stanzas and lines is clear throughout.

3. At the bottom of the page after stanza 6 there is a large L, indicating that the MS was written by Landstad.

4. T3 has every appearance of being an original.

T8

(25) 1. Eg drak ejn Dreyk om Joleftaen
for Folkej fek seg Madt
dæ, kjenner eg paa Brono-mine
at dette fjasar Adt.—

(26) 2. Eg Drak ejn Dryk af Sløkjefri
den jore meg soe lejt.
eg lae meg nepaa aa- Sovna
soe ondeleg Droum eg fek.—

(5) 3. Eg la meg te Sova om Joleftaen
eg Sterke Svevnen fek
æg Vaknakje før om Trettandagjen
daa Folkje i Kyrkja gjek.—

(8) 4. Vakkre deg Olav Aasteson
no heve du sove lænje
Folkje heve i Kjørkja geengje
aa Fuglan heve stilt sine Vejengjer.—

(83) 5. Thii heve fare fort fe meg
eg heve Vore i Verden Vie
eg heve sedt hejte Helvete
aa jen deel af Him*m*erikje

Alterations: 1.3 dæ *altered from* da*(?)*; 2.1 af *added above line*; 2.4 Droum *first written* Drom, *but* u *added above line*; 3.3 Vakna *altered from* Vakne*(?)*; 3.4 Kyrkja *altered from* Kyrkje*(?)*; 5.1 fe *altered from* fo.

Other notes on the MS:

1. 1.3 the line after *Brono* may be a dash rather than a hyphen, cf. 2.3; 3.3 first letter of *æg* is very difficult to read, but resembles *æ* more than anything else; 4.3 *geengje* may read *genngje*.

2. The stanza numbering 1–5 is found in the MS; the stanzas are not separated into lines, and this feature has been added by the editor.

3. It is difficult to tell whether or not T8 is an original. The writing appears slow and spidery rather than fast and clumsy, and the MS is neatly separated into five stanzas. However there are several mistakes (chiefly those giving rise to the alterations noted above) and two cases of transposition (1.2 *Folkej* and 5.4 *jen*) as well as the odd *Vejengjer* (4.4) which may have occurred because the writer at first forgot *ng* and failed to cross out *ej* when he noticed his mistake and completed the word properly.

Individual stanzas from a number of variants

(80) V8,1. Eg hev vore uppunde Skjy
aa av ne paa Havi svarte;
den som vi mine Fotspor fygje,
maa inkji have Kaave hjarta.

(96) V8,2. Ormen sting aa Bikkja bit
aa Stuten stend aa stangar;
mi slepp 'kji ive den Gjallarbrui,
fe Draugann' e so mange.

(103) V9,7. Eg hev gjengji Gjalarbroì,
aa der va' krokane paa,
verre va' dei gaglemyrane
Gud bære den dei skò gaa.

---

(99) V ?12,1. Bikkja bit'e aa òrmen steng'e
aa stuten han stend aa stangar.
De gjeng engjen te endes paa Gjaddarbrui
fòr der æ fòr mange taggar.

---

(20) M9a,7. Hesten min stende på Nórnesi
han æ blakk'e på den eine sía
han tar ikkje beisli hava
hi han æ' då so hǿg å ríe

(88) M9a,9. Eg hev— [fari meg uppte mæ å]
å ne mæ en bergestein,
Gud råde no fy mínom færi,
eg ha snært 'kji hitta heim

---

(85) M14,1. Eg hev vore i Himerik
sæl han, som kom der inn
der va allting so blankt
og mange rare Ting.

---

(62) M15b,3. Eg va meg eigong på Bjærdingens hald
eg strei der mæ ei løve,
løva trådde meg under seg
å reiv meg mæ sine kløver.

---

(110) M20,1. Sume fér'e øystrevegjen
å sume Skålestrònde
å sume fér'e Gjæddarbróé
dei fér ikkjé alt so fórt,
dei kåma kji att'e førr um trettandagjen,
når me hava drukkjé ei ònó jól.

---

(22) F1,2. So sala eg ut hesten min
o ville ăt kjyrkjunne rie
o då eg kom meg på vegjen fram
skjein solæ langt nedaa lìå.

---

(35) L1,2. Presten sto for Altaren
Les up Textine sine
Olaf Haakenson stænd i Kjyrkedynne
Fortæle han Draumane vie.

(106) L1,16. Gjængje saa hæv e Gjæddarbroe
O tost 'ponde Skye Hange
Aa vassa saa hæv eg Vaassemyrane
Vægane faldt saa vrange

---

(131) L3,5. Daa kom æg meg te Maanno dei
Dei vrei sine Hænder i Blo
Gud naae dei fattike Saaline
Som her kun' for Ronine raa

---

(113) L10a,1. Aa some fere Geitarheii
Aa some Skaalestraand
Men dei som fere Jolehylen,
[dei] koma vaate fraa.

---

(81) L12,3. Eg hev vore høgt uppunder skjy
o ne att i jupe dalar.
O trøst o bære den arme mann
som i mine fotspor ska fara.

---

(141) K2,4. sæl æ' dæn i denne Heimen
dæn Fatike gjeve Mat.
Han tar 'kje ræddas i anen Heimen
anten før Spott hell Hat.

---

(136) K3,3. Eg kom meg te sýslehúse
der va' sýslinne inne,
de tótte eg va' allefælaste,
í raue blóe di kinna.

(127) K3,5. 'Eg ha' meg eigång eitt líte bån,
eg ville 'kje mæ dæ kanne
derfor må eg i denne heimen
líe den stóre vande.

---

(125) K5,11. [S]aa kom eg til Mannen den
Kappa va [g]jord af Blo
de æ den stoste Sond som æ te
aa myre Mannen i Skog.

(163) K5,20. De va Sante Sæle Mekkjel
han bles i Luen den Lange
Dei ska fram alle Sjæline
fe Dommen skaa dei gange

(166) K5,21. De va Sante Sæle Mekkjel
han blæste i Skaalevekt
dei skaa vek alle Sjælene
he[n] ti Hemmerik.

---

(4) S6,2. [Olaf han var i voxtro (véne)
han var som ein] liljurunni
[faðir og moðir ant 'om vel]
så lengje han í heimen ha vori

(133) S6,8. dær såg eg dei ormanne tvo,
dei hogge kvarandre í tanne;
dæ sill vera dei syskini,
som ha kverandre burtbanna.

---

(23) N1,4. Daa 'n kaam te kjørkja fram
batt 'n sin hest i stettì.
Alle som visst' han i dròumo ha legje
paa haannom ville deì helse

---

(159) T5,4. Der kom Færi sonnate
de tottes æg væra bedst
fyri rei Sancte Saale Mechael
han rei paa kvitan Hest.

---

(121) T6,1. Eg var meg i Anheimen
i mange nettar og trá
ded veit Gud i himerik
hossi mang ei naud eg ság.

---

(137) Sæl,1. Dei rei yvi Dømmingfossen,
aa der stoge Keddingann' kinna;
der sveitta dei det kalde Bloi;
det var so tong ei Vinna.—

---

(53) By1,2. E[g va meg me Gaglemyre]
Der gjor aa saa vondt eit Veir
Kjeddigje [laante meg Øyro si]
Elles meine eg, eg ha døytt.

---

(7) By2,1. Eg la meg ne um Joleptdagjen,
de va i so go 'n Timi;
eg vakkna 'kji fyrr um trettande Dagjen,
daa Fokkji at Kyrkja vi rie.

Alterations and variant readings: V9,7.3 *first written* men eg totte ve, *but this crossed out and the existing* l.3 *written below it*; M9a,9.3 råde *altered from* rå'e; fy *first written* for, *but* o *altered to* y *and* r *apparently crossed out*; M15b,3.2 løve *altered from* løvr*(?)*; 3.3 u *of* under *altered from* o*(?)*; M20,1.3 *note on* Gjæddarbróé*:* opgav isteden også: Jóleh$\overset{ø}{\text{y}}$len *([The informant] also used [the word]* Jóleh$\overset{ø}{\text{y}}$len *instead)*; 1.5 kj *of* kji *altered from* ik; F1,2.3 me*(?) written before* o, *but crossed out*; L1,2.1 Altaren *underlined and* Predikstolen *added after it, presumably as variant reading*; 2.2 Textine *altered from* Lexune*(?)*; 2.3 Kjy *of* Kjyrkedynne *begun as* Ko*(?)*, j *added and* o *given tail to form* y*(?)*; 2.4 D *of* Draumane *altered from* d*(?)*; 16.1 a *of* Gjæddarbroe *altered from* e; 16.3 o *written above* aa *of* Vaassemyrane *with a sign indicating its position (in place of* aa*?)*; 16.4

el. (Domane faldt saa mange) *written below this line as variant reading*; L3,5.3 syndige *written above* fattike, *presumably as variant reading*; L12,3.1 r *of* uppunder *underlined and apparently later addition*; 3.4 ska *altered from* sko; K2,4.3 M *written before* Heimen, *but crossed out*; K5,11.3 aa *written after* Sond, *but crossed out*; 20.1 S *of* Sante *altered from* s; 21.4 ti *first written* til, *but* l *crossed out*; S6,8.2 *first* a *of* kvarandre *altered from* e; T5,4.4 (næste Jesum Christ) *(S.160) written above this line, possibly as variant reading, cf. Section 3.2, p. 83*; By1,2.2 gjor aa *first written as one word, but divided by vertical line*; 2.3 o *of* Øyro *altered from* e.

Other notes on the MSS:

1. V8 the text is that found in Skar 3,5; V ?12,1 a large L (= Landstad ? fifty ?) written in l.1 before *b* of *bit'e*; M9a,7.3 *ikkje* could read *ikkji*, final letter has shape of *i*, but no dot; 7.4 *hi* may have been written in mistake for *ha* and not subsequently crossed out, it is otherwise difficult to explain; 9.3 *æ* of *færi* underlined, apparently for stress reasons; M14,1.1 *vore* could read *vori*; 1 this stanza was written first in pencil and subsequently in ink in such a way that ll.2–4 of the ink version cover ll.1–3 of the pencil version, making the latter very difficult to read with any accuracy: for this reason the ink version is followed here; M15b,3.1 *Bjærdingens hald* underlined and *Bjærtinggjens* written above *Bjærdingens* and bracketed together with this; 3.4 *kløver* underlined with reference to note in margin: *tostavelses* (tone two); M20,1.4 and 6 *ikkjé* and *drukkjé* could read *ikkji* and *drukkji*, cf. however l.3 *Gjæddarbróé*; L10a,1.4 the word *dei* is no longer visible owing to a tear at the edge of the page and has been supplied by the editor; L10a the text is that found in Ross 3,76; K2 the text is that found in Bugge's original MS; K3,3.1 *(trollkjeringh.)* (witches' house) written under *sýslehúse* by way of explanation; 5.2 *(svara dæ fra dæ)* — first *dæ* added above line — written above line as an explanation, possibly in mistake for *svara for dæ* (take responsibility for it); K3 the text is that found in Bugge's original MS; K5,11.1 and 2 and 21.4 the letters in square brackets are no longer visible owing to wear at the edges of the pages and have been supplied by the editor; T5,4.3 *Mechael* could read *Michael*; Sæ1 the text is that found in Skar 2,3; By1,2.1 and 3 these lines consist of the letter and word printed and a long horizontal stroke, indicating that ll.1 and 3 of the preceding stanza are to be repeated: in 3 this stroke has (inadvertently ?) been run through the *gje* of *Kjeddigje*; By2 the text is that found in Skar 3,21.

2. In the MSS words and/or lines may often be omitted from a stanza since the reading can be inferred from the preceding stanza or stanzas. In the two cases above where this occurs (M9a,9, By1,2) the missing text is supplied from the preceding stanza and placed in square brackets. In S6,2 Bugge has simply written *liljurunni* and *så lengje han í heimen ha vori* by stanza 3 of Landstad A in his copy of *Norske Folkeviser*. The words in square brackets are therefore Landstad's text.

3. Diacritic marks: an attempt is made to follow the usage in each MS where this is reasonably clear.

4. The language of Draumkvæde

The form of Norwegian found in most texts of *Draumkvæde* is the dialect of western Telemark as it was about a hundred years ago (a few fragments come from Sætesdal of which Sæ1, By1 and By2 are printed wholly or partially in this edition). It is coloured to a greater or lesser degree by the ability of each collector to hear the phonemic distinctions of the dialect and his ability or willingness to portray them in writing. Less experienced collectors tend to be somewhat inconsistent and are often influenced by Danish spelling habits. Prior to the appearance of Ivar Aasen's dictionary and grammar there was no norm for writing Norwegian and it was up to the individual collector to construct his own orthography. Niels Svenungsen, for example, who wrote V1a and V1b used a number of spellings which often startle the modern reader. Landstad began by basing his orthography fairly closely on the Telemark dialects, but changed in the mid 1840s to an etymological spelling reminiscent of Faroese (compare K1,28, a later addition, with the other stanzas of this variant). Mistakes occur fairly frequently in the MSS, though in the absence of any norm it is not easy to define these. Cf., however, *sa* (L4,1), *Dramæn* (K1,6), *Ta* (K1,8), *Foesheimen* (K1,12), *Vejengjer* (T8,4), *stoste* (K5,11).

The following notes are an attempt to outline the more unusual linguistic and orthographical features the reader will encounter in this work. The norm against which these are measured is conservative *nynorsk*, and anyone attempting to read the texts should be tolerably familiar with this form of Norwegian (a useful grammar is Leiv Heggstad, *Norsk grammatikk*, 1914, 2nd edition 1931, reprinted 1966). It must be stressed that it is not the dialect of western Telemark (or Sætesdal) that is being described, but its appearance in the texts of this edition. Orthography and phonology are therefore treated under the same heading and described largely in orthographical terms.

4.1 Orthography and phonology

a) 'e' and 'æ' are virtually interchangeable in both stressed and unstressed syllables. Exs.:

Svevnæn (V1a,5) — Svævnen (V1a,3)
heve (M6,1) — hævæ (V1a,1)
meg (M6,2) — mæg (V1a,1)
ler (M1,1) — lær (M6,11)
bles (K5,20) — blæs (K1,26)
der (L6,3) — dær (M6,31)
Fuglanne (M6,6) — Fuglanæ (V1a,4)
Sole (V1a,13) — solæ (F1,2)

b) double and single consonants are virtually interchangeable; double vowels occur sporadically, even where the vowel sound is short. Exs.:

fek (V1a,6) — fekk (M6,2)
Ete (L4,14) — ette (K9,2)
Qvase (L4,19) — kvasse (K1,12)
Jedarbroi (L4,13) — Jeddar broi (L4,12)
Bikja (V1a,39) — Bikkja (M6,14)
Soli (K1,5) — Solli (K1,4)
Domen (K1,20) — Dommen (K5,20)
vakna (M6,6) — vakkna (By2,1)
Skarlakens (V1a,29) — Skarlakkens (V1a,28)
Draumane (L1,2) — Draumanne (M6,8)
Syskjenboni (K1,10) — Syskjenboonne (V1a,53)
fér (M20,1) — feer (V1a,39)
skene (V1a,22*refr.*) — skeene (V1a,2*refr.*)
viæ (V1a,40*refr.*) — viiæ (V1a,1*refr.*)
Gronne (V1a,31) — Gronnee (V1a,31)

c) 'ej', 'ey' and 'ei', 'ou' and 'au', 'øi' and 'øy', 'aa', 'á' and 'å', and 'qv' and 'kv' are interchangeable. Exs.:

ejn (T8,1) — ein (M6,10)
hejte (T8,5) — heyte (V1a,33)
dey (V1a,2) — dei (M1,2)
Droumane (V1a,14) — Draumane (L1,2)
høire (K1,heading) — høyre (M6,5)
qvea (V1a,1) — kvea (M6,1)
saag (K1,18) — ság (T6,1) — såg (M6,30)

Standard 'au' appears as 'o' in, e.g., *Dromkve* (M1,heading), possibly, like 'ou', an attempt to render more clearly the dialectal pronunciation ([öu] rather than [æu]) in writing.

d) etymological *g* or *k* ± *j* when followed by a front vowel may be written in the following ways: 1. 'g' ('k') + 'j' + FV; 2. 'g' ('k') + 'i' + FV; 3. 'g' ('k') + FV; 4. (in the case of *g*) 'j' + FV. These spellings reflect standard (Danish or Aasen) orthography, etymological knowledge, varying dialectal pronunciation (cf. especially, e.g., [iɲjən] and [eɲd͡jən], [dɑjən] and [dɑd͡jən]) and a good measure of uncertainty. Exs.:

'gj'/'kj'	'gi'/'ki'	'g'/'k'	'j'
gjæk (K1,3)	Giek (L4,8)	gek (L4,2)	jek (K9,1)
dagjen (L6,1)			-dajen (V1a,3)
fygje (V8,1)	fygie (M1,1)		fyje (V1a,32)
ingjen (M6,2)			injen (L4,20)
gjøy (M6,43)			jøyr (V1a,51)
Skjye (T3,1)		Skye (V1a,30)	
Kjæm (L4,9)	Kiæm (L4,8)		
inkje (V1a,44)		inke (L4,24)	

Cf. also *Fye* (L4,5) and *Skjæfte* (L4,10). Etymological *g*(*g*) + etymological or analogical *j* + vowel sometimes appears as 'j' or 'i'. Exs.: *knejar* (V1a,51), *Hoie* (L4,10), *jore* (T8,2). Etymological *skj* appears once as 'sj' and once as 'si': *sjuse* (V1a,22), *siæve* (L4,17).

e) 'e' and 'i' are in many cases interchangeable in weakly stressed syllables. The appearance of /e/ and /i/ in inflexional endings was regulated by two different morpho-phonemic systems in the dialects of western Telemark, but the distinctions of these systems are by no means always reproduced in the texts and this often results in ambiguity. In certain cases 'i' does not occur (weak and *pl.* forms of the *adj.*, verbal inflexions excluding the supine, the svarabhakti vowel (cf. point *f*), the *def.m.sing.*), but 'e' then alternates with 'æ'. The *pl.* of *i*-stem substantives is almost always written '-ir', '-in(n)e'. Exs.:

indef.m.sing.	*def.m.sing.*	*dat.m.sing.*
Reendi (V1a,29)	Svevnæn (V1a,5)	Fingre (V1a,29)
Rygge (V1a,60)	Hujen (L4,22)	Munni (M6,12)
Snjore (M6,40)		Munne (M6,68)
vande (K3,5)		manni (L6,8)

m.pl.
Drenjir (V1a,1)
Vægjene (K1,7*refr.*)
Vegjine (K1,20*refr.*)

def.f.sing.
Sole (V1a,13)
Hui (M6,9)
soli (L4,3)

f.pl.
tekstinne (L6,2)
Sjæline (K5,20)
Sjælene (K5,21)

indef.n.sing.
Dikje (V1a,32)
Hæi (K1,16)

def.n.sing.
Vatne (V1a,44)
Fókkji (M6,71)

indef.n.pl.
Klæi (M6,19)
Klæi (L4,17)

def.n.pl.
Votne (V1a,45)
? Fokkje (M6,7)

strong adj.
(*m.sing.*) trøyttæ (V1a,44)
(*f.sing.*) besleje (V1a,25)
(*n.sing.*) liti (M6,31)
(*n.sing.*) Lite (L4,8)
(*pl.*) blie (L4,5)

weak adj.
bliæ (V1a,32)
vene (L4,23)

v. pres. and imp.
fyjer (V1a,31)
fere (M6,74)
sættæ (V1a,12)

supine
sovi (V1a,1)
Sove (L4,1)
gjængje (K1,11)
stai (K1,11)

adv.
lengje (M6,1)
lengji (M6,6)
att'e (M20,1)

pron.
denni (K1,2)
denne (K1,22)

solæ (F1,2) represents the pronunciation in this area of Telemark: [æ].

f) a svarabhakti vowel written 'e' or 'æ' occurs irregularly in the following cases: 1. *indef.nom.sing.* of strong *m.* substantives; 2. *indef.nom.sing. m.* and *f.* of adjectives (not possessives); 3. monosyllabic *pres.sing.* verb forms (including compounds); 4. certain adverbs. Exs.:

subst.	*adj.*	*v.*	*adv.*
Snjoræ (V1a,38)	addæ (V1a,25)	riæ (V1a,14)	sondæ (V1a,28)
Fóte (M6,9)	Håge (M6,15)	heve (M6,1)	atte (K1,19)
Fugle (M6,23)	bærføte (L4,19)	Rye (L4,3)	
Orme (M6,23)	blakk'e (M9a,7)	fortele (L4,4)	

In some cases it is impossible to distinguish between the svarabhakti vowel and a) a *dat.* ending, e.g., *Gronne* (V1a,30), b) the *def.* form of the *adj.*, e.g., *dyre* (K1,22). *míne* (M6,63) would appear to be an ungrammatical form rather than *min* + svarabhakti; *Flutte* (L4,9) is probably due to a confusion of tenses and *mange* (L6,3) is presumably *def.sing.*

g) standard 'u' mostly appears as 'o' when followed by a nasal (though conversely we find 'u' for 'o' in the *def.pl.* of weak feminines, cf. older *-urnar*) and in some cases where a following nasal has been lost. Exs.:

Ongæ (V1a,14)	brone (L4,22)
-bro(e) (<brú(na)) (V1a,23–6)	ont (K1,1)
Monne (V1a,30)	om (K1,3)
Hond (V1a,51)	tong (Sæl,1)

An occasional *def.dat.* (or *acc.*?) *sing.f.* ends in '-un(n)e' or '-un'. The *u* may have been introduced on analogy with the *def.pl.* which has identical forms.

h) standard 'y' often appears as 'ø' when historically short, especially if followed by a nasal. Exs.:

Kjørkjune (L4,2)	søndige (L4,9)	fø (V1a,3)
tønner (L4,7)	Sond (= Sønd?) (K5,11)	før (K2,4)

i) in stressed syllables standard 'o' mostly appears as 'å' ('aa') when followed by a nasal, though not where this is of late origin, cf. *Konn*, *-honn* (M6,20). This is due to a dialectal development whereby [ö] (< *o*, *ǫ*) > [ɔ], [ǫ] in this position. Collectors sometimes ignore the difference between [ö] and [ɔ], [ǫ], however, and we can find either sound represented by both 'o' and 'å' ('aa'). Exs.:

eingaang (V1a,37) — eigong (M15b,3)
kaam (V1a,38) — kom (M14,1)
aanno (V1a,57) — ònó (M20,1)
Håge (M6,15) — hoge (K1,13)
Kaan [kön:]? (K1,14) — Konn (M6,20)
skaa [skö]? (K5,20) — sko (M6,28)
Aaspelauv (K1,27)

In unstressed syllables standard 'o' is written 'o' and 'å' ('aa') (normally pronounced [o]). Exs.:

aanno (V1a,57) — aannaa (V1a,56)
Maanno (L3,5) — lìå (F1,2)
haannom (N1,4)

og is written 'å' ('aa'), 'o' and 'og'; the former two spellings often occur in contrast to the normal representation of sounds in Norwegian, e.g., *å* (M6,11), pronounced [ö] in Mo, *o* (F1,2), pronounced [ǫ] in Fyresdal.

j) standard 'i' sometimes appears as 'e' ('ee') when followed by a nasal (though conversely we find 'i' for 'e' in the *def.pl.*, cf. older *-irnar*, *-irnir*) or where a following nasal has been lost. The sound change which lies behind these spellings is largely confined to the most westerly dialects. This is the main reason for the confusion of 'i' and 'e' in endings referred to under point *e*). Exs.:

skjeene (V1a,1*refr.*)	Styjeengs (V1a,60)	me (V1a,28)
seenæ (V1a,12)	engjen (V ?12,1)	Sole (V1a,13)
Veende (V1a,24)	steng'e (V ?12,1)	Votne (V1a,45)
Hemmerikje (V1a,33)		

k) standard 'a' appears sporadically as 'aa' or 'o' before 'l' and 'ng' [ŋ]. Exs.:

fortaaldæ (V1a,12)	vraange (L4,13)	skolv (K1,27)

l) in stressed syllables standard 'je' appears as 'ja', 'je' ('jæ'), 'jo' and 'jø'. It is not possible to formulate any rule about the occurrence of these forms which would be of help in reading the texts. Exs.:

Gjeddar (V1a,22)	Jønni (V1a,24)	gjønni (M6,36)
Gjaddar- (V ?12,1)	jonni (T3,2)	norafjølls (M6,40)
sjellan (M6,48)		

m) progressive and regressive vowel assimilations cause certain words to have different forms from standard *nynorsk*. Exs.:

fyry (K1,23)	oto (M6,33)	ivi (V1a,22)	Tynnyr- (M6,9)

n) standard 'll' often appears as 'dd' ('d'). Exs.:

addæ (V1a,25)	eismadd (M6,33)	Keddingann' (Sæl,1)
hadde (M6,22)	Jeddar (L4,12)	Mod (K1,11)

o) standard 'ld' often appears as 'll' ('l'). Exs.:

halle (M6,28)	alli (M6,33)	sjellan (M6,48)	hel (V1a,60)

In one case [l:] derived from [ld] > [d:] (cf. point *n*): *addi* (M6,32).

p) standard 'rn' and 'rst' normally appear as 'nn' ('n') and 'st'. Exs.:

gjønni (M6,36)	bonno (L4,11)	jonni (T3,2)	støste (M6,55)
Bjønnir (M6,50)	konn (L6,4)	Hon (K1,14)	Fyste (L4,6)

Båne (M6,26b), *bån* (K3,5) etc. reflect a development [arn] > [ɔ:n].

q) in the dialects of western Telemark [l] is lost between a vowel and certain consonants and the quality of the vowel is sometimes changed. This gives rise to a number of unfamiliar forms in the texts. Exs.:

fygje (V8,1)	Fókkje (M6,7)	Kaave (V8,1)
Fye (L4,5)	siæve (L4,17)	

r) words which in Old Norwegian had the sequence *vowel* + *ð* + *r* exhibit a variety of forms in the texts. Exs.:

are (M6,10)   aurom (M6,17)   -fjøirir (M6,48)   Veir (By1,2)

The forms *Fair* and *Moir* (K1,2) should also be noted. These words are pronounced both mono- and disyllabically, the latter pronunciation presumably reflecting normal loss of intervocalic [ð].

s) many words appear in the texts without the final '-r' they have in standard spelling. Exs.:

fø (V1a,3)	unde (M6,28)	He (L4,15)	òno (M20,1)
ette (V1a,25)	mei (M6,28)	noko (K1,15)	yvi (Sæ1,1)
va (V1a,38)	oto (M6,33)	Gudmo (K1,19)	

t) certain words appear in the texts without the final '-n' they normally have in standard spelling. Exs.:

Heyma (V1a,28)   Gama (M6,27)   (with *def.art.*) joleftá'en (L6,1)

u) etymological *hv* appears as 'h' in two words:

hot (M6,36)   hossi (T6,1)

v) an 'h' appears in a number of words (mostly in V1a) where it is not found in standard spelling. It is likely that in most cases this represents an attempt to mark aspiration, but 'th' for 't' may be due to Danish spelling habits (cf. Section 4.4). Exs.:

Vhii (V1a,1)	thi (V1a,23)	sheeh (V1a,38)
ægh (V1a,1)	dher (V1a,37)	Thii (T8,5)

4.2 Morphology

a) **Substantives** have the following inflexions (Ø = zero):

	singular		plural	
	indefinite	definite	indefinite	definite
		strong m.		
nom./acc.	-Ø -e -æ	-en -n -æn	-Ø -ar -e -er -ir -r	-an(n) -an(n)e -anæ -ene -in(n)e -ne -æne
gen.	-s			
dat.	-e(e) -i		-o	
		weak m.		
nom./acc.	-e -i(i)	-e(e)n	-ar	
gen.	-s			
dat.		-a		
		strong f.		
nom./acc.	-Ø	-e -i -æ	-ar -er -ir	-an(n) -an(n)e -en(e) -in -in(n)e
gen.				-enes -ernes
dat.	-e		-o -å	
		weak f.		
nom./acc.	-a -e -æ	-a	-ur	-un(n)e -unæ
dat.		-un -un(n)e		
		strong n.		
nom./acc.	-Ø	-e -i	-Ø	-e -i
gen.	-s	-ets -sens	-s	
dat.			-o	
		weak n.		
nom./acc.	-a -e	-ai	-ne	-o
gen.		-as		

There are obligatory (i.e., affecting all words) changes in the root vowel in the following cases: 1. *nom./acc.n.pl.* 'a' > 'o' ('å'), e.g., *Votne* (V1a,45), *Laand* (L4,23), cf. also *baan, sing.* (L4,8), *Syskjenboni, pl.* (K1,10); 2. *dat. pl.* 'a' > 'o' ('å'), e.g., *votno* (L4,22), *Båndo* (M6,33), cf. also *bonno* (L4,11).

Such changes are not normally given in Section 5.3 (glossary). There are optional (i.e., affecting some words) changes in the root vowel in the following cases: 1. *nom./acc.m.pl.* 'a' > 'e', 'o' > 'ø', e.g., *Neglan* (V1a,29), *Føtar* (M6,45); 2. *dat.f.sing.* 'å' > 'æ', e.g., *hænde* (L4,20); 3. *nom./acc. f.pl.* 'a' > 'e', 'o' > 'a', 'o' > 'ø', 'å' > 'æ', e.g., *Tennar* (M6,39), *Kasir* (V1a,37), *Ørnekløanne* (M6,60), *Hændan* (L4,9). Such changes are given in Section 5.3 (in standard spelling) under the word concerned.

There are certain forms which are difficult to distinguish. Neuters which end in '-e' or '-i' (*Dikje*, *Helviti*) have this ending in *sing.* and *pl.*, *def.* and *indef.* *Draumkvæi* (L6,heading) could thus represent standard *Draumkvæde* (*sing.* or *pl.*), *Draumkvædet* or *Draumkvædi*, and indeed the title of the ballad has at one time or other been taken in each of these four ways. Because of the impossibility of deciding whether both '-e' and '-i' occur in all four positions, neuters of this type have been omitted from the above table. The difference between *def.* and *indef.* use is difficult to establish with regard to a number of other endings (cf. Section 4.3). There is, however, little doubt about the function of the weak feminines with a *nom./acc.sing.* in '-a', e.g., *Bikia* (L4,13), *Kyrkja* (T8,3), *Vinna* (Sæl,1), and it is clear that the weak neuters with *nom./acc.pl.* in '-o' are all *def.*

It is often impossible to distinguish between a svarabhakti vowel and a *dat.* ending in the case of strong masculines, e.g., *paa Havsens Gronne* (V1a,30), *då møtte [eg] en Manne* (M6,26b). That there is a *dat.* form is clear from a number of examples: *uti Kjæfte* (V1a,53) is almost certainly *def.*; the writing of '-ee' and '-i', e.g., *Gronnee* (V1a,31), suggests a pronunciation different from the [ə] of the svarabhakti vowel; the form *Fingre* (V1a,29) contrasts with the *nom./acc.* which is usually *fing(e)*. It is also worth noting such phrases as *af qvorjum Fingre* (V1a,29), [*av bliom*] *Munni* (M6,12), *at manne dei* (L4,8) where the *adj.* or *pron.* qualifying the *subst.* has a *dat.* form, although this in itself proves nothing. It nevertheless seems clear that not all strong masculines ending in '-e' ('-æ') are datives where they have a historically *dat.* syntactic function: *av kvor min Fóte* (M6,9) and *av kvor min Finge* (M6,10) contrast with the datives *føte* (fairly common in the Telemark dialects) and *Fingre* (V1a,29).

Strong *neut.* substantives have not been given a separate *dat.sing.* ending in the table. In the few cases where a *dat.* may occur it cannot be distinguished from the *def.sing.* and *nom./acc.pl.* ending, e.g., *mæ Jønni* (V1a,24), *mæ Havi* (M6,11), *mæ Båne* (M6,26b). Weak neuters have no separate *dat.sing.* form.

It is not difficult to distinguish between the *dat.sing.def.* and *nom./acc. pl.def.* of weak feminines, but whether the *sing.* endings '-un', '-un(n)e' should be regarded historically as *gen.* or *dat.* (or even *acc.*) is hard to say.

It has been suggested that *seene Droumme* (V1a,61) is a modern form of the Old Norwegian *acc.pl. sína drauma.*[371] This is possible, but *Droumme* may equally well be an anomalous form determined by the rhyme word *Attegoumme.* Unusual words and endings occur several times at the end of the second and fourth line, e.g., *har* (M6,3), *upptraktar* (M6,35), *grý* (L6,8).

There are certain individual endings which are difficult to place in the table and have therefore been omitted from it.

1. *Viso* (V1a,52) appears to be *def.nom./acc.sing.* of *vise,* while *Svolo* (V1a,15) could be *def.nom./acc.sing.* of *svola,* although it is perhaps more likely to be *dat.pl.* of *svol.* If the '-o' ending in these two words is the *def.nom./acc.sing.*, corruption, either scribal or oral, has to be assumed. The *sing.def.art.* of weak feminines with a historically long root syllable (*vísa*) is always *-a,* and *Svolo* would indicate confusion between *svola* 'swallow' and *svol* 'open passage way' (cf. Section 5.3, **kyrkjesvol**).[372]

2. *Texten din* (K1,6) can be taken as *m.sing.*, but a variant reading gives *dine,* and the example should perhaps be compared with *Voxmyren* (K1,11), which is presumably *f.pl.*, although the normal *def.pl.* forms of *myr* in the texts are *-myran(e), -myrann(e).*

3. *Skarlakskåpi* (M6,10) is presumably *indef.nom./acc.sing.* with '-i' for the more usual '-e', but cf. *Skarlakskåpa* (M6,9) with the same syntactic function.

b) **Adjectives** are inflected much as in conservative *nynorsk.* The following points should, however, be noted:

1. The strong *m.* and *f.sing.* can end in '-e' ('-æ'), e.g., *Håge æ den Gjæddarbrói* (M6,15).

2. Adjectives of the type *open* and past participles of strong verbs end in '-e', '-en' ('-æn') or '-i' in the strong *f.sing.* and in '-e' or '-i' in the strong *n.sing.*, e.g., *ho vha . . . besleje* (V1a,25), *líti Gama* (M6,27*var.*).

3. The old strong *acc.* and *dat.m.sing.* (or strong *dat.pl.*) endings *-an* and *-um* occur frequently as '-an' ('-en'), '-om' ('-um') respectively, but unattached to any particular gender, case or number and with both *def.* and *indef.* function, e.g., *dey nyttan Drenjir* (V1a,1), *på viddan Hei* (M6, 49), *fy mínom færi* (M9a,9).

4. A number of adjectives are indeclinable or may lack certain endings, e.g., *trá* (T6,1), *glóands* (L6,8).

Comparatives and superlatives as well as the forms of irregularly inflected adjectives (e.g., *annan*) are given in Section 5.3.

It is sometimes difficult to distinguish between strong and weak forms of the *adj.* and between *def.* and *indef.* function. This matter is discussed in Section 4.3.

There are certain individual adjectival endings which require comment.

1. *søndugu* (V1a,53), in contrast to *syndige*, *søndige* elsewhere, has preserved the *u* of the middle syllable (Old Norwegian *syndugr*). The final vowel appears to have been influenced by this *u* (cf. Section 4.1, *m*).

2. *eismadd* (M6,33), apparently used attributively, has nevertheless retained the inflexion which follows the predicative function this word normally always has. Alternatively *eismadd* may stand in apposition to the preceding *dæn*, although this seems less likely.

3. *den gnýren mange* (L6,3) appears to involve the *def.* use of *mange*, which is unusual. The final syllable is of course needed if the rhyme with *stanga* is to be preserved.

c) **Verbs** are inflected much as in conservative *nynorsk* and Section 5.3 contains forms not readily identifiable from the *inf.* The following points should, however, be noted:

1. The *inf.* ends in '-a' or '-e' ('-æ') according to whether the root syllable was short or long in Old Norwegian. There are virtually no exceptions to this rule (*have* (V8,1) seems to be the only genuine one), but verbs which in Old Norwegian had a short root syllable followed by *-ja* in the *inf.* appear with '-je', e.g., *fortællje* (K1,4). This may be the reason for the '-e' in *kvele* (M6,31), but it is more likely to be a Danish form of a Danish word (cf. 8 below and Section 5.3, **kvela**).

2. Single-syllable *pres.* forms (except where the *inf.* is also monosyllabic or in the case of most auxiliaries) can end in '-e' ('-æ'), e.g., *skeene* (V1a,2*refr.*), *fedde* (M6,14), *bit'e* (V ?12,1). A number of verbs can thus have the same form in the *inf.* and *pres.*, e.g., *skeene* (V1a,2*refr.*), *skeene* (V1a,13).

3. Separate *pl.* forms occur sporadically in both the *pres.* and *imp.* The *pres.pl.* has the same form as the *inf.* and is mostly confined to verbs with historically short root syllables, e.g., *gala* (V1a,51), *fara* (M6,74), *falle* (L4,1*refr.*), *hava* (M20,1). The *imp.pl.* is confined to strong verbs and ends in '-e' ('-æ'); sometimes the *pl.* has a different root vowel from

the *sing.*, e.g., *skokæ* (V1a,4), *brone* (L4,22), *vore* (K1,17). It is occasionally impossible to distinguish between the form of the *pres.sing.* and the *pres.* or *imp.pl.*, e.g., *bite* (K1,9).

4. The supine ends in '-e' or '-i'.

5. The imperative consists of the root form of the verb with zero ending or '-e'.

6. *-st* forms end in '-st' or '-s'.

7. It is difficult to distinguish between the *pres.* and *imp.* of *gråta* and *blåsa* since the use of 'e' and 'æ' is anything but consistent and the normal sequence of tenses is often not observed.

8. Danish inflexions occur sporadically, e.g., *erfaret* (M6,57), *vaagnede* (K1,29), *faldt* (L1,16).

There are certain individual verbal forms which require discussion.

1. *vakne* (V1a,3) would seem to be due to an error by the collector.

2. *kjænne* (V1a,3*refr.*) could be *pl.*, but such forms are not common in verbs with historically long root syllables (cf. 3 above). It can hardly be an error since the form occurs again in V1b,2*refr.*, M13,1*refr.* and T7,1*refr.*

3. *læer* (V1a,30–2) is doubtless meant to represent a monosyllable with a long vowel, cf. *ler* (M1,1), *lær* (M6,11) etc.

4. *haag* (M1,3) would appear from the context to be *pres.*, but the normal form in the dialect is *høgg*(*e*). The *imp.* in standard *nynorsk*, as well as in many dialects outside western Telemark, is *hogg* and this is perhaps what is intended.

5. *vaddi* (K9,4) is unique in having an '-i' ending. This suggests that it may represent *vadd' i* which would be perfectly grammatical.

6. [*ant*] (S6,2) is Landstad's form and occurs nowhere in the texts, the form there being *ont* with the same vowel as the *inf.* and *pres.*

7. *meine* (By1,2) has an unusual *pres.* ending (without '-r') which is, however, common in the dialects to the south of Bygland.

d) Adverbial and pronominal inflexions are dealt with in the vocabulary.

4.3 Syntax

There is little in the syntax of the texts which deviates widely enough from what is accepted in standard *nynorsk* to cause difficulty to the reader. The following points do, however, deserve mention:

1. The use of the *indef.* and *def.* articles is freer than in the standard language. Both are sometimes omitted where we would normally expect them, e.g., *Fuglanne skóke Vengjir* (M6,6), *hae Flutte deild i Skog* (L4,9). The *def.art.* can occur where a *subst.* is qualified by a preceding possessive *adj.* or by another *subst.* in the *gen.*, e.g., *meene Fotspore* (V1a,31), *mine Føtanne* (M6,38), *annensmans Hjarta'i* (M6,36). The uncertainty as to where one may expect to find the *def.art.* makes it difficult to discern the function of a number of endings: *af blie Monne* (V1a,30) could be the *indef.nom.m.sing.* (in '-e'), the *indef.dat.m.sing.* or the *def.dat.m.sing.*; *i Lie* (K1,5) could be the *def.nom.f.sing.* or the *indef.dat.f.sing.*; *mæ Jønni* (V1a, 24) could be the *def.nom.n.sing.*, the *indef.dat.n.sing.*, the *def.dat.n.sing.* or the *def.nom.n.pl.* Where neuters end in '-e' ('-i') in the *indef.nom.sing.* it is difficult to distinguish the *nom.sing.* (*def.* or *indef.*) from the *dat.sing.* (*def.* or *indef.*) and the *indef.* from the *def.nom.pl.*, e.g., *paa svarte Dikje* (V1a,33), *sine Foreldri* (M6,34).[373]

2. Strong forms of the *adj.* are sometimes used with *def.* function, e.g., *dey nyttan Drenjir* (V1a,1), *Annom Heimen* (L4,17), *den anen heim* (L6,4), *fljotan Folen* (K1,5), *annen Heimen* (K1,16); *den enlig Fugl* (M6,37) seems likely to be an error by the collector. Weak forms of the *adj.*, presumably with *def.* function, appear to occur more widely than in standard *nynorsk*, but the optional '-e' ('-æ') ending in the strong *m.* and *f.sing.* and the difficulty in many cases of recognising the *def.art.* often makes it hard to know what form or function one is dealing with, e.g., *af blie Monne* (V1a,30), *i dyre Ti* (K1,22);[374] *af bliæ Hjarta* (V1a,32), *av bliom Hjarta* (M6,11) which would appear to be syntactically parallel to *af blie Monne* have a weak(?) and strong form of the *adj.* (with *indef.* or *def.* function?) qualifying an *indef.nom.* or *dat.n.sing.* (*def.* normally *hjartai*).

3. The sequence of tenses is somewhat freer than in standard *nynorsk*, e.g., L4,10, K1,5, K9,7, T3,2. For the influence of Danish syntax on the language of the texts cf. below.

4.4 Danish

A number of Danish forms and spellings are found in the texts and occasionally whole stanzas appear in Danish. Isolated forms and spellings may often be due to the collector, but complete Danish phrases and stanzas, in the midst of Norwegian, must clearly come from the informant (cf. Section 3.3, pp. 97–8 and 102). Exs.:

a) double vowels and 'oe': *Soomæ* (V1a,43), *beer* (M6,55), *Paradiis* (K1,18), *foer* (V1a,43).

b) monophthongs: *en* (M6,26b), *dør* (M6,45), *røde* (K1,19). Before two consonants partial or complete monophthongisation usually takes place in the dialects of western Telemark too. This explains a form such as *Rest* (L4,23) in an otherwise Norwegian stanza, but *hørde* (M6,56) in a mixed Danish and Norwegian stanza may be either Danish or dialect.

c) 'g', 'd' for 'k', 't': *tog* (V1a,13), *Fodspor* (V1a,32), *mødte* (K1,21).

d) 'ld', 'nd' for 'll', 'nn': *Norafjølds* (V1a,38), *Grund* (K1,11).

e) additional 'd': *bedst* (K1,24), *Madt* (T8,1).

f) various Danish forms: *Øine* (M6,38), *Huggormen* (M6,42), *langsomme* (M6,56), *Verden* (M6,56), *verandre* (L4,10).

g) Danish words: *Klippi* (M6,29), *grumme* (M6,39), *hinaen* (L4,10), *he*[*n*] (K5,21).

h) Danish inflexions: *Havets* (M6,38), *Øine* (M6,38), *Løvernes* (M6,39), *Lerken* (M6,67), *sang* (M6,67), *vaagnede* (K1,29).

i) the frequent use of the *acc.m.sing.* ending of the *adj.* is doubtless modelled on usage in Danish ballads: *nyttan* (V1a,1), *Fjottan* (L4,3), *sterken* (L6,1), *svartan* (K1,23).

j) most of the *gen.* constructions are modelled on Danish syntax, as is probably the *def.* use of the *acc.m.sing.* *-an* ending: *Hjartas* (V1a,31), *Havets* (M6,38), *Løvernes* (M6,39), *Foreldres* (M6,57), *stærkan* (K1,3).

Bibliographical note. The dialects of western Telemark are described in detail in Hans Ross, *Norske bygdemaal II*, *Vest-Telemaal*, Videnskabs-Selskabets Skrifter. II. Hist.-Filos. Klasse. (1906) No.3. Brief notes on the language of the Norwegian ballads will be found in Sophus Bugge, *Gamle norske Folkeviser* (1858, reprinted 1971), pp. VI–XI, Richard Berge, *Norske Visefugg* (1904), pp. 10–12, and Einar Lundeby, *Overbestemt substantiv i norsk og de andre nordiske språk* (1965), pp. 228–35.

5. Notes, glossary and indices

5.1 General notes

It should be observed that the bibliographical references in these notes are selective.

1. *Anheimen* (T6,1) has been taken as meaning both 'the other world' and 'the spirit world' (Landstad (1853), pp. 77–8, Moltke Moe, *Forelæsninger over norske ballader og folkeviser fra middelalderen II*, pp. 36–7, FM, pp. 54b–55, Aasen (1873), Mortensson, *Grunnsteinen*, p. 27, Ssk., pp. 257–8). As Moe points out in his lectures, one would expect a form *andar-* or *ande-* if 'the spirit world' were the correct interpretation, though *and-* [ɑn:] is perhaps not entirely impossible. Formally *Anheimen* is very like *anen* [ɑən ?] *Heimen* (K2,4) and *aen Hejmen* (T9,1) which are clearly parallel to *annen Heimen* (K1,16), *den anen heimen* (L6,9), *Annom Heimen* (L4,17), *aanno Være* (V1a,57), *aurom Væri* (M6,17) etc. There is, however, no stanza in the variants we now have in which *Anheimen* and *anen Heimen* (or one of the other forms) appear as alternative readings. Moltke Moe (FM, p. 55) asserts that *annheimen* occurs in S.150 and this is presumably why he felt able to substitute *aurom heimi* in MM 14 and 25, but the variant containing this form no longer exists. Mortensson's contention (*Grunnsteinen*, p. 27) that *andheimen* developed from Old Norwegian *anda-himinn* appears to be unsupported by any evidence. The use of the strong *nom./acc.m.* form *annan* with *def.* function in the above examples seems likely, because of the frequency of its occurrence in *Dr* as opposed to elsewhere, and because of the parallel *dat.* forms, to be a traditional usage rather than a Danicism (cf. Section 3.3, pp. 102–3).

2. *gjæv(a) Attegoum(m)e* (V1a,14, 61) seems to be a development of Old Norwegian *gefa at því gaum* 'pay attention to'. The form in V1b is *Ettegoumme* which corresponds better with the dialect phrase *gjeva gaum ette*. Moltke Moe began by using *gjeve atte gaume* (accompanied by a long note in FM, p. 39b, which see), but changed to *etti gaum'e* in his text of 1904. As Moe points out in the above-mentioned note, a substantive *attegaum* is not otherwise recorded; Aasen's suggestion in his dictionary that it means 'renewed attention' ('fornyet Opmærksomhed') seems unlikely.

3. *dei Laugevatni bar* (M6,3). It was the practice in Telemark as elsewhere in Norway for the whole family to bath on Saturday evening, prior to relaxing and enjoying themselves, and for this purpose water was fetched and poured into a large tub. The *Laugevatn* together with *Kling å Kakur* and *Øl i Skål* (M6,4–5) therefore suggests preparation for a festive occasion.

4. *bergestein* (M9a,9) seems to be a corruption of *dvergestein*. The stanza concerned occurs in another ballad: *Margjit og Targjei Risvollo* (Liestøl and Moe (1920–4), 13, cf. also Bugge (1858), pp. 29–35) where *dvergestein* has a clear function in suggesting that a maiden was lured away from home and into the embraces of a (supernatural ?) lover by magic. The *prep.* used in this ballad: *ikringum* (for *ne mæ*) also seems to give better sense.

5. *betlarstyen* (L4,23), *Vetters Ti* (K1,17–18). Various suggestions have been made as to the meaning of these two words or phrases. Bugge (1854–5), p. 117, rejected Landstad's view (1853, p. 79) that they were both corruptions of *vette-stíg* ('Gudevei' – 'divine path'? 'path of gods'?, cf. Norwegian *vett f.*, *vette n.*, *vetter f.*) and finally (p. 192) suggested that they might represent an earlier *vetrarstígen* 'Milky Way' (cf. the common word *vetter-braut* with the same meaning), widely held in popular belief to be a path taken by the souls of the dead. Moltke Moe (*Forelæsn. II*, pp. 58–60) considered that the two words were unconnected. *Vetters Ti* was a corruption of *vetterstig* 'Milky Way', while the first element of *betlarstyen/Betlarstigen* (L1,22) was a corruption of the *gen.pl.* of *bitel* or *betel* 'bit', and the word meant 'bridle path' ('ridevei', 'hesteveien'), the path on which dead souls rode – cf. *Tunge va dæn Granastigjen å gange* (M6,16a). *vetterstig* was the form Moe adopted for his reconstructed text, but in Ssk., p. 279, he suggests that *betlarstigjen* (cf. Section 3.7, L4, Alterations) may be a corruption of Anglo-Saxon or Middle English *Wætlingastræt*, *Wætlingstreet* 'Milky Way', in which case *vetterstig* must be secondary. Moe does not explain how *Wætlingstreet* could become *betlarstigjen*, and his view, in support of this etymology, that there were several Anglo-Saxon loan-words in *Dr*, carries little conviction. He rejects the simplest explanation, that *betlarstyen* means 'beggar's path', 'poor man's path', the straightest way to Heaven, because, so he says, the *v. betle* is a late loan and not generally found in Norwegian dialects. Mortensson uses the form *vette-stig* in his texts and explains it as 'spirit path' ('ånde-vei', *Draumkvedet i ny uppsetjing*, p. 30). Ådel Blom (1971), p. 261, follows Moltke Moe, but assumes corruption by the collector: what appears in K1,17–18 as *Vetters Ti* may well have been sung *vettersti*. In K5,16 we find the form *Ventersti* (presumably another form of *Vetters Ti*) which would appear to support this view, but is it likely that *-stig* would have been sung *-sti* in both cases? There is also the problem of the *f.indef.art.* in K1,18, although it is *m.* in K1,17 and *Ventersti* is qualified by *min*. We cannot rule out the possibility that *ei Vetters Ti* means 'a winter's time', 'in winter' (i.e., meant this to Maren Ramskeid), but *ein Vetters Ti* which is clearly the same expression can hardly have this meaning a) because of the *m.indef. art.* (although *tíð* could be *m.* in Old Norwegian/Icelandic, there is no indication that the word was anything but *f.* in later Norwegian), and b) because it renders the first two lines of this stanza meaningless. It is not certain either that *Vetter(s)-* means 'winter', although purely linguistically this seems more likely than the alternative 'spirit' and would appear to be supported by the form *Ventersti*.

6. *de blei mæg daa Fyste ve* (L4,8), *då blei eg fyste grý (ve)* (L6,8, 10). These phrases have proved difficult to interpret. According to Moltke Moe (*Forelæsn. II*, p. 77, (1899), p. 12, Ssk., p. 313) *verta ve* means 'begin to move'?, 'feel' ('komme i bevægelse', 'bli til mode'), neither of which seems to give good sense here, and indeed in Liestøl and Moe (1920–4), I, p. 196, this explanation was replaced by the laconic: 'What the second line means is uncertain' ('Kva andre lina tyder, er uvisst'). Mortensson (*Draumkvedet i ny uppsetjing*, p. 30) explains the phrase as meaning 'noticed' ('la merke til') without further comment. In Old Norwegian *verða við* normally means 'react (to)', 'respond (to)' with or without an object in the *acc.* or *dat.* A change of meaning to 'notice', 'become aware of' seems very possible here, and it may be that Mortensson's explanation is correct. It is worth noting, however, that in Old Norwegian/Icelandic we do not seem to get a construction of the type: *þá varð ek við* except where the object is strongly implied; normally the phrase contains either an object or an *adv.* such as *hversu* or *vel*. With the postulated change of meaning an object would appear more or less essential. The fact that we do not find it in some of the *Dr* variants could be due to textual corruption. In

L6,10 we may have *då* for *det* or the object may be understood: 'then I first noticed (my surroundings, what was going on).' In L1,10 *Dei blei naa fyste ve* makes little sense unless the subject (*eg*?) has been lost and *Dei* refers to man and child. As the text stands it certainly looks as though *dei* in the first line (*Kjæm e meg aat Manne dei*) has been taken as *pl.* and repeated mechanically in the second line. L4,8 *de blei mæg daa Fyste ve* appears to mean 'then it first noticed me' or 'then it noticed me first of all', but this is meaningless in the context and *mæg* may well be a corruption of *eg*. The most readily understood reading is found in T5,6–7: *dæ va dæ fyste æg vart ve, dæ andre æg vart ve* 'it was the first thing I noticed', 'the second thing I noticed'. The informant of L6 herself did not know the meaning of *grý*, and the collector, Bugge, offers no explanation either (cf. Section 3.7, L6, note 3). The demands of rhyme may have caused an earlier form of this word, which made better sense, but which rhymed poorly with *blý*, to be altered; alternatively *grý* may be a genuine word which had gone out of use by the nineteenth century. It is tempting to see *grý* as a corruption of *gru*, but the syntax of L6,8 forbids such an interpretation. The same objection applies, at least in most variants, to the equation of *ve* with the *subst.* meaning 'pain', 'suffering' (German *Weh*).

7. *blæste* (K5,21) would appear to be the *imp.* of the Danish *v. blæse*, unless a weak ending has been added analogically to the *imp.* of *blåsa.*

8. *dæ mone mæg inkje bære hænde* (K1,19), *dæ mone mæg kje bete gange* (K1,20). Moltke Moe who commented on the latter of these two phrases asserted that it referred to the third line in this stanza: *reis du dæg te Broksvalin* and considered that this commandment was necessarily displeasing to the visionary (*Forelæsn. II*, p. 63, FM, p. 60, Ssk., p. 281). Moe's view found its way into the school edition of the Norwegian ballads in the form of the following explanation of MM 28, ll.2–3 (cf. Liestøl (1971), p. 89): 'Things did not go any better for me than that she said I should leave Paradise and go to *Brokksvaline*' ('det gjekk meg ikkje betre enn så at ho sa at eg skulle fara frå Paradis og til Brokksvaline'). It is, however, far from certain that this is the correct interpretation. The two lines under discussion, which only occur in K1, are clearly parallel. Irrespective of whether Moe is right in thinking that the second line in K1,20 refers to the third, the events in K1,19, which he does not discuss, can hardly have been displeasing to the visionary, and the second line of this stanza must rather mean 'better things will not happen to me'. Given this, it seems unlikely that *dæ mone mæg kje bete gange* in K1,20 means the opposite. It probably refers to the first line, but could also indicate that the visionary was eager to get to the judgement which was to have such a happy outcome. This is apparently the view of Ådel Blom who translates the two lines much as I do (1971, pp. 261–2).

9. *bær* (M6,59) can hardly be the *pres.* of *bera* with the text as it stands. It rhymes with *kjær* in the third line, and one feels tempted to suggest that it may be a corruption of *er* (*æ*), or possibly *her*, though why or how such corruption should or could have occurred is hard to say.

10. *Dyrering* (K1,7), *Dyretraa* (K1,8), *Tyner Skog* (V1a,28), *Tyners Reendi* (V1a,29), *Tynnyrmóge* (M6,9), *Tynnyr*(*e*)*ring'e* (M6,10), *tøner Ring* (L4,6), *tønner mog* (L4,7). These words or phrases have provoked much comment, too much to go into here in depth (cf. Landstad (1853), pp. 73–4, 76, Bugge (1854–5), pp. 105–8, Moltke Moe, *Forelæsn. I*, pp. 181–3, Ssk., pp. 259–64, Mortensson, *Grunnsteinen*, pp. 24–7, Liestøl (1946), pp. 51–4). If all the variants are examined, several clearly related stanzas can be found describing a journey in which the protagonist's scarlet cloak is torn and, in most cases, he suffers damage to his hands or feet. The place across which the journey was made is described by what appears to be a compound, the first element of which has three basic variations and the second five. The possible combinations are as follows (in normalised spelling):

1st element	2nd element
dynne- (dura-)	-ring, -trå
dyre-	-ring, -trå
tynner-	-mo, -rinde, -ring, -skog

-mo rhymes with *for, fot* and *tå, -rinde* with *fingre, -ring* with *fing, -skog* with *for, fot* and *drog* and *-trå* with *tå*. It seems difficult to say anything useful about the relationship of the various words to each other (although this has not deterred previous scholars from declaring some 'original' and others 'secondary'), and it will perhaps be sufficient to discuss what they mean. *Dynne-* (*dura-*) can hardly signify anything but 'door', and compounded with *-ring* is used of a door-handle which takes the form of an iron ring. In T5,1 this gives good sense: *Æg helt i Dynne Ring* 'I held onto the door-handle', but K5,5: *eg gjek ivi Dy*[*nne*] *Ring* 'I walked across the door-handle' suggests textual corruption, unless *Dy . . .* should be expanded to *Dy*[*re*], which seems unlikely given *Dynne-Tra* 'doorstep' in the preceding stanza. *Dyre-* would appear to mean 'animal', although Landstad points out that his informants either did not understand or misunderstood the phrase, those who misunderstood it taking it to mean 'door'. He adds that some informants imagined that Olav was dragged through the iron ring on the door, '. . . just as people say the devil can be exorcised through a key-hole' ('. . . ligesom man siger den Onde kan manes ud igjennem et Nøglehul'). Of the MSS we now possess it is only K1 which contains *dyre-* as the first element. If Maren Ramskeid told Landstad that this meant 'door', then as far as we are concerned in the 1840s it meant 'door'. She may, however, have been one of those who did not understand the phrase, and certainly 'door' gives no sense in her variant. If we are right in translating *dyre-* as 'animal', then *Dyrering* and *Dyretraa* mean 'circle of animals' and 'animals' path'. Those who subscribe to this interpretation connect the phrases either with the animals on *Gjallarbru* or with the zodiac (cf. Landstad (1853), pp. 73–4, Bugge (1854–5), p. 106, Mortensson, *Grunnsteinen*, pp. 24–7). By far the most common first element is *tynner-* 'wild rose', with the emphasis clearly on its thorny nature. (Landstad (1853), p. 76, took *tynner-* as *tyner-* 'from [Old Norwegian] *þyna . . .* or *týna*' ('af þyna . . . eller týna'), and interpreted *tyner-rende* as 'the path of perdition or oblivion' ('Fortabelsens eller Forglemmelsens Bane'), but this seems improbable, if for no other reason than that it is hard to see what part of either *v. tyner-* might be.) *Tynner-mo, -rinde, -ring, -skog* then mean 'heath, ridge, circle, wood of wild roses' and these clearly represent either an obstacle which hinders the protagonist or a punishment he must suffer on his way. *Tynnermo* occurs again in S.147 (cf. L4,19), though some variants here have *heklemo* (e.g., K1,12) 'hackle heath', i.e. 'spiky heath' and *hellemo* (e.g., K5,8) 'rocky heath'. In related stanzas we find *Heklenou* (S.146 – V1a,58) 'spiky danger' and *Hæklebro* (S.148 – V1a,59) 'spiky bridge' which like *tynnermo* etc. in S.147 clearly refer to obstacles and/or punishments described elsewhere in the ballad.

11. *men enten i Plage hell stóre Ve,/ som mig i Verden erfaret* (M6,57). In the MS Bugge has written *ingen har* 'no one has' above *enten i* and placed a question mark in the margin after *Ve*. As it stands the third line of this stanza certainly makes no sense together with the first two and the fourth, and the fourth itself exhibits a most unusual construction: *det erfarer mig* for *jeg erfarer det* (possibly on analogy with *det hænder mig*, if *erfaret* is not to be taken as *er faret* = *er gått* (*gjenge*), 'the way things have gone for me in the world'). Some meaning can perhaps be extracted from the stanza if one assumes *men* to be a corruption, namely: 'My parents' upbringing, so good it is (it has stood by me), in either torment or great suffering which I have experienced in the world.'

12. *som sterkan* (*sterke*) *Svevnen fanga* (M6,33, 37) appears to mean 'whom deep sleep ensnared'. 'Trapped' is clearly the sense of *fanga* in the fourth line of M6,37. It is, however, hard to ignore the parallel with M6,2, particularly in view of the similarity of meaning of *få* and *fanga* (in Danish ballads they are often used synonymously), and it may be more correct to render the phrase 'who fell into a deep sleep'.

13. *fesla(r)* (M6,45–6) has been interpreted in two ways. According to Moltke Moe (Ssk., p. 355) the informants (he heard S.45 with ll.3–4 preceding 1–2 from Hæge Leirebrekk in Mo, cf. notes 21 and 37 below and Section 3.5, M20, note) in his day understood *fesla* as meaning 'tie', 'bind' ('binde'). However, both he and Liestøl (1946), pp. 53–4, point out that *fesla* normally means 'bind up', 'bandage'. Liestøl disregards the informants' interpretation entirely, but in oral literature primary consideration must be given to what the informants intended the word to mean, and this was, according to Moe, 'tie', 'bind'.

14. *men Gaukjen fyrutta Meining* (M6,52) puzzled Bugge, who entered two question marks in the right-hand margin of his fair copy. The line does indeed defy interpretation. *fyrutta Meining* could be translated 'without meaning', and this certainly seems apt.

15. *Føesheimen* (*Foes-*) (K1,12, 15) is said to have developed from Old Norwegian **fœðisheimr* 'the world into which one is born and in which one lives' ('Den verden, man fødes til og lever i', Moltke Moe, *Forelæsn. II*, p. 36) or 'the world in which one lives' ('den verden man har sit ophold i, lever i', Ssk., p. 334). This is not well supported by Old Norwegian (or Icelandic) evidence (what word can the first element be other than *fœði*, which is more suggestive of a world in which one needs bodily sustenance?), but the expression is clearly parallel to *denne Heimen* (L4,17–19, 24), *denne Være* (V1a, 56–9) etc., and can therefore reasonably be taken as 'this world'. Furthermore, *Føesheimen* contrasts with *andre Heimen* (K1,15) and *annen Heimen* (K1,16), and these and the equivalent phrases *aanno Være* (V1a,57–9), *aurom Væri* (M6,17, 19 etc.) plainly mean 'the other world'. *Føesheimen* does not only occur in K1; it is also found in S5 and V9,9 (*fødeheimen*) as well as in other ballads and *stev*. Another expression used in its place is *Fyriheime(n)* (K5,7–10). This is presumably synonymous with *fyrre*[*heimen*] (S6,5), and both forms may well have been inspired by the antonym *annan*.

16. *Gråduva* (M6,23) is not a high-flying species of pigeon, but a variation on *grågåsi*, the bird normally mentioned in this stanza which occurs widely as a *gamlestev* (cf. Bø (1964), pp. 30 and 65).

17. *Gudmo(er)* (L4,20–1, K1,19–20) is normally explained as a reference to the Virgin Mary, Old Norwegian *sæl guðs móðir* (cf. Bugge (1854–5), pp. 117–8, Moltke Moe, *Forelæsn. II*, pp. 51–7, FM, pp. 55–56b, Ssk., pp. 273–4, Mortensson, *Grunnsteinen*, p. 14, Liestøl (1946), pp. 88–90). Landstad (1853), p. 79, has the form *gullmór* and takes it to mean 'precious mother' ('dyrebare Moder'), presumably on the basis of the dialectal expression *gulle mor*. However, as Moe points out (*Forelæsn. II*, p. 51), *gullmor* is not otherwise known as a synonym of *gulle mor* and is better interpreted as 'godmother', *gullmor* being a common form of *gudmor* (cf. Aasen (1873), p. 251). In any case *gullmor* now only occurs in one, apparently garbled, variant (S4,2b): *dær såg eg mi gode gullmor/ hó stó kinna bló*. Another form found in two variants (L1 and L2) is *Sjukmo(e)r* 'step-mother'. It seems very likely that the *gudmor* of the variants did at one time refer to Mary, but by the nineteenth century it had clearly come to mean godmother, and it was doubtless in this sense that it was replaced in L1 and L2 by *Sjukmo(e)r*, although in the context of Norwegian folklore it is strange to find a step-mother described as 'good', as she is in L1,19.

18. *mæ salte Tårir har* (M6,3) makes little sense unless we assume that *har* means 'hard' and that the *pl.* ending has been dropped for reasons of rhyme. In his fair copy Bugge writes *har'*.

19. *hald* (M15b,3) could as it stands be one of a number of substantives (*hall n.* 'slope', *hall m.* or *f.* 'hall', *hall m.* 'stone'), but appears to be part of a place-name (cf. Section 5.2, Bjærdingens hald).

20. *Heere mo* (V1a,44) is difficult to interpret. No easier are the various other words which can appear in its place. S7,1 has *feddemó* and T11,1 *Færemoen,* while in Jørgen Moe's reconstructed text (stanza 17) we find *Herrefær* which was presumably the reading in V1b. Landstad (1853), p. 73, prints *hermo,* probably a 'normalised' form of *Heere mo,* and *felmo,* neither of which is found in any variant. He explains these words as (having developed from?) *harmr* 'sorrow', 'lamentation' ('Sorg Jammer') and *felmr* 'horror' ('Forfærdelse'); the final *-o* is presumably the *dat.pl.* ending. Bugge (1854–5), p. 105, considers *herreferð* (i.e., *Herrefær*) to be a corruption of *helferð* 'journey to Hel', but has no suggestions as to the meaning of *hermo* or *felmo.* In FM, p. 43b, in a note attributed to Bugge, *trøytte af hermo* (*felmo*) is explained as a corruption of *trøytt å færemó* '[tired and] weary of the journey' ('mødig av færden'), and *feddemó* as a possible corruption of *ferlamóðr, fellamoðr,* the first element of which would be Old Norwegian *ferill* 'track', 'path'. The text in FM is emended accordingly; *trøytt å færemo* appears in subsequent texts too, but there only with the laconic comment: 'from Old Norwegian *ferðamóðr,* weary of the journey' ('av gln. *ferðamóðr,* mødig av færden'). Certainly there seems to have been corruption of some sort in the shaping of *Heere mo* and the other words, and since it is difficult to make sense of them as they stand (unless they are place-names – or could *Heere* be *her* 'army' and *Heere mo* mean something like 'weary of struggle'?), it is legitimate to bring in Old Norwegian *ferðamóðr,* especially in view of the reading in T11,1. Whether it is reasonable to suppose that *trøytt å færemo* would develop into a number of different expressions, none of which appear to make much sense, is another matter.

21. *unde míne Føtanne helle* (M6,44) can be taken either to mean 'supports my feet' or 'clings to the bottom of my feet', according to one's understanding of *fesla* and thus the motivation of *Smådrengjinne* (cf. note 13 above and 37 below and Ssk., pp. 354–6).

22. *hi* (M9a,7) may well be a scribal error, *hi-* for *ha-*, which was not crossed out when *han* was re-written in full. Grammatically the only word somewhat like *hi* which could be used here appears to be *ti,* but it hardly accords with the style of this or the other stanzas of M9a.

23. *dæn hægste i Himmerig vera* (M6,61) gives little sense in the context in which it is found. Mortensson (*Grunnsteinen,* p. 30) explains that *den hægste* is Christ, but this hardly illuminates the problem. Similar phraseology is employed in a stanza in *Sigurd svein* which in Liestøl's version (Liestøl and Moe (1920–4), III, p. 53) runs: '*Høyre du snarpe Sigurd svein,/ kvåre vil du no gjera :/ anten den hægste i Oskorrei/ hell den minste i Himmerik vera.*' Whether this is a possible source of the fourth line in M6,61 is hard to say. There are, however, certain other points of similarity between M6 and *Sigurd svein,* most notably the use of the name *Granastigjen* in M6,16a, 18. What appears to be a snatch of *Sigurd svein* is also found in V8 (cf. Section 3.5, V8, note).

24. *Kjellar Bræi* (M6,19, 34) has been explained as Old Norwegian *keldna breði* 'glacier of springs' in modern guise (cf. Moltke Moe, *Forelæsn. II*, p. 46, Ssk., pp. 343–4, Liestøl (1946), pp. 59–60). On the face of it the first word means 'cellar', but this makes no sense in the context. We are given no indication of how Anne Skaalen understood the expression, but Bjørguf Rofshus, the informant of the only other variant in which it occurs (M3), stated that he did not understand it. Moe's explanation has the advantage that S.144 then ties in with other parts of the ballad (SS.116-17 and possibly 115), as do many of the *sæl* stanzas, although neither M3 nor M6 contain the relevant material (cf., however, M6,40–1). Mortensson (1920), p. 50, explains *Kjellar Bræi* as based on a place-name: Kjeldenut, two peaks to the south east of Hardangerjøkulen.

25. *kvesste* (M6,38). In a marginal note in Bugge's fair copy Moltke Moe suggests that this may be an alternative (Norwegianised?) form of Danish *kvæstede* 'hurt' (an older form of *kvæste -ede* in Danish was *kvesse -te*, although it had become completely obsolete long before the nineteenth century). Without some such explanation the line means 'and sharpened my feet' (or 'legs'). It is perhaps possible that there is confusion between *kvæste* and *kvessa* and the line is meant to mean 'and cut my feet on something sharp'.

26. *Lindarormen* (M6,18 etc.) is the name given to a fabulous snake of great size which appears in a number of Scandinavian ballads and tales (cf. Old Norwegian/Icelandic *linnormr*). It (they) appears in its usual role as a dangerous, menacing figure in M6,18, 31, but in M6,39 seems to help the protagonist.

27. *aa ennaa maa me brænnæ* (V1a,44) seems to be an unusual impersonal construction meaning 'and still I must burn', although *me* could be the *pl.pron.* 'we'. A number of variants contain this stanza: S7,1 (basically Landstad A 19 with the second line as in his note 24, cf. Section 3.5, S7, note) has *at innan sá má (mone) deð brenne* and S8c,1, S9a,1 and T11,1 have *(Aa) inna so (saa) monne eg brænne (brenne)*. This last reading is the one adopted by Moltke Moe in MM, and the meaning is clearly 'I am burning inside', 'there is a burning sensation inside me'. *ennaa* may possibly be a corruption of *enna*, the Vinje form of *inna*. It is unlikely to be a scribal error since Jørgen Moe's reconstructed text, based here on V1b, also has *ennaa*.

28. *Milir* (K1,5) is problematic. From the context one would expect a word which like *Greeme/Grime* in S.21 referred to a piece of riding gear, and *mile* or *mila*, *pl. milur* 'rings at the side of a bit' at once springs to mind. Interestingly enough Landstad seems to have altered *Milir* to *Mile* in the MS of K1, and *mile* (without *dei*) is the only form which appears in his printed texts. However, 'and put on a golden bit-ring' is not the likeliest of lines (one would at least expect him to put on two). It is conceivable that *Mile* here refers to the whole bit (if it really was a form Maren used), or perhaps has an entirely different meaning. The only other variant to include this stanza (K5) has the form *Mile* with the explanation: *ɔ: Sale* 'saddle'. *Milir* as it stands must be the *pl.* of *mil* '(Norwegian) mile', but then to make sense of the line one has to assume corruption of either this word or some of the others. An earlier reading could have been *la ut på . . .* (?) *milir*.

29. *myre* (K5,11), because of the context, seems to mean not just 'murder', but 'murder secretly', 'murder and hide the body', which is the sense in which the word was most often used in Old Norwegian.

30. *myrke Hús* (M6,70) may simply mean 'dark buildings' in a general sense, but is perhaps a compound synonymous with *myrkestova* 'a house in darkness'. *sat í myrke*

Hús would then mean '[I] sat in a building without lights', the image being of someone alone in a deserted farmhouse.

31. *då møtte en Manne mæ Båne på Armen bar* (M6,26b) seems to lack one or more subjects or objects. In Bugge's fair copy *[eg]* has been inserted between *møtte* and *ein*; *meg* is also possible. It is even conceivable that the clause is complete as it stands and means 'a man appeared, came forward'. In the second clause *mæ* is probably the *prep.*, but could also be the *conj. med*; in either case *han* seems to be lacking. If *mæ* is the *prep.* we would expect *mæ Båne* (*som*) *han . . .* , if the *conj. mæ han Båne . . .* In the latter case, of course, *Båne* could grammatically be the subject (*mæ Båne han . . .*), but in the context this seems unlikely.

32. *nedaa* (F1,2) appears to be a compound the first element of which is the *adv. ned*, the second the *prep. å*. This is unusual since the *prep.* used both in ballads and everyday speech in connection with *li* 'slope', 'hillside' is *i*.

33. On occasions *no* seems to be used merely to fill out the line, e.g., M6,2–5, but it can also serve to give emphasis or otherwise modify the sense of what is being said. In such cases translation is often ineffectual, e.g., *Aa den Rei naa so tvist* (L4,14) 'and it rode so very slowly', 'and indeed it rode so slowly'. It is sometimes very difficult to judge the exact function of *no* (cf. K1,6*var.*, K9,4, M9a,9), and the attempts at elucidation in the glossary should be considered as no more than a rough guide.

34. *Norafjøl(d)s* (V1a,37–8), *norafjølls*, *nórafjølls* (M6,40–1, 64–7). When used in *stev* this expression normally refers to the country north and west of Hardangervidda, but in spite of the fact that V1a,37–8 and, in a slightly different form, M6,40 occur frequently as *stev*, this can hardly be the meaning here, if, as it appears, we are dealing with ballads about life after death. Mortensson (*Grunnsteinen*, p. 17) asserts that in M6 '*nordanfjells*' must mean 'in the other world' ('i den andre verdi'), but it is hard to see on what evidence this is based. Perhaps the word simply gives an impression of great distance.

35. *næste* (K1,24) may be either an *adj.*: *aa* [*den*] *næste* [*var*] . . . or an *adv.* 'next', 'then'. The latter interpretation is supported by the readings of other variants, e.g., *Ete kom Jesom Christ* (L4,14), *og dernæst Jesum Krist* (K5,19). T5,4*var.* reads *næste Jesum Christ* where *næste* could be a *prep.* as well as *adj.* or *adv.*, 'next to Jesus Christ'. This might be one of the reasons for the form *Jesum.*

36. *mæ rapa Mod i Mun* (K1,11) according to Moltke Moe is 'the mark of the dead man' ('kjendemærket på den afdøde', cf. *Forelæsn. II*, p. 11, FM, p. 51b), and in Ssk. and other editions of MM a note on this line states (with varying form): 'with the earth of the grave in my mouth, i.e., as a dead man' ('med gravmuld i munden, d. v. s. som død mand'). *Mold* is certainly often used metaphorically of deaths, graves and burials, but it is difficult to find an example of *rapa* ('fall', 'plunge', 'collapse') in this connection. Nor, if Moe's explanation is correct, is the literal meaning of the line entirely clear. The image is perhaps that of earth being thrown onto a corpse or a coffin during burial, or of a coffin rotting after many years in the ground, causing earth to fall onto the corpse. The line may of course simply indicate that while he was wading through the bottomless *Voxmyren*, earth or mud fell into the visionary's mouth.

37. *i Tynnyrringjen meg refsa* (M6,46) appears to lack a subject, unless the protagonist punished himself or we are to understand *Smådrengjinne* of the first line as subject (cf. notes 13 and 21 above). Over *refsa* Bugge has written *rispa??* 'scratched ?', 'tore ?' in his fair copy, and in 'Limbus puerorum', (1908), p. 248, (1927), p. 347, Moltke Moe demonstrates the existence of this reading by printing the following version of S.45, together with a second stanza, from an otherwise unrecorded variant by Hæge Leirebrekk (cf. Section 3.5, M20, note): *Eg sleit sund'e mi skarlakskåpe,/ i tynnyr-ringjen meg rispa;/ kome dei fram smådrengjinne/ å mine finganne fesla.* This gives better sense than M6,46. If *rispa* is a more original reading, corruption may at first have been caused by confusion with *rifsa*, although neither in Old nor newer Norwegian does this word appear to have meant simply 'tear', cf. Fritzner (1883–96) and Ross (1971).

38. *Rest eg* (L4,23) probably indicates that *reste* and *eg* were pronounced as one word: *resteg.*

39. *r[æast]* . . . *på* (M6,21), instead of the usual *ræ(dd)ast fyre*, may be due to confusion with *høyra på* since sound is the principal element of the ordeal.

40. *eitt Skógesnar så tykt* (M6,50) stands apparently unconnected with the preceding line. What seems to be lacking is a *prep.*, *i*, *yver*, or perhaps *igjenom*. Grammatically it is possible to take the phrase as being in apposition to *Hei*, but a *hei* is not a *skogesnar*.

41. *Sløkjefri* (T8,2). According to Landstad (1853), p. 382, several informants understood this to mean 'the drinking horn' ('Drikkehornet'). The word may, as Landstad suggested, come from Old Danish *sløkæfrith*, 'concubine' (modern Danish *slegfred*), but it is not easy to see how the change of meaning occurred. It must have been a fairly early loan judging by the form of the word in Norwegian, and since the meaning 'drinking horn' is not recorded in Danish sources, was probably borrowed in its original sense. Possibly the drinking horn was in some way compared to a concubine. It may have been thought of as equally exciting or perhaps even considered a substitute (cf. that one of the names of Lady's bedstraw (*galium verum*) in Swedish is *slägfrid* 'concubine', a relic of the days when this plant was widely used for bedstraw). Alternatively there may have been some association with *sløkkja* 'quench'.

42. *Straumo* (T3,3) appears to be *dat.pl.* of *straum* 'stream', 'current', which gives little sense. Landstad (1853), p. 75, prints S.102 without comment, but Moltke Moe (*Forelæsn. II*, p. 9) tacitly admits that the word is in need of explanation. He also states (*Forelæsn. II*, p. 11) with reference to Landstad A 25 that *Gjallarbru* has a 'covering of gold' ('gulddække'), but this must be based on a variant reading Landstad gives to his A 24 (S.101): *hon er fast með gullið slegin*, or perhaps on the description of *Gjallarbrú* in Snorri's *Edda*. The third line of Landstad A 25 (almost identical with the first – or third – line of T3,3) can hardly be taken to mean that *Gjallarbru* was 'covered' with gold. Reidar Christiansen (*Norske folkeviser* (1957), p. IV) interprets *etter straumo lagt* as 'gold laid as in streams' ('gull lagt som i strømmer'), but this does not accord with any known meaning of *etter*. Could *Straumo* in some way be a corruption of *saum*?

43. *svala* (M6,31) means '[to] cool' and gives no sense in the context. In the right-hand margin of his fair copy Bugge has written *svalla?* 'chat?'. Against this it must be said that according to Aasen's dictionary the form of this *v.* in Telemark is *svælle* or *svelle*, which it would be difficult to confuse with *svala*. However, there scarcely seems to be a better explanation.

44. *sýslehúse*, *sýslinne* (K3,3). Under *sýslehúse* Bugge has written *trollkjeringh.* 'witches' house', which is presumably the informant's interpretation of the word. In his fair copy Bugge writes '*trollkjeringanne*' 'the witches' in brackets after *sýslinne*, but since no such explanation occurs in the original MS, this is probably his own interpretation. Moltke Moe has written extensively about this and another stanza (Sæl,1) which form the basis of MM 44 (cf. *Forelæsn. II*, pp. 68–70, Ssk., pp. 326–8). He considered *sýsle-* to be a combination of the Old English *susl* 'torment' and the Old Norwegian *sýsla* 'work'.

According to Moe *sýsle-* had, to begin with at least, the meaning of *susl* (cf. Old English *susla hus* 'house of torment', 'hell'), but the form of the Norwegian word. Later the sense probably shifted somewhat towards that of *sýsla*, and *sýslehúse* may have been looked upon as a kind of purgatory – with hard labour. Liestøl (1946), pp. 75–6, prefers to 'explain the name in the Old Norse sense', 'labour', 'toil', but this is largely on the basis of a line in Sæl,1 *det var so tong ei Vinna* which does not occur in connection with *sýslehúse* or *sýslinne*. As we have the stanza now, *sýslehúse* means 'witches' house' and *sýslinne*, presumably, 'witches' (from *sysl f.* ?). All we know about these witches is that they churned blood, an activity which, as Moltke Moe points out, is probably connected with their practice in legend of stealing milk from cows; these they milk so dry that finally only blood comes out, whereupon they set about churning the milk. Suggestions as to the 'original meaning' of *sýsle-*, however well argued, founder for lack of evidence. It is perhaps reasonable to suppose that the word is connected with Old Norwegian *sýsla*, but discussion about whether purgatory or hell is meant seems futile when we do not even know for sure that *sýslehúse* is a place of punishment. Mortensson (1920), p. 50, explains it as a place-name: Sys (cf. Sysendalen) + lo + huset.

45. *dæn må mæ Tunga tala* (M6,49) makes sense, but states the obvious in a way uncharacteristic of the Norwegian ballads. In a marginal note in his fair copy Bugge suggests two possible emendations: *må 'kje* 'must not', i.e., he must remain silent, or: *mæ Tungom* 'in tongues', i.e., in an unknown language, the power to speak which comes from God, cf. 1 Kor. (Cor.) 12–14, Ap. gj. (Acts) 2. The latter is more likely since there seems to be some emphasis on *Tunga*.

46. *upptraktar* (M6,35) is difficult to understand. The word is a *hapax legomenon*, and it is impossible to make sense of it by analysing its component parts. Furthermore it appears to be ungrammatical. On the evidence of other *sæl* stanzas we would expect an *inf.* In a marginal note in his fair copy Bugge suggests four possible emendations: *oprakte*, *udrakte*, *opstrakte* and *udstrakte*, but if any of these is accepted, one has to take *fyr* as the *conj. fyre* 'for', or *fyrr* 'before', and the meaning becomes little clearer. A *pp.* **utrakta* in apposition to *Tann* would give good sense, but such a form is unknown and not very like *upptraktar*.

47. *pivi* (V1a,60). The meaning is that they hung a cauldron of tar up over a fire or some source of heat.

48. *utreisa, Utreisa* (M6,9–10), *utreisi* (L4,6–7), *Utreysning* (V1a,28–9), *Uttexti* (K1,7–8). The interpretation of the first three of these words is clear. They can only mean 'outward journey', 'journey hence, away'. It is the fourth, which is used in the same context, that has given rise to much speculation, cf. Landstad (1853), p. 73, Bugge (1854–5), p. 106, Moltke Moe, *Forelæsn. I*, p. 181, Ssk., pp. 259–60, Myhren (1968). Myhren's article is discussed in Section 2.16, and there is little to add to what is said there. '*Utekst*' according to him means 'riding', 'journey', or possibly 'outfield', 'outlying place' – to which one journeyed ('køyring', 'ferd', 'utmark'). *Fyst va æg i Uttexti* (K1,7) must then mean 'First I was journeying along' or 'First I was in an outlying place'. Myhren translates (p. 62): 'I have been out travelling' or 'I have been far away in outlying places' ('eg har vore ute og ferdast', 'eg har vore langt uti utmarkene'), but this rendering is based on his own line: *Eg var meg i uteksti*, which is nevertheless presumably derived from K1,7–8 or the similar K5,4–5. It is worth noting that *Uttexti* is not an exact parallel to *utreisi* etc., and it is therefore a trifle rash to state, as Myhren does (p. 61): '. . . there is no doubt that singers interpreted *i uteksti* = *på utferd*' ('. . . det er ingen tvil om anna tradisjonen har tolka *i uteksti* = *på utferd*'). There is no evidence for this, except what can be found among the readings of other variants, but an examination of these shows that none of them has **Fyst va eg på utreisi* or the equivalent. Typical is *Dæ va fyste* (*are*) *utreisa* (*Utreisa*) *mi* (M6,9–10); other phrases are: *På dæn are reisa* (M3,6), *Den fyrst*[*e*] *reise han dergjen*[*om*] *for* (L11,2), *Æg va mæg eigaang utregst* (T5,2) (the reading *utreksti* mentioned by Myhren (p. 59) does not seem to occur in any of the variants). If the contention is that *Fyst* (*Saa*) *va æg i Uttexti* (or the *De fyste va me i Utext*, *De fyste me va i Uttext* of K5,4–5) gave birth to all the other phrases, it is strange that we find nothing closer to it than *På dæn are reisa* which occurs only once in one variant.

49. *vigde Votne* (V1a,45) is interpreted by Moltke Moe as 'holy water' ('det viede, hellige vand') and is said to be 'one of the streaming rivers in the netherworld' ('en av de strømmende elver i underverdenen', cf. Ssk., pp. 254–6). Why the water in such a river should be 'holy' is not explained. In FM (p. 45b) Moe suggests that it may be 'the river of punishment' ('straffefloden') over which *Gjallarbru* leads, but remarks that it is unusual (in visions) for such a river to be invisible. Liestøl (1946), pp. 50–1, considers it unlikely that this stanza belongs to *Dr* (i.e., 'originally' formed part of it). He notes: 'The epithet '*vigde*' (holy) does not seem to suit in a *stev* about an ordinary journey', but asks: 'Could it be meant as a place-name: *Vigdevatnet? (Cf.* Vigdesjå [*-sjå* = *sjø*] in Brunkeberg [Kviteseid] and Vigdarvatnet in Sunnhordland).' The answer must be no, in the context in which we find the stanza. The form *Votne* also fails to tally with either place-name (Jørgen Moe prints *Vatne* in his reconstructed text, but this is no guarantee that V1b from which the stanza (18) is taken had exactly the same reading). Whether the stanza once existed as an individual *stev* about a journey is another question and one it is at present impossible to answer. If a real or fictitious earthly journey were what was once described, *vigde Votne* can hardly be synonymous with the water running under the earth, especially if a place-name is involved. A person travelling across a lake would hardly have failed to see it.

50. *de ville eg ynskje* (M6,13) may mean the same as *det ynskjer eg*, but could also be less direct, 'I could wish', implying a certain deference (to God).

51. *vinne* (M6,32) is queried by Bugge in the right-hand margin of his fair copy, and underneath the word he has written *ɔ: komme frem?* 'arrive ?', 'get there ?'. An examination of the meanings of the word in Aasen's dictionary reveals no example of this usage, but as a *tr.v. vinna* can mean 'carry out', 'complete', 'do', 'manage'. We should perhaps understand *det*, *meg upp* or some such expression as object. The line might then mean: 'I thought I should manage to get up', 'I thought I should make it'.

52. *i voxtro veenæ* (V1a,2), *i Voxtern* (K1,1–2), [*i voxtro* (*véne*)] (S6,2). Landstad notes (1853, p. 68): 'The word *vene* is omitted by some. The meaning then is that he was in his youth when he experienced the events described' ('Ordet *vene* udelades af Nogle. Meningen bliver da, at han var i sin Opvæxt, da det Beskrevne vederfores ham'). In fact the inclusion or omission of *vene* has little to do with the meaning of *voxtro*/*Voxtern*. 'Olav was handsome in his youth, like . . .', 'Olav was like . . . in his youth', 'Olav was handsome in appearance, like . . .' and 'Olav was like . . . in appearance' are all possible interpretations. Aasen's dictionary gives the phrase *han er væn i Vokstren* under the heading 'shape, form which has developed in the process of growth' ('Skikkelse, Form som har udviklet sig ved Væxten'), and the comparison with the 'willow shoot' etc. points towards appearance rather than age; on the other hand the image of the doting parents suggests that Olav was still fairly young.

53. It can occasionally be difficult to distinguish between *og*, which is almost always spelt 'aa' ('å'), and the *int. o, å* 'Oh!'. From the point of view of form and syntax it is impossible to be certain that, for example, *Aa* (L10a,1, 1st occ.) means 'and' or that *O* (L12,3, 2nd occ.) means 'Oh!'. Except in this latter case, however, it is probably more reasonable to take 'o' or 'aa' ('å') as 'and' where there is any doubt.

5.2 Index and glossary of personal and place-names

Certain words which could be considered place-names appear in Section 5.3 (*helvite, himmerike, paradis*), while others which might be thought of as ordinary substantives are included in this index (*Pilegrims Kjørkje, øystrevegjen*). The former three are felt to be concepts rather than places. *Pilegrims Kjørkje* may or may not be a place-name; it seems to refer to a particular church (what, after all, are pilgrims' churches ?), although it lacks the *def.art.*; *øystrevegjen* is an exact parallel to *Skålestrònde* and *Gjæddarbróé*, and other names often take its place in the variants (*Eikjaråsen* (M6,24), *Geitarheii* (L10a,1) etc.).

It should be noted that the bibliographical references in this index are selective.

Bjærdingens (*var.* ? Bjærtinggjens) hald (M15b,3): The whole stanza is found in *Vidrik Verlandsens Viise* (Peder Syv, *Et Hundrede udvalde Danske Viser* (1787), p. 419, cf. DgF, 10F) where the name reads *Birtings-Hald. Birting, Bjærting, Bratten* etc. are names which occur frequently in Danish heroic ballads (*kæmpeviser*), and they seldom seem to refer to an identifiable place. It is reasonable to see the stanza in Syv as the source of M15b,3. The name must then mean: Bjærdingen Hall, the hall at Bjærdingen.

Broksvalin (K1,20, 21*refr.*–25*refr.*, 27*refr.*): Halls of the clouds ('Skyernes Sale', Landstad (1853), p. 79); Vestibule of misery, distress ('bedrøvelsens, trængselens forhal', Ssk., p. 281). Cf. also Mortensson (1920), p. 50, Liestøl (1946), pp. 76–8.

Dømmingfossen (Sæl,1) – other texts have *Donning-* (for *Dønning-* ?, NFS Skar 46,2, 62,58), *Dømning-* (Skar 51,16) and *Døningfossen* (Skar 1,16): Judgement Falls ?, Thunder Falls ? Cf. Ssk., pp. 255 and 277.

Eikjaråsen (M6,24, 74): Oak Ridge. Cf. Landstad (1853), p. 72, Moltke Moe, *Forelæsn. I*, p. 174, FM, p. 56c, Liestøl (1946), pp. 55–6, Bø (1955), pp. 81–2, Alver (1971), pp. 124–6.

Gaglemýr (M6,44), gaglemyrane (V9,7), Gaglemyrann (M1,2), Gaglemyranne (M6,15), [Gaglemyre] (By1,2): Gjoll Swamps ('gjallarmýrann ?', Landstad (1853), p. 75); (Wild) Goose Swamps (Bugge (1854–5), pp. 116 and 192); Mud Swamps ('Goglemyrane', Liestøl (1924), pp. 65–9). Identified by the informant, Hæge Aarmote as 'inaccessible swamps where the wild goose lays its eggs' ('Utilgjængelige Myrer, hvor Gaglen værper', M2, Bugge I,115); for Anne Skaalen's interpretation cf. Section 3.7, M6, note 4 and for that of the informant of M1, Section 3.7, M1, note 4. Cf. also Ssk., pp. 270–1, Liestøl (1946), pp. 72–5.

Geitarheii (L10a,1): Goat Heath. Cf. Landstad (1853), p. 72, Moltke Moe, *Forelæsn. II*, pp. 8–9 (Geitir's Heath ?), Liestøl (1946), pp. 55–6, Bø (1955), pp. 81–2, Alver (1971), pp. 124–6.

G. B. (T3,4, 6), Gjaddarbrui (V ?12,1), Gjalarbroì (V9,7), Gjallarbrui (V8,2), Gjeddarbro (V1a,25), Gjeddarbroe (V1a,23), Gjeddar Broe (V1a,22), Gjeddarbroi (K1,9, 11, 14,

T3,2), Gjeddar Bru (K1,13), Gjæddarbro (V1a,24, 26), Gjæddarbroe (L1,16), Gjæddarbróé (M20,1), Gjæddarbroi (M1,3, M6,16b), Gjæddarbrói (M6,14–15), Gjæddar bru (V1a,56), Jedarbroi (L4,13, 16), Jeddarbro (V1a,39), Jeddar broi (L4,12), Jeddarbrui (K9,5–7), Jæddarbroe (M1,2): Gjoll Bridge. Cf. Snorri's *Edda*, ed. Finnur Jónsson (1931), p. 66. Most scholars who have written on *Dr* have had something to say about *Gjallarbru*. The essential material can be found in Bugge (1854–5), pp. 108–15, Mortensson (1920), p. 50, Ssk., pp. 264–8, Liestøl (1946), pp. 64–70, Strömbäck (1946), pp. 51–68, Alver (1971), pp. 103–8.

Granastigjen (M6,16a, 18, 29): Grani Path (a path in the world of the dead along which one rides – parallel to *betlarstyen*?). Cf. *Sigurd svein* (Liestøl and Moe (1920–4), 115), stanzas 9, 12–14 etc., Moltke Moe, *Forelæsn. II*, pp. 33–4, Mortensson (1920), p. 50.

Grutte graasiæje (L4,15), Grutte Graaskjæggje (K1,23): Snorter greybeard – the devil, Óðinn (Bugge (1854–5), p. 119); Fierce-eye greybeard or Squinter greybeard – the devil, Óðinn (Ssk., pp. 285–93). Cf. also Landstad (1853), pp. 82 and 400, where it is stated that the name *grutte* (*gráskeggi*) is said to be used of the devil, Mortensson (1920), p. 50, Liestøl (1946), pp. 70–1.

haddanbrú (L6,6), haddanbrúi (L6,3, 7): Haddan Bridge, a clear parallel to and possibly corruption of *Gjallarbru*. There are no farms, rivers or lakes called *Haddan* in Telemark, but in Sætesdal we find the name *Halland*(*sfossen*) and, in connection with this (?), *Hallandsbrui* (cf. Johannes Skar, *Gamalt or Sætesdal* (1961–3), I, p. 288, II, pp. 99, 132, 179, 246 and 255–6, Per Hovda, 'Fossenamn', *Maal og minne* (1945), pp. 109–10). By normal phonetic processes *Halland-* develops from Old Norwegian *haldandi*, which is an unusual name for a waterfall. *Haddan-*, on the other hand (almost certainly from Old Norwegian *hallandi*), provides a more adequate description of falling water. Whether *haddanbrú*(*i*) in L6 and *Hallandsbrui*, *-fossen* are in any way connected and, if so, which is the more original form, is difficult to say.

Jesom Christ (L4,14), Jesum Christ (K1,24), Jesum Krist (K1,28): Jesus Christ.

Jolehylen (V1a,43, L10a,1), Jólehylen (M6,24, 74): Christmas Pool. The informant Steinar Gibøn told Bugge that *Jólehylen* 'is said to be *Tottak*' ('sko vera Tottak', R2b), and in H2 a note on the same line as *jólehølen* states: 'jóli = Dale gjætstgiverst.' Cf. also Section 3.7, M20,1, Alterations and variant readings, Landstad (1853), p. 72, FM, p. 57c, Berge (1940–4), I, p. 21: '*Jolehylen* is said to be *Totak*' ('Jolehylen er Totak, skal vera'), Bø (1955), pp. 81–2. One variant (V9,6) has *Gjaddarhylen*, but with the note: 'only the form I used when asking [if the informant knew the stanza]' ('berre mi spyrjeform').

Nórnesi (M9a,7): North Nes. Quite commonly used in *stev*, but apparently without reference to a particular place. Some of these *stev* may once have formed part of a Norwegian ballad of *Margrete* of which several Faroese variants exist. In this case *Nórnesi* must originally have meant Nordnes in Bergen. Cf. Landstad (1853), pp. 391–2, Gustav Storm, 'Audun Hestakorn og St. Margrete paa Nordnæs', *Historisk Tidsskrift*, *2. R.*, *4* (1884), pp. 209–52, Bø (1964), pp. 33–4.

Ó. (L6,2), Olaf (K1,1–2), [Olaf] (S6,2), Olav (V1a,2, 13, 15, M6,8, L4,3, L6,1, K9,1–3), Ólav (M6,72–3), Olaf Haakenson (L1,2), Olav Åknesi (M6,1), Olaf Aakneson (K1,29 *refr.*), Olav Aakneson (L4,1, 4), Olaf Aaknesonen (K1,3*refr.*), Olav Aasteson (V1a,1, 61, 61*refr.*, T8,4), Olav Aastesonen (V1a,54*refr.*): Olav, son of Åkne etc., or Olav Åknesi (farm name ?, cf. Section 3.7, M6, note 4: the farm mentioned is not listed in *Norske Gaardnavne*, but must be identical with Åsnes, a tenant farm belonging to

Vå nordre on the shores of Lake Totak in Rauland); Ansgarius (Landstad (1853), pp. 90–4); St Ólafr, son of Åsta (Jørgen Moe (1850), p. 279, Paasche, *Edda I*, pp. 46–7, (1924), p. 485); St Ólafr and/or someone else or several others (Bugge (1854–5), pp. 103–4, Mortensson, *Grunnsteinen*, pp. 38–42, the German commentators with the exception of Trummler who regards the protagonist as an otherwise unknown Olav Aasteson, cf. Steiner (1958), pp. 35–6, 40–1, 46, Trummler (1927), p. 9, Hoffmann (1954), pp. 16–20); Olav, God's beloved son and/or Olav, son of a poor farmer ('guðs ástsonr', (Old English) '*æcer-esning', FM, pp. 38–40, Ssk., pp. 248–9). Cf. also Liestøl (1946), pp. 24–5. In L8,1 and H3,1 the protagonist's first name is *Ola* (*Óla*), and in T9,3 *Peder*. His second name has numerous different forms, for the most part apparently variations on *Aakneson*, cf., however, *Aasneson* (L8,1), *Ånisón* (H3,1).

Pilegrims Kjørkje (L4,20–1): Pilgrims' Church. Cf. Mortensson, *Grunnsteinen*, p. 14, Ssk., pp. 282–4 (*Pilegrims Kjørkje* = *Broksvalin*), Liestøl (1925), pp. 119–23, (1946), pp. 77–8 and 88–90. Grammatically there is no compelling reason to take *Pilegrims Kjørkje* as a place-name; in none of the existing variants does the *def. -kyrkja* or *-kyrkjun* of the reconstructed texts (or Liestøl's 'variant' J (1946), pp. 134–7) occur.

Rodelaande (V1a,3*refr.*): Rogaland? ('Rógelándo, Rogernes Lande'), Rolanda socken? (Landstad (1853), p. 70, cf. Section 2.1, p. 5); Rauland (Mortensson (1920), pp. 51–2).

Skålestrònde (M20,1), Skaalestraand (L10a,1), Skålestrånd (M6,24, 43), Skaalæstraand (V1a,43): Bowl [-Lake] Shore (Mortensson (1920), p. 50); House Shore ('husstranden', Ssk., pp. 276–8); Hut (*Sæter*) Shore (Berge (1940–4), I, p. 21: 'The south-eastern side of *Totak* is called *Skaalestrondi*, with *Skaalen* [a *sæter*] and *Sandstaul*' – 'Sudaustsida av Totak kallast *Skaalestrondi*, med Skaalen og Sandstaul'). Cf. also Liestøl (1946), pp. 55–6, Bø (1955), pp. 81–2, Alver (1971), pp. 124–6. Several informants identify *Skålestrånd* with a specific place: 'at the end of *Tottak*' ('i Enden af Tottak', R2b), 'Skålestrand – Raulandstrand' (M5), 'paa Raulandstr.' (M9b), and cf. Section 3.7, M6, note 4.

Sæle Mekkjel (K5,20–1), Saale-Mechael (K1,24), Saale Mechael (K1,25–6, T5,4), saale Mikjel (L4,14), sále Mikkjel (K1,28): Blessed Michael and Michael of the souls. Cf. Paasche, *Edda I*, Ssk., pp. 294–309.

TveitarAasen (V1a,43): Tveit Ridge (*tveit* is a very common farm name; for the meaning of the word cf. *Norske Gaardnavne* (1897–1936), *Forord og Indledning*, p. 83). Cf. Landstad (1853), p. 72, FM, p. 56c, Liestøl (1946), pp. 55–6, Bø (1955), pp. 81–2, Alver (1971), pp. 124–6. In H2,1 the first line runs: *Sóme fór í Tveitaråó* and under the last word of this line is written 'Tinn'.

vossemyran (L4,16), Voxmyren (K1,11), Vågslimýrann (L6,7), Vásmyran (T3,6), Vaasmyrane (K9,5), Vaassemyrane (L1,16), VaaæMyran (V1a,26): Dampness Swamps?, Toil Swamps? (Landstad (1853), pp. 75–6, 858, Bugge (1854–5), pp. 115–16, *Vås-*); Danger Swamps (Bugge (1854–5), p. 116, *Vå-*); Mud Swamps (FM, pp. 52–52b, Ssk., pp. 269–70); Toil Swamps (Liestøl (1946), p. 71). According to Liestøl '. . . *Vå-*, *Vogs-*, and *Vågsli-myran* are connected with place-names in Telemark and are evidently secondary'. There is nothing in the MSS to connect these names with specific places in Telemark, though *Vå*, *Vaag* and *Vågsli* all occur or have occurred as farm names in western Telemark, and *Vågsli* (*Norske Gaardnavne* (1897–1936), VII, *Bratsberg Amt*, Vinje Herred 99) and *Myrane* are now the names of two guest-houses between Haukeligrend and Haukelisæter. Since Liestøl fails to mention which place-names are meant, it is likely that he was making an assumption rather than stating a fact.

øystrevegjen (M20,1): Eastern Way. Cf. Landstad (1853), p. 72, Ssk., p. 276 ('the path of the dead' – 'de dødes vei'), Liestøl (1946), pp. 55–6, Bø (1955), pp. 81–2, Alver (1971), pp. 124–6.

Åmlivollen (L6,1*refr.*): Åmli Meadow. *Åmli* (<**Almlíð*, 'Elm Slope') is the name of a farm in both Lårdal and Mo.

5.3 Glossary

Notes on using the glossary.

1. The glossary contains two kinds of entries: standard and non-standard. Standard entries are those under which a translation or a reference to a note is given (e.g., **ganga**, **betlarstyen**). Occasionally where a standard entry forms part of a set phrase or consists of an unfamiliar inflected form the reader may be referred to another word (e.g., **til** (2), **totte**). Non-standard entries are those which record abnormal (non-standard) spellings and refer the reader to the standard entry of the word he is looking up (e.g., **geengje** see **ganga**, **hoge** see **håg**, **kon(n)** see **korn**). Occasionally where a non-standard entry forms part of a set phrase or a compound the reader may be referred to these (e.g., **adt** see **fjasa**, **kjøru** see **tjørukjetel**). Non-standard entries are always given just as they occur (subject to 3 below, e.g., **jøn(-ni, -no)** see **jarn**, rather than **jønn** see **jarn**. There are no non-standard entries for compounds whose first element occurs separately in the same (non-standard) form and which therefore is already entered. The compound *Bjønnehamen* will thus only be found under the standard entry **bjørneham** since there is already a non-standard entry **bjønnir** which refers the reader to **bjørn**).

In choosing the form of most standard entries an attempt has been made to follow a conservative *nynorsk* norm. This policy has not, however, been carried out consistently. Where the *nynorsk* form does not occur anywhere in the texts or is very uncommon in these, the dialect or *riksmål*/Danish forms used are normally preferred or given as an alternative, except where it is purely a question of spelling (e.g., **hot** (norm: *kva*), **kvor** (*kvar*), **skjelva** – **skolv** (*skalv*), **sleppa** – **sluppe** (*sloppe*), **syngja** – **sang** (*song*), **tykkjast** – **tykkjest** or **tyst** etc., **hossi**). This means that the root of related words may sometimes have more than one standard form (e.g., **sakna**/**savn**). Where *nynorsk* itself allows two forms of the same word, both are sometimes used (e.g., **bort**, **burtbanna**). The use of so-called 'silent' *d* is far from consistent in the *nynorsk* norm and its inclusion or omission in the words in the glossary has been dictated by practical considerations: the need to keep down the total number of entries at the same time as ensuring that all standard entries have a recognisable form.

2. Some entries are partially bracketed. Such brackets have two functions: 1) in standard entries to indicate that a word may have a long and a short form (e.g., **bli(va)**, **ræ(dd)ast**); 2) in non-standard entries to give in the most economical way the various abnormal forms and spellings which occur in the texts (e.g., **fortæl(-e, -lje, -æ)**, **kjæn(-d, -ne)**, **kon(n)**, **kåm(a)**, **vej(i)ne**). It should be noted that bracketed letters follow the same strictly alphabetical order as the rest of the glossary (e.g., **bli** see **bli(va)**, **blid**, **bli(-e, -om)** see **blid**, **bli(va)**; the *adj. bli* does not occur without inflexion – had it done so, an additional entry, **bli** (2), would have been necessary).

3. In the texts there are a number of spellings which vary according to a regular pattern. Such spellings are regarded as interchangeable. Users of the glossary should therefore bear in mind the following points:

a) 'ej' and 'ey' appear as 'ei', 'ou' as 'au', 'qv' as 'kv', 'øi' as 'øy' and 'aa' as 'å' (e.g., for *Heyma, høire, qvasse* read *heima, høyre, kvasse*). However, where a word with one of these combinations occurs as a non-standard entry, the original spelling is retained except in the case of 'aa' which always appears as 'å' (e.g., **douen** see **daude**, **qvæa** see **kveda**, but **båte** see **både**).

b) Double and single consonants are interchangeable (e.g., for *Dryk, Dommen, nyttan, Qvase* read *drykk, domen, nytan, qvasse*). Non-standard entries retain the consonant spelling found in the texts (e.g., **sjuse** see **skjussa**, **et(t)e** see **etter**). Where a deviation from the norm occurs with both normal and abnormal consonant spelling (cf. **et(t)e** above) and separate non-standard entries would be required to accommodate both forms, only the form with normal consonant spelling appears in the glossary (e.g., **annen** see **annan**; a separate entry would be required for *anen* since *anheimen* and *annan* intervene alphabetically).

c) The combinations etymological *g* or *k* ± *j* when followed by a front vowel may be written in one of three ways in the texts: 1) 'g' ('k') + 'j' + FV; 2) 'g' ('k') + 'i' + FV; 3) 'g' ('k') + FV. Both standard and non-standard entries follow the *nynorsk* norm in these cases and there are no non-standard entries exclusively for spellings which deviate from it (e.g., for *drukkjé, festingji, Giek, giæve, gjøy, inke, kie, kjeimar, Kjyrkjunne, Kjyrkedynni* read *drukke, festingi, gjek, gjæve, gøy, inkje, kje, keimar, kyrkjunne, kyrkjedynni* and see **gjæve** and **kje** for reference to the standard entries **gjeva, ikkje**). In addition etymological *g* ± *j* followed by a front vowel, or etymological *g(g)* + etymological or analogical *j* followed by any vowel is often written 'j' + V (e.g., *dajen, Drenjir, fyje, jore, jøyr, knejar*); such forms are given non-standard entries.

d) 'e' and 'i' and 'e' and 'æ' are interchangeable in weakly stressed syllables, especially in inflexional endings. In non-standard entries it is usually possible to accommodate both forms (e.g., **fortæl(-e, -æ)**, **jore** (2), **jori**), but in standard entries and where separate non-standard entries would otherwise be required, the *nynorsk* norm, or the form closest to this, is followed (e.g., for *denni, kji, Kaapæ, riæ* read *denne, kje, kåpe, rie* and see **kje** and **rie** for reference to the standard entries **ikkje, rida**). Occasionally 'ee' and 'ii' occur in endings. For these read the single vowel equivalents.

4. Under standard entries the following forms are normally given:

Substantives: *indef.sing.*; the *indef.pl.* is given where this cannot easily be predicted from the *sing.* (e.g., **fot** (*pl.* **føtar**), **hond** (*pl.* **hendar, hender**), but for *votn, pl.* of **vatn** cf. Section 4.2*a*). *Def.* forms and other endings are not normally given, even where they deviate from the *nynorsk* norm (e.g., *Dage, Kjyrkjun, solæ, Hændan*). For such forms cf. Section 4.2*a*.

Adjectives: *indef.m.sing.*; irregular forms are given where they occur (e.g., **annan, liten, nokon** (2), **min**).

Verbs: the *inf.*, which ends in *-a*; in addition the principal parts of strong or irregular verbs, including plurals where these occur (e.g., **koma, standa, telja**; in the case of compounds this only applies where the simple form is not found, e.g., **uppeta**). The *-st* form appears as *-st*, never as *-s*.

Pronouns: those forms which occur, though normally only one *spelling* of each form appears as a standard entry (e.g., **andre, den, han, nokon** (1)).

Adverbs are always entered separately from adjectives (e.g., **håg** *adj.*, **hågt** *adv.*).

Regular inflexions (including svarabhakti *-e*) are not given since it is assumed that the reader will be familiar with these (cf. Section 4.2).

5. In the translations normally only those meanings of a word are given which are found in the texts (e.g., **driva** drive, drift, **søkja**; *søkja på* rush at, attack).

6. No abbreviations (except **st.**) are given in the glossary since they normally only occur if the complete word appears in an earlier stanza (e.g., M6,7).

7. Apostrophes, accents and capital letters are ignored in both standard and non-standard entries. They are, however, retained in direct quotations.

8. Instead of 'weak' and 'strong' the terms 'definite' and 'indefinite' are used of adjectives. These should be taken as referring to function rather than form (e.g., *annan/annen* and *are* are both 'strong' – historically speaking, at least – but the former has *def.* and *indef.*, the latter *def.* function).

The term 'dative' is retained where form is the primary consideration (e.g., in substantives), but 'oblique' is preferred where case distinction still has syntactic function (e.g., in some personal pronouns).

9. Unless otherwise stated references to notes are to the general notes in Section 5.1.

10. Words from the non-*Dr* stanzas of V1a are not included in the glossary.

11. The following grammatical and general abbreviations are used in the glossary and elsewhere in the work:

acc. accusative
adj. adjective
adv. adverb
art. article
aux. auxiliary
coll. collective
comp. comparative
conj. conjunction
dat. dative
def. definite
defct. defective
f. feminine
fut. future
gen. genitive
imp. imperfect
indef. indefinite
inf. infinitive
int. interjection
intr. intransitive
m. masculine
n. neuter
nom. nominative
norm. normally
num. numeral
obl. oblique
occ. occurrence
part. particle
pers. person
pl. plural
pp. past participle
prep. preposition
pres. present
pret. preterite
pron. pronoun
refl. reflexive
refr. refrain
rel. relative
siml. similarly
sing. singular
subj. subjunctive
subst. substantive
sup. superlative
sv. strong verb
tr. transitive
undecl. undeclined
v. verb
var. variant reading
wv. weak verb

a *prep.* see **av (1)**.
ad *prep.* see **at (1)**.
adde (1) *pron.* M1,3 see **alle**.
adde (2) *adj.* V1a,25, M6,30, 47, 63 see **all**.
addi *adv.* see **aldri(g)**.
adt *adv.* see **fjasa**.
af *prep.* see **av (1)**.
aldri(g) *adv.* never.
all *adj.* all V1a,25, M6,27 ?, 27*var.* ?, 30, 47, 63, 73, K1,26–8, K9,6, K5,20–1.
alle *pron.pl.* all (of them) M1,3; everyone N1,4.
allefælaste *adj.sup.* as *subst.* the most horrible thing of all K3,3.
alli *adv.* see **aldri(g)**.
allting *n.* everything.
alt (1) *adv.* all the way, entirely L4,8.
alt (2) *expletive part.* V1a,1, M6,27 ?, 27*var.* ?, 67, L4,1, 15, K1,18, M20,1.
altar *m.* altar.
altraren *m.* see **altar**.
andre *pron.pl.* others M6,69, L6,9.
anheimen *m.* (see note 1).
annan *m.sing.*, **onno(r)** *f.sing.*, **annom** or **aurom** *dat.sing.*, **andre** or **are** *def.*, *adj.* other, second; *i aanno Være, i aurom Væri, i Annom Heimen, i den anen heim, i andre Heimen, i annen Heimen* V1a,57, M6,17, L4,17, L6,4, K1,15, 16 etc. (see note 1).
annen *adj.* see **annan**.
annensmans *m.gen.* another man's.
ant *wv.* see **unna**.
anten *conj.* either; *men enten i Plage hell stóre Ve* M6,57 (see note 11).
are *adj.* see **annan**.
arm (1) *m.* arm M6,26b etc.
arm (2) *adj.* poor, wretched K1,22 etc.
at (1) *prep.* to V1a,14, L4,3, 8–12 etc.; *egh hæv seet ad heyte Helviti* I have looked towards hot hell V1a,33.
at (2) *conj.* that M6,13, 25, 32, 55, 59, 62, T8,1.
at (3) *inf. marker* K1,29–30 see **å (4)**.
att *adv.* again, back; K1,19 see **kjenna**; L12,3 see **nedatt**.
atte *adv.* see **att**.
attegaum *m.* attention (see note 2).
auka *wv.* increase.
aurom *adj.* see **annan**.
av (1) *prep.* (1) from, off V1a,29, 31, M6, 9–10, 32, 38, 59 etc.; (2) of V1a,52, M6,2, 5, 33, L6,8 etc.; (3) by M6,20, K1,heading; (4) about, of V1a,14, K9,3; (5) with V1a,30, 32, M1,1 etc.; *av Hjarta stúre*, sorrow from the heart, be full of sorrow M6,69; V1a,44 (see note 20); M6,19*var.* see **ræ(dd)ast**.
av (2) *adv.*; *av ne paa Havi svarte* away down onto the black sea V8,1.

band *n.* bond, chain.
banga *adj.* afraid, fearful.
banna *wv.*; *banna bort* curse L4,11 (see **burtbanna**).
bare *adv.* only.
barn *n.* child.
be(da) (ber, bad, bede) *sv.* ask, pray.
bedst *adj.* see **best**.
beer *sv.* M6,55 see **be(da)**.
behalda *sv.* keep, preserve.
beisl *n.* bridle; *n.sing.* ? *beisli* M9a,7.
bera (ber, bar, bore) *sv.* (1) bear, carry M6,4–5 etc.; *dei Laugevatni bar* they brought the bath water M6,3 (see note 3); *bera på* L6,8 = *bera* (1); (2) wear, be clothed in M6,48; (3) suffer M6,63.
bere *wv.* K9,4 see **betra**.
berg *n.* mountain.
bergedal *m.* mountain valley.
bergeknapp *m.* mountain top.
bergestein *m.* mountain stone, mountain rock (see note 4).
bergetopp *m.* mountain top.
berrføtt *adj.* bare-foot.
besleje *sv.* see **beslå**.
beslå *sv.* mount, overlay, cover.
best *adj.sup.* best.
bete *adv.* see **beter**.
beter *adv.comp.* better, see **ganga** (& note 8).
betlarstyen *m.* (see note 5).

betra *wv.*; *bære, Gud bère* God help! M6,32, K9,4 etc.; *O trøst o bære* (God) comfort and help L12,3.

betre *adj.comp.* better, see **henda** (& note 8).

bevara *wv.* keep, preserve.

bibra *wv.* shake.

bikkje *f.* dog.

binda (**bind**, **batt**, **bunde**) *sv.* bind, tie.

bita (**bit**, **beit**, **bite**) *sv.* bite.

bjønnir *m.* see **bjørn**.

bjørgeklippe *n.* (norm. *m.*) mountainous cliff.

bjørn *m.* bear.

bjørneham *m.* bear-skin.

blakk *adj.* white.

blanda *wv.* mix; *dei blandar eg alt isama* I mix them (all ?) up, confuse them M6,27; *dæ blandast alt í dæ sama* it (all ?) gets mixed up into the same thing M6,27*var.*

blank *adj.* bright, shining.

blaut *adj.* wet, boggy.

bli *sv.* M6,20, 45 see **bli(va)**.

blid *adj.* cheerful, happy.

bli(-e, -om) *adj.* V1a,30, 32 etc. see **blid**.

bli(va) (**bli(v)** or **blir**, **blei**, **blive**) *sv.* (1) be, become M6,48; *de blei mæg daa Fyste ve, då blei eg fyste ve* that was the first thing I noticed L4,8, L6,10 (see note 6); *då blei eg fyste grý* L6,8 (see note 6); (2) as *aux.+pp.* be M6,20, 56; will be M6,45.

blod *n.* blood.

blo(-e, -i) *n.* see **blod**.

bly *n.* lead.

blæsa ? *wv.* blow K5,21 (see note 7).

blå *adj.* blue, dark.

blåsa (**blæs**, **bles**, **blåse**) *sv.* blow; *imp.* ? *blæs* K1,26 (see Section 4.2*c*).

bonnar *m.* see **bunn**.

bonno *n.* see **barn**.

bort *adv.* see **banna**.

bratt *adj.* steep.

brau *n.* bread.

brei *adj.* see **breid**.

breid *adj.* broad.

brenna (**1**) (**brenn**, **brann** *pl.* **brunne**, **brunne**) *sv.* burn (*intr.*); *den va' brunnen blå* it had burnt (and turned) blue L6,13.

brenna (**2**) *wv.* burn (*tr.*).

brone *sv.* see **brenna** (**1**).

brono-mine *f.+adj.* see **brun** & **min**.

brun *f.* brow, eyebrow; *dæ, kjenner eg paa Brono-mine* I can feel it on my brows, my head is telling me T8,1.

brykja *wv.* see **brytja**.

brytja *wv.* chop into small pieces; *aa brykja ni, ein Styjeengs Rygge* and chopped up a wicked person's back (and let it fall) down into it V1a,60.

bræi *m.* M6,19, 34 (see note 24).

brænnæ *wv.* see **brenna** (**2**).

bu *wv.* live, dwell.

bunn *m.* bottom; *havsens bunn* (*bunnar*) the bed (depths) of the sea M6,12, L4,5, L6,12.

bur *n.* cage.

burtbanna *wv.* curse.

bær M6,59 (see note 9).

bære (**1**) *adj.* K1,19 see **betre**.

bære (**2**) *wv.* M6,32, V9,7, L12,3 see **betra**.

bærføt(t)e *adj.* see **berrføtt**.

bå *conj.* see **både**.

både *conj.* both.

bån *n.* see **barn**.

båndo *n.* see **band**.

båne *n.* see **barn**.

båte *conj.* see **både**.

d *pron.* see **den**.

dag *m.* day; *13 dagjen* L6,1 see **trettanddag**.

da(g)jen *m.* see **dag** & **trettanddag**.

dal *m.* valley.

daude *m.* death.

de(d), **dee** *pron.* see **den**.

deel *m.* see **deil**.

deil *m.* part.

deild *f.* boundary stone, boundary marker.

den *m.* & *f.sing.*, **det** *n.sing.*, **dei** *dat.sing.*,

dei *pl., pron.* (1) he, him, she, her, it, they, them, that, those thing(s) or person(s); *den som mine Fotspor vi Fye* he who would follow in my footsteps L4,5; *Dæ va St Saale Mechael* it was St Michael of the souls K1,26; *Dei vrei sine Hænder i Blo* they wrung their hands in blood L3,5; *Fatike dæn kann gjeva* who can give it to the poor (?), he (who) can give to the poor (?) M6,61; *dæ = det er* (?) V1a,53; *de n.sing.* ? M6,60; *di pl.* L4,11, K3,3; *de pl.* ? L6,9, 11; (2) that, those; *Håge æ den Gjæddarbrói* that Gj. is high M6,15; *Kiæm eg mæg at manne dei* I come to that man L4,8; *kvòr den Tinde* every spike K9,6; *fraa dhee han kom i Heimee* from the time (that occasion when) he came into the world V1a,2; (3) there; *dæ dreiv så mykje Snjore* there was so much snow blowing (drifting) M6,40; (4) as *art.* the; *dei store Klippi* the great cliffs M6,29; *den einaste* the only person M6,37.

denne *m. & f.sing.*, **dette** *n.sing.*, **desse** *pl., pron.* this; *i dessi Væri* (*dat.f.sing.* or *n.pl.* ?) in this world M6,17, 19 etc.

der (**1**) *pron.* there, it V1a,38 ?, 60, M6,14, 31, 71, K1,18, By1,2 ?; *dheer feer injen Jeddarbro* there is no one travels (crosses) *J.* V1a,39.

der (2) *adv.* (1) there V1a,3*refr.*, 37, 38 ?, M6,67, By1,2 ? etc.; *der va* (which) was there K1,27; *der... utpå* out onto it L6,13; *der ifraa* from there K1,17; (2) *rel.* where L4,22, K1,17.

derfor *adv.* see **derfyre**.

derfyre *adv.* therefore.

derifrå *adv.* from there.

dhe(e) *pron.* see **den**.

dhe(e)r (**1**) *pron.* V1a,38 ?, 39, 60 see **der** (**1**).

dher (2) *adv.* V1a,37, 38 ? see **der** (2).

dherfø *adv.* see **derfyre**.

di *pron.* see **den**.

dikje *n.* pit, hole, morass.

din *adj.* your; *pl.* ? *dine* K1,6*var.* (see Section 4.2*a*).

djup *adj.* deep.

djupt *adv.* deep.

dom *m.* judgement.

domedag *m.* the Day of Judgement.

douen *m.* see **daude**.

draga (**dreg**, **drog**, **drege**) *sv.* go, travel.

dramæn *m.* see **draum**.

draug *m.* ghost, spirit.

draum *m.* dream; *dat.pl. Draumo* K1,4; *pl.* ? *Droumme, Drømme* V1a,61, K1,30 (see Section 4.2*a*).

drekka (**drekk**, **drakk**, **drukke**) *sv.* drink; *drekka jol* celebrate Christmas M20,1.

dreng *m.* man, young man.

drenjir *m.* see **dreng**.

dreyk *m.* see **drykk**.

driva (**driv**, **dreiv**, **drive**) *sv.* drive, drift.

drykk *m.* drink.

drænjr *m.* see **dreng**.

drømme *m.* see **draum**.

drøyma *wv.* dream.

du *nom.*, **deg** *obl.*, *pron.* you.

dynn(-e, -i) *f.* see **kyrkjedynn**.

dyr (**1**) *n.* animal V1a,37.

dyr (2) *adj.*; *i dyre Ti* in hard times K1,22.

dyrering *m.* (see note 10).

dyretrå *f.* (see note 10).

dæ *pron. & art.* see **den**.

dæg *pron.* see **du**.

dæn *pron. & art.* see **den**.

dær (**1**) *pron.* M6,14, 31, 71 see **der** (**1**).

dær (2) *adv.* M6,67 see **der** (2).

døma *wv.* judge, pass judgement.

dør *wv.* see **døy**.

døy *wv.* die; *d'æ som 'en kunna døy* it is as if he should die, an experience like death M6,43.

då (**1**) *conj.* when V1a,3, M6,6(2nd occ.), 7, 25 etc.

då (2) *adv.* then M6,3, 6(1st occ.), 26b, L4,3, 8 etc.

då (3) *emphatic part.* M9a,7.

e (**1**) *pron.* L4,7, L1,16 see **eg**.

e (2) *sv.* K9,5, V8,2 see **vera**.

eg *nom.*, **meg** *obl.*, *pron.* I, me, to me; *æg Heyma drog* (when) I left home V1a,28;

aa ennaa maa me brænnæ and still I must burn (?) V1a,44 (see note 27); *Dæ va meg* it was me, it happened to me M6,26a; *De va mæ den Fyste* (*Andre*) *utreisi* it was for me the (was my) first (second) journey hence (?) L4,6–7 see **med (1)**; *refl.*? myself M6,46; K3,5 (4th occ.) = *til meg* (?); *meg i Hælanne, meg . . . av Minne, meg te Møia, mæg . . . i Hujen* M6,18, 32, 66, L4,22 see **hæl, minne, møye, hug** & **skjota**; L4,8 (3rd occ.) see **bli(va)** (and note 6); K1,11 see **standa**; K1,20 see **ganga**.

egh *pron.* see **eg.**

ei *adv.* not M6,35, 59–60.

ei(-gong, -gång) *adv.* see **eingong.**

ein (1) *m.*, **ei** *f.*, **eit(t)** *n.*, *art.* a, an V1a, 2–3, 33?, 37–8, M6,9–10, 26b (see note 31), 31–2 etc.

ein (2) *num.* one V1a,33?, M9a,7; *aa Gud bevare En og Her* God save each and everyone, one and all K1,29; *kvor ein Tinde* every (single) spike T3,2.

einaste *adj.* only, single; as *subst.* M6,37.

eingong *adv.* once.

eingång *adv.* see **eingong.**

einki *adv.* see **inkje.**

eismadd *adj.* only, solitary (see Section 4.2*b*).

ejendeyl *art.*?+*m.* see **ein (1)** & **deil.**

ekta *wv.* marry.

elles *adv.* otherwise.

en (1) *art.* V1a,3, 60, M6,26b (see note 31), 32, 36, L6,9, K1,30, M9a,9 see **ein (1).**

en (2) *num.* K1,29 see **ein (2).**

en (3) *pron.* M6,1, 43?, 45?, L4,1, K1,1–2 see **han.**

en (4) *pron.* M6,41, K1,14? see **den.**

end *adv.* see **enn.**

ende *m.* end; *i Enda* at the end V1a,24; *te endes* to the end, right across V?12,1.

endå *adv.* even, still, yet; *enddaa vær'* still worse M1,2.

engjen *pron.* see **ingen (1).**

enkje *adv.* see **inkje.**

enlig *adj.* single, solitary; *def.* M6,37 (see Section 4.3).

enn *adv.* still.

ennå *adv.* still.

enten *conj.* see **anten.**

er *sv.* see **vera.**

erfara *wv.*; *som mig i Verden erfaret* M6,57 (see note 11).

et(t)e (1) *adv.* L4,14, K9,2 see **etter (1).**

ette (2) *prep.* V1a,25, L6,3 see **etter (2).**

etter (1) *adv.* (1) after, behind L4,14; (2) *resste te Kjyrkja ette* went along to church K9,2.

etter (2) *prep.* along, across L6,3, T3,3; *aa Soum ette qvorjum Teende* and nails along every spike V1a,25.

fadd(-e, -æ) *sv.* see **falla.**

fa(-der, -ðir, -er) *m.* see **far.**

fager *adj.* beautiful, pretty.

fair *m.* see **far.**

fald(-e, -t) *sv.* see **falla.**

falla (fell *pl.* **falle, falt, falle)** *sv.* (1) fall K1,30 see **i (1)**; (2) extend, run; *Vejine faddæ so viiæ* the roads stretch out so far V1a,1*refr.*, siml. V1a,22*refr.*, 40 *refr.*, M6,1*refr.* etc.; *Aa vejne falle lange* and the roads stretch out far (?) L4,16; (3) be(?), seem(?) L4,16; *Vægane faldt saa vrange* the roads were so awkward (?) L1,16; (4) be pronounced L1,16*var.*; *fyr Dómanne fedde vrånge* for unjust judgements are pronounced M6,14.

falsk *adj.* false.

fang *n.* embrace; *Lite baan i Fanie bar* he carried a small child in his arms L4,8.

fanga *wv.* sieze, capture, trap, imprison; *som sterkan* (*sterke*) *Svevnen fanga* M6,33, 37 (see note 12); *pp.*? M6,37 (2nd occ.).

fanie *n.* see **fang.**

far *m.* father.

fara (fer *pl.* **fara, for, fare)** *sv.* go, travel, walk; *fara seg* = *fara* M9a,9.

farleg *adj.* dangerous.

fast *adv.* firmly.

fat *n.*?; *få fat i* get hold of M6,40–2.

fatig *adj.* poor.

fat(t)i(-ge, -ke, -kæ) *adj.* see **fatig.**

fe (1) *prep.* L4,4, 18, K1,14–15, 26, T8,5, K5,20 see **fyre (1).**

fe (2) *conj.* L4,2–3 see **fyrr (1).**

fe (3) *conj.* L4,13, K1,20, V8,2 see **fyre (2).**

fedde *sv.* see **falla.**

feer *sv.* see **fara.**

fella *wv.* pass, pronounce (judgement) V1a,39.

ferd *f.* (1) journey, travels M9a,9; (2) group of riders, host L4,14–15, K1, 23–5, T5,4.

fesla *wv.* bandage (see note 13).

festarfolk *n.* betrothed couple.

festing *f.* betrothal; *i festingji ha' dei døytt* they had died while still betrothed L6,14.

fing(-anne, -e) *m.* see **fing(er).**

fing(er) (*pl.* **fing(r)ar**) *m.* finger.

fisk *m.* fish.

fjasa *wv.* catch fire; *dette fjasar Adt* things are catching fire, my head is burning (because of the drink) T8,1.

fjottan *adj.* see **fljot.**

fjuka (fyk, fauk, foke) *sv.* fly (at great speed), sweep through the air.

fljot *adj.* fast, speedy.

flytja (flyt, flutte, flutt) *wv.* move.

fo *conj.* see **fyrr (1).**

fodspor *n.* see **fotspor.**

foer *sv.* see **fara.**

foesheimen *m.* see **føesheim.**

fok(k)j(-e, -i) *n.* see **folk.**

fole *m.* foal, colt.

folk *n.* people.

folkej *n.* see **folk** (& Section 3.7, T8, note 3).

for (1) *prep.* M6,16a*var.*, L4,24, L6,4, K1,16, 27, 29, L1,2, L3,5 see **fyre (1).**

for (2) *conj.* K1,7*refr.*, 9*refr.*, V ?12,1(1st occ.) see **fyre (2).**

for (3) *conj.* T8,1 see **fyrr (1).**

for (4) *adv.* too V ?12,1(2nd occ.).

forakta *wv.* despise.

foreldre *n.pl.* parents.

forgylt *adj.* golden.

fort *adv.* quickly.

fortelja *wv.* tell, relate.

fortæl(-e, -lje, -æ) *wv.* see **fortelja.**

fortål(-dæ, -t) *wv.* see **fortelja.**

fot (*pl.* **føtar**) *m.* foot.

fotspor *n.* track, footprint, footstep.

fram *adv.* forward, forth K5,20; *koma fram* (1) arrive, get (somewhere) V1a,43, M6,24, N1,4; (2) come out, come forth M6,31, 39, 42, 44–7; (3) get across T3,4; *då eg kom meg på vegjen fram* when I got onto the road, or: when I had gone some distance down the road F1,2; *ganga, fara fram* proceed along M6,43–4; *fram fe Domen stande* step forward to be judged, come to the judgement K1,26.

fri *adj.* free.

fro *adj.* learned, wise.

frå (1) *prep.* from V1a,2 see **den.**

frå (2) *conj.* from the time K1,2.

frå (3) *adv.*; *koma frå* come out, away L10a,1.

fugl *m.* bird.

fuglebur *n.* bird cage.

fugleflokk *m.* flock of birds.

full *adv.* certainly, surely.

fullenda *wv.* complete, finish.

fullna *wv.* complete, finish; *den som fulnar meene Fotspore* he who completes the same path as me, follows in my footsteps V1a,30.

fy *prep.* see **fyre (1).**

fydder *wv.* see **fylla.**

fy(gi)e, fy(g)je(r) *wv.* see **fylgja.**

fylgja *wv.* follow; *den som fyjer meene Fotspore* he who follows in my footsteps V1a,31, siml. V1a,32, M1,1 etc.

fylla *wv.* fill; *dæn som mi' Fotspori fydder* he who 'fills' my footprints, follows in my footsteps M6,11–12, siml. M6,45, 48 etc.

fyr (1) *prep.* M6,8, 19, 22, 34–5, 72–3 see **fyre (1).**

fyr (2) *conj.* M6,14 see **fyre (2).**

fyre (1) *prep.* (1) for T8,5; (2) in front of,

before M6,8, 72–3, L4,4, K1,6, 26, L1,2; (3) because of V1a,22–3; *som Aaspelauv for Vinde* like aspen leaves in the wind K1,27; *fe Dommen skaa dei gange* they must go to the judgement K5,20; *bevare . . . for* preserve from K1,29; V1a,56–7, 59, M6,19, 22, 34–5, L4,18, 24, L6,4–6, K1,14–16, K2,4 see **ræ(dd)ast**; V1a,58 see **fæla**; M9a,9, L3,5 see **rå(da)**; K1,27(2nd occ.) see **gråta**.

fyre (2) *conj.* for, because M6,14, L4,13, K1,7*refr.*, 9*refr.*, 20, V8,2, V ?12,1.

fyre (3) *adv.* in front L4,14–15, K1,23–5, T5,4.

fyrr (1) *conj.* before V1a,3–6, M6,6–7, 25 etc.

fyrr (2) *adv.* earlier, sooner K9,1–2.

fyrst (1) *adj.* first V1a,28–9 etc.

fyrst (2) *adv.* first, first of all L4,8 ?, K1,7; first, for the first time L4,8 ?, L6,8, 10.

fyrutta *prep.* ? (see note 14).

fyry *adv.* see **fyre (3)**.

fyst *adv.* see **fyrst (2)**.

fyste (1) *adj.* V1a,28–9 etc. see **fyrst (1)**.

fyste (2) *adv.* L4,8, L6,8, 10 see **fyrst (2)**.

fæk *sv.* see **få**.

fæla *wv.*; *fæla fyre* fear V1a,58.

fæller *wv.* see **fella**.

fælæ *wv.* see **fæla**.

fær(i) *f.* see **ferd**.

fø (1) *conj.* V1a,3–5 see **fyrr (1)**.

fø (2) *prep.* V1a,23 see **fyre (1)**.

fødey *prep.+pron.* see **fyre (1)** & **den**.

føe *f.* food.

føesheim *m.* this world, this life (see note 15).

før (1) *prep.* L6,6, K1,6, K2,4 see **fyre (1)**.

før (2) *conj.* K1,3–5, T8,3 see **fyrr (1)**.

før (3) *adv.* K9,1–2 see **fyrr (2)**.

førr *conj.* see **fyrr (1)**.

få (fær, fekk, fenge) *sv.* have, get, obtain; *stærkan Svævnen fæk* fell into a deep sleep V1a,3, siml. V1a,6, M6,2, 7 etc.; *fek seg Madt* ate T8,1.

gala (gjel *pl.* **gala, gol, gale)** *sv.* sing, crow.

gama *n.* see **gaman**.

gamal *adj.* old.

gaman *n.* fun; as *adj. så Gama* so amusing, funny M6,27.

gang *m.* walk, journey, passage.

ganga (gjeng, gjekk, gjenge) *sv.* go, walk, cross; *ganga seg* = *ganga* M6, 38–9, 49–51, 63; *Gak no dæg* go (now ?)! K1,6*var.*; *gjekk mæ* wore L6,8; *dæ mone mæg kje bete gange* things will not go better for me, this is the best that could happen to me K1,20 (see note 8).

gangar(e) *m.* steed.

gard *m.* farm, house.

gauk *m.* cuckoo.

geengje *sv.* see **ganga**.

give *sv.* see **gjeva**.

giænom *prep.* see **igjenom**.

gjera (gjer, gjorde, gjort) *wv.* (1) do, make; *gjære han lexune lange* he makes the scriptural readings long, or: he takes the long scriptural readings V1a, 15; *som Fuglanne gjer ti Nøgjes* who does what the birds want, pleases them M6,53; *Der gjor aa saa vondt eit Veir* the weather turned so bad By1,2; (2) as *aux. han gjer 'kje annten kve hell kjeimar* he does not sing or sway M6,51.

gjerne *adv.*; *som gjønni vil* who wants very much M6,36.

gjeva (gjev *pl.* **gjeva, gav, gjeve)** *sv.* give; *gjæv Attegoume* pay attention! V1a,14; *Gud give* God grant M6,58.

gjor *wv.* see **gjera**.

gjæk, gjæn(-gje, -ji) *sv.* see **ganga**.

gjære *wv.* see **gjera**.

gjæv(-a, -e) *sv.* see **gjeva**.

gjønni *adv.* see **gjerne**.

gla *adj.* see **glad**.

glad *adj.* cheerful, happy.

gla(-e, -ere, -este) *adj.* see **glad**.

glede *f.* joy.

glei *f.* see **glede**.

gloands *adj.* glowing, red-hot L6,8.

glod *f.* red-hot embers.

gloe *f.* see **glod**.

gløyma *wv.* forget.

gnyr *m.* noise, turmoil.

go *adj.* see **god**.

god *adj.* (1) good M6,57; (2) good, kind L4,20–1; (3) nice, pleasant V1a,52, K1,9 ?; (4) easy(?) K1,9; *so go 'n Timi* so early (?) By2,1; L4,22 see **skjota**.

go(-e, -t) *adj.* see **god**.

gram *adj.* wild, angry.

greeme *f.* see **grime**.

grime *f.* halter.

gronne(e) *m.* see **grunn**.

grum *adj.* cruel, ferocious.

grund *m.* see **grunn**.

grunn *m.* bottom; *Havsens Gronne* the bed of the sea V1a,30–1; *pl. grunnar* depths T3,1; *å ne mæ klare Grunnar* and down in the clear depths M6,68.

gry *adj.* ? *adv.* ? *subst.* ? (see note 6).

grå *adj.* grey.

gråduve *f.* grey pigeon (see note 16).

gråta (**græt**, **gret**, **gråte**) *sv.* cry, weep; *gråta fyre* bewail K1,27; (see Section 4.2*c*).

gud *m.* God; L4,11 see **herregud**.

gudmo(er) *f.* see **gudmor**.

gudmor *f.* godmother (see note 17).

gull *n.* (1) gold T3,3; (2) gold ring or bracelet K1,19.

gullband *n.*; *Rødegulband* rings (or: bracelets) (a ring ?, bracelet ?) of red gold L4,20.

gulmo *f.* see **gudmor**.

gylden *adj.* golden.

gøy *wv.* bark, howl.

gå *sv.* see **ganga**.

går *m.* see **gard**.

ha *wv.* see **hava**.

hadde *wv.* see **halla**.

hae *wv.* see **hava**.

hald *subst.* (see note 19).

halda (**held**, **helt**, **halde**) *sv.* hold, keep; *ti glaere sko eg halle meg* I shall remain (be) the happier M6,28; *unde míne Føtanne helle* holds the bottom of my feet M6,44 (see note 21).

halla *wv.* tip, tilt; *Vikti kan hadde ne* can push the scales down, favour people when weighing goods M6,22.

halle *sv.* see **halda**.

han *nom.*, **han** or **honom** *obl.*, **honoms** *gen.*, *pron.* he, him, his, it; *nom. 'n* N1,4; *nom.* & *obl. en* M6,1, L4,1, K1,1–2; *obl.* ? *han* N1,4; *obl. ho* K1,2; *obl. haannom* N1,4; *obl. -o* (*onto*) V1a,2; *obl.* [*'om*] S6,2; *obl. æn* V1a,1.

hanga (**heng**, **hekk**, **hange**) *sv.* hang (*intr.*).

har *adj.* ? M6,3 (see note 18).

harm *m.* grief.

hat *n.* hate K2,4.

hatt *m.* hat L4,15.

haugetuss *m.* pixie, goblin, gnome.

hav *n.* sea, ocean; *def.sing. Havi* M6,11, 13, V8,1; *def.gen.sing. Havsens* V1a, 30–1, M6,12, L4,5, *havsens* L6,12.

hava (**hev** *pl.* **hava**, **hadde** or **ha**(**e**), **hatt**) *wv.* (1) have, own; *hava seg* = *hava* (1) K3,5; (2) as *aux.*+*pp.* V1a,1, 4, 25 etc.; *ha egh tot den Douen goe* if I had thought that death pleasant, if I had liked that death V1a,52; *eg ha snært 'kji hitta heim* I almost did not find the way home M9a,9; *imp.* or *inf.* ? *ha* N1,4.

havsensbotn *m.* the bed of the sea, see **bunn**.

he *adv.* see **her**.

heera *adv.* see **her**.

heere *subst.* ? (see note 20).

hei *f.* heath.

heim (**1**) *m.* (1) world V1a,2, L4,17–19 etc.; (2) home M6,62.

heim (**2**) *adv.* home T3,6, M9a,9.

heima *adv.* from home.

heimate *adv.* see **heimatil**.

heimatil *adv.* from home.

heit *adj.* hot; *comp. heytar* V1a,60.

heklebru *f.* spiky bridge (see note 10).

heklemo *f.* spiky heath, thorny moor (see note 10).

heklemoe *f.* see **heklemo.**

heklenau *f.* spiky danger (see note 10).

hell *conj.* (1) after *comp.* than V1a,60, K9, 1–2; (2) or M6,51, 57, L4,17, K1,16, K2,4.

helle *sv.* see **halda.**

helsa *wv.*; *helsa på* meet, talk to N1,4.

helvete *n.* see **helvite.**

helvite *n.* hell.

hemmerik(je) *n.* see **himmerike.**

hen *adv.* away, off over.

henda *wv.* happen; *dæ mone mæg inkje bære hænde* better things will not happen to me, this is the best that could happen to me K1,19 (see note 8).

hengja *wv.* hang (*tr.*).

her (1) *adv.* (1) here L4,14–15(1st occ.); here, in this life V1a,53, M6,36 ?, L3,5; (2) *expletive part.* ? M6,40–1, 64–8, L4, 14–15(2nd occ.).

her (2) *pron.* K1,29 see **kvor (1).**

herre *m.* see **herregud.**

herregud *int.* God!, O God!

hest *m.* horse.

hi *conj.* ? (see note 22).

him(m)eri(-g, -k) *n.* see **himmerike.**

himmerike *n.* heaven.

hinaen *pron.* see **hinannen.**

hinannen *pron.* each other.

hind *f.* hind.

hindeham *m.* hind-skin.

hitta *wv.*; *hitta heim* find the way home M9a,9.

hjarta *n.* heart.

hjerte *n.* see **hjarta.**

ho (1) *nom.*, **hæna** *obl.*, *pron.* she, her, it V1a,24–5, 28, M6,15 etc.; *nom. O* L1,16.

ho (2) *pron.* K1,2 see **han.**

hoge *adj.* see **håg.**

hogga (høgg, hogg or **ho(gg)je, hogge)** *sv.* (1) cut, chop V1a,37; (2) lunge, strike L4,10, L6,3, K1,10; *pres.* or *imp.* ? *haag* M1,3 (see Section 4.2*c*); *imp.* ? *hogge* S6,8; *refl. hoggast* strike at each other; *dey hojis uti Kjæfte* they tore at each other's mouth V1a,53.

ho(-ie, -jis) *sv.* see **hogga.**

hon *n.* see **stutehorn.**

hond (1) (*pl.* **hendar, hender)** *f.* hand, arm L4,9, 23 etc.; *dat.sing. hænde* L4, 20, *Hænde* K1,19.

hond (2) *m.* V1a,51 see **hund.**

hossi *adv.* how.

hot *rel.pron.* what.

hud *f.* skin.

hug *m.* mind, thoughts.

huggorm *m.* adder.

hui *f.* see **hud.**

hujen *m.* see **hug.**

hull *adj.* faithful.

hund *m.* dog.

hundegau *m.* baying of dogs.

hundegaul *n.* baying of dogs; *m.* or *f.* M6,56.

hus *n.* house, building.

hyggja (*pres.* **hygger** or **hygg)** *wv.* think.

hæe *n.* scorn.

hægste *adj.sup.* see **håg (1).**

hæklebro *f.* see **heklebru.**

hæl *m.* heel; *som tist meg i Hælanne hange* who seems to be dogging my footsteps M6,18.

hæna *pron.* see **ho (1).**

hændan *f.* see **hond (1).**

hænde (1) *f.* L4,20, K1,19(2nd occ.) see **hond (1).**

hænde (2) *wv.* K1,19(1st occ.) see **henda.**

hænder *f.* see **hond (1).**

hængde *wv.* see **hengja.**

hænge *sv.* see **hanga.**

hær *adv.* see **her (1).**

hæv(-e, -æ) *wv.* see **hava.**

høg *adj.* easy, comfortable M9a,7.

høgre *adj.* right (hand).

høgt *adv.* see **hågt.**

hørde *wv.* see **høyra.**

høyra *wv.* hear, listen; *høyre på* = *høyra* M6,5.

håg (1) *adj.* high M6,15, 19, 34 etc.; *sup. hægste* M6,61 (see note 23).

håg (2) *sv.* M1,3 see **hogga.**

hågt *adv.* high; *di Stoge so Høgt paa Gloe* they stood so high on red-hot embers L4,11.

hånd *f.* see **hond (1).**
hånnom *pron.* see **han.**

i (1) *prep.* (1) in, into V1a,2, 3*refr.*(2nd occ.), 12 etc.; (2) on V1a,3*refr.*(1st occ.), M6,65(2nd occ.), L4,3, 19(2nd occ.), K1,4–5, 7–8 ?, 26, K9,2, K5,20; (3) at V1a,24(1st occ.), K1,29; (4) of V1a,33, M1,3, M6,40–2; (5) for T6,1(2nd occ.); (6) to N1,4(1st occ.); *i Kyrkja* to church V1a,3 etc.; *i dròumo* dreaming, having dreams N1,4; *í stór Sút å Savn* in a situation of great grief and sorrow (?) M6,66; *at falde i saadan Drømme* to fall asleep and have such dreams K1,30; *í raue blóe di kinna* they churned red blood K3,3; *i* = *ei*(?) L4,14; M6,60(3rd occ.) see **taka**; L4,6 see **igjenom.**
i (2) *adv.* inside, in it L6,14(1st occ.).
idag *adv.* today.
ifra *conj.* see **ifrå (2).**
ifrå (1) *prep.* from K1,17.
ifrå (2) *conj.* from the time K1,1.
ifrå (3) *adv.* away, off M6,42.
igienem *prep.* see **igjenom.**
igjenom *prep.* through, across.
igjænom *prep.* see **igjenom.**
ikkje *adv.* not.
ikorn *n.* squirrel.
ikring *prep.* round, on.
imot *prep.* against.
ingen (1) *pron.* none, no one V1a,39, M1,2, M6,2 etc.
ingen (2) *adj.* no, not any M6,23, 36, L4,20–1.
injen (1) *pron.* V1a,39 see **ingen (1).**
inj(e)n (2) *adj.* L4,20–1 see **ingen (2).**
inkje *adv.* not V1a,44–5, 51, 57–9, M6, 53, L4,17–19, 24, L6,13, K1,3, 9, 12–16, 19, T3,4, V8,1.
inn *adv.* in.
inne *adv.* inside K3,3.
inni *prep.* into L4,23.
is *m.* ice; *isanne*, *Isæne* the surfaces of ice, the ice L4,22, K1,17.
isama *adv.* together.
iv(-e, -i) *prep.* see **yver.**

ja *int.* well.
jaga *wv.* chase, drive.
jarn *n.* iron; *dat.pl. Jønno* pieces of iron, iron fittings K9,6; *pl.* ? V1a,24–5, T3,2.
jase *m.* hare.
jeg *pron.* see **eg.**
jek *sv.* see **ganga.**
jen *art.* see **ein (1).**
jengji *sv.* see **ganga.**
jkon *n.* see **ikorn.**
jol *f.* Christmas.
joleftaen *m.* see **joleftan.**
joleftan *m.* Christmas eve.
joleftanskveld *m.* the evening of Christmas eve.
joleftdag *m.* Christmas eve.
joleptdagjen *m.* see **joleftdag.**
jolæftansqvællen *m.* see **joleftanskveld.**
jonni *n.* see **jarn.**
jor *f.* see **jord.**
jord *f.* earth, ground; land L6,9.
jordtorv *f.* clod, lump of earth.
jore (1) *wv.* T8,2 see **gjera.**
jore (2), **jori** *f.* V1a,44–5, M6,26b, L4,8, L6,10, K1,21, K9,4 see **jord.**
jupe *adj.* see **djup.**
jupt *adv.* see **djupt.**
jøn(-ni, -no) *n.* see **jarn.**
jøyr *wv.* see **gøy.**

kake *f.* cake (or: bread).
kald *adj.* cold.
kalvehjarta *n.* calf's heart; *have Kaave hjarta* be chicken-livered, easily frightened V8,1.
kanna *wv.* acknowledge; *eg ville 'kje mæ dæ kanne* I refused to acknowledge it as mine K3,5, see **eg.**
kappe *f.* cloak.
kasir *f.* see **kos.**
keddingann *f.* see **kjerring.**
keima *wv.* sway, swing back and forth (with joy).
kinna *wv.* churn.
kje *adv.* see **ikkje.**
kjeddigje *f.* see **kjerring.**

kjeft *m.* mouth, jaw.

kjellar *m.* M6,19, 34 (see note 24).

kjenna *wv.* (1) know, recognise; *der va meg injen man kjænd* no one there was known to me L4,20; *kjenna att* recognise K1,19; *kjenna til* know (of, about) K9,4; *pl.* ? *kjænne* V1a,3*refr.* (see Section 4.2*c*); (2) feel T8,1.

kjerring *f.* old woman.

kjæfte *m.* see **kjeft**.

kjæm *sv.* see **koma**.

kjæn(-d, -ne) *wv.* see **kjenna**.

kjær *adj.* dear.

kjærinje *f.* see **kjerring**.

kjættil *m.* see **tjørukjetel**.

kjørkje *f.* see **kyrkje**; L4,4 see **kyrkje-dynn**.

kjøru *f.* see **tjørukjetel**.

klar *adj.* clear.

kling *m.* buttered (and norm. sugared) 'lefse' (thin pancake made of rolled, unleavened dough).

klippe *n.* (norm. *m.*) cliff, crag.

klo (*pl.* **kløver**, norm. **klør**) *f.* claw.

klæde *n.pl.* clothes.

klæi *n.* see **klæde**.

kløver *f.* see **klo**.

kne *n.* knee; *te Knes, te knés, under Knè* up to his knee M6,26b, L6,10, K9,4; *alt unde Kne* right up to his knee L4,8; *dat.* ? *pl. te Knio* up to his knees K1,21.

kneggja *wv.* neigh.

knejar *wv.* see **kneggja**.

knekkja *wv.* break, snap (*tr.*).

knio *n.* see **kne**.

koma (**kjem** *pl.* **koma**, **kom**, **kome**) *sv.* come, arrive, get (somewhere), see also **fram**; *koma seg* = *koma* L4,8–12, 20–2, L6,7–8, 10, 13–14, F1,2, L3,5, K3,3; *fe domane dei kom vraange* because unjust judgements were passed L4,13; *eg kom der inkje utpå* (and) I did not go out onto it, or: I should not go out onto it L6,13.

kon(n) *n.* see **korn**.

konne *pret.pres.v.* see **kunna**.

koon *n.* see **korn**.

korn *n.* corn.

kornmål *n.* measure of corn (that will fill a utensil); *Konnmåli den kan auke* he (who) can give more corn to beggars than custom dictates (?) M6,21.

kos (*pl.* **kasir**) *f.* piece of land on which the vegetation has been burnt and the ash used as a fertiliser; *hogge Kasir* hoe such pieces of land so that they are ready for sowing V1a,37.

kringum *prep.* (a)round.

krok *m.* hook.

krøkja *wv.* bend, curl; *som Ørnekløar krøkte* which crooked their eagles' talons M6,30.

ku *f.* cow.

kulde *m.* cold, coldness.

kull *m.* see **kulde**.

kun *pret.pres.v.* see **kunna**.

kunna (**kann**, **kunne** or **kunna**, **kunna**) *pret.pres.v.* (1) can, be able V1a,1, M1,2, M6,1–2, 5, 13 etc.; (2) may, might, should M6,43; (3) know V1a,52.

kvarandre *pron.* see **kvorare**.

kvass *adj.* sharp.

kvast *adv.* (1) sharply, badly; (2) hard, fast L4,15.

kve(a) *sv.* see **kveda**.

kveda (**kved**, **kvad**, **kvede**) *sv.* sing, recite.

kvela *wv.* choke, strangle (or: torment = *kvelja* ?) M6,31 (see Section 4.2*c*).

kverandre *pron.* see **kvorare**.

kvesste *wv.* M6,38 (see note 25).

kvide *m.* (norm. *f.*) distress, agony.

kvie *m.* see **kvide**.

kvist *m.* branch.

kvit *adj.* white.

kvitt *adj.* rid of, free of, past.

kvor (1) *pron.* each person, everyone K1,29.

kvor (2) *adj.* each, every M6,9–10, 47 etc.; *dat. qvorjum, Kvorjom, kvorjum* V1a,24–5, 29, 52, L4,12, T3,3; *kvor den, kvor den Sjæl* every single soul K1,27.

kvorare *pron.* each other.

kvorkjen *conj.* neither; *inkje . . . Qvorkjen . . . hel* neither . . . nor L4,17.

kyrkje *f.* church; V1a,12 see **kyrkjedynn**; V1a,15 see **kyrkjesvol.**

kyrkjedynn *f.* church door, church doorway.

kyrkjesvol *f.* church porch, open passage way (with waist-high exterior wall) round outside of stave-church (see Section 4.2*a*).

kåm(a) *sv.* see **koma.**

kån *n.* see **korn.**

kåpe *f.* cloak.

kåt *adj.* (1) frisky V1a,22–3; (2) gay, jolly L4,1.

kåve *m.* see **kalvehjarta.**

land *n.* land, country.

lang *adj.* long.

langsam *adj.* slow, dreary, unchanging; *i míne langsomme Dagar* in my unchanging life (?), in those never-ending days (?) M6,56.

langsomme *adj.* see **langsam.**

langt *adv.* far.

lappa *wv.* mend, sole.

laugevatn *n.* bath water (see note 3).

leggja (legg, la(e), lagt) *wv.* lay, put, place; *leggja seg (ned, nedpå)* lie down, go to bed V1a,4–6, M6,6–7 etc.; *leggja ut* discuss, interpret, hold forth about M6,8, 72, K1,6, K9,3.

lei (1) *f.* path, road M1,3.

lei (2) *adj.* unpleasant, nasty; as *subst. den jore meg soe lejt* it had such a bad effect on me T8,2.

leika *wv.* play.

leksa *f.* scriptural text, piece of Scripture.

lenge *adv.* for a long time, long; S6,2 see **sålenge.**

ler *sv.* see **læ.**

lerke *m.* (norm. *f.*) lark.

lesa (les, las, lese) *sv.*; *lesa upp* read out, read aloud V1a,12 etc.

lette *n.* relief; *dæ va' meg te Letti* it was a relief to me M6,67.

lexune *f.* see **leksa.**

li *f.* slope, hillside; *dat.pl.* ? *lìå* F1,2.

lida (lid, leid, lide) *sv.* suffer.

lie *sv.* see **lida.**

liggja (ligg, lå, lege) *sv.* lie, rest.

like *m.* match, equal.

liljurunne *m.* lily shoot, branch of a lily.

lindarorm *m.* mighty snake (see note 26).

lindegrein *f.* branch of a lime tree.

lisle *adj.* see **liten.**

liten (*def.* **lisle**) *adj.sing.* little, small; *n. líti* M6,27*var.*

liv *n.* life.

livande *adj.*; as *subst. livandes* living person M6,36.

ljota (lyt, laut, lote) *sv.* must, have to; with *inf.* omitted *sonde lout mi Skarlags Kaapa* my scarlet cloak had to get torn, I could not avoid getting my scarlet cloak torn L4,6–7.

longe *adv.* long ago, long since.

lu(r) *m.* horn, trumpet.

lya *wv.* listen, hear.

lysa *wv.* shine; *der lyser* there is a shining light K1,18.

læ (lær, lo, lætt) *sv.* laugh.

læer *sv.* see **læ.**

læg(ge) *wv.* see **leggja.**

læn(g)je *adv.* see **lenge.**

løve (*pl.* **løver**, norm. **løvur**) *f.* lion.

løveflokk *m.* band of lions.

løverkula *f.* band of lions (?).

løvetann *f.* lion's tooth.

løysa *wv.* free, release.

låna *wv.* lend.

lånd *n.* see **land.**

långæ *adv.* see **longe.**

madt *m.* see **mat.**

mang *adj.* many V1a,15, V8,2 etc.; *den gnýren mange* L6,3 (see Section 4.2*b*).

mange *pron.* many (people) M6,71.

mann (*pl.* **mennar**) *m.* man; *dat.pl. Maanno* L3,5.

mannetunge *f.* human tongue.

mat *m.* food.

me (1) *pron.* we V8,2, M20,1.

me (2) *pron.* V1a,44, K1,25 see **eg.**

me (3) *adj.* V1a,28–9 see **min.**

me (4) *prep.* M1,1, K9,6, By1,2 see **med (1).**

me (5) *conj.* M6,32 see **men.**

med (1) *prep.* (1) with V1a,24–5 etc., M6,26b ? (see note 31); (2) in, on, among M1,1, M6,11–13, 68, L4,5, K9,6(1st occ.); *De va mæ den Fyste (Andre) utreisi* it happened on the first (second) journey hence (?) L4,6–7 see **eg**; *Aa nagle mæ Kvorjom tinde* and a nail on every spike L4,12; (3) by, at By1,2; (4) along M9a,9(1st occ.); (5) round(?), by way of (?) M9a,9(2nd occ.) (see note 4); L6,8 see **ganga.**

med (2) *conj.* while V1a,61 etc., M6,26b ? (see note 31).

meen(e) *adj.* see **min.**

mei *adv.* see **meir.**

mein *n.* harm, damage.

meina *wv.* think.

meining *f.* meaning(?), intention(?) M6, 52 (see note 14).

meir *adv.comp.* more.

men *conj.* but.

mest *adj.sup.*; as *subst. dæ meste* the most, all M6,55.

mi *pron.* V8,2 see **me (1).**

midnatstid *f.* midnight.

midt *adv.* in the middle.

mig *pron.* see **eg.**

mil ? *f.* ? K1,5 (see note 28).

min *m.sing.*, **mi** *f.sing.*, **mitt** *n.sing.*, **mine** or **mi** *pl.*, *adj.* my V1a,12, 14, 22–3, 28–32 etc.; *pl. mi* M6,11, 45, 48–9, 51, 55, 64, 68–9, K1,4; *m.sing.* ? *mine* M6, 63; *kvor min Fóte (Fót'e)* each foot M6,9, 47; *kvor min Fing(e)* every finger M6,10 etc.

minne *n.* memory, recollection; *dæ gjenge meg addi av Minne* it will never leave my memory M6,32.

mjødde *f.* see **mjøll.**

mjøll *f.* light, powdery snow, fresh snow.

mo *subst.* (see note 20).

mod *f.* see **mold.**

mo(-der, -ðir, -er) *f.* see **mor.**

mog *m.* see **tynnermo.**

moir *f.* see **mor.**

moka *wv.* shovel; *i Molle moka* shovelled into the earth, buried V1a,52.

mold *f.* mould, earth.

molle *f.* see **mold.**

mon *pret.pres.v.* see **mun.**

monar *m.* see **munn.**

mon(n)e (1) *pret.pres.v.* M6,54, 57, 62, K1,10, 19–20 see **mun.**

monne (2) *m.* V1a,30, M1,1 see **munn.**

mor *f.* mother.

morgon *m.* morning.

mot *prep.* against, towards.

mun (munde) *defct.pret.pres.v.* (1) will (surely) K1,19–20; (2) as *expletive part. som Skorpejonen monne fara* where the scorpion wanders M6,54, siml. M6,57, 62–3; *dei mone kvorare ægte* they (i.e., who) marry each other (?) K1,10.

munn *m.* mouth; *af blie monar* with cheerful lips L4,5.

mykje *adj.* (*undecl.*) much.

myrda *wv.* murder; *myre Mannen i Skog* K5,11 (see note 29).

myre *wv.* see **myrda.**

myrk *adj.* dark; *myrke Hús* dark buildings (?), a house in darkness (?) M6,70 (see note 30).

mæ (1) *prep.* V1a,24–5, M6,3, 11–12, 23, 26b ?, 31, 49, 66, 68, 70, 73–4, L4,5, 6–7 ?, 12, 15, 20, L6,8, K1,11, 19, M9a,9, M15b,3 see **med (1).**

mæ (2) *conj.* V1a,61, M6,4, 26b ?, 51, 54, 67, 69 see **med (2).**

mæ (3) *pron.* L4,6–7 ?, K3,5 see **eg.**

mæg *pron.* see **eg.**

mæn *conj.* see **men.**

mænnar *m.* see **mann.**

mødte *wv.* see **møta.**

møta *wv.* meet; *då møtte en Manne* then I met a man M6,26b (see note 31); *imp. møte* K1,22.

møye *f.* trouble, difficulty; *dæ va' meg te Møia lagt* it was placed on me as a burden (?), it was arranged (done) to give me trouble (?) M6,66.

måkje *pret.pres.v.+adv.* see **måtta** & **ikkje**.

mål (1) *n.* speech, voice M6,5, 74.

mål (2) *n.* measurement, measure M6,60.

måne *m.* moon.

månno *m.* see **mann**.

måtta (må, måtte, mått) *pret.pres.v.* (1) must, have to V1a,44–5, 61, M6,15 etc.; with *inf.* omitted *då måtte eg på Havsensbotnen* then I had to go to the bottom of the sea M6,3, siml. M6,4, 29; (2) may, might M6,58; (3) can(?) M6,53.

n (1) *pron.* N1,4 see **han**.

n (2) *art.* By2,1 see **ein (1)**.

nagel (*pl.* **neglar**) *m.* (finger- or toe-) nail.

nagle *m.* (metal or wooden) nail.

natt (*pl.* **nettar**) *f.* night.

nau *f.* see **naud**.

naud *f.* need, want K1,15; *hossi mang ei naud* how much distress, wretchedness T6,1.

ne *adv.* see **ned** & **nedatt**.

neat(t) *adv.* see **nedatt**.

ned *adv.* down.

nedatt *adv.* down again.

nedi (1) *adv.* down into it V1a,60.

nedi (2) *prep.* down into M6,29.

nedpå *adv.*; see **leggja**.

nedå *prep.* down on (see note 32).

nee *adv.* see **ned**.

nekta *wv.* reject, repudiate, disown.

neri *prep.* see **nedi (2)**.

ni *adv.* see **nedi (1)**.

nie *num.* nine.

no *adv.* (1) now V1a,4, 26 etc., K1,6*var.* ?, M9a,9 ?; (2) as *expletive part.* M6,2–5, 27, 44, 62, L4,14–15, K1,6*var.* ?, K1,12, M9a,9 ? (see note 33).

nok *adv.* probably, all right.

noken (1) *pron.* M6,33 see **nokon (1)**.

noken (2) *adj.* M6,41 see **nokon (2)**.

nokon (1) *m.sing.*, **noko** *n.sing.*, **nokon** *pl.* ?, *pron.* any(one), something V1a,60; *Egh kan noko af qvorjum Viso* I know a bit of every song, or: I know something of every custom V1a,52; *men alli noken av mine Vinir* but (there were) never any of my friends M6,33.

nokon (2) *m.sing.*, **noko** *f.sing.*, *adj.* any, a, an M6,41, K1,11, 15.

nora *adv.* see **nordavind**.

norafjøl(-ds, -ls) *adv.* see **nordafjølls**.

norate *adv.* see **nordatil**.

nordafjølls *adv.* north of the mountains (see note 34).

nordatil *adv.* from the north.

nordavind *m.* the north wind.

ny *adj.* new.

nyt *adj.* able, doughty.

nægte *wv.* see **nekta**.

næste *adj.* ? *adv.* ? (see note 35).

nøgje *n.* satisfaction; *ti Nøgjes* as they want M6,53 see **gjera**.

nå *adv.* see **no**.

nåda *wv.* have mercy on.

nåe *wv.* see **nåda**.

når *conj.* when.

o (1) *int.* Oh! L12,3(2nd occ.) (see note 53).

o (2) *conj.* F1,2, L12,3(1st & 3rd occ.) see **og**.

o (3) *pron.* L1,16 see **ho**.

oddu *intensifying adv. before sup.* of all M6,28*var.*

og *conj.* and (see note 53); *Aa ny e Heimate for* and (it was) new (when) I left home (?) L4,7.

om (1) *prep.* (1) on V1a,3–6, M6,2–7, 25–6 etc.; (2) about V1a,1, 12, M6,1, L4,1; (3) in V1a,13; (4) for M6,55; M6,62 see **tenkja**.

om (2) *pron.* S6,2 see **han**.

omkring *adv.* around, about.

omtrent *adv.* around, approximately.

onde *prep.* see **under**.

ondeleg *adj.* see **underleg**.

ond(-er, -æ) *prep.* see **under**.

ong(-e, -æ) *adj.* see **ung**.

ont *pret.pres.v.* see **unna**.

onto *pret.pres.v.+pron.* see **unna** & **han**.

oppdragelse *m.* education, upbringing; *Mine Foreldres Opdragelse* the upbringing my parents gave me (?) M6,57.
orm *m.* snake, serpent.
ormevrimmel *m.* mass of snakes.
ospelauv *n.* aspen leaves.
oto *prep.* see **utor.**
ottefugl *m.* early bird.

paradiis *n.* see **paradis.**
paradis *n.* paradise.
pivi *adv.* see **uppyver.**
plaga *wv.* torment.
plage *f.* affliction, torment.
podde *f.* toad.
ponde *prep.* see **uppunder.**
predikstol *m.* pulpit.
prest *m.* priest, pastor.
prækestolen *m.* see **predikstol.**
præsten *m.* see **prest.**
punde *prep.* see **uppunder.**
på (1) *prep.* (1) on, onto V1a,30, 39*refr.*, 56*refr.*, 60*refr.*, M1,3, M6,13 etc.; (2) in, into V1a,12, 15, 32–3, M6,8, 72, 73 (1st occ.), L6,1*refr.*, 2, K9,3, M15b,3 ?; (3) to M6,3–4, 17, 56; *paa mi Høgre haand* (*Haand*) to my right L4,23, to (on) my right (hand) K1,18; F1,2 see **fram**; M6,5 see **høyra**; M6,21 see **ræ(dd)ast**; M6,30 see **søkja**; M6,39 see **setja**; M6,73(2nd occ.) see **stagga**; L6,8 see **bera**; K1,17, 18(1st occ.) see **taka**; N1,4 see **helsa.**
på (2) *adv.* on (it) V1a,13, K1,5, V9,7.
pådda *f.* see **podde.**

qvæa *sv.* see **kveda.**

rapa *wv.*; *mæ rapa Mod i Mun* K1,11 (see note 36).
rar *adj.* strange, fascinating, exciting.
raud (1) *m.* reddish coloured horse, bay V1a,22–3.
raud (2) *adj.* red.
raue *adj.* see **raud (2).**
reendi *m.* see **tynnersrinde.**
refsa *wv.* punish (see note 37).
rei (1) *n.* nest M6,52.
rei (2) *sv.* L4,14–15, K1,23–5, T5,4, Sæl,1 see **rida.**
reisa *wv.* go, travel; *reisa seg* = *reisa* K1, 20; *Rest eg* L4,23 (see note 38).
renna (renn, rann, runne) *sv.* (1) run; (2) rise (of the sun); *Sol(l)i ran i Li(e)* the sun rose (and shone) on the hillside K1,4–5.
res(s)t(e) *wv.* see **reisa.**
rett *adv.* justly, correctly.
rida (rid, reid, ride) *sv.* ride; *rida seg* = *rida* V1a,14.
rie *sv.* see **rida.**
ring *m.* see **tynnerring.**
riva (riv, reiv, rive) *sv.* tear.
rjoda (ryd, raud, rode) *sv.* redden; *soli ho Rye i lie* the sun casts a red glow onto the slope L4,3.
ronine *f.* see **runer.**
rosenslund *m.* grove of roses.
rou *m.* see **raud (1).**
rug *m.* rye.
runer *f.pl.* runes, rune magic.
rye *sv.* see **rjoda.**
rygg *m.* back.
ræ(dd)ast *wv.* fear, be afraid of; *ræ(dd)ast av, fyre* = *ræ(dd)ast* V1a,56–7, 59, M6,19, 19*var.*, 22 etc.; *ræast på* = *ræast*(?) M6,21 (see note 39).
rænnæ *sv.* see **renna.**
røde *adj.* see **raud (2).**
rødegulband *adj.+n.* see **raud (2)** & **gullband.**
rå(da) *wv.* control, rule; *rå(da) fyre* be master of, guide M9a,9, control, use L3,5.

sa *adv.* L4,1 see **so (1).**
sakna *wv.* miss.
sala *wv.* saddle; *sala ut* saddle up V1a, 22–3 etc.
salt *adj.* salt.
same *adj.*; as *subst.* *dæ sama* the same thing M6,27*var.*
samla *wv.* collect, gather.
sancte *adj.* see **sankte.**

sandeleg *adv.* see **sanneleg.**
sankte *adj.* Saint.
sanneleg *adv.* certainly, indeed.
sanning *f.* truth.
sannong *f.* see **sanning.**
sante *adj.* see **sankte.**
saum *m.* (metal) nail(s).
savn *n.* want(?), loss(?).
se *sv.* see **sjå.**
sedt *sv.* see **sjå.**
seen(-e, -æ) *refl.adj.* see **sin.**
see(-r, -t) *sv.* see **sjå.**
seg *refl.pron.* him(self), her(self), it(self), them(selves).
seljeteine *m.* see **seljutein.**
seljuronne *m.* see **seljurunne.**
seljurunne *m.* willow shoot, willow branch.
seljutein *m.* willow shoot.
setja *wv.*; *setja seg* sit down V1a,12; *setja på* rush at, attack M6,39.
sheeh *refl.adj.* see **sin.**
shæl *adj.* see **sæl.**
sia *f.* see **side.**
side *f.* side.
silkeseng *f.* silken bed, bed with silk sheets and covers.
sill(e) *pret.pres.v.* see **skula.**
sin *m.sing.*, **si** *f.sing.*, **sitt** *n.sing.*, **sine** or **si** *pl.*, *refl.adj.* his, her, its, their; *pl. si* V1a,38, By1,2.
sitja (sit, sat, sete) *sv.* sit.
siæve *sv.* see **skjelva.**
sjel *f.* soul.
sjeldan *adv.* seldom.
sjelefristelse *m.* temptation of the soul.
sjellan *adv.* see **sjeldan.**
sjuse *wv.* see **skjussa.**
sjæl(-ene, -ine) *f.* see **sjel** & **syndesjel.**
sjå or **se (ser, såg, set)** *sv.* see, look; *sjå seg = sjå* M6,30, K1,19.
ska *pret.pres.v.* see **skula.**
skaka (skjek, skok *pl.* **skoke, skjeke)** *sv.* shake, flap.
skarla(-gs, -k(k)ens) *n.* see **skarlakskåpe.**
skarlakskåpe *f.* scarlet cloak; *indef.sing.* ? *Skarlakskåpi* M6,10.
ske(e)ne *sv.* see **skina.**
skina (skin, skein, skine) *sv.* shine.
skjebne *m.* fate.
skjelva (skjelv, skolv, skolve) *sv.* tremble, quake.
skjn *sv.* see **skina.**
skjota (skyt, skaut, skote) *sv.* shoot, push, throw; *gud Skout mæg so got i Hujen* God gave me such a good (happy) idea L4,22.
skjussa *wv.* give (someone) a ride, transport, carry.
skjæbnen *m.* see **skjebne.**
skjæfte *m.* see **kjeft.**
sko (1) (*pl.* **sko** or **skor)** *m.* shoe V1a,38, 59, M6,40 etc.
sko (2) *pret.pres.v.* M6,16*avar.*, 28, 32, 43, L6,1*refr.*, 12, K1,20, 21*refr.*, 24*refr.*, 26, V9,7 see **skula.**
skoe *m.* see **sko (1).**
skog *m.* forest, wood; V1a,28 see **tynnerskog.**
skogesnar *n.* copse, thicket (see note 40).
skorpejonen *m.* see **skorpion.**
skorpion *m.* scorpion.
skrål *n.* shout(ing), racket.
skula (ska(l) or **sko, skulle** or **sille, skula)** *pret.pres.v.* (1) *fut.* shall, will, should, would M6,25, 32(1st occ.), 52 ?, L6,1*refr.*, K1,20, 21*refr.*, 24*refr.*; (2) be going to, intend to, shall M1,1, M6,28, L6,12, L12,3 ?; (3) have to, is to M6, 16*avar.*, 32(2nd occ.) ?, 43 ?, K1,26, V9,7 ?; with *inf.* omitted *Dei ska fram, dei skaa vek* they must come forth, they are to go hence K5,20–1; *dæ sill vera* it represented S6,8.
sky *n.* (*f.coll.* ?) cloud.
skå *pret.pres.v.* see **skula.**
skål *f.* bowl, large drinking vessel.
skålevekt *f.* see **skålevikt.**
skålevigt *f.* see **skålevikt.**
skålevikt *f.* balance, pair of scales.
slange *m.* snake, serpent.
slej(-en, -i, -æn) *sv.* see **slå.**
sleppa (slepp, slapp, sluppe) *sv.* escape from, get out of L6,7, K9,5; *sleppa*

yver (be able to) get across V1a,22–3, V8,2; *eg slap ikje af* I could not get off L4,13.

slita (slit, sleit, slite) *sv.* tear.

slæjæn *sv.* see **slå.**

sløkjefri *f.* ? drinking horn (see note 41).

slå (slær, slo, slege) *sv.* overlay, cover, fit; *ho va Fast mæ krokar sleji* it was firmly fitted with hooks, hooks were firmly driven into it L4,12.

smerta *wv.* grieve.

smådreng *m.* little boy.

snaka *wv.* take, steal.

snill *adj.* kind, nice.

snjor *m.* snow; *so stor ein Snjoræ* such a big snowfall V1a,38.

snært *adv.* almost.

so (1) *adv.* so, such a V1a,1, 1*refr.*, 4, 22*refr.*, 24–5, 38, 40*refr.* etc.; thus(?) M6,56.

so (2) *adv.* then, and then, and V1a,12, 14, M6,4 etc. see **så (2)**, L6,9(2nd occ.), 11, F1,2.

so (3) *conj.* as M6,23.

so (4) *expletive part.* V1a,44(2nd occ.), 45, M6,18 etc. see **så (4)**.

soe *adv.* T8,2 see **so (1)**.

sol *f.* sun.

solænje *adv.+adv.* see **so (1)** & **lenge.**

som (1) *rel.pron.* who, which, that V1a,1, 30–2, 39, 43, 53, 54*refr.*, 56–9, 61*refr.*, M1,1, M6,1–2, 11–12, 15, 18 etc.; M6,54 ? see **som (4)**.

som (2) *conj.* like, as V1a,2, M6,23, 36 (1st occ.), 37(2nd occ.) ?, K1,1–2, 27, S6,2; as if M6,43(2nd occ.).

som (3) *conj.* when, as L6,3, 7–8, 13–14.

som (4) *rel.adv.* where M6,52, 53(1st occ.), 54 ?, 63.

some *pron.* see **sume.**

somloug *adj.* see **sumlug.**

sond *f.* see **synd.**

sonde *adv.* see **sund.**

sondesleyt *adv.+sv.* see **sund** & **slita.**

sonnate *adv.* see **sunnatil.**

soomæ *pron.* see **sume.**

sorg *f.* sorrow.

soten *m.+art.* the dark brown, or black horse.

sova (søv, sov, sove) *sv.* sleep.

sovna *wv.* fall asleep.

spiker *m.* (metal) nail; *pl.* ? T3,2.

spott *m.* ridicule.

st. *adj.* see **sankte.**

stagga *wv.*; *stagga på* stop (from leaving) M6,73.

stai *sv.* see **standa.**

standa (stend, sto(d) *pl.* **stoge, stade)** *sv.* (1) stand; *Stat up* get up! arise! V1a,54*refr.*, 61*refr.*; *dæ hæv kje stai mæg nokon Grund* there was no ground under me, my feet did not touch bottom K1, 11; K1,26 see **fram**; (2) be held, take place L6,1*refr.*, K1,20, 21*refr.*, 24*refr.*

stanga *wv.* butt, gore.

stenge *sv.* see **stinga.**

sterk *adj.* deep V1a,3, 5–6 etc.

stett *f.* (& *n.* ?) door-step, small flight of steps leading up to outer door or entrance K9,2, N1,4, or: gate(way) into churchyard (?) N1,4.

stikka (stikk, stakk, stukke) *sv.* bite, sting.

stilla *wv.* still, quieten.

stinga (sting, stakk, stunge) *sv.* bite, sting.

stoge *sv.* see **standa.**

stor (*sup.* **størst**) *adj.* (1) big, mighty, great V1a,38, M6,29 etc.; *pl.* or *def.* ? M6,57; (2) powerful, loud M6,21, L4, 24.

stoste *adj.* see **stor.**

strand *f.* shore.

straum *m.* current, stream (see note 42).

strei *sv.* see **strida.**

strida (*imp.* **streid**) *w.* & *sv.* fight.

stura *wv.* mope, sulk, grieve.

stut *m.* ox, bull; K1,14 see **stutehorn.**

stutehon(n) *n.* see **stutehorn.**

stutehorn *n.* bull's horn, ox's horn.

stygging *m.* wicked, sinful person.

styjeengs *m.* see **stygging.**

stænd(-e, -æ) *sv.* see **standa.**

stærkan *adj.* see **sterk.**

støste *adj.* see **stor**.

sume *pron.pl.* some people, some.

sumlug *adj.* giddy, dizzy; *han tar inkje somloug gange* he need not feel dizzy when walking K1,13.

sund *adv.* in(to) bits, pieces.

sunnatil *adv.* from the south.

sut *f.* grief.

svala *wv.* (see note 43).

svara *wv.* answer.

svart *adj.* black.

sveipa *wv.* wrap.

sveitta *wv.* sweat; *sveitta dei det kalde Bloi* they sweated cold blood Sæl,1.

svevn *m.* sleep.

svolo *f.* see **kyrkjesvol** (& Section 4.2*a*).

svævnen *m.* see **svevn**.

synd *f.* sin; K1,27(1st occ.) see **syndesjel**.

syndesjel *f.* sinful soul.

syndig *adj.* sinful.

syngja (**syng**, **sang**, **sunge**) *sv.* sing.

sysken *n.pl.* brother and sister.

syskenbarn *n.* cousin.

syskini *n.* see **sysken**.

syskjenbo(**-ni**, **-onne**) *n.* see **syskenbarn**.

syskjni *n.* see **sysken**.

sysl *f.* ? witch(?) (see note 44).

syslehus *n.* witches' house (?) (see note 44).

sæg *refl.pron.* see **seg**.

sæhl *adj.* see **sæl**.

sæl *adj.* (1) blessed V1a,56–9 etc.; K5,20–1 (see Section 5.2); (2) lucky, happy M14,1.

sættæ *wv.* see **setja**.

søkja *wv.*; *søkja på* rush at, attack M6,30.

sønd(**-ige**, **-ugu**) *adj.* see **syndig**.

søvne(**n**) *m.* see **svevn**.

så (**1**) *adv.* M1,2, M6,1, 1*refr.*, 6, 25, 27 (2nd occ.) etc. see **so** (**1**).

så (**2**) *adv.* M6,4, 28*var.* ?, 31–2, 38–9, 42–3, 44(1st & 3rd occ.), 45–6, 48(1st occ.), 49, 50(1st occ.), 51–4, 58, L6,9, K1,6, 8, 17–22, 24–5, 28–30, K9,2, K5,11 see **so** (**2**).

så (**3**) *conj.* M6,23 see **so** (**3**); S6,2 see **sålenge**.

så (**4**) *expletive part.* M6,18, 27(1st occ.), 28, K1,14, K9,5 ?, T3,6, L1,16(1st & 2nd occ.) see **so** (**4**).

sådan *adj.* such; *pl.* ? K1,30.

sål *f.* soul; L4,14, K1,24–6, 28, T5,4 (see Section 5.2).

sålenge *conj.* as long as, all the time S6,2.

ta *f.* see **tå**.

tagge *m.* barb, prong, sharp point.

taka (**tek**, **tok**, **teke**) *sv.* take; *stærkan Svevnæn tok* fell into a deep sleep V1a,5; *taka til* begin V1a,13, M6,43; *taka i* touch, take hold of M6,60; *taka på* set off, start out K1,17–18.

tala *wv.* speak.

tann (*pl.* **tennar**) *f.* (1) tooth M6,35, 39 etc.; (2) prong, tine T3,3.

tar *pret.pres.v.* see **turva**.

te (**1**) *prep.* M6,26b, 66–7, L4,2, 21 etc. see **til** (**1**).

te (**2**) *adv.* K5,11 see **til** (**2**) & **vera**.

teende *m.* see **tind**.

tekst *f.* scriptural text, piece of Scripture; *m.* or *pl.* ? *Texten din* (*dine*) K1,6 (K1, 6*var.*) (see Section 4.2*a*).

telja (**tel**, **talde**, **talt**) *wv.* tell, relate.

tenkja *wv.* think, consider, feel; *tenkja om* = *tenkja* M6,62.

text(**-en**, **-ine**) *f.* see **tekst**.

theele *wv.* see **telja**.

thi *prep.* see **til** (**1**).

thii *f.* see **tid**.

ti (**1**) (+*comp.*) *conj.* the (-er) M6,28.

ti (**2**) *f.* see **tid**; K1,17–18 (see note 5).

ti (**3**) *prep.* V1a,38, M6,40, 53, K5,21 see **til** (**1**).

ti (**4**) *adv.* V1a,13, M6,43 see **til** (**2**) & **taka**.

tid *f.* period, time(s).

tikjes *wv.* see **tykkjast**.

til (**1**) *prep.* (1) to V1a,23, L4,2, 21, L6,7 etc.; (2) towards, at K1,18–19; (3) up to, below M6,26b, L6,10(2nd occ.), K1, 21; (4) as *prep.* & *inf. marker* to V1a,38, M6,40, T8,3; M6,53 see **gjera** & **nøgje**;

M6,66 see **møye**; M6,67 see **lette**; K9,4 see **kjenna**.

til (2) *adv.* K5,11 see **vera**; as *adv.* & *inf. marker* to V1a,13, M6,43 see **taka**.

tilje *f.* board, plank.

time *m.* time, hour, see **god**.

tind *m.* spike, sharp point.

ting *n.* thing M14,1; creature M1,3.

tis(-s, -t) *wv.* see **tykkjast**.

tjørukjetel *m.* cauldron of tar.

tog *sv.* see **taka**.

tong *adj.* see **tung**.

tonga *f.* see **tunge**.

torvunne *f.* see **jordtorv**.

tos(-e, -se, -t) *wv.* see **tykkjast**.

totte *wv.* see **tykkja**.

trang *adj.* tight, miserly.

trettan *num.* see **trettanddag**.

trettanda(g)jen *m.* see **trettanddag**.

trettanddag *m.* thirteenth day (of Christmas, 6th Jan.), epiphany.

trettande *num.* thirteenth; as *subst. den Trettende* the thirteenth (day) K1,29 see **trettanddag**.

trettende *num.* see **trettande**.

tri *num.* three.

tro *adj.* faithful.

trygt *adv.* safely.

trøa *wv.* tread, tramp; *den som mine fótspor sko' trøa* he who would tread in my footsteps L6,12.

trøsta *wv.* comfort.

trøytt *adj.* tired.

trå (1) *adj.* persistent(?), tireless(?) K1, 25; long(?), prolonged(?) T6,1.

trå (2) *wv.* trample.

tung *adj.* (1) heavy Sæl,1; (2) hard, difficult M6,16a, 18 etc.; (3) weary, muted M6,74; sad(?), distressing(?) M6,25.

tunge *f.* tongue; *dæn må mæ Tunga tala* he must have the gift of tongues (?) M6,49 (see note 45).

tura *wv.* celebrate.

turva (tar(v), turvte, turvt) *pret.pres.v.* need.

tut *n.* howl, cry.

tvei *num.* see **tvo**.

tvist *adv.* quietly, calmly.

tvo *num.* two; *m. tvei* V1a,53, K1,10.

tykk *adj.* thick.

tykkja (tykkjer, totte, tott) *wv.* think, consider.

tykkjast (tykkjest or **tyst, tottest, tost** or **tosse, totst)** *wv.* (1) seem V1a,51, M1,2, M6,15, 16b, 18, L4,16, K1,24–5; (2) think, consider M6,27*var.*, K1,23, T5,4; (3) *refl.* consider oneself V1a,52.

tyner(s) *m.* see **tynnerskog** & **tynnersrinde**.

tynnermo *m.* moor of thorns, thorny moor (see note 10).

tynnerring *m.* circle of thorns (see note 10).

tynnerskog *m.* forest of thorns (see note 10).

tynnersrinde *m.* ridge of thorns (see note 10).

tynnyreringe *m.* see **tynnerring**.

tynnyrmoge *m.* see **tynnermo**.

tynnyrring(-e, -jen) *m.* see **tynnerring**.

tyst *wv.* see **tykkjast**.

tøn(n)er *m.* see **tynnerring** & **tynnermo**.

tå *f.* toe.

tår *f.* tear.

ulvetut *n.* howl of wolves.

um *prep.* see **om (1)**.

unde *prep.* see **under**.

under *prep.* (1) under V1a,44–5, M1,2, M6,28, 53, K1,21, 25; *under seg* under itself, down M15b,3; (2) up to, below L4,8, K9,4; M6,44, 47 see **halda**.

underleg *adj.* strange, unusual.

ung *adj.* young V1a,61; as *subst.* young (people) V1a,14.

unge *m.* chick M6,23.

unna *wv.* love; [*ant*] S6,2 (see Section 4.2*c*).

upmæ *prep.* see **uppmed**.

uponde *prep.* see **uppunder**.

upp (1) *prep.* up M6,29.

upp (2) *adv.* up M6,11–13, 32, 52, 68, L4,5; V1a,12, L4,4, L1,2 see **lesa**; V1a, 54*refr.*, 61*refr.* see **standa**.

uppeta (uppet, uppåt, uppete) *sv.* eat up.

uppmed *prep.* up among.
uppreida *wv.* make (bed).
uppte *adv.* see **upptil**.
upptil *adv.* upwards.
upptrakta *wv.* ? (see note 46).
uppunder *prep.* up under, up beneath.
uppvakna *wv.* wake up (*intr.*).
uppvekkja *wv.* wake up (*tr.*).
uppyver *adv.* up (above), up over (it) (see note 47).
uppå *prep.* up on.
ut *adv.* see **leggja** & **sala**.
utav *prep.* (1) of L4,9; (2) of, about M6,8; (3) on account of M6,72; *de ville eg ynskje utav Gud* I wish God would grant M6,13.
uti *prep.* in, see **hogga**.
utivi *prep.* see **utyver**.
utleggja *wv.* discuss, interpret, hold forth about.
utor *prep.* from.
utpå *prep.* out on(to).
utreis(e) *f.* journey hence, away (see note 48).
utreisning *f.* journey hence, away (see note 48).
uttexti *m.* or *f.* ? (see note 48).
utyver *prep.* out across.

va *sv.* see **vera**.
vada *wv.* wade; *vaddi* = *vadde i* (?) K9,4 (see Section 4.2*c*).
vaka *wv.* surface, jump.
vakna *wv.* wake up (*intr.*); *imp.* ? *vakne* V1a,3.
vaknakje *wv.*+*adv.* see **vakna** & **ikkje**.
vakra *wv.*; *vakra seg* wake up, rouse oneself.
vande *m.* distress, torment.
vandra *wv.* wander, roam.
vassa *wv.* wade.
vatn *n.* (1) water V1a,44, 45(2nd occ.); (2) water, lake V1a,45(1st occ.) (see note 49), L4,22.
ve (1) *m.* ? pain, suffering; *sing.* or *pl.* ? M6,57.
ve (2) *prep.* & *adv.* see **bli(va)** (& note 6).
ved *prep.*; *omtrent ved* round about K1,29.
veende *m.* see **vind** & **nordavind**.
veenæ *adj.* see **væn**.
veg *m.* road, path.
vega (veg, vog, vege) *sv.* weigh.
veir *n.* weather.
vejengjer *m.* see **veng** (& Section 3.7, T8, note 3).
vej(i)ne *m.* see **veg**.
vekk *adv.* away, hence.
vekkja *wv.* wake up (*tr.*).
vel *adv.* (1) well L6,14; (2) dearly V1a,2, K1,1–2, S6,2; (3) rather (too) M6,24; (4) no doubt, I imagine M6,71.
venda *wv.* turn; *venda seg* = *venda* L4,22–3; *eg vænte meg, æg vendte* (and) I turned (?), that I should turn (?) L4,22, K1,17.
vene *adj.* see **væn**.
veng *m.* wing.
vente *wv.* see **venda**.
vera (e(r), va(r) *pl.* **vore, vore)** *sv.* (1) be V1a,2, 13, 26, 28–33, 44, 51, 56–60, M1,1–3, M6,9–10 etc.; *vera seg* be V1a,37–8, M6,11–13, 40–1, 64–8, M15b, 3, T6,1, By1,2; *Eg va* I would have been V1a,52; (2) be, happen M6,2–5, L4,6–7 ? see **med (1)**; *Dæ va meg* M6, 26a see **eg**; (3) as *aux.*+*pp.* be V1a, 24–5, M6,66, 71, L4,12, 20, L6,13–14, K9,6, T3,2–3, K5,11; *vera til* exist K5, 11.
verandre *pron.* see **kvorare**.
verd *f.* world.
verden *m.*±*art.* world.
verre *adj.comp.* worse.
verst *adj.sup.* worst.
vetters *m.* ? (see note 5).
vha *sv.* see **vera**.
vhi(i) *wv.* see **vilja**.
vi *wv.* see **vilja**.
vid *adj.* (1) wide V1a,26, K1,18 etc.; (2) far-reaching L1,2.
viddan *adj.* see **vill**.
vide *adv.* widely, far V1a,1*refr.*, 22*refr.*, 40*refr.* etc.
vie (1) *adj.* K1,18, T8,5, L1,2 see **vid**.

vie (2) *adv.* V1a,22*refr.*, M6,1*refr.* etc. see **vide.**
vigja *wv.* hallow (see note 49).
vigt *f.* see **vikt.**
vii *adj.* see **vid.**
viiæ *adv.* see **vide.**
vikt *f.* (1) weight M6,60; (2) scales, weighing apparatus M6,22.
vilja (vi(l), ville, vilja) *wv.* want to, intend to, will, would (like) V1a,1, 22–3, 32, 37, 53, M6,1, 31 etc.; with *inf.* omitted *Idag vil æg te Kjyrkjune* today I want to go to the church K1,4; *expletive part.* ? M6,13 (see note 50).
vill *adj.* wild.
villande *adj.* wild.
vin *m.* friend.
vind *m.* wind, air.
vinna (1) (vinn, vann, vunne) *sv.* succeed(?), manage(?) (see note 51).
vinna (2) *f.* work, task Sæl,1.
visa *f.* song(?), ballad(?), custom(?) V1a,52 (see Section 4.2*a*).
visst (1) *adv.* certainly, indeed M6,64.
visst (2) *pret.pres.v.* N1,4 see **vita.**
vita (veit, visste, visst) *pret.pres.v.* know.
viæ *adv.* see **vide.**
vokster *m.* (1) growth, development; (2) shape, appearance; (3) youth; *Olav han æ i voxtro veenæ* Olav is handsome in appearance (?), Olav is handsome in his youth (?) V1a,2, siml. K1,1*var.*, S6,2 (see note 52); *Olaf han va i Voxtern* Olav was in appearance (?), Olav was in his youth (?) K1,1–2 (see note 52); *f. dat.def.* ? *Voxtrun* K1,1*var.*
vond *adj.* bad, unpleasant V1a,51, By1,2; difficult(?) M6,44, K1,9.
vont *adj.* see **vond.**
voxt(-ern, -ro) *m.* see **vokster.**
voxtrun *f.* ? see **vokster.**
vraka *wv.* reject.
vrang *adj.* (1) unjust, wrong V1a,39, M6,14 etc.; (2) difficult, awkward L1,16.
vrei (1) *adj.* angry; *pl.* ? M1,3 (see Section 3.7, M1, note 1).
vrei (2) *sv.* L3,5 see **vrida.**
vrida (vrid, vreid, vride) *sv.* wring.
vrånge *adj.* see **vrang.**
væg(-ane, -jene) *m.* see **veg.**
væl *adv.* see **vel.**
væn *adj.* handsome, beautiful.
vænjo *m.* see **veng.**
vænte *wv.* see **venda.**
vær *adj.* see **verre.**
væra *sv.* see **vera.**
vær(-e, -i) *f.* see **verd.**
værst *adj.* see **verst.**
vågne(-de, -r) *wv.* see **vakna.**
våt *adj.* wet.

ynskja *wv.* wish.
yver *prep.* over, across.
yvi *prep.* see **yver.**

æ *sv.* see **vera.**
æg(h) *pron.* see **eg.**
ægte *wv.* see **ekta.**
æn *pron.* see **han.**
æra *wv.* honour.

øl *n.* beer.
ørnefjøirir *f.* see **ørnefjør.**
ørnefjør *f.*; *som Ørnefjøirir bar* who bore eagles' feathers, who turned out to be eagles (?) M6,48.
ørneklo (*pl.* **ørnekløar**) *f.* eagle's talon.
øye (*pl.* **øyne**) *n.* eye.
øyra *n.* ear.

å (1) *f.* river M9a,9.
å (2) *adv.* By1,2 see **gjera.**
å (3) *conj.* V1a,1*refr.*, 2, 2*refr.*, 12–15 etc., M6,4(2nd occ.) ? see **og.**
å (4) *inf. marker* to M6,4(2nd occ.) ?, 16a, 17–18, 22, 29(1st occ.), 44, L6,4, K1, 9(3rd occ.), 29–30 (*at*), M9a,7, K5,11.
ånn(-o, -å) *adj.* see **annan.**
årle *adv.* early.
åspelauv *n.* see **ospelauv.**

5.4 Index of stanzas published in the texts of this edition

127 K3,5
128 K9,4
129 L4,9
130 L6,9, 11
131 L3,5
132 L4,11
133 S6,8
134 L4,10
135 V1a,53; K1,10
136 K3,3
137 Sæl,1
138 L6,14
139 M6,23
140 M6,56
141 K2,4
142 K1,16
143 L4,17
144 M6,19, 34
145 K1,15
146 V1a,58
147 L4,19; K1,12
148 V1a,59
149 V1a,56; L6,6; K1,13
150 V1a,57; M6,20; L4, 18; L6,4; K1,14
151 M6,17
152 M6,21; L4,24; L6,5
153 M6,61
154 M6,35
155 M6,22
156 M6,60
157 L4,15
158 K1,23
159 T5,4
160 L4,14; K1,24
161 K1,25
162 K1,26
163 K5,20
164 K1,27
165 K1,28
166 K5,21
167 K1,29
168 K1,30
169 V1a,61

Postscript 1

Since this book was written a number of new *Dr* MSS from Rikard Berge's collection have been made available. They date from between *c.* 1911 and 1922 and nearly all seem to be fair copies by Berge himself. The variants they contain are from most areas of Telemark where *Dr* had previously been recorded, with the possible addition of Heddal. There is little fresh textual material in these variants. Some three or four new stanzas occur, all variations on existing stanzas. The most interesting of the new variants is TFM Berge CCXLVII,83–5, recorded by Berge in 1913 from Ingebjørg Vislandskosi, a daughter of Anne Skaalen. Unlike Anne's *Draugkveen*, Ingebjørg's variant contains only eleven stanzas: SS.1,5,8,34,39,43,98,111,139,144,150. These occur in *Draugkveen* too, but apart from SS.139,144 and, to a lesser extent, 43, they are among the most common of all *Dr* stanzas. The lack of any trace in Ingebjørg's variant of the other sixty-three stanzas of *Draugkveen* strengthens the supposition made on pp. 97–9 that Anne was improvising rather than transmitting material she had learnt. A statement in TFM Berge CCXLVII,87, attributed by Berge to Ingebjørg, may give us some indication of the esteem in which Anne was held as a ballad-singer, although it is perhaps more likely to be an expression of popular wonderment that anyone should wish to collect folk material: '"*Bugge* va' ti mor aa samla. Aa so som dei forondra seg alle menneskjen hott i jøss nam han ville mæ de"' ('Bugge came to mother collecting. And how surprised they all were, they wondered what on earth he wanted to do that for').

When Berge's great collection of ballad MSS has finally been catalogued in its entirety I hope to publish a brief article or supplement to this volume dealing with all the new material that has emerged.

Postscript 2

Two contributions to *Dr* studies have recently appeared, too recently for inclusion in Section 2. Olav Bø's chapter on 'Draumkvedet' in his book *Utsyn over norsk folkedikting* takes the form of a general survey of the ballad and some of the problems connected with it. Bø affirms his belief in the pre-Reformation origin of *Dr*, but is inclined to date it to the last part of the middle ages. Magne Myhren's article in the first volume of *Tradisjon* deals with the expressions *dyrering*, *dyretrå*, *betlarstig* and *vetterstid.* His conclusions about the meaning of these words do not differ greatly from certain of the suggestions made in Section 5.1 of this book.

The first element *dyre-* means 'animal' and the *dyrering* and *dyretrå*, like the thorny moor, are torments Olav must suffer on his journey; *betlar-stig* means 'beggars' path' and is an indirect expression of the humility Olav had to show before he was allowed to see paradise; *vetterstid* means 'winter' and is to be seen in connection with the blue ice and the fact that Olav made his journey in the middle of winter. (Cf. Section 2.19.)

Postscript 3

With the kind assistance of Bjarne Hodne of Institutt for folkeminne-vitskap in Oslo I have recently managed to discover a little about Maren Ramskeid, Anne Lillegaard and their parentage. Maren was born Hegg-tveit 30.6.1817. In 1848 she married Bjørgulv Olavsson Epletveit and subsequently emigrated with her husband to the United States. Maren's father, Olav Gunnleiksson Ramskeid, born Heggtveit, was christened 27.12.1757 and died 22.12.1834. His father, Gunnleik Jørundsson, lived from 1725 to 1804 and was a direct descendant of the first owner of Hegg-tveit of whom we hear, one Tormod, who lived in the (latter half of ?) the sixteenth century. Gunnleik Jørundsson was also the great-great-grandfather of Hallvard Gun(n)leiks(s)on Heggtveit, the collector (and in-formant ?) of K5 which shows such remarkable similarity to K1, Maren's variant. The dates of Maren's birth and her father's death do not tally entirely with the information given us by Landstad. In *Norske Folkeviser* (p. 66) he describes Maren as being about thirty years old, presumably, though perhaps not necessarily, on the occasion she sang *Draumekvæi* for him, yet at the same time he tells us that her father died 'a score of years ago' ('for et Snees Aar siden' – 'fifteen years ago' ('for 15 Aar siden') in the MS of K1). For the reasons stated on p. 74 of this book, and since she was married in 1848 – Landstad describes her as a 'Pige' (young, unmarried woman) – it seems likely that Maren was indeed about thirty years old when she sang for Landstad and that the other figures are wrong. It is interesting to note that in the MS of K1 Landstad originally made the same mistake as the parish registers of Brunkeberg, describing Olav Gunnleiksson as seventy years of age at his death. Seventy was, however, corrected to seventy-seven by Landstad himself.

Clear facts about Anne Lillegaard are less easy to come by. 'Anond Larsen' and 'Else Dalen' in Lårdal had a daughter, 'Anne', who was christened 4.5.1794 (Anne 1). Almost exactly nine years later 'Aanund

Larsøn' and 'Else Vraalsd. Dahlen', who are clearly the same couple, had another daughter, 'Ane', who was christened 8.5.1803 (Anne 2). These are the only two female children born in Lårdal who can possibly be identified with Anne Lillegaard, the ballad-singer. Furthermore, in the slips of Norsk stadnamnarkiv, Lillegaard in Lårdal has the following entry (abbreviated): 'hpl. under Kleppo. Skal høyre til Dalen' ('tenant farm under Kleppo. Is supposed to belong to Dalen'). It is of course no more than conjecture, but it seems likely that after their marriage Aanund Larsen and Else Dalen moved to Lillegaard and that both Anne 1 and Anne 2 were born there. They would then both have been called Anne Lillegaard. Anne 1 appears to have lived in Lårdal all her life. In 1820 she married 'Aasmund Halvorsen Kleven', a tenant farmer. They may have moved to Kleven for a time, but at some stage they must have returned to Lillegaard for the parish registers record the death of 'Aasmund Halvorsen, Lillegaard' 10.3.1836. 'Anne Aasmundsdatter, Lillegaard' died 20.10.1863 (the pastor seems to have made a mistake about the father's name, there can hardly be any doubt as to the identity of this 'Anne'). Anne 2 ('Anne Anundsdatter') moved to Skafså (Mo) at the age of seventeen and worked there as a 'Tjenestepige' ('servant girl') until her marriage 11.11.1821 to 'Osmund Olsen Bilstad'. She appears to have lived at Bilstad (Mo) for the rest of her life for the parish registers of Mo record the death of 'Anne Anundsdatter, Gaardmandskone. Opholdssted Bilstad i Skafse' 25.4.1861. Her husband died 30.7.1875.

It is clear that Jørgen Moe's informant in 1847 was Anne 1. She is described by him as a widow, and there is nothing in what he says to suggest other than that Eidsborg (Lårdal) was her home (i.e., it was not Anne 2 on a visit to her sister). Sophus Bugge in *Gamle norske Folkeviser* describes one of his informants as 'Anne (Aanundsdatter) Lillegaard i Eidsborg' on three occasions (pp. 22, 67, 117). This, too, must be Anne 1, since he would hardly have described Anne 2 as 'i Eidsborg'. In his introduction to *Dr* in *Norske Folkeviser* (p. 66), Landstad states that one of his informants was: 'Anne Lillegaard i Mo Præstegjeld'. He is probably though not necessarily here referring to the informant of L4, recorded by Olav Grasberg. If so, it may be that what Landstad says in *Norske Folkeviser* is a mistake, for in the MS of L4 he has written: 'Af Anne Lillegaard paa Esborgberget', without doubt a reference to Anne 1. It is of course possible that Anne 2 also knew *Dr* and was one of Landstad's informants, but any record of her version that may once have existed is now lost. The mistake in *Norske Folkeviser* – if mistake it is – may have been caused by Grasberg's giving false or garbled information to Landstad (perhaps Anne 1 was visiting her sister when she sang for Grasberg), though this hardly squares with the unambiguous note in L4 which was presumably added before the publication of Landstad's edition. On the basis of such information as we now have it would seem to me reasonable to conclude that Anne 1 was the ballad-singer Anne Aanundsdatter Lillegaard, of whom mention is often made, and that she was the informant of L1 and L4 (might her sister have been responsible for L2 which shows such strong similarity to L1/4?). It is in any event impossible to trace either Anne's line of tradition back very far, since all we know is that Anne learnt the ballads she sang from her grandmother, but whether this was Aanund Larsen's or Else Dalen's mother we are nowhere told.

The information in this postscript can be found in the relevant parish registers of Brunkeberg, Eidsborg, Kviteseid, Lårdal, Mo and Skafså, and in Torjus Loupedalen and Olav Bakken, *Kviteseid bygdesoge* (1956–62), I–II, especially I, pp. 218–23.

Postscript 4

The following additions should be made to the bibliography on pp. 63–8:

Articles etc.

Ekornes, Anne, 'Tankar og teoriar om Draumkvedet', *Olivant 1–3* (1972), pp. 6–8, 8–10, 8–9.

Lindholm, Dan, 'Draumkvedet. Litt om dets opprinnelse og skjebne gjennom tidene', *Steinerskolen 4* (1967), pp. 13–29. Includes the text of 1896 expanded with stanzas from Landstad A.

Lindholm, Dan, *Das Traumlied vom Olav Åsteson* (1967). Includes the text of 1896 expanded with stanzas from Landstad A and a German verse translation of the Norwegian text.

Editions

draumkvedet, en julehilsen fra Bergen Faktorforening (1971): Christiansen's text of 1957.

Blom, Ådel & Bø, Olav, *Norske Balladar* (1973), pp. 104–8: K1; pp. 109–11: L1; pp. 112–14: L4.

Translations (German)

Trummler, Erich, *Das norwegische Traumlied des Olaf Åsteson* (1965): the text of 1896 (verse).

Notes

1 Hereafter abbreviated *Dr* in text and notes.

2 Ivar Mortensson, *Grunnsteinen i norsk bokheim* (1927), p. 4, makes a clear distinction between the two, and Karl-Ivar Hildeman, 'I marginalen till Draumkvædet', *Medeltid på vers* (1958), p. 233, states that it was not only in its early stages that the ballad genre could have influenced 'the poem which became *Draumkvædet*' ('... den dikt, som blev Draumkvædet'), which perhaps indicates that he sees *Dr* as a poem that was reshaped as a ballad. Most scholars use the two terms synonymously.

3 Cf., however, *Sante Jakup* (Knut Liestøl and Moltke Moe, *Norske folkevisor* (1920–4), 42) or *Sancte Jeppe* (*Danmarks gamle Folkeviser* (hereafter abbreviated DgF), 100) which shows certain similarities with *Dr*.

4 The exact number of variants is difficult to determine. It depends on the definition of variant and on the criteria used to define *Dr*, cf. Section 3.1 (especially pp. 71–8) and 3.5. Nor is it always clear how many stanzas a variant contains, cf. Section 3.2, p. 83.

5 Olav Bø, 'Draumkvædet og Gamle-stevet', *Norveg 5* (1955), pp. 77–102.

6 Cf., however, Hildeman (1958), pp. 222–3, who suggests that it may be a combination of several closely related poems, and Moltke Moe, *Forelæsninger over norske ballader og folkeviser fra middelalderen I*, p. 158 and *II*, p. 3, who thinks it could originally have been two ballads, *Droumkv.* and *Drougkvæi.* This idea never appeared in any of Moltke Moe's published works.

7 Jørgen Moe, 'Indberetning ...', *Norske Universitets- og Skole-Annaler* (1850), pp. 278–86.

8 For an explanation of the system by which variants are classified in this edition and the abbreviations used cf. Section 3.1, pp. 79–80 and 3.4, p. 103.

9 For details of these and all other variants cf. Section 3.5.

10 In a letter to Moe (now apparently no longer extant) Svenungsen stated that his MS contained sixty-two stanzas.

11 Jørgen Moe (1850), pp. 279–80: 'Romance'; 'Indholdets Natur'; 'Vanskeligheden har været forøget derved, at alle ældre Stev og flere andre Kjæmpeviser ere lagte til Draumkvætonen og at Opskriften C har, for at være ret fuldstændig, medtaget en stor Deel af disse heterogene Stoffer.'

12 In his introduction to *Draumekvæði* Landstad mentions a number of informants. The names of two of these, Olaf Glosimot and Anne Golid, do not appear in any of the extant variants, but there are several MSS of *Dr* in Landstad's collection for which the informant is unknown, and they may very well be the source of one or more of these, cf. Rikard Berge, *M. B. Landstad, Norske folkeminnesamlarar II,2* (1920), p. 113.

13 Landstad (1853), p. 66: 'det fuldstændigste og meest ordnede'.

14 The corresponding stanzas of Landstad A and B are as follows (brackets indicate similar, but not identical stanzas, the final rhyme word and in some cases other features being different; for a definition of the difference between variants of the same stanza and separate stanzas cf. Section 3.2):

B	A	B	A	B	A	B	A
1	3	9	26	17	38	25	56
2	2	10	[50]	18	41	26	57
3	4/13	11	29	19	42	27	58
4	–	12	33	20	43	28	59
5	6	13	34	21	[45/46]	29	–
6	11	14	36	22	47	30	–
7	22/31	15	[35]	23	53		
8	23	16	37	24	55		

15 V1b,1–14 contains more or less the same stanzas as V1a,1–14, but in very different order from both V1a and Landstad A 1–12.

16 Landstad (1853), p. 90: 'den Blanding af hedenske og kristelige Forestillinger'.

17 Landstad (1853), p. 65: 'Kristendommens første Aarhundreder i Norden'.

18 This name does not occur in any extant variant.

19 Landstad (1853), p. 70. In fact there is no *Rolanda sokn* in Älfsborgs län. The nearest approach to this is Råglanda, a curate's glebe in Gärdhems socken, Väne härad.

20 Landstad (1853), pp. 65–6: 'Stump'; 'flere hundrede Vers'; 'Nils Svenungsen havde indblandet mange uvedkommende Ting, men da Meget deraf gjenkjendtes som tilhørende andre Viser, var det Uvedkommende her ikke saa vanskeligt at udskille'; '... næsten Enhver, som endnu interesserer sig for de gamle Viser, har hørt det omtale, eller kan nogle Vers deraf. Men disse løsrevne og spredte Vers blandes med og benyttes som Stev, og ere som saadanne udsatte for at undergaa de Endringer, som den Stevjende finder passende til Tid og Sted.'

21 Cf. Erik Dal, *Nordisk folkeviseforskning siden 1800* (1956), pp. 187–8.

22 *M. B. Landstad, Folkeviser fra Telemarken,* ed. Knut Liestøl (1925).

23 Liestøl/Landstad (1925), p. XII: '... ikke ... restituerte – ialfald ikke i nævneværdig grad'.

24 The corresponding stanzas of *Droumekvæi* and V1a (those marked * are unique to this version) are as follows (there are occasionally slight differences in wording, probably due to emendations by Landstad; in stanza 25 the final rhyme word is the same as in K1,15, but the rest of the line is different from both this and V1a,58):

Droum	V1a	*Droum*	V1a	*Droum*	V1a	*Droum*	V1a
1	1	8	24/25	15	60	22	52*
2	2	9	–	16	43	23	56
3	13	10	26	17	45*	24	57
4	14	11	28*	18	44	25	[58]
5	3/6	12	29	19	51	26	61*
6	4	13	30	20	39		
7	12	14	33	21	53		

25 *No hæv æg gjængje Gjaddar-Broi,/ aa sliti mæg mæste sonde,/ ho va adde mæ Jønni slæjen/ aa Draugane dei va vonde.*

26 'Mythologiske Oplysninger til Draumekvædi', *Norsk Tidsskrift for Videnskab og Litteratur VII* (1854–5), pp. 102–21 and 192.

27 Cf. Bugge (1854–5), pp. 102–3, 106, 111 and 118.

28 Bugge (1854–5), pp. 103–4: 'Navnet ... kan her ikke have Betydning uden for saa vidt, at derved af Folket selv en Mening om Kvædets Ælde udtales.'

29 SS.118–20 = stanzas 118–20 according to the numbering of this edition, cf. Section 3.2.

30 Old Norwegian *ð* is regularly lost after vowels, but can also, in one or two cases, develop to *l*(*l*), cf. Ivar Aasen, *Norsk Grammatik* (1864), § 127, Anm.

31 Peter Christen Asbjørnsen and Jørgen Moe, *Norske Folkeeventyr* ... (1852), No. 16 'Hanen og Hønen i Nøddeskoven', cf. also No. 8 'Jomfru Maria som Gudmoder'. Moltke Moe suggests that it is possibly a golden head-band, used as a sign of virginity, that is meant in No. 16, cf. FM (see p. 11 below), pp. 56–56b.

32 *Grímnismál* 48 and 49.

33 *Gylfaginning*, chap. 42.

34 Bugge (1854–5), p. 113: 'Den, der i levende Live gavmild har skjænket den Fattige en Ko, finder nu paa sin Vandring til de Dødes Boliger en Ko, der leder ham over Gjallarbroen; den Ubarmhjertige derimod faar ingen Leder, bliver svimmel og styrter fra den høie, bratte Bro ned i den dybe Gjallarhyl.'

35 This vision was translated into Old Norwegian/Icelandic (usually known as *Duggals leizla*), probably in the thirteenth or fourteenth century. The Norse translation appears in *Heilagra manna søgur*, ed. C. R. Unger (1877), I, pp. 329–58. It seems to be generally considered by those who see a connection between Tundale and *Dr* that the author of *Dr* was familiar with *Duggals leizla* rather than with a Latin text of the vision.

36 Cf. *Heilagra manna søgur* I, pp. 340–1.

37 Cf., however, *Moltke Moes samlede skrifter*, Instituttet for sammenlignende kulturforskning, Serie B, I, VI, IX (1925–7), III (hereafter abbreviated Ssk. in the notes and after Section 2), pp. 337–8, where S.149 and the relevant passage in Tundale's vision/*Duggals leizla* are seen as positive and negative aspects of the same motif.

38 Cf. *The Poetical Dialogues of Solomon and Saturn*, ed. R. J. Menner (1941), p. 102.

39 *Olafs saga hins helga*, ed. O. A. Johnsen (1922), pp. 1–2.

40 *Jómsvíkinga saga*, ed. N. F. Blake (1962), pp. 3–4; *Íslenzk fornrit X* (1940), p. 85; *Íslenzk fornrit XI* (1950), pp. 48–9.

41 Landstad (1853), p. 78: '"*den brændende Svovelsø*" eller ... Skjærsilden'.

42 Bugge (1854–5), p. 120: 'i Draumekvædi er det ... ved Dommedag, at de to Skarer ride sammen'; 'den hedenske Mythe om Ragnarøkk'.

43 Henning Frederik Feilberg, 'Et Kapitel af Folkets Sjæletro', *Aarbog for dansk Kulturhistorie* (1894), pp. 116–18.

44 Amund Helland, *Norges land og folk VIII, Bratsberg amt* (1900), I, pp. 429–31. On the question of authorship cf. Leiv Heggstad and Hakon Grüner Nielsen, *Utsyn yver gamall norsk folkevisedikting* (1912), p. 29, Axel Olrik, 'Moltke Moe ... ', *Danske Studier* (1915), p. 38, *Grunnsteinen*, p. 1.

45 Hjalmar Christensen, 'Et moderne draumkvæde', *Vort litterære liv* (1902), pp. 189–202.

46 Christensen (1902), p. 195: 'stilløst'; 'naivere, men lige usmagelig'; 'løse brudstykker af kristelig tro og moral'; '... trækker ingen bestemt grænse mellem den katolske luttringsild og den såkaldte evige ild.' Christensen seems to have had much

the same view of the ballad as the parson, Hans Mathias Abel, who in the 1770s did all he could to stamp it out in Skafså (Mo) (cf. Landstad (1853), pp. 65–6).

47 Christensen (1902), p. 195: 'Helheim er nu engang ikke noget straffested for dem, der ikke har spæget sit kjød med hunger'.

48 Cf. the bibliography in Section 2.19.

49 For details cf. Section 2.19.

50 Ssk., p. 359: 'utjevnet'.

51 The commentary from Moe's lectures of 1891–2, FM, the proofs of the commentary volume planned by Forening for norsk bogkunst and from Moe's MS where these leave off; the notes from the text of 1899 (stanzas 32–52) and the commentary volume (stanzas 1–31), cf. Ssk., p. 359. The fact that the text is that of 1912, while the notes belong partly to the text of 1899 and partly to the commentary volume has, in at least one case, led to a discrepancy, cf. p. 250, text: *vengjir*, note: '*vengjo* . . . old dative plural' ('gammel dativ flertal'). There is also a curious discrepancy between the uninterrupted text on pp. 199–208 and that which accompanies the commentary; the former has fifty-two stanzas, the latter fifty-one. This is due to the fact that Moe did not add stanza 52 to his text until 1906, after he had completed his commentary.

52 Knut Liestøl, *Draumkvæde . . .*, *Studia Norvegica 3* (1946), p. 131.

53 Bø (1955), p. 79: 'Rett nok er det ei ramme for Draumkvædet, slik vi kjenner det frå Moltke Moes meisterlege restitusjon, men denne ramma var lite kjend og lite fylgd av kvedarane på den tid då oppskrivinga gjekk for seg.'

54 Bø (1955), p. 80.

55 Cf. Ssk., p. 235.

56 FM, p. 37: 'Den her givne tilrettelægning av digtet er ikke fremkommet uden vilkaarlighed. Men denne vilkaarlighed har vist sig nødvendig for at faa en enhed i de indbyrdes lige til ukjendelighed avvigende optegnelser, og for at skabe en tankesammenhæng i teksternes paa forskjellig vis omskiplede versorden.'

57 Cf. the three stanzas in Ssk., p. 347.

58 Although it is often difficult to show that Moe preferred Landstad A to genuine variants in specific cases, there is no doubt that Landstad's text had some influence on the shaping of MM. In Ssk., for example, the first two lines of MM 41 read: *Kjem eg meg åt bònno dei,/ dei støje so hågt på glo.* This agrees with Landstad A 49, to which a note is appended: 'I have written *støje* for *støðe* (stode) in accordance with the pronunciation.' ('Jeg har skrevet efter Udtalen støje for støðe (stode).') Moe also has a note (Ssk., p. 320): '*støje* (*stod*) is the Old Norse 3rd *pers.imp. subj. stæði* (sound change as in *støyl* from Old Norse *stǫðull*). The subjunctive is used here as in Old Norse about that which one thinks one sees in a dream.' ('*støje* (stod) er gn. 3 pers. impf. konj. *stæði* (lydovergangen som i støyl av gn. stǫðull). Konjunktiv er her brukt likesom i gn. om det man tror at se i drømme.') The only variant which includes a form of the verb *standa* in the second line of this stanza is L4, where it reads (11): *di Stoge so Høgt paa Gloe.* It is almost certain that Moe took the form *støje* from Landstad A, particularly in view of the fact that Liestøl finally (in Moe's text in the fifth edition of (*Utval av*) *norske folkeviser til skulebruk*, 1939) changed it back to *stoge*.

59 Apart from being among the oldest of the genuine variants, K1 and L1, as pointed out above, also formed the basis of Landstad's and Jørgen Moe's texts respectively.

60 The 'sections' and 'episodes' referred to here and in the following are not necessarily the same as the seven or eight parts into which Moe divided the ballad, cf. Section 3.2, pp. 84–5.

61 This division is made for a purely practical purpose: to demonstrate more clearly the ways in which MM differs from the variants. It has no significance beyond this. The five categories can sometimes overlap.

62 Cf. Ssk., p. 251.

63 Moe (1899), p. 13, cf. also Ssk., p. 320.

64 1896: stanza 24, 1901: 24, 1902: 28. Cf. the bibliography in Section 2.19.

65 The proof of FM is wanting at this point.

66 Ssk., p. 324.

67 FM, p. 43b.

68 Moe (1899), p. 4: '*Færemo* av gln. *ferðamóðr*, mødig av færden.'

69 FM, p. 43b.

70 Cf. FM, p. 50b and Ssk., pp. 266–7.

71 FM, p. 58: 'Den vei han vandrer kaldes "*vetterstíg*" (hos Landstad forvansket til "vetters ti") eller "betlarstígjen.'

72 Moe (1899), p. 8: 'Istedenfor *vetterstig* forekommer stundom varianten *betlarstig*'.

73 Ssk., p. 301: 'I Maren Ramskeis version av avsnittet har han efter en anden kilde optat to strofer som varierer to av hendes: 52 og 54.'

74 There are other variants which contain stanzas belonging to the judgement section, V9, S6 and T5. The latter two are older than MM, but none of them contains the word *brass*.

75 Ssk., p. 257: 'i den anden verden; forældet dativ ental hankjøn, gammelnorsk *í ǫðrum heimi*'.

76 Landstad (1853), p. 78: '(andheimen ?)'.

77 The word itself does not appear in K4 which consists of references to the relevant stanzas of Landstad A with variant readings where the informant differed from this text.

78 FM, p. 55: '"aandeverdenen . . ."'. It is impossible to say what reading FM had in stanzas 48, 50–1 since the proofs of 38–51 are wanting.

79 Moe is here presumably referring to his stanza 49, but there is no extant variant which has the form *annheimen* in this stanza.

80 FM, p. 55: '"Annheimen" forstaar jeg ikke som "aandeverdenen", men som "den anden verden". Herfor taler annheimen v. 49^3, der er ensbetydende med og en variant til aurom heime 50^3. Herfor taler ogsaa udtrykket "i den anen heimen" i optegnelsen s. (Bugge).' As can be seen, the proof is defective. What is intended is perhaps a reference to variant L6 (recorded by Bugge) where we find *i den anen heimen* in a punishment stanza (9) and *i den anen heim* in a *sæl* stanza (4). It is also conceivable that a suggestion of Bugge's is the source of the note.

81 Ssk., p. 258: '*kvorjom* er en uregelret dativ ental i intetkjøn av *kvar* (i Telemarken *kvor*)'.

82 Moe (1899), p. 13: 'den ældre form *dessom* kan også forekomme i viserne.'

83 It has proved impossible to find a copy of Moe's text of 1912 on which that in Ssk. is based so we cannot be sure whether *dessom* first appeared here or was one of the inconsistencies 'ironed out' by Liestøl.

84 Ssk., p. 359.

85 In V9 l.3 of S.135 (12) runs: *de va' dei sønduge systkjìnì* which is closer to Moe's *de va synduge syskjini* than the reading of any other variant, but V9, of course, post-dates MM.
86 Cf. Ssk., pp. 337–8.
87 Landstad (1853), pp. 71–2.
88 Cf. Ssk., pp. 269–70.
89 S6,10 consists of a reference to Landstad A 28 which has *vosemyrann*, but without written evidence there is, of course, no certainty that it was precisely this form the informant used.
90 Cf. Section 2.9, p. 39.
91 Ssk., p. 343: '. . . forlikes . . . ikke vel sammen med vor strofe 50'.
92 Cf. Section 2.6, 9, 11, 12 (especially), 13 and 15.
93 Cf. Ssk., pp. 209 and 334.
94 Cf. Section 3.1 and 3.
95 Ssk., p. 277: '. . . kun Godskalks vision kjender disse tre veier: en steil som leder op til himlen, og skinner som luende ild; en bred og behagelig mellemvei som fører frem til fagre husbygninger, og en stinkende, trang, stupbrat vei nedover, med bundløst dynd i.'
96 Ssk., p. 277: '. . . dyndveien er derfor her avløst av vadningen over den underjordiske elv.'
97 Ssk., p. 275.
98 Landstad (1853), p. 72, Liestøl (1946), pp. 55–6, Bø (1955), pp. 81–2. According to Bø Moe may have based his stanza 26 on a variant from Sætesdal. Such a variant, however, does not now appear to exist.
99 Ssk., p. 276.
100 Cf. Rikard Berge, *Vinje og Rauland* (1940–4), I, p. 21 and Section 5.2.
101 In FM (p. 57c) Moe states: '. . . in placing this stanza [26] where it is we have been guided by vision literature: in Thurcill's vision, for example, all paths meet at the *congregatio animarum*, the beginning of the realm of the dead itself.' ('. . . naar vi har sat dette vers paa denne plads, da har visionslitteraturen været vor ledesnor: i Thurchils vision f. eks. samles alle veier i Congregatio animarum, selve dødsrigets begyndelse.') On p. 59 of the same work MM 27 (*So tok eg av på vetterstig/ alt på mi høgre hònd*) is compared with the three paths in Gottskalk's vision: 'The expression *på mi høgre hand* [sic] indicates that the visionary comes to a *cross-roads* where he takes a path which branches off to the right. The only vision in which such a cross-roads is clearly portrayed is Gottskalk's.' ('Udtrykket "på mi høgre hand" viser, at visionæren her har staat ved en *korsvei*, hvor det tar en vei av til høire, som han følger. Vi kjender bare én vision hvor dette veiskjel kommer klart frem, og det er Godskalks syn.') And in Ssk., p. 280 *vetterstig* and 'the steep path leading up to paradise [from Gottskalk's vision]' ('den bratte sti som leder op til paradis') are identified as one and the same.
102 Ssk., p. 282: '. . . en av forutsætningerne for den rolle Draumkvædet tildeler Maria i den hinsidige kirke.'
103 Cf. Liestøl (1946), pp. 88–90 and 95 and 'Til Draumkvædet', *Heidersskrift til Marius Hægstad* (1925), pp. 119–22. Apart from there being similarities between Gundelin's vision and the stanzas in question it is also noteworthy that this vision was translated into Old Icelandic/Norwegian (cf. *Maríu saga*, ed. C. R. Unger (1871),

pp. 534–41 and 1162–8), whereas Gottskalk's survives only in one MS, probably the original according to Liestøl, and no translations of it are known. It seems to have passed almost unnoticed.

104 Liestøl (1946), p. 88.

105 K4,1 and T6,2 (S.119) corresponding to MM 25 are considered to be the same stanza as K5,17, L4,20, L2,6 etc. corresponding to MM 29, since, in effect, it is only the first line which differs. In FM (pp. 55–55b) Moe compared *Anheimen* ('aandeverdenen'), the reading of T6,2, with Thurcill's *animarum congregatio,* but with his replacement of the word by *auromheimi* the relevance of MM 25 to the matter under discussion is only slight.

106 The order is different in the text of V9 printed by Berge in *Vinje og Rauland* (I, pp. 142–3). According to Berge the informant did not recite the stanzas in any particular order.

107 Cf. Section 5.2.

108 This is one of the rare occasions on which Moe discusses the variants, and is the fullest account he gives of any variant readings.

109 Cf. also Section 3.1, p. 79 and 3.5, By4, note.

110 Ssk., p. 301: '. . . vort avsnit har bevaret så mange reminiscenser om længst forgangne tiders tro – likefra Grutte Gråskjeg med hans halvhedenske Odins attributer til st. Mikaels skålevegt – og av Kristi bakgrundsfigur, som ikke lar sig forlike med Johannes-åbenbaringens fremstilling.'

111 Ssk., p. 304: '. . . vil i virkeligheten si det samme, da broen jo kun betegner overgangen fra de levendes til de dødes verden.'

112 Concerning the possible dependence of K5 on Landstad's printed texts, cf. Section 3.1, p. 79.

113 Cf. Section 3.5, L5, note.

114 Cf. Ssk., p. 300.

115 Cf. Dag Strömbäck, 'Om Draumkvædet och dess källor', *Arv II* (1946), p. 57.

116 Cf. Ssk., pp. 309–11.

117 Liestøl (1946), p. 38.

118 Cf. *Njáls saga, Íslenzk fornrit XII* (1954), p. 257: 'hann [Michael] skal meta allt þat, sem þú gerir, bæði gott ok illt, ok er svá miskunnsamr, at hann metr allt þat meira, sem vel er gǫrt.' Further examples of such sentiments can be found in Fredrik Paasche, *Kristendom og kvad* (1914), p. 44, reprinted in *Hedenskap og kristendom* (1948), p. 74.

119 Cf. Ssk., pp. 301 and 304–5.

120 Ssk., p. 299: '. . . hvordan Mikael fører de retfærdiges sjæle ind til herligheten'.

121 Cf. Ssk., p. 313.

122 Ssk., p. 324: '. . . er øiensynlig en fri, eiendommelig tillempning av et træk i Turkills vision.'

123 Cf. Ssk., p. 334.

124 Ssk., p. 340: 'Jeg ser ingen anden mulighet end at tyde vort vers ut av fortællingen hos Tundal'.

125 Cf. Ssk., pp. 292–3.

126 Hjalmar Falk, *Sólarljóð,* Videnskapsselskapets Skrifter. II. Hist.-filos. Klasse. (1914) No. 7, p. 55: 'de mange likheter lar sig meget vel opfatte som gjenspeilinger av fælles kilder.' In contrast to this Moe asserts (Ssk., p. 211) that *Dr* is one of the sources

of *Sólarljóð*, but unfortunately the necessary arguments to support such a theory are lacking.

127 Fredrik Paasche, 'St. Michael og hans engle', *Edda I* (1914), pp. 33–74.

128 Paasche, *Edda I*, p. 46: 'sterkt visionær'.

129 Cf. Paasche, *Edda I*, p. 47.

130 Cf. Paasche, *Edda I*, p. 47.

131 Ssk., p. 248: '. . . utænkelig, at Hellig-Olav, landets nationalhelgen, ved den tid, Draumkvædet blev til, skulde kunne betegnes uten sit helgennavn, og oven i kjøpet efter sin *mor*.'

132 Paasche, *Edda I*, p. 46: '. . . er . . . det negative bevis – de indvendinger, som kan reises mot andre tydninger – det sterkeste.'

133 Cf. Bugge (1854–5), p. 120 and Ellen Jørgensen, *Helgendyrkelse i Danmark* (1909), p. 6.

134 Moltke Moe demonstrated much the same thing in Ssk. (pp. 294–307), although he was not arguing against heathen influence on the portrayal of St Michael. Paasche's views about the identity of the visionary and the origins of *sankte såle Mikkjel* are reiterated in the article on *Dr* in Bull and Paasche's *Norsk litteraturhistorie* (1924–55), I, pp. 485–8.

135 Ivar Mortensson-Egnund, 'I andre heimen', *Vidar I* (1917), pp. 431–8 and 'Draumkvædet', *Vidar I* (1917), pp. 406–14. 1917 was the date of publication of the complete volume which consisted of many parts. These began appearing in 1915. The text was also published separately in 1916.

136 The *utgreidingar* consist of a crude glossary (containing only twenty-eight words) which also accompanies the text in *Gjallarbrui*.

137 Cf. *Grunnsteinen*, p. 22 and the title of this work.

138 Mortensson (1920), p. 31: '. . . som berre er aandlause hermingar av halvlærde munkar'.

139 *Grunnsteinen*, p. 2: 'innre organiske prinsip'.

140 Liestøl (1925), p. 113: '. . . so mykje må vera burtkome at det er ovleg vandt å setja broti saman att til noko heilt.'

141 Landstad (1853), p. 65: 'Originally our *Draumkvæde* appears to have had a greater similarity to *Sólarljóð* than is the case now, since people who heard it in their childhood relate that it contained among other things a description of how the sun turned black before the visionary, the *helgrind* thundered and he came upon some women who were grinding mould as food for their husbands etc. (*Sólarljóð* 57).' ('Oprindelig har vort Draumkvæde vistnok havt en større Lighed med Solarljod, end det nu har, da Folk, der have hørt det i deres Barndom, berette at det blandt andet indeholdt en Beskrivelse om hvorledes Solen sortnede for Drømmeren, Helgrinden larmede, og han kom til nogle Koner, som mol Muld til Mad for sine Mænd o. s. v. (Solarljod 57 V.).') The relevant stanza and refrain are (1916 41, 1926/7 52): *Kjem eg meg i den andre halli,/ der inne troll-kjeringar sat,/ molo på so tunge steinar/ monnom mold til mat*, and (1926/7 following 16): *Soli ho svortna,/ og helgrindi dunde.* The stanza is taken from the 1926/7 text.

142 Landstad (1853), p. 74: *Deð fyrste eg fór, dá førðe dei meg/ igjønnom den dýraring,/ neglanne spratt af kvor mi tá/ og bloðið af kvor min fing.* This is Mortensson's stanza 22.

143 In contrast to most previous editors of *Dr* Mortensson lists the sources on which his reconstruction is based and the alterations he made to these sources (*Grunn-*

steinen, pp. 28–9). Unfortunately, however, his source list leaves much to be desired, and his list of alterations (only nine items in all) gives a totally misleading impression of their real extent. Furthermore the stanza numbering in these lists does not tally with any of Mortensson's *Dr* reconstructions known to me.

144 In Mortensson (1920) there seems to be some doubt about this (p. 44), but in *Grunnsteinen* it is stated quite clearly that Olav and Rúnólfr are one and the same (cf. pp. 38–9).

145 Cf. *Grunnsteinen*, p. 42: 'Christmas 1147 would seem to be the right time for the *draumkvede* poet.' ('Jol 1147 skulde ein tenkje laut vera rette tidi for draumkvedeskalden.') It is not entirely clear whether it is the date of the vision, the date of the composition of *Dr*, or both that is meant.

146 *Grunnsteinen*, p. 12: 'innvigsle-former og rettleidingi frå diktaren'. I am not entirely sure of the meaning of *innvigsle-former*. It could perhaps be translated 'types of initiation'.

147 *Grunnsteinen*, p. 4: '. . . ein original diktar, og det ein mann so rik og stor at han skulde ikkje trengje å låne so mykje av andre.'

148 Cf. *Olafs saga hins helga* (1922), pp. 2–4.

149 Cf. the ballad of *Ásmund Fregdegævar*, Landstad (1853), pp. 15–17.

150 Cf. *Grunnsteinen*, p. 41: 'According to the old teachings of the *Edda* a man had to be born on earth three times before he became free.' ('Etter den gamle læra i Edda måtte eit menneskje fødast tri gonger på jord fyrr han vart fri.') This is presumably a reference to *Helgakviða Hundingsbana II* and *Helgakviða Hjǫrvarðssonar*.

151 This is Mortensson's final explanation of the name which is given to the visionary in *Dr*. He considered it possible that originally he was called Rúnólfr in the first part of the ballad, but Ólafr after the belt had been retrieved; then, over the years, the less common name was forgotten. In addition *det varranolv* (an alternative form of Rúnólfr) could easily have become *det var an olav* when the ballad was sung (cf. *Grunnsteinen*, pp. 38–9); Mortensson's earlier theories about the origin of the name Olav in *Dr* are found in Mortensson (1920), pp. 44–5.

152 Stanzas 28–34, 114 (last two lines) and 116–17 in the text of 1926/7.

153 Cf. Landstad (1853), pp. 73–4 and S.39. This word presumably forms part of the 'guidance of the poet' mentioned above.

154 *Grunnsteinen*, p. 24: '. . . må det vera meint den same vegen gjenom dyre-ringen, som ogso månen fêr. [new §] Fylgjer me denne rettleidingi fell ordningi av bolkane av seg sjølv, dei svarar til dei "dyreheimar" som månen skrid gjenom frå *Taurus* (stuten) til *Sagittarus* (skyttaren).'

155 *Grunnsteinen*, pp. 27–8: 'Då eg hadde skipa ihop Draumkvede-vers som finst i ymse uppskrifter og stelt dei saman i bolkar etter denne planen og teki burt slikt som berre tyktest vera variantar og tildiktningar og dertil fyllt ut med vers frå stev og visur som eg hadde grunn til å tru kunde eller måtte vera lån frå Draumkvedet, då fekk eg som ei stadfesting på at eg var på rett veg, med di at det vart ein bolk for kvar dag drøymaren var burte.'

156 Liestøl (1946), p. 20.

157 Torkel Ofteli, 'Draumekvæde-skalden', *Telesoga 46* (1920), pp. 3–10.

158 *Grunnsteinen*, p. 19: 'Å skjera burt noko av det som tradisjonen hev rekna med til Draumkvedet det vågar ikkje ein utgjevar å gjera no, utan han hev sers gode grunnar.'

159 Of Steiner's three lectures devoted principally to *Dr* that of 1913, *Olaf Åsteson. Das Wachen des Erdgeistes*, was first published in 1916, that of 1914, *Weltenneujahr. Das Erwachen der Menschenseele aus dem Geistesschlaf der finstern Zeit*, in 1932 and that of 1912, *Neujahrsfeier. Über das Traumlied des Olaf Åsteson* in 1958 together with a reprint of the two previously published lectures. The editions of 1932 and 1958 included Steiner's translation. It seems virtually certain that it also appeared in 1916, but I have been unable to check this.

160 Erich Trummler, *Traumlied des Olav Aasteson* (1927).

161 Ludwig Hoffmann, *Das Traumgedicht* (*Der Traumgesang*?) (1917), *Licht aus dem Norden* (1924), *Im Traumlicht der Ewigkeit* (1954). I have been unable to locate copies of Hoffmann (1917) and (1924) and do not, therefore, know whether the 'literal' translation in these works was the same as that in Hoffmann (1954). The author gives the title of his 1917 publication as *Der Traumgesang*, but according to *Deutsches Bücherverzeichnis* it is *Das Traumgedicht*. Hoffmann (1954) also includes a free translation provided by 'ein begeisterter Freund' (p. 7).

162 Cf. Section 2.19.

163 Cf., for example, Steiner, stanza 35 and refrain and Lammers (1901), stanza 39 and refrain: *Wie selig ist, wer im Erdenleben/ Den Armen Kleider reicht!/ Ihn können nicht erfrieren/ Die Eisesmassen in Brooksvalin./ Da spricht der Waage Zunge,/ Und Weltenwahrheit/ Ertönt im Geistesstand.*; *Sæl er den, i føisheimen/ fatike gjeve klæi;/ han tar 'kje ræddast i aurom heimi/ fyr høge kjellar-bræi./ Tunga talar, –/ og sanning svarar på domedag.*

164 Steiner (1958), p. 42.

165 Steiner (1958), p. 36.

166 Steiner (1958), p. 19.

167 Steiner (1958), p. 36.

168 Steiner (1958), pp. 40–1.

169 Steiner (1958), pp. 35–6.

170 Steiner (1958), p. 36.

171 It would be charitable to assume that this is a printing error, but it accords with the abysmal standard of accuracy elsewhere in the book.

172 Steiner (1958), p. 46.

173 Steiner (1958), p. 46.

174 Cf., for example, Hoffmann (1954) and Lammers (1901), stanza 10, ll.1–2 and refrain to stanzas 7–20: *Ich überfuhr den Todesfluß,/ kam über Schluchten abgrundtief;/ Rot glänzte der Mond/ und weithin liefen die Wege.*; *Eg hev fari yver vigde vatne/ og yver djupe dalar,/ Fyr månen skine/ og vegjinne falla so vie.* (*Fyr* = *Feuer* = *rot*?)

175 Trummler (1927), pp. 7, 8, 19 and 23.

176 Hoffmann (1954), pp. 5, 19, 104 and 106–7. Concerning *Frau Holle* cf. the article of this title in *Handwörterbuch des deutschen Märchens* (1930–40).

177 Knut Liestøl, 'Draumkvædet', *Syn og Segn 54* (1948), pp. 49–65.

178 Knut Liestøl, 'Gaglemyrane', *Festskrift tilegnet . . . A. Kjær . . .* (1924), pp. 65–9, and (1925).

179 The introduction was reprinted in Olav Bø and Svale Solheim, *Folkeviser I*, *Norsk folkedikting VI* (1958, 2nd edition 1967), pp. 253–5 and in abbreviated form in the various editions of (*Utval av*) *norske folkeviser til skulebruk.*

180 Liestøl (1946), Preface.

181 Liestøl (1946), Preface.

182 Cf., for example, Axel Olrik, *Danske Folkeviser i Udvalg I* (1899), p. 50: 'In Norway the solemn and serious *Drømmekvæde* came to be the greatest work of literature of the thirteenth century and the whole middle ages' ('I Norge blev det alvorstunge "Drømmekvæde" det 13de Aarh.s og hele Middelalderens ypperste Digtning'); Ssk., p. 210: '. . . *Draumkvædet* is somehow raised several degrees above the ordinary level of narrative' ('. . . Draumkvædet ligger likesom både ett og to trin løftet over det vanlige episke nivå'); Ssk., p. 246: 'But of the whole endless array of visions there are only *three* which have attained the sublime: the vision of Tundale, Dante's *Divina Commedia* and *Draumkvædet*' ('Men av den hele, uoverskuelige række av visioner er der bare *tre* som har nådd det høieste: *Tundals syn, Dantes* Divina Commedia, og *Draumkvædet*'). In later literature on *Dr* it has become almost traditional to quote one or more of these statements, usually accompanied by Moltke Moe's description of how moved he was the first time he heard *Dr* sung (cf. Ssk., pp. 246–7).

183 Liestøl (1946), p. 26. While it is undoubtedly true that there is no such limit, however one interprets 'belongs to', it seems questionable whether the differing number of stanzas in editions of *Dr* proves this.

184 Liestøl (1946), p. 28.

185 Cf., however, 'Limbus puerorum', *Sproglige og historiske afhandlinger viede Sophus Bugges minde* (1908), pp. 247–57 (reprinted in Ssk., pp. 346–56), and Moe's text of 1906. The importance of MM for Liestøl's view of what was and what was not genuine can be seen in the unsupported statement (Liestøl (1946), p. 33): 'Moltke Moe's text contains, in fact, everything that there is cogent reason to ascribe to *Draumkvæde.*'

186 Liestøl (1946), p. 34.

187 Liestøl (1946), p. 35.

188 Liestøl (1946), p. 35.

189 Cf. Jørgen Moe (1850), pp. 275–6, Landstad (1853), p. 66 and note 305 below. There is nothing in what Moe says which indicates that the prototype of L1/4 was necessarily older than about 1780.

190 Cf. Liestøl (1946), p. 36 (concerning K1): 'The tradition, then, in the family, extends to the earlier half of the 18th century, and this is one of the main reasons why the song was so complete and genuine.'

191 Cf. note 190 above.

192 Liestøl (1946), pp. 36–7.

193 Cf. Liestøl (1946), chap. II.

194 Ssk., p. 270: 'Ved siden av Våsemyran forekommer også *Gaglemyran* som navn på myrstrækningerne i den hinsidige verden.'

195 Cf. Liestøl (1946), p. 72.

196 Liestøl (1946), p. 27.

197 Cf. Liestøl (1925) and (1946), chap. VII.

198 Liestøl (1925), p. 114: 'Berre den ting at ein må søkja fyrebiletet for dei einskilde dragi i Draumkvædet stundom hjå Gottskalk og stundom hjå Thurkill, syner at ingen einskild av desse visionane kann ha gjeve inspirasjonen.'

199 Liestøl (1946), pp. 91 and 117.

200 Cf. Liestøl (1946), pp. 50–1 and 55–6, also pp. 29–30 and 32–3.

201 Ivar Mortensson's search for *gamlestev* which might once have formed part of *Dr* (cf. Section 2.7) can hardly be rated a serious contribution to our understanding of the problem.

202 Liestøl (1946), p. 50.

203 Liestøl in effect parallels Dag Strömbäck's remarks on *Gjallarbru* which appeared in the same year in his article in *Arv*.

204 Cf. Liestøl (1924) and Section 5.2.

205 Cf. Liestøl (1946), p. 128.

206 Liestøl (1925), p. 123 and (1946), p. 130.

207 Cf. Hildeman (1958), pp. 225–6, 228 and 231.

208 Magnus Olsen, 'Gjøre bro for ens sjel', *Maal og minne* (1936), pp. 210–12, Berge (1940–4), I, pp. 142–4, 254, 257 and 268–70, Anders Bugge, 'Dommedagssvalen ved verdens ende', *Museum I* (1948), pp. 56–7.

209 Olsen (1936), p. 212: 'i den eldste kristne tid gjorde man ferden over myrer og elver i den annen verden lett for den efter hvem der i denne verden var ryddet vei eller gjort bro.'

210 Cf. Section 3.5, V9 and note. Hildeman's statement (1958), p. 222: 'No other variants [than K1 and Liestøl's combination of L4 and L1] have been printed' ('Inga andra uppteckningar har nått trycket') is thus incorrect.

211 Strömbäck (1946).

212 Strömbäck (1946), p. 35: 'acceptabel'.

213 Strömbäck (1946), p. 40: 'De olika stadierna på visionärens väg skildras här klarare och konsekventare än i den version, vars innehåll vi nyss relaterat.'

214 The original texts are found in Strömbäck (1946), pp. 65 and 67–8, the last also in Liestøl (1946), p. 65 together with an English translation. Beyond commenting: 'This is, satirically used, the idea in *Draumkvæde* that the giving of alms will help the soul on the Gjallarbru', Liestøl draws no conclusions from this text.

215 Cf. Strömbäck (1946), p. 67.

216 Cf. Strömbäck (1946), p. 51.

217 Cf. *Biskupa Sögur*, ed. Guðbrandur Vigfússon and Jón Sigurðsson (1858–78), I, pp. 451–4 and II, pp. 9–11.

218 Strömbäck (1946), p. 70: 'Över dessa skakande upplevelser, som berättats i bygden, har sedan kvädet uppbyggts och sjungits i folkviseton under århundraden i Telemarken.'

219 Strömbäck (1946), p. 70: 'reminiscenserna'.

220 Cf. Liestøl (1946), p. 65.

221 Midbøe (1949), p. 32: 'dikterens stilling, hans opplevelse, og fram for alt: hans intensjon?'

222 Midbøe (1949), p. 41: '. . . den praktiske, livsnære holdning som til stadighet kommer til uttrykk i skildringen'.

223 Cf. Midbøe (1949), pp. 121–2.

224 Hildeman (1958) takes a different view. He thinks Midbøe's candidate is a certain Jwar, *vicegardianus* of the Franciscan monastery in Oslo in the late 1200s, possibly identical with a 'friar Ivoer of the order of Minors' (Midbøe (1949), p. 122), who visited England in 1297.

225 Cf. Midbøe (1949), p. 120.

226 Cf. Midbøe (1949), pp. 30–1 and 119. He seems to misunderstand Strömbäck's point that motifs from these and other visions may have become part of folk-belief.

227 Midbøe (1949), p. 64: '. . . går . . . stort sett sine egne veier'.

228 Cf. Midbøe (1949), pp. 68–9, also pp. 86, 89 and 111–12.

229 Cf. Midbøe (1949), pp. 113–15.

230 Cf. Midbøe (1949), p. 118.

231 Cf. Midbøe (1949), pp. 45, 48, 59–60, 64, 81, 88–9, 92–4 and 105.

232 Midbøe (1949), p. 104: 'Avgjørende kan dette argument . . . ikke være.'

233 Midbøe (1949), p. 88: 'ganske nær grenseområdet mellom skjærsilden og det egentlige helvetet.'

234 Cf. Ssk., p. 327.

235 Midbøe (1949), p. 93: 'Er det ikke riktig å oppfatte denne skjærsildskildring som en presisering av det som *ikke* førte til frelse?'

236 Midbøe (1949), p. 77: 'teoretisk og abstrakt'.

237 Cf. Midbøe (1949), pp. 77–8, 93–4 and 105–9.

238 Midbøe (1949), p. 41: '. . . den syntese, den sammensmelting, av nesten ekstatiske syner og praktisk, realistisk livsinnstilling som kommer til uttrykk i skildringen.'

239 Midbøe (1949), p. 36: 'Så sant Draumkvedet er et særpreget, personlig dikterverk, og hvem vil egentlig benekte det . . .'

240 Cf. Midbøe (1949), pp. 35–6.

241 Cf. note 5 above.

242 Cf. Bø (1955), pp. 79–80.

243 Cf. Bø (1955), pp. 81–4. It is interesting to note the author's suggestion that MM 45 may be a mixed stanza, and that the last line, which was of great significance for Midbøe's theories of Franciscan or Dominican origins, displays the caustic humour characteristic of so-called *ølstev* (*stev* most probably sung at alcoholic parties). Bø seems in general to favour the idea that *Dr* was composed by a layman, rather than a member of the Church (cf. pp. 82–4).

244 Bø (1955), p. 99: 'ei Draumkvæde-strofe i sterkt utvatna form'.

245 Bø (1955), p. 80: '. . . gjorde den store likskapen mellom ekte Draumkvæde-strofer og gamle-stev til at kvædet vart tynna ut.'

246 Bø (1955), pp. 82, 84 and 98: 'nokså frie'.

247 It is interesting that of the six stanzas Bø mentions as probable or possible *gamle-stev*, five do not belong to any common episode or section in *Dr* (cf. Section 3.2, pp. 84–5) and four are not found in any variant defined as a ballad in Section 3.3.

248 Bø (1955), p. 78: '. . . svært mykje . . . har falli bort.'

249 Bø (1955), p. 80: '. . . kanskje størsteparten . . . har blitt gløymt.'

250 Cf. Bø (1955), pp. 81 and 89–91, Liestøl (1946), pp. 29–30 and *Grunnsteinen*, especially pp. 15–17 and 19.

251 Cf. Liestøl (1946), pp. 29–30.

252 Cf., for example, Landstad (1853), p. 65.

253 Cf., however, Landstad (1853), pp. 65–6 and 379 and *Grunnsteinen*, pp. 15–19.

254 Bø himself does not suggest this and therefore makes no attempt to define the difference between separate stanzas and variants of the same stanza (for such a definition cf. Section 3.2). He nevertheless seems to recognise the distinction since he states, for example, that two remarkably dissimilar stanzas are one and the same (p. 100).

255 Karl-Ivar Hildeman, 'I marginalen till Draumkvædet', *Medeltid på vers* (1958), pp. 216–55.
256 Hildeman seems to have been misled by Liestøl into believing that L1 and L4 are one and the same variant (cf. Hildeman (1958), p. 221). V9, printed in Berge (1940–4), I, pp. 142–3, appears to have escaped Hildeman's notice (cf. note 210 above), otherwise he would doubtless have included it in his survey.
257 This section of the ballad Hildeman declares to be 'the least attractive to the modern reader' ('. . . som lämnar en nutida läsare minst tilltalad') and 'aesthetically of least account' ('. . . som estetiskt väger lättast', cf. Hildeman (1958), pp. 218–19 and 254). Such statements, however, surely tell us more about the climate of modern Swedish society than about *Dr*.
258 Hildeman (1958), p. 222: 'en sammanfogning av flera närbesläktade [dikter]'.
259 Hildeman (1958), p. 220: '. . . drar slutsatserna ur de erfarenheter Olav meddelar från landet hinsides.'
260 Hildeman (1958), p. 254: '. . . då den generation, som följde ärkebiskop Olav Engelbrektsson i den sista revolten för Noregsväldets gamla tro, bör ha varit ur räkningen.'
261 Hildeman (1958), p. 229: 'Och om *en* variant har existerat i katolsk tid, så har *visan* också gjort det.'
262 Cf. Andreas Holmsen, *Norges historie* (1964), pp. 402–3.
263 Hildeman (1958), p. 242: '. . . en sammanställning, ett rationaliseringsförsök av i princip samma slag, som det Moltke Moe utförde.'
264 Cf. Liestøl (1946), p. 44 and Hildeman (1958), pp. 235–7.
265 Liestøl (1946), p. 44.
266 Hildeman appears to have been unaware of this fact. On p. 245 of his article he states that *Dr* was sung by Niels Svenungsen.
267 K11, which Hildeman did not know, is little more than a fragment, and there are reasons for regarding it with some circumspection (cf. Section 3.1, p. 73).
268 Cf. Liestøl (1946), p. 40.
269 Hildeman states (Hildeman (1958), p. 245) that Moltke Moe considered all the refrains to be late and secondary. This does not, however, seem to be the case, cf. Ssk., p. 282.
270 Cf. note 3 above.
271 Cf. Midbøe (1949) and Section 2.12. Even if Midbøe were right about the Franciscan authorship of *Dr*, he fails, as Hildeman points out, to produce any convincing arguments in favour of a fourteenth-century dating: 'All the characteristics which can be ascribed to the Franciscans in 1300 apply equally well in 1400 or 1500' ('Alla de drag, som kan tillskrivas franciskanerna år 1300, har alldeles samma relevans år 1400 eller år 1500', cf. Hildeman (1958), p. 251).
272 Cf. Hildeman (1958), pp. 229, 237 and 240.
273 Cf. Hildeman (1958), p. 253.
274 Giovanni Gonnet, 'Il Draumkvaede e la Divina Commedia', *Atti, I° Congresso degli Italianisti Scandinavi* (1963), pp. 63–78. Both forms of the title occur, cf. pp. 63 and 223.
275 Giovanni Gonnet, 'Draumkvædet og Divina Commedia' and Mattias Tveitane, 'Draumkvædet og Divina Commedia . . . ', *Edda LXVI* (1966), pp. 25–40 and 217–22.
276 Cf. Gonnet (1963), pp. 72–3.

277 Mattias Tveitane, 'En norrøn versjon av Visio Pauli', *Årbok for Universitetet i Bergen. Humanistisk serie* (1964), No 3.

278 Cf. Tveitane (1966), p. 218.

279 Cf. Tveitane (1966), pp. 219–20 and (1964), p. 23.

280 Cf. Tveitane (1966), p. 218.

281 Magne Myhren, '"I uteksti" – eit utolka ordlag i Draumkvædet', *Maal og minne* (1968), pp. 59–62.

282 Cf. Ssk., p. 259.

283 Alver (1971), p. 45: 'viktigaste'.

284 In my review of Alver (1971) (*Maal og minne* (1972), pp. 82–92) the grosser errors of fact are listed, the page references corrected and an attempt is made to throw light on a number of obscurities.

285 Alver (1971), p. 85: '(gamle)stevrekkjer'.

286 Cf. Alver (1971), pp. 47 and 81.

287 Cf. Alver (1971), p. 60.

288 Cf. Alver (1971), p. 131: 'funksjon som gamlestev'.

289 Alver (1971), p. 129: 'originaloppskrift . . . '.

290 Alver (1971), p. 130: 'Samanblandinga er så sterk at ein utan vidare kan seia at ein stor del av Draumkvedetradisjonen *må* vera gamlestev eller rekkjer av gamlestev, og at dei fleste *kan* vera det.'

291 Cf. note 288 above.

292 Cf. Alver (1971), pp. 130–1.

293 Cf. Alver (1971), p. 87.

294 Alver (1971), p. 135: '. . . kunne . . . få høyra om menneske som hadde vore i den andre verda og sett korleis det var der, at vonde gjerningar i dette livet ville få konsekvensar for det neste tilværet og at gode gjerningar her på jorda ville bli rekna ein til fordel når ein skulle gå over grensa til dødsriket.'

295 Cf. Landstad (1853), pp. 65–6.

296 Cf. Alver (1971), pp. 81–3, 127–8 and 134. On p. 83 Alver suggests that five or six of the 'most important' variants (K1, L1/4, L3/5, M9a, M6, V9) had no fixed stanza order, but this seems only to be true of two of these (L3/5 and V9, cf. Section 3.5, L3, L5 and V9, notes) in the sense of real disorder that Alver apparently means. In the case of M6 all the evidence he can adduce (p. 82) is a remark in the fair copy by Bugge to the effect that: 'The order of the last six lines uncertain according to her [Anne Skaalen's] own statement' (cf. Section 3.7, M6, note 4). An unfortunate misprint, 'Versordene' for 'Versordenen', renders the quotation meaningless, but even if we insert the correct form, of what significance is it? The stanza order of the last six lines was uncertain – in a variant that consisted of seventy-four stanzas.

297 Cf. Alver (1971), pp. 45–79 and 89–126.

298 These thirty-four (+ V1a–b) are to represent *Dr* in the forthcoming critical edition of the Norwegian ballads (cf. Section 3.4–5).

299 In connection with Solheim's textual work mention is made (pp. 251–2) of his lectures on *Dr* (unfortunately unpublished), in which he suggested that it was a socio-political rather than a religious ballad, comparable in this respect with Dante's *Divina Commedia*, but from a later age (*c.* 1500), just as the social changes which gave birth to both works came later to Scandinavia than to Italy.

300 Blom (1971), p. 254: 'tradisjonelle vandrestrofer'.

301 Interest in *visions* clearly persisted. One example of many, also mentioned by Alver (1971, pp. 137–8), is the so-called *Sunnmørsk Draumkvæde*, a ballad from 1769 (reprinted 1961). One cannot, however, fail to be struck by the complete dissimilarity between this work and *Dr*. It will suffice here to quote one stanza: *Dernæst Gud ogsaa klager paa Den Uskik, der i svang nu gaa Med syndig Jule-Glæde, Da Højtids-Dage blive brugt Til dantsen, Kortspil og Utugt, Og Bachi-Skaal påtømmes, Men Herrens Lov forsømmes.*

302 Cf. Blom (1971), p. 254. On p. 255 it is suggested that this variant (K1) is the only one with a narrative thread.

303 The use of the 'I' form does not seem to be very common in medieval vision literature. In all the visions on which *Dr* has been thought to be based the visionary is described in the third person.

304 'Long' is, of course, a relative term, but a ballad of thirty stanzas would hardly seem to require this unique usage of the varying refrain. The third feature discussed by Hildeman, the introductory stanza, does not occur in K1 (cf., however, Section 3.7, K1, note 7).

305 Cf. Blom (1971), p. 270. There is nothing in what Landstad says to suggest that *Draumekvæi* was sung in the beginning of the 1700s (cf. Section 3.7, K1, note 6 and Landstad (1853), p. 66). All he tells us is that Maren's father (who died about 1830(?) aged seventy-seven) learnt it from his father. Maren's father must have been born shortly after 1750, but it is only an assumption that the grandfather knew the ballad at this time. It is also difficult to see why Blom concludes that *Draumekvæi* must be older than the earliest date at which we can be reasonably sure that it existed (1780–90?). (Cf. Postscript 3.)

306 Cf. Blom (1971), pp. 270–1 and 278–9.

307 Blom (1971), pp. 263–72.

308 Cf. note 302 above. Even T8, with its five stanzas, forms or *can* form a narrative: the protagonist drinks (a potion?) on Christmas eve, falls asleep and has a strange dream; he does not awake until epiphany when people at last manage to arouse him; he marvels at how quickly time has passed and tells briefly of what he has dreamt.

309 Blom (1971), p. 271: 'I *Draumkvæi* finner vi den offisielle katolske lære om himmel, helvete og skjærsild.'

310 Cf. note 189 above.

311 Cf. Alver (1971), pp. 45–79.

312 Cf. Alver (1971), pp. 89–126; 'som gamlestev'.

313 Cf. Alver (1971), pp. 45–6.

314 Cf. note 288 above.

315 Cf. Alver (1971), p. 11.

316 Cf. Berge (1940–4), I, p. 268, and Section 3.4–5.

317 The first two lines of 5 are unparalleled in the variants, but are found in Landstad A 15 in a slightly different form. Landstad may have based this stanza on T8.

318 Alver (1971), p. 128: 'rekkje av gamlestev'.

319 Alver (1971), p. 129: 'Også dette har fleire forskarar rekna som ein variant av Draumkvedet.'

320 Cf. Alver (1971), p. 60, variant 19 and Section 2.17, p. 56.

321 Cf. Landstad (1853), pp. 384 and 408 and Olav Bø, *Stev, Norsk folkedikting V* (1964), p. 83 where stanza 1 and something reminiscent of 2 are printed as such. Cf., however, Bø (1955), p. 97 (about T8): 'The introductory stanzas are probably new, on the model of *gamlestev*' ('Innleiingsstrofene er truleg nydikting etter gamle-stev mønstret').

322 Cf. Bø (1964), p. 9.

323 Whether Crøger asked Svenungsen specifically to collect *Dr* or merely to collect ballads in general is not entirely clear from his letter, although the former seems more likely.

324 Some general knowledge of the ballad by informants is presupposed by the stories Landstad heard about it, cf. Landstad (1853), pp. 65–6.

325 'Alt anna hjaa Landst er ukjent.'

326 Stanzas 7–11, 16–21 = *Mit belte* (*Beltevisa*) (Landstad 89); 40–2 = *Ásmund Fregdegævar* (1); 46–7 = *Fránar ormen og Yslands galten* (10); 48–50 = *Steinfin Fefinson* (4).

327 Stanzas 34–5, 54–5.

328 Cf. Landstad (1853), p. 423.

329 Jørgen Moe includes SS.86,90,148 in his reconstructed text with an indication that they come from V1b.

330 Cf. Landstad (1853), p. III.

331 Cf. Berge (1920), pp. 49–65. T4 may have been written late in 1846 or early in 1847, since it has some features of the etymological spelling, notably 'ð' and accents over certain vowels. The orthography in V2 also seems to be late, but the MS shows signs of being a fair copy. If, as is suggested in Section 2.2, *Droumekvæi* in Liestøl/Landstad (1925) is an abbreviated version of V1a, none of the longer variants are likely to pre-date 1845, since otherwise Landstad would presumably have used them in his early draft too – especially K1.

332 Complete in the sense that they form a recognisable section or unit in the MS (i.e., are preceded and followed by a break or some sign to indicate where they begin and end) and do not contain matter incompatible with what we know about the ballad (cf. p. 73 above and pp. 75–7 below).

333 Cf., however, note 308 above.

334 'Variant' is used widely in both senses in this edition. Where it is necessary to contrast the two meanings, the terms 'complete variant(s)' and 'incomplete variant(s)' are used (cf. note 332 above).

335 In V1a–b the original numbering is maintained since these are not incomplete variants, but reconstructed (or edited) texts which were numbered by the editor/collector, Svenungsen. In most MSS the stanzas are not numbered, and where some or the majority are omitted from a variant in this edition, it serves no practical purpose for the editor to base his numbering on the order in which the stanzas included occur in the MS, and can even be misleading since those which are omitted do not form any part of the *Dr* ballad variant.

336 It is possible to take By1 as *stev* (thus Alver (1971), p. 75), but the two stanzas form a complete variant in the MS, mention *Gaglemyre*, and By1,1 is paralleled by M6,40; they have therefore been included as a *Dr* ballad variant in this edition.

337 Liestøl and Moe (1920–4), 127.

338 Liestøl and Moe (1920–4), 13; also printed by Sophus Bugge, *Gamle norske Folkeviser* (1858), pp. 29–35, under the title *Margjit aa Jón í Vaddelíó.*

339 Peder Syv, *Et Hundrede udvalde Danske Viser* (1787), pp. 419–22 (cf. DgF, 10F).

340 *Dei som koma den øystre Vegjen/ fara 'kje alt så skjót,/ dei koma inkji åt Gjeirufsgaren,/ fyr drukkji ei onnå Jol.*

341 While S.87 occurs in V1a, S.137 is found only in Sæl and appears to have no connection with the ballad.

342 Although the varying parts, even pages, of Landstad (1853) apparently circulated widely among the people of Telemark (cf. Dal (1956), p. 186 and Knut Liestøl, 'M. B. Landstads "Norske Folkeviser"', *Edda XXVI* (1926), p. 2), it is difficult to demonstrate that his A text of *Dr* had a direct influence on any informant.

343 The fact that Bugge often abbreviates stanzas with reference to Landstad A does not prove that he used this text 'as a basis when he interviewed his informants' ('som grunnlag for sine intervju av informantane', Alver (1971), p. 46). In fact in some cases (e.g., M2,1, K3,2) we can see that it is only in the fair copy that the abbreviation and reference to Landstad A occurs.

344 Cf. Section 3.7, M6, note 4; 'nyt', 'fuldnyt'.

345 'Var. til "*Draumkvæde*".'

346 'berre mi spyrjeform.' V9 (from 1910) also includes two stanzas (7, 13, possibly also 10) which only occur once elsewhere, and in each case in a pre-1853 variant; 13 consists simply of the words: 'v.54 = L. kvit*e* hest.'

347 Cf. Alver (1971), pp. 74–5 and Section 3.5, By4, note.

348 Ramskeid was a small tenant farm which belonged to Heggtveit, cf. Postscript 3.

349 Cf. Alver (1971), p. 81.

350 Cf. Section 3.3. The provenance of the variants and its significance are also dealt with by Alver (1971), pp. 89–126.

351 Cf. Section 3.4. Where the provenance of a variant is very uncertain (normally when nothing definite is known about the informant), a question mark follows the letter and the variant is placed last in the geographical section to which such evidence as there is suggests it may belong. Some variants can only be localised to Telemark.

352 Occasionally stanzas consist of more or less than four lines, cf. Section 3.6, notes.

353 The episode in a narrow sense is used by Alver, cf. (1971), pp. 40–4. On pp. 84–5 below an attempt is made to divide the *Dr* ballad material into sections or episodes in the wide sense.

354 It might also appear that K1,6 and V1a,12 ought to be two separate stanzas, but cf. K5,3b: *Stat naa du Prest for Altaren din/ aa leg ut Textine* [*dine*]/ *mæ eg stænd i Kjorkjedynni/ fortel*[*e Drau*]*manne mine* and M20,2: *Presten stænd'e på predikstolen/ å les upp tekstine sine/ å eg sit'e i kyrkjedynni/ fortél'e droumó mine.*

355 Cf. Liestøl (1946), pp. 31–2. Landstad and Moltke Moe suggest it indirectly by printing the same stanza twice (Landstad A 4, 13; MM 2, 7) with the variation *Han/seg – Eg/meg.* Cf. also Moe's headings in MM: 'The frame of the vision' ('Visionens ramme') 1–6, 'The visionary's introduction' ('Visionærens indledning') 7–15.

356 'Endnu meddelte han Landst. A V.24 Var.2; 17. (Eikjaråsen, jólehylen). 14.'

357 Cf. Bengt Jonsson, 'Balladdiktning', *Kulturhistorisk Leksikon for nordisk middelalder* (1956–), I, col. 316.

358 Cf., e.g., Bugge (1858), Nos. IV and V, Bø (1964), pp. 32 and 36 and Alver (1971), p. 131.

359 Cf. Berge (1940–4), I, p. 268.

360 The value of the title is less certain for the reasons given above.

361 Cf. Bugge (1858), p. 15.

362 Only an approximate figure is given because of the difficulty of deciding in some cases whether or not a stanza has something in common with matter in V9 etc.

363 Cf., however, pp. 87–8 above.

364 Cf. Landstad (1853), p. 400.

365 Cf. Alver (1971), pp. 59–60.

366 Alver (1971), p. 59: 'store delar'.

367 Cf. Johannes Skar, *Gamalt or Sætesdal* (1961–3), I, p. 124 and Bø (1955), pp. 86–7.

368 Cf. Alver (1971), pp. 59–60.

369 Cf. Johan Fritzner, *Ordbog over Det gamle norske Sprog* (1883–96, reprinted 1954), *heimr* 2.

370 Cf. Einar Lundeby, *Overbestemt substantiv i norsk og de andre nordiske språk* (1965), pp. 114–15.

371 Cf. Ssk., p. 251.

372 Jørgen Moe prints *-svalo* and *Vise* in his text. V1b,15 appears to read *-svolo*; the other relevant stanza of this version is missing.

373 The editor of the most recent edition of *Norske folkeviser til skolebruk* (Aslak Liestøl, 1971) appears able to distinguish between a number of these forms, but it is hard to see how (e.g., *Draumkvedet*, stanza 4 *i lie*; 8 *med havet svarte*; 9 *av blidom munne*; 10 *på svarte dikje*; 19 *på leii*).

374 Liestøl (1971) prints *i dyre tid*, but why not *i dyr'e tid*? In the other examples discussed here the '-om' ending is used in this edition.